BRACE YOURSELVES BOYS

Over a 2 year period I am subjected to five court cases which result in two consecutive injunction orders plus I am ordered to pay huge council costs and thousands of pounds in fines. Eventually I stand trial for committal to prison to serve the maximum sentence of two years.

My crime? Advertising my café on an A-board at the end of a quiet side street.

Yet in these troubled times of global recession, unemployment and County Council cutbacks, small businesses such as mine are struggling to survive. We would expect local government support but in my case instead of help I fall victim to an unscrupulous County Council employee - his job title 'Licensing and Enforcement Manager' for East Sussex Highways. I stand up to this bully and when he realises that he has taken on much more than he anticipated, he commandeers other members of staff to join his crusade and uses tax payers' money to fund his obsession in his determination to wreck my business.

BRACE YOURSELVES BOYS

By Sally Pattinson

Edited by Elizabeth Hojlund
Contact: info@elizabethhojlund.com

FOR
'MERCHANT BANKERS EVERYWHERE'

Contents

ACKNOWLEDGEMENTS

Many thanks to Cindy, Lesley, Jenny, Lily, Tim, Diana, Tony, Eve, Sean, Chris, Stephen, Danny, Jimmy, Ronette, Hayley, Jan and customers whose names I do not know, for contributing to the making of the sound tracks and videos of 'Team Fluffit' and 'The Fluffits Can Stuff It'.

To Molly for putting together the videos 'What's This?', 'The 1980's Fluffit's Act' and 'The Final Fluff'.

To Danny, for technical information.

To Lesley and Jenny for their support.

Special thanks to my partner in crime, Lily.

Special thanks to Elizabeth for her help in editing this book.

To East Sussex Highways Department for providing endless amusement and laughter which I hope will be passed on to the readers of this book.

BRACE YOURSELVES BOYS

CHAPTER 1

This story is the truth the whole truth and nothing but the truth.

I was 60 years old and on Friday 15th April 2011 I was in Hastings County Court, standing before HH Judge Hollis to be committed to prison for a maximum of two years at the request of East Sussex County Council.

My crime, deemed worthy of such punishment, was that I had placed, not far from my café, an A-board which advertised that there was an open café.

The definition of 'authority' is *'The power to enforce laws, exact obedience, command, determine or judge. One that is invested with this power as a public agency or corporation with administrative powers in a specified field'.*

Most of us dutifully respect the law of the land and abide by the rules and regulations which are imposed upon us by various authorities that run the country, counties, towns and villages. No one is exempt from authority, not even the ones who enforce it. However, there are certain individuals who work in local authorities with job titles that warrant the power to enforce. Sometimes, in fact quite regularly, there will be an unscrupulous employee who falls victim to temptation and abuses the privilege with which he has been entrusted. Councils often choose to employ ex-policemen to fill these middle-management jobs, as they have heavy-handed and intimidating dispositions and the misconception of being upright and honest. In November 2008 East Sussex Highways Authority tried to enforce themselves upon my humble café by confiscating the café sign which indicated that my café was situated down a side street in Camber. The café would perish without one. It was imperative to have this sign for the café and I was determined to have one there, so all the heavy-handedness and intimidation they enforced upon me proved futile, as this time they had picked on the wrong woman.

I was aware from a young age that I was determined, and always felt that I had been born into the wrong family; I didn't look like them, speak like them, think like them or perceive life in general like them. I was fed, clothed and well educated; but that is where it ended. As a teenager I rebelled at the restrictions put upon my social life, the dislike of my choice of friends they had never met, the length of my skirts, the way I wore my hair, the amount of Mary Quant make-up and the art of painting lashes round my eyes and the dotties I stuck all over my face. I was constantly being corrected on the pronunciation of nearly every word I uttered. One was expected to speak with a plum in one's throat especially having had a private education and was subjected to even more pressure to use that one special voice which only applied when answering the telephone. I was constantly being reminded of how much money had been wasted on educating me.

I had a sister, four years my elder; we were as different as any two sisters could be. She was constantly unkind to me when we were little and as we grew up nothing changed. She was mean, spiteful, painfully shy, lacked personality and was caked in orange make-up. She was undoubtedly my mother's favourite daughter; she could do no wrong, whereas I could do no right. She bleached and curled her hair and wore tight fitting knitted dresses down to her knees and beyond. I on the other hand would give a stranger my last penny, I wore mini-skirts that were barely twelve inches in length, I had wild hair, and I was out-going and loved excitement and adventures. On rare occasions my sister and I would end up in the same night club, albeit before ten thirty. She would be with her friends in a corner dancing on the spot, stepping from side to side in time to the music, her arms bent rigidly with her handbag hanging off one elbow and both her index fingers pointing upwards twirling in time to the music. In contrast I was an exhibitionist, my dancing occupied the whole dance floor; I threw myself about, did roly-polys across the floor and did a lot of head shaking. My sister would always ignore me when we were out, which suited me for I was a modern girl who did my own thing and I wanted independence and freedom more than anything else in the world. One thing was certain; I was not, under any circumstances, in any shape or form, going to be a replica of my spiteful sister.

Contrary to my mother's belief I did have morals and despite her accusing me of being a prostitute when I was still a virgin because I got home late one night, I had no desire to be promiscuous. I liked to show off my dancing to the boys, that was all.

I believed that as an individual I had the right to think for myself and make my own decisions and if I wanted to ruin my life by mixing with the 'wrong type of people' then that was going to be my choice and no one was going to stop me. So inevitably, two weeks after reaching the grand old age of seventeen, I packed my belongings into a few brown paper carrier bags with string handles and moved out of my parents' beautiful home to live in a tiny bed-sitter half a mile up the road which cost £2.00 a week. So I had my freedom at last.

Having had, but not appreciated, my expensive education, I realised that one's accent, although distasteful to my mother, made little difference in expressing oneself or holding an intelligent conversation. I was able to get jobs through interviews, and my cockney accent, which I had acquired purposely to annoy my mother, was never going to be a hindrance in achieving. I was not academic, I was never going to be a highly paid executive, but I was grammatically correct and knew how to conjugate verbs and amazingly and not something that had to be learned, I had been gifted with personality and an incredibly strong will-power.

So my life rolled on, uphill and down dale. I had countless jobs, telephonist, cabaret dancer, waitress, bar maid, cook, rep. SEN training, care assistant, delivering car parts, supermarket night shift shelf-packer to name a few. I had been married and divorced twice and I had two beautiful children. I was on my third marriage and in the early hours of the morning on March 18th 1990 we upped and moved to France for a 'better life' according to my husband. He was working at Shakespeare Cliff on the construction of the Channel Tunnel, but four years after moving to France my husband who by that time had gone to work in Germany after the tunnel was complete, had disappeared from our lives never to be seen or heard of again. I continued to live in France for 12 years and at the time he abandoned us I was selling official T-shirts and stuff for young people from a little shop that I rented in Boulogne and from various markets during the week and Brocantes on Sundays.

I enjoyed the challenge of learning a foreign language and I wanted to learn to speak French just to prove to myself that I could. It took five years, but I did it. Just in time too as I was unable to pay the bills and mortgage payments on the small amount of income from the shop and therefore it was easier to plead my case to the growing amount of debtors that were waiting for their money that I did not have. Inevitably in 1998 I was declared bankrupt and as the French police had failed to

5

locate the missing spouse after a two year search, I was granted a divorce on the grounds of abandonment and he was ordered to pay 2500 francs a month to me and my son. As he was not present and oblivious to the fact he was divorced I never received anything in the way of maintenance. We endured five years of utter struggle and poverty and eventually lost the home which had been the dream of a better life. The process of losing the house was pretty miserable we were forced to leave it in the middle of January 1999 when it was freezing. The final trip to the new accommodation was the worst as we had the dog Annie, the little Staffordshire bull terrier who hated the two cats. The two cats also hated each other but had to share one cat basket together during transit. We had the mop and bucket and the hoover, bags of clothes, house plants and any other belongings we were able to cram into the very old Astra.

The new accommodation was near to Etaples which was one of the places we used to sell our stuff at the market so we knew the area quite well. The new home was an ancient cow shed which had been minimally converted to a kind of fermette. There was a great hole in the living room wall and brambles growing down from the eaves in the roof. There were snails crawling up the walls and the floor covering in the bedrooms was concrete. There was no electricity apart from one light bulb in the kitchen and certainly no home comforts apart from the log burner I had managed to retrieve from our house. The rent for this place was 2500 francs a month so that's the way it was for the time being and we just had to put up with it.

I had been working in Calais in the notorious English owned beer and wine warehouse for a year before we were turfed out of our home. There were amazing job opportunities in this pirates paradise. I became a cashier and was not only taught how to count money quickly but also shown only once how to use a hand gun of which there was a choice of two ready and loaded in the checkout booth One of them was placed on a shelf directly overhead and the other just lying casually on the right hand side of the till. I was certainly expected to shoot to kill if there was ever an attempted robbery. However the opportunity never arose for me to kill a potential thief in cold blood to save the master's fortune to which I had contributed by means of slave labour. My twelve hour shift with a twenty minute lunch break paid £20 a day, but compared to how it had been before I felt like a millionaire. I learned to drive a fork lift truck, without a licence of course, but I never dropped a pallet and I could unload a lorry in twenty minutes. I worked there for two years; I met gangsters and smugglers, rough and readies, all out to earn a quick buck, the "white van brigade'. So when I was offered a job driving from Calais to Luxembourg for £300 a day three times a week I gratefully accepted. It was not for greed but after five years of struggling to afford to eat apart from anything else it was truly out of sheer desperation that I became a tobacco smuggler with excellent pay. So I was living the life of Riley for the duration. I could pay the bills, I ate and was driving around in expensive hired cars used for the dastardly deed I was doing. Sadly nothing lasts forever and just over a year later my luxurious way of living came to an abrupt end owing to my French counterpart being nabbed in Dover. He ended up in Canterbury jail for eighteen months which consequently ended the best paid job I had ever had. The money I had left from my well paid job was stuffed inside carrier bags under my bed. It was not possible to bank it and besides I had lost my bank accounts when I went bankrupt and you were not allowed to have one ever again I seem to remember. Anyway it soon ran out and regrettably I returned to slave labour in a beer and wine ware house driving a forklift truck again but this time for a different establishment and I was paid £30 a day.

Both my children had moved back to the UK and I had started to wish that I was back there too but I had my German Shepherd 'Nicor' who I had acquired from a French security guard who worked occasionally on the industrial estate where I had been working in a warehouse. Nicor was a trained guard dog, but he had been sacked for not biting a burglar who had been breaking into an establishment there on the industrial estate and his owner needed to re-home him. I said I would take him and so the security guard had just handed him straight to me. I was terrified of this dog as he was huge. I drove so slowly going home for fear he would attack me, but within a very short time I managed not to be scared of him and I loved him. I did want to go back to the UK but I could not afford to put him into quarantine and even if I could I wouldn't have been able to be separated from him for the six months that was required.

Then there was talk of changes regarding quarantine for animals. And so it was announced in 2000 that the UK quarantine law had been abolished and all that was required now was a passport, a microchip, a tattoo which he already had and certain last minute health checks. So six months later with Nicor attended to I happily abandoned that French dream and boarded the ferry in Calais, and as the French coast line disappeared on the horizon the white cliffs of Dover came into view. It's true, there is no place like home. I had no home to go to but getting back to England was a start. I was 50 years old and I knew it wasn't going to be easy but I was ready to start again.

CHAPTER 2

At 10.30 am on Saturday 15th September 2001 I arrived back
in the UK, broke, with a few clothes, 3 house plants, £19 and
the dog. Unfortunately my Renault 21 had no MOT, the tax
had expired in '98, the petrol tank was hanging down as one of
its straps had snapped in two, there was a great crack across
the entire width of the windscreen and both the electric
windows had got stuck at an angle and were permanently
open to the elements.

So I was back in East Sussex, embracing the challenge that
lay ahead of me to re-establish myself here and get back on
my feet and the only way I knew how to do that was to work
hard. So I stayed with friends that first week-end and on the
Monday I not only scrapped the Renault 21, on the advice of
my friends, I also got myself a job as a bar person in a Private
Members Club in Pett Level known as The New Beach Club.
I soon found accommodation and moved into a converted
garage where I lived for a year. In 2002, a year after I got back
to the UK, I bought my flat in Camber, a small village about
10 miles up the coast from the New Beach Club. Camber has
a fabulous sandy beach and in 2004 won a Blue Flag Award.

I continued working at the New Beach Club and was
promoted to Club Steward after a couple of years of service,
but because of the lack of funds within the club caused by the
dwindling number of members (mostly from them departing
to a more spiritual place) I voluntarily took on the role of
social secretary, and booked bands and organised special
social events.

After five years I felt that I had outstayed my time there
and was wondering what to do next. I had for some time
fancied buying my own business. I looked for commercial
properties for sale and was pleased to see that Camber Café,

only two doors away from my flat, was for sale. It was
September 2006 and not a good time to be buying a seasonal
business, but I made enquiries regarding the sale of Camber
Café and I was duly sent the details. I told the agent that I
might be interested in buying the café and then I
waited....until one cold bleak day in January I made my offer,
it was not accepted so after a bit of negotiating a price was
agreed. My flat had doubled in value, and it seemed a good
idea at the time to take a loan secured on my property, so I
borrowed enough money to buy the Café and pay the agent
and legal fees. So that was it, I had wanted my own business
and now I had one. I took on the lease of Camber Café on
Monday 16th April 2007.

Camber Café was built in 1974 and was part of a row of
three shops with flats above. My flat was the other end of the
block and had been a craft shop before it was converted to a
flat. The middle one had been a greengrocer and had also been
converted to a flat, and that just left the café, which had been
there since 1984, so I had bought a well-established business
with a good turnover.

At first glance the café looked as if it had been a living
room conversion with the extra-large double glazed sliding
patio door which occupied nearly all the entire front of the
building. There was a door to the right which accessed the
café behind the counter. It was a good sized café which seated
52 inside and 20 outside. There was an ample forecourt with
enough space to park four cars. On the north side of the car
park was the access to Beaky's flat which was hidden behind
two huge wooden gates with a 'No Parking' sign attached.
Unfortunately the patio furniture was that horrible cheap
green plastic, bottom of the range stuff and not very stable,
the three tables rocked on the broken tarmac and the chairs
were no better. Some of the arms of the chairs were broken.
The inside of the café was very 70's. Formica tables on two

pedestals which were screwed to the carpeted floor with two-seater benches either side on metal legs. There was a reasonably sized back kitchen with two large sinks, a dish-washer, and a chest freezer which was placed right across the back door and would be the only way of escape if there was ever a fire at this end of the café. Along the next wall was a gas cooker used to make Sunday roast, a chest freezer and then work top space. This small area led into the main café. There was an electric cooker, seven microwave ovens and a griddle. There were three fryers standing in a row sitting on a strange wooden structure. At the end of the extensive work top there was a huge drinks fridge with a lump of wood slightly bowed wedged across the bottom. The toilets were at the back of the café and compared to the rest of the establishment were in a reasonable state. There were no disabled facilities at all.

It was evident to me that the café had been neglected over the years, and it was in urgent need of a deep clean. The carpet was disgusting; full of grease and sand, and it had been there for over twenty years. I could not imagine why anyone would put a carpet in a greasy café next to a sandy beach. Luckily there was lino behind the counter.

The evening before I took over the café there was a knock at my front door. It was Beaky, the landlady of the Café and the person to whom I would be paying the rent which was at that time £9,250 per annum divided into quarterly payments. Although we were potential neighbours I had never seen Beaky before. She was certainly getting on in years; I'd say in her early seventies. She proceeded to tell me that I must deduct 25% off my takings every day and if I didn't I would get her and the previous owner into serious trouble. I asked her what I would do with the deducted money, and she told me to imagine all the things I could spend it on. I presumed she wanted me to declare less revenue for the purpose of tax evasion. I was amazed at her suggestion. I did not want to start doing that. I told her that I would not agree. She clearly was not happy about me rejecting her suggestion, so she handed me a piece of paper she had flapping in her hand and reminded me that the rent is reviewed every three years and this July she was putting the rent up to £12000 a year, an increase of £3000. I was flabbergasted by the huge increase she had proposed. She insisted that I signed the agreement there and then. There was no way I was going to agree to that. Ridiculous! 'What a greedy woman' I thought. £9,250 a year was too much already for a seasonal café in a side street, never mind putting it up to £12,000. I said ok to her because I wanted her to go but I took the piece of paper and I already had an excuse in mind to not agree to it.

As part of the café purchase, I became the proud owner of two dilapidated A-boards which the previous owner had placed - one at the top of the road on the corner at the junction of Lydd Road, to attract passing motorists and holiday makers, and the other by the roundabout on the main road to attract the builders at the 'White Sands' housing development project. The A-board that was placed at the top of the road was in such a sorry state I was concerned that it could easily blow into the road as it was quite flimsy, so I decided that I would make two new signs and zap them onto the telegraph pole that was conveniently installed at the same junction where the dilapidated A-board was situated. I would put one facing east and the other facing west. I did ring Rother District Council to ask if this was permissible and whoever I spoke to took my number and said someone would contact me. I did not hear back from them so I contacted them twice more and was told the same thing again. I also contacted Open Reach who owned the BT pole but the guy I spoke to said I needed written permission to attach a sign on the pole. I didn't expect them to come and check, so I ignored him, and made two

signs and wrote on each one 'CAFÉ OPEN 7.30 am' with an
arrow pointing in the direction of the café. I zapped them onto
the BT pole, high enough not to cause an obstruction to
motorists at the junction and high enough not to cause injury
to anyone, and there they stayed.

Wow, that first day was so hectic. I had my friends to help
me. There were six of us behind the counter, bumping into
each other and not knowing where anything was or how much
it all cost. There had been a punk venue at Pontins that week-
end and check out or chuck out time was by 10 o'clock in the
morning...it seemed they had all descended upon Camber
Café at the same time, and the queue was out of the door and
across the forecourt... it was manic. I was cooking and I was
taking forever doing it, someone was taking the orders,
someone washing-up, someone serving and clearing tables. I
think a lot of customers had waited over an hour and a half
before they got their breakfasts. It was a challenge but we got
through the day. Thank goodness for my friends and patient
punks. It was a great first day and I was really happy, but I
had a lot to learn - especially having to improve my cooking
speed.

Having survived week one of life as a café owner it was
imperative for the sake of the customers that I improved the
cooking time in readiness for the long summer season which
was rapidly approaching. I was glad that there was the gas
cooker in the back kitchen, as it would have been too much
making breakfasts, roasting meat and potatoes, boiling
vegetables, making stock, frying eggs and making the
occasional omelette all on the same cooker in the main
cooking area. So the arrangement to have a separate cooker
away from the main cooking area was a good idea. However,
as there was no town gas in Camber, anyone wanting to have
a gas cooker or heating in the village would have to use gas
bottles. The arrangement, which had been Beaky's suggestion,

was the same as when she worked the café herself, with a gas bottle situated in her driveway on the other side of the kitchen wall where the connection from the cooker to the gas bottle went through a hole in the outside wall. Beaky's boyfriend Bodger told me to purchase a double connector that would attach to two gas bottles, so when one ran out the other automatically took over. I spent a fair bit of money on two new 47 kilo Propane gas cylinders and a double switch-over regulator. I purchased the necessary bits and two gas bottles were delivered. Bodger attached the new connector to the outside wall and connected the gas bottles to it. I decided that I would wait a couple of weeks before I started to do the roast dinners, as I needed to speed up with the breakfasts first.

Six weeks later I was sitting in the café after a busy day when a very slim pretty young girl came into the café and said she was looking for a job and that she had had experience working in a jewellers. I asked her how old she was and she replied that she was thirteen. She looked a nice girl and her name was Lily. Lily started work the following Saturday and her duties were to serve the food to the customers, clear the tables and wash up. My job was to take the orders and cook the food and anything else that needed doing when I got the chance. We got very busy; Lily was working very well and she was on the ball and didn't need any prompting. I had so many orders queuing up at the griddle I had to give Lily a crash course on how to work the till which she mastered in seconds. As well as writing the orders, she managed to find all the correct prices to charge the customers. What a clever girl, plenty of common sense. I don't know what I would have done without her that day.

Four days after Lily had started working for me I popped home at 2 o'clock as usual to take Nicor for his pee walk. He was always waiting at the door for me and I sometimes had trouble getting in as he wouldn't move away. This day as I opened the front door he wasn't there. I saw him lying on the floor in the living room by the sofa, so I called him and asked him what he was doing there on the floor. He didn't respond and then I saw his tongue was hanging out of his mouth and he wasn't breathing. He was still warm. I was devastated I couldn't believe my best pal was gone. I had loved him so much, he was my mate. He died six weeks before his tenth birthday.

A friend buried Nicor in his field facing him toward France.

Beaky continued to pester me to sign and agree to the £3000 rent increase to start in the following July. I was not prepared to pay that amount of rent for a seasonal café down a side street in Camber so I told her that my solicitor said it was too much. She was clearly annoyed as she realised that I was not going to agree to the huge increase. Shortly after that, one Sunday morning as I got to work at the regular time of 7 o'clock, there on the patio in front of the café where the two full bottles of gas, the regulator and screws were lying in a heap beside them having been ripped off the external wall, and I hadn't even done a roast dinner yet.

It was clear that I was not going to have a pleasant relationship with Beaky.

Following this incident, there then ensued a year long legal battle to agree on a fair increase in the rent which incurred much unnecessary expense. I continued to pay the rent of £2,250 a quarter whilst it was battled out between their Chartered Surveyor and my solicitor. Beaky had told the Chartered Surveyor that my turnover to date was £100,000 pounds. That was rubbish; it was barely £50,000 after nine months. So I realised why the blind in her living room above the café was always twitching; because she was spying on us. She had obviously counted the number of customers coming into the café on a daily basis and she had thought she could

work out how much they had spent. She never left her flat
other than a Thursday morning to go shopping, the rest of the
time she spent with her nose poking through the blind. Her
window would open if people sitting outside were having a
private conversation or someone was speaking on their phone.
This intrusion into other people's privacy was extremely
irritating.

Finally, after a long and expensive battle, an increase of
£750.00 every three years plus £500.00 a year towards the
building insurance (which I was apparently obliged to
contribute) was agreed. I also had to reimburse the back-dated
payments of the new increase. Luckily I had saved something
towards it.

This was the first of many annoyances I was to be dealing
with in the future from Beaky and Bodger.

CHAPTER 3

That first summer season was great fun, hot and tiring, but my cooking speed had improved. Lily was amazing. She learnt very quickly for a girl so young and soon I was able to rely on her to get on with her jobs. In fact that first season she learnt to do every job available, even helping me with the food preparation, as in preparing the scrambled eggs and jacket potatoes. Not once did I ever have to tell her to find a job to do. She was always busy doing something constructive during the quiet times.

At the end of each day when we were clearing up all the greasy utensils and cooker bits she used to make a concoction to wash all the stuff in, which included washing-up liquid, bleach and toilet cleaner to name a few..

Lily and I got on well together despite a forty-three year age gap. She told me all her woes and I told her mine. Other staff came and went - good ones, lazy ones, old ones, daft ones, but Lily stayed and was the best employee any employer could have wished for.

The café became my social life as well as my livelihood. I always loved meeting and talking to people, but although I had lived in Camber for five years already, I didn't really know many of the residents, apart from my immediate neighbours, so after a few months I had become acquainted with quite a few of the locals.

The customers were mostly very nice and quite often very patient when they were waiting ages for their food - not many complaining. But one Sunday afternoon when it was pouring with rain and the forecourt was full of puddles, five ladies came into the café soaking wet having trudged around Camber in the turbulent weather. After some deliberation they ordered and paid for five cream teas. These ladies it transpired were members of the WI.

We made the scones ourselves as I liked to make them quite large, and because we cooked a few dozen at a time they were kept in the freezer and then defrosted in the microwave when they were needed. Our cream teas consisted of two home-made scones, freshly whipped cream, a good helping of jam in a ramekin dish and four butter portions per person. The cost of the cream tea was £2.50.

So we set about defrosting ten scones, whipping up the cream remembering to add a little sugar at the end, setting the plates with serviettes, butter portions, knives, and ramekins filled with jam and finally the warm scones. The mugs of tea were made and we served the ladies their cream teas. Within a couple of minutes after serving the teas to the table one of the ladies came to the counter and asked for their money back. I asked her why she wanted their money back and she said the cream was off. I told her we had just opened a new pot of cream it couldn't possibly be off. She insisted on having a refund. The other customers in the café were listening and I started to get annoyed. The cream was not off. I fetched the bowl we had whipped the cream in and I wiped my finger round it to taste it and it was fine. I made the other staff wipe their fingers round the bowl too and then I made the nearest customer wipe his finger round the bowl to taste and he agreed there was nothing wrong with it. We all unanimously agreed the cream was not off. I told the woman it was quite all right but she said they didn't want to risk eating it. I was furious, we had put a lot of effort into the preparation and presentation of those cream teas and they were complaining for no reason. I noticed that the other four WI ladies sat quietly with sheepish expressions on their faces as the one at the counter insisted that they got their money back. I went to the till and got their £16.50 out and flung it in the woman's hand and told them to clutter off out of the café. As they all got up to leave one of the old dears croaked 'I'm not coming here again' so I hastily added to her comment that they would not be let in if they did come back. Out they filed into the pouring rain and the puddles on the forecourt and they didn't even thank us for the five free mugs of tea they had managed to drink in that short time.

I asked the other customers who had been watching the fiasco if they would all like a scone with jam and sour cream for nothing. They all said they would so I shared them between everyone. A lady with her family who were on the table next to where the WI ladies had sat told me that the ladies had been talking about the price of the cream teas and decided that it was too expensive and were discussing how they could get their money back and one of them had suggested that they say the cream was off.

It is true to say that in Camber the seagulls outnumber the residents, and every roof on every building in Camber is home to a pair of seagulls plus chicks in the summer months. People that are born and bred by the coast, as I was, happily accept the seagulls as part of everyday life. Unfortunately many of the folk who have chosen to move to the sea-side from inner cities take a dislike to these gulls. They brand them as dangerous, dirty and noisy. Of course they are noisy, they are birds and that is the sound of the coast, the sea is noisy when the waves crash onto the shore, that is what you get living in a coastal town.

A seagull's life span is up to fifteen years. They are very intelligent and they mate for life. They are protected as well. We loved the gulls and indeed we had our own pair which we called Fred and Freda. We used to put the left-overs into an empty butter box every day for Fred and Freda, and when their lunch box was placed outside for them it also encouraged dozens of neighbouring seagulls that would swoop down to try and get themselves a taste of Fred's lunch, only to be chased away or attacked by Fred. He considered all areas of the café as his territory and no gulls were permitted to land there. Strangely, he did not object to other wild birds helping themselves like the sparrows, starlings and wagtails. Even Quigley the cat from over the road was permitted to come onto the café forecourt without being squawked at.

Fred and Freda had always nested on the café roof but unfortunately there were Beaky and her boyfriend Bodger in between. Apparently, the previous year the boyfriend had destroyed Fred and Freda's nest which they had built on their roof. He had also chucked rocks at the nest and broken the eggs. Sadly such a horrible act of cruelty by them did not surprise me. So that was the reason Fred and Freda built their nest on the garage roof in my back yard this year. The roof was flat with a couple of extension ladders lying to one side and so the nest was built right in the middle of the roof. Although visible from Beaky's balcony it was far enough away not to come to any harm. And this year Fred and Freda were the proud parents of two chicks we called Snitch and Snatch.

That summer was hot, busy and tiring, but it was nearing its end and one Sunday we had the hottest day of the year. It was so hot that people came from far and wide to spend the day on the beach. I got the first customers early and I was cooking the first breakfasts by a quarter past seven that morning. Before long the queue was out of the door onto the forecourt. The orders were coming thick and fast, I was struggling to keep up and the waiting time was an hour or more, but the customers patiently waited. The more I cooked the more grease splattered. I had forty or more numbered order tickets laid out on the work top, so when the number of the ticket jumped up two numbers it meant that the missing ticket was possibly stuck on the bottom of someone's plate by the grease it had been covered in on the work top. I shouted across the café to the customers if they would be so kind as to check the bottom of their plates for the missing ticket as we had no idea what the order consisted of. They all obligingly lifted up their plates to look for the missing ticket, and there it was stuck to the bottom of a plate of smoked kippers. So the delay had caused another delay, but we carried on regardless. I did not stop cooking until twenty minutes past six that evening. There were only three of us working that day and we were all shattered by the time we had cleared up. I went home feeling like a rancid lump of melted lard and got straight in the bath. It was nine o'clock; I had worked nonstop for fourteen hours.

That first summer passed and the winter was rapidly approaching. Pontins did have a few week-end venues and the last week-end in November with the Rockabilly Rave hailed the end of the season. So I closed the café for my well-deserved winter break. I had not had a day off since I took over the business on 16th April. This meant the long awaited opportunity had finally arrived to redecorate the café and rid it of the old yellow walls and continuous blue freeze half way up it and remove the disgusting carpet which had apparently lain there for at least twenty years.

I was going to brighten the place up and had chosen my favourite colour to re-paint the café which was bright lime green, the MDF which extended all around the café and formed the front of the counter was to be painted white along with the ceiling and door frames. The floor was to be painted garage floor grey.

I employed a friend to do the work. He started by removing the tables as they were screwed to the floor through the carpet. This carpet had probably been a brown and green paisley pattern in its prime but it was so filthy it was not even worth guessing what had gone before. It took him two days to take the carpet up which after two decades had become brittle being encrusted with grease and sand, he could only break it up in small segments, it was like snapping caramel. Then more horror, for beneath the first carpet there was another, filthier than the first. This one had probably been cream coloured in its original state but was now stained with dark brown and yellow rusty matter. So the poor guy progressed slowly and eventually removed the second filthy carpet, but removing both carpets had revealed thousands and thousands of mice droppings. Goodness knows how long they had been there. They were quickly disposed of.

So eventually the café was decorated and looked beautiful ready to open at the end of January 2008.

When the time came to close for the winter I had saved enough money to upgrade my little yellow Smart car. I had loved this car; it was a special edition and had 'smart arse' written across the side, but I had been fancying a Smart Roadster convertible. I had been looking on line for a couple of months and then one day shortly before I closed the café for the winter I saw my dream car for sale. So I went all the way to Surrey to buy it, and it was my pride and joy. I had enough money put by to pay the bills and live comfortably for a couple of months. So that is what I did. I never forgot that miserable time I had spent in France and now here I was in Camber. I had been back in the UK for six years. I had bought my flat and the business and I had a decent car for the first time in my life.

CHAPTER 4

2008 began quietly but as Easter approached Pontins started
to get holiday makers and off we went again. I had become
much quicker with my cooking skills and Lily was as keen as
ever. She asked me one day if she might cook herself some
breakfast on the griddle. I was happy to let her do that but I
didn't want her to get burnt. As she proceeded to cook her
breakfast, I was amazed to see that she arranged the breakfast
items in exactly the same position on the griddle as I did. She
had been observing the way I cooked and she copied the way I
did things. She was confident and capable, so from then on we
shared the cooking which was a great relief to me as all day in
front of a griddle was quite tiring.

Fred and Freda had produced three chicks that year and as
soon as the babies had learned to fly they were ushered to the
café entrance by their devoted parents for me to feed and if I
did not provide them with food straight away they would
squeak until their demands were met. They made one hell of a
noise, the only way to stop them was to feed them and Fred
and Freda knew it. They were a source of great interest and
were often photographed by the customers.

All was well and we were chugging along nicely. The
weather was good and business was fine. All of a sudden one
morning in April there appeared red and white balls and
chains on legs draped around the café forecourt.
Unfortunately it was not just for that one day it was a daily
occurrence. The daily display of red and white balls and
chains would be in place when I arrived for work at 7 o'clock
in the morning and would be hastily removed shortly after I
closed. Surely Beaky would not purposely interfere in my
business with this ridiculous behaviour?
As well as these balls and chains Bodger parked their huge

mobile home on the forecourt. I guessed the object of this daily routine was to give the impression that the car park was full so some customers just carried on driving rather than try to park in front of the café. Beaky had legal access to the entrance of their property, but only access, and according to the lease nothing was allowed to be stationary on this area which not only applied to my customers' vehicles but also to their car and this huge mobile home.

I had never defaulted on the rent for the café which I paid every three months, so I did not understand why she was trying to disrupt the running of the business. If she didn't want me there why did she sell the lease? She certainly was the most extraordinary person I had ever encountered. Last year she had cost me nearly £3000 in legal fees over the huge increase in the rent she had demanded and now this. I had no choice but to go and seek advice from a solicitor and incur more unnecessary expense.

I went to a solicitor in Hythe in Kent and provided him with the lease. Over a period of a few weeks and correspondence with questions and answers back and forth from the solicitor it became quite obvious that the terms of the lease were being breached by Beaky.

Then one day in July Bodger the boyfriend started dismantling the red balls and chains in the middle of the day and after a few moments they were gone never to be seen again. Hooray! I had now incurred another huge bill and had a £2500 solicitor's fee to pay.

After the balls and chains episode ended we were able to get back to the normal routine. Although the café had been decorated, the pictures which hung on the walls all around it were quite drab, old and faded prints in broken plastic frames, pictures of metal tables and chairs beside nondescript shrubs. I hated them and they needed to be replaced. I decided to hold a painting competition for the local children; the subject was

'Summer in Camber'. I love children's paintings; they use bright colours and are full of imagination. The children had the summer holidays to create their masterpieces and the winner would get £10 and a party for all the entrants.

After a while the paintings started to arrive. There were large and small ones but they were all beautiful paintings by the local children. The oldest competitor was nine and the youngest was two. The beautiful seaside paintings were of sea, sand and starfish, break-waters, buckets and spades, surfers, mermaids and rough seas. The local play group had painted a seagull, which looked very much like our Fred, and they had put their little hands in paint to make a feather effect body. It was very impressive. Another family had painted the sea with great waves crashing onto the sand and they too had put their hand-prints all over the sandy bit and written 'We live here in Camber 2008'. It was difficult to choose a winner, as they were all so good. However we could only choose one and the winning painting was of a girl on a surfboard skimming along on the sea, painted by a little girl of seven. I presented her with a £10 note and a few weeks later gave all the children a party. We even got a write-up and photo of the paintings in the local paper.

I happily chucked those horrible faded pictures away and had all the children's paintings framed and hung them round the café and they looked fabulous. I was so pleased with them.

One day Lily and I were sitting out in the sunshine having our early morning coffee and we noticed that one of the oval plastic tables was broken. Two of the legs were broken and had caved in and were lying underneath the table, the other end was still standing on the two remaining legs. We laughed as it looked so funny and wondered how it had come to be in that state and how we would be able to dispose of it as it was probably too big for the dustman to take. When we got up to go back into the café I noticed with horror lying on the patio a pink condom which looked very much as though it had been used as it was neatly tied in a knot. It was clear that the broken table had been used for some vigorous night time activity, but unfortunately for the lovers the old plastic table was not the best choice for a night of passion. Neither Lily nor I had any wish to remove the condom so it stayed where it was until Bob, a regular customer, kindly disposed of it for us, earning himself a free coffee.

That September my mother passed away having reached the grand old age of 89 and for all my sins mother had left me a little bit of money, so I invested it in making some improvements in my flat.

October was pretty uneventful. There were a couple of week-end bashes at Pontins and one in November, after which I closed the café for the winter. Now was a good time to make some urgently required improvements. The green plastic tables were replaced with wooden picnic tables with benches attached, two four seaters and one six seater. Inside, the electric glass display cabinet and the metal shelf unit were removed and were replaced with one long work top the whole length of the counter, which looked so much better and provided more space.

I dared to think that finally I had reached my goal and was firmly back on my feet and so pleased with a successful second year. Sadly those thoughts were short lived as this was the last time I closed the café for a winter break. For what was about to unfold in 2009 put paid to my recently acquired peace of mind and the tranquillity that I had worked so hard for.

CHAPTER 5

By the middle of January 2009 I was bored with not working and despite it being very cold I decided to go back to work earlier than the previous year with joyful optimism that this year there would be no unnecessary legal expenses inflicted upon me. There was no heating in the café as it was only intended to be a seasonal business from April to September and thereafter just open at the week-ends when there were things going on in Pontins.

I did open despite the cold, and there were not many customers that first week and by the end of the second week there were none at all. I guessed it was due to the time of year. Then a friend came to tell me that my café signs on the telegraph pole at the end of the road had been removed a few days ago along with two laminated signs which had been put there only a couple of months beforehand by the owner of the Wine Bar which was down on the sea front. I asked him if he knew who had removed them and he said he thought the council probably had. Great, that meant that any potential customers would never know that my café was here, yet alone open, if there were no signs to see.

The next morning I phoned Rother District Council and had great difficulty trying to locate someone who might know something about my missing signs. Having spoken to three people who each passed me on to another person who might be able to help but couldn't, I finally gave up after I was told that Rother District Council would never remove business signs. So I was none the wiser and I wondered if my friend was right about the Council taking them or maybe someone just pulled them down. I decided to phone the owner of the Wine Bar. I was surprised that he apologised and said that a rival business had reported the Wine Bar for putting their signs on the BT pole and that it was just a private vendetta between the two businesses and nothing to do with me or my signs at all. He also said that he had received a letter from East Sussex Highways in Bexhill asking him to remove his laminated signs but he had ignored the letter. He suggested that I didn't put new signs back on the BT pole until Easter and in the meantime to put an A-board at the top of the road instead. I took his advice and took the A-board from the forecourt and put it at the top of the road beside the BT pole.

The following day I rang the Highways Department in Sidley. I did not ask if they had my café signs because I knew they had. Instead I politely asked for their return. I was told I needed to speak to Kilkenny, the Highways Inspector, but he wasn't there at the time and would be asked to call me back. Call me back he did, but I was out this time and he left me a short message, spoken in a gentle Irish brogue, that I should call him. So I called him again and eventually after nearly a week trying to track down my missing café signs discovered that they were in the Highways yard in Sidley. I asked him why he had taken them and he actually denied taking them by saying 'Oh, he took yours too did he'? I don't know who he was referring to and I told him I didn't care who had taken them but they were my property and I would like them back as my business relied upon them for passing trade. He said that my café signs were a danger to motorists and I must not attach them to the BT pole again. I asked him what was dangerous about them, as I had screwed them onto the pole securely with six inch screws and that they had been there for nearly two years. He replied that they were a distraction and could cause a fatal accident. I said they only had two words written on them and that was 'Café Open' and an arrow underneath, so how could that distract a driver to the point of crashing his vehicle? He avoided answering that question so I asked him how would anyone know where my café was if I didn't have a sign at the top of the road. He said that wasn't his problem. I told him he was unreasonable and that I would have to have something there. He said something about reading between the lines, I didn't understand what he meant by that remark. He said he would look for my signs and if he found them he would bring them back the next time he was in Camber.

A couple of days later I was at home in the afternoon and there was a knock on my window and there were my café signs being returned by Kilkenny the highway man with the Irish accent. He was clothed from head to foot in high visibility gear; his face hidden by the high collar which was zipped right up to his nose with the hood pulled so far forward it covered his eyes. I wondered if, although he couldn't hide his accent, was he trying to hide his identity. He muttered something about fly-posting. I loved his accent and thought it such a shame I couldn't see what he looked like. I asked him to leave the signs at the café.

As soon as I put the A-board at the top of the road again customers were coming to the café, much to my relief. It was ridiculous for any authority to expect a business which was down a side street to function without any signs advertising its whereabouts. I thought maybe the Irish man was new to the job and had taken his authority to extremes beyond reason.

It was a pain taking the A-board up and down the road everyday so in the end I just left it there and did not hear any more from the Irish man Kilkenny from East Sussex Highways. In the meantime I gave the returned café signs a makeover which they badly needed. At the beginning of Easter week that April I screwed the newly painted signs back onto the BT pole but used a lot more screws than before just in case the Irish man tried to take them down again. I had noticed that the Wine Bar had relocated their laminated signs some time ago onto the back of a large signpost which was conveniently placed opposite the top of a sandy old road full of pot-holes which lead to the beach and the Wine Bar was directly at the bottom of that road. These advertisements had been placed side by side. They had different things written on them. In fact the two signs had more than thirty words written on them. So it was all right to advertise on a signpost belonging to the Highways but it was not all right to advertise a two-worded sign on a BT pole. It didn't make sense. In fact I couldn't see that the BT pole was even anything to do with the Highways especially as the OpenReach engineer had said I could put my signs on the pole.

I was not bothered who advertised where as long as I could have my café signs visible on the main road.

After I put my signs back on the BT pole all was well for the first three days. On the fourth day an East Sussex Highways van pulled up outside the café and Kilkenny the Irish Highway man got out. Despite the warm weather he was still engulfed in his high-vis gear and apart from his hands there was no part of his body exposed. He was accompanied by another man in high-vis gear too and the other man was hobbling with a walking stick. It seemed odd that someone so reliant on a walking stick would be working. They both sat down at one of the benches outside. Before I could say anything, Kilkenny reminded me that he had told me not to put my café signs back on the BT pole. I asked him how he expected me to run a business if nobody knew it was here. He said his boss had seen them and that they would give me seven days to remove them. I told him that I was not going to remove them because I didn't know how else to advertise my business other than putting an A-board at the end of the road. He said I couldn't have an A-board either. I tried to politely argue with him that all the previous owners had put an A-board at the end of the road and never had a problem with it. He said no one had complained about it before and now there had been a complaint made they had to follow it up. I had no idea that there had been a complaint about my signs. I suggested that he should tell the person that had complained that he had followed up his complaint and that he had decided that my signs were not a distraction and it was fine for them to be there. I explained to him that it was the Motel who had a private vendetta with the owner of the Wine bar and that it was nothing to do with me. He compared my café signs to the dangers of flowers put on the highway by grieving families when a loved one has been killed in a traffic accident. I asked him if he removed the flowers people leave in memory of a deceased person and I was shocked when he said he did. I told him that people lay flowers as a mark of respect and they were not a hazard. He said people look at them as they drive past and it was dangerous. I suggested that although the flowers represented the tragic death of somebody's loved one, maybe it stood as a warning to other motorists of the danger on that particular section of the highway.

I then brought to Kilkenny's attention and indicated in the direction of the main road that was clearly visible from where he was sitting, the recently constructed wind-farm in the field literally behind the houses on the main road. A wind-farm of twenty-six windmills erected to provide thousands of homes with electricity but not for us in Camber. These wind-mills were huge and could be seen clearly from the main road into Camber and everyone who drove along it felt compelled to count how many of the wind-mills were going round. I said that in my opinion the wind-mills were a much bigger distraction than flowers on a fence. He made no comment, instead he got up to leave and muttered that it was like being married coming to my café talking to me. He repeated that I had seven days to remove the signs off the BT pole and I repeated that I would not remove them. The man with him had not said one word. They got back into their van and drove off down the road.

I had not mentioned to Kilkenny about the Wine bar's adverts on the signpost and I had no intention of removing mine off the BT pole either. I thought that would be the end of it; there must be far more important things for the Highway men to attend to.

The weather was getting warmer and people were arriving in Camber for one reason or another. I decided as a precaution in case my signs were removed again by the over-enthusiastic Kilkenny, I would make a few spare ones. I went into Rye and purchased a panel of cheap plywood from the timber merchant which they sawed into six equal parts. I also bought a box of long screws and a packet of cable ties. I had a full tin of lime green paint left over from when I had my kitchen decorated, so Lily and I painted the boards lime green and when they were dry I wrote CAFE OPEN and an arrow pointing towards the café.

All seemed well; we were getting busier as the summer approached. We were hoping for a long hot summer which up till now had been quite acceptable as British summers went. We had no more visits from Kilkenny so I hoped he had been assigned to something else other than driving round the county looking for business signs with the possibility of wrecking someone's livelihood. Alas, three weeks later that East Sussex Highways van pulled up outside the café again. I couldn't believe it. Out got Kilkenny and even on that warm day in May he was still wearing his huge high-vis winter uniform zipped up to his chin; but the hood had been detached exposing his face. He had very close-set beady eyes and a little mouth and the most ghastly hair style comparable to a sixteenth century Franciscan Monk; how very disappointed I was.

There were no hands visible, as they were up inside the long sleeves his jacket provided and the long trouser legs only exposed the toe caps of his boots. He must have been sweltering in all that clobber. He had a young girl in tow too; she only had the high-vis jacket unzipped over her own clothes. I thought she might have been on work experience.

As soon as he came into the café he asked me why my signs were still on the BT pole when he had told me to take them down. I asked him what made him think they were my signs, they had not got Camber Café written on them so it could be any of the cafés in Camber, and he said he had followed the arrows on them and they had lead him here to my café. He said he would remove them if they were still there in seven days' time. I then invited him to accompany me to the back kitchen which he did. I showed him the six new café signs Lily and I had made. I told him that for each of my signs he removed I would replace it with two more. I hoped this slight threat of more work would deter him from taking the two signs off the BT pole. Time would tell.

CHAPTER 6

There was something about Kilkenny that fascinated me. I liked his Irish accent, but he wasn't good looking and he was quite old. I found him strangely mysterious and I felt that I wanted to see him again. Maybe under different circumstances, without the high-vis uniform and with a pint of Guinness in his hand, he might be quite an interesting guy to talk to. So I speculated that if he did take my signs down and I did replace each one with two more, that would give him plenty of reason to come over to Camber and maybe I'd get the opportunity to talk to him properly and have a good look at him as well.

Precisely one week later Kilkenny stuck to his word and removed my café signs from the BT pole; he did not pay a visit to the café this time, he just took the café signs away. We never saw him do it though; in the morning they were there and then by the afternoon they were gone. As soon as we had closed, Lily and I loaded the car with four of the six signs we had prepared in readiness, along with the cordless drill, a box of screws and a packet of cable ties, and we went off to fly-post.

As I replaced the two signs back onto the BT pole I was concerned about the number of holes I was making in it. Kilkenny had not unscrewed the ones he had taken but had just ripped them off the pole; consequently some of the screws were left embedded into the wood. And because of the force he had applied it had bent the screws and they were sticking out of the pole.

Afterwards we drove round Camber to choose the next locations for the other two signs. I noticed that the other businesses that had signs on the highway including the Wine Bar's on the signpost were all in their usual places. So why was Kilkenny just taking mine I wondered? As other people advertised on various council property. I decided to put one of my café signs onto a highway lamppost opposite Pontins main entrance where there was usually a queue of traffic waiting to go in, so hopefully the people waiting to book in to Pontins would see the café sign. I had to drill four holes in the board first to thread the cable ties through. We put it as far up the lamppost as possible, luckily Lily was taller than me so she was able to push it up another few inches. We pulled the cable ties as tight as we could so it would not be possible for someone to turn it round to face the wrong way. The second one we put outside the village on the back of a signpost next to the golf course.

So there were four of the six new signs used already. I went back to the timber merchants and bought another panel which they cut into six pieces for me again. As I had only recently bought the last panel the salesman was interested to know what I was doing with the wood. I told him it was to advertise my café and that the highway man Kilkenny had threatened to take them if I put them on the BT pole so I was stocking up in case he took them again.

Lily and I set about painting the six new panels of wood with the lime green paint and wrote Café Open on them in readiness for the next time. In each sign I drilled four holes big enough to push the cable ties through. We now had eight in reserve ready to be put to use when necessary. It worried me that if there was no sign at the top of the road I would lose so much business and I couldn't afford for that to happen.

It was not just the new signs that were being painted lime green. In our enthusiasm and rush to get them ready the paint was splashing everywhere mainly on the seat part of the benches outside as it was easier to do the painting leaning the wood against them. The concrete beneath the tables was also getting covered in lime green paint as were the black pinnies we wore for work. Customers arriving wondered what we were doing and when we told them they were amazed why I would not be allowed to advertise the café at the top of the road. Beaky had stuck her head out of her top window asking what we were doing. I told her we were making new signs, but I did not give her the reason why we were. I did not wish to communicate with her at all and besides I did not trust her. Kilkenny was one of those 'jobs worth' morons and I had a feeling he was new to this roll as Highways Inspector and I was correct for shortly after Kilkenny's last visit a smartly dressed man came for breakfast. I was chatting with him and it transpired he worked for the local Environment Agency. I mentioned Kilkenny had forbidden me to put café signs at the top of the road despite all the previous owners doing it since 1984. The guy had heard of Kilkenny and told me that he had been employed just to drive hundreds of miles a week round the county looking for signs to take back to the yard in Bexhill. I would have understood a man being employed to drive round Sussex to remove debris and dead animals off the road but not to remove business signs that people relied upon to earn a living and this job was funded with tax payers' money. The guy agreed with me but there was nothing he could do about it. He finished his breakfast and went on his way to check a drain in a field somewhere.

Needless to say, a week later all four café signs had gone. From then on I took a photo of every café sign I put on the road or attached to something. I was losing count of how many cafe signs had been taken already but I was now going to log how many I made.

There were several seasonal businesses in Camber along the main road. One of them was based in the council owned car park. It sold food, drinks, buckets and spades, inflatables and all things needed for a day out on the beach. Every day the owner of the kiosk would place directly either side of the car park entrance two large metal signs, one advertising fish and chips and the other food and drinks. He placed them right at the edge of the curb stones. His signs were only a few hundred meters up the road from mine. Opposite the central car park was the motel that had made the complaint about the Wine bar signs but nevertheless they put their A-board advertising rooms and food on the council owned grass verge adjacent to the entrance of the motel, also on the main road. The local pubs all put A-boards on the pavements and various signs displaying food menus, ice creams and the usual things found in a seaside village. The Wine Bar still had their signs stuck onto the back of the signpost, so why was Kilkenny just targeting mine?

He had taken the four signs just a week after we had put them up. If this was going to be a battle of will power he had one hell of a challenge facing him and although I knew I was probably going over the top with the advertising, I had to keep to my threat. That meant we had to put eight signs up this time. Although I was full of determination, I was concerned that what I was actually doing was most likely illegal. One thing was certain, I was not afraid of the council, although it annoyed me that I had to do what I was doing just to keep my signs on the BT pole, and if this was going to be a battle of wits then I would rise to the challenge.

I wanted to make it harder for Kilkenny to take my signs. It was obviously too easy to cut through a plastic cable tie so I bought some metal ones from Rye Hire and hoped that he would not be able to cut through those. Lily and I went out with the eight signs, metal cable ties, drill, screws and a stool to stand on so we could push the signs as high as possible out of Kilkenny's reach.

This time I collared the tallest man in Camber, six feet seven inch Rob, who put the signs onto the BT pole high above the screws that were sticking out of the wood from the previous signs. Keeping the friend in tow we went back to the lamppost opposite Pontins, and he stood on the stool and was able to push the sign nearly to the top of the lamppost. He then made a hasty getaway worried he might get done for fly-posting. Lily and I put another sign on the signpost by the golf course, and there, lying on the ground, were the previous plastic cable ties cut into several pieces. The metal cable ties were extremely sharp and could have easily sliced into our fingers, so we were cautious when tightening them up but optimistic that Kilkenny would be unable to cut them off with his knife. We drilled one onto a telegraph pole, then we reached the end of the road at the junction of the A259. There were two large signposts so we put one facing the traffic coming from Ashford and another facing the traffic coming from Rye. On the way back I attached one onto a chevron post. Then I drove to the far end of the village where, opposite the entrance to the caravan park, was a telegraph pole by a bus stop where I attached the last café sign. So it was back to the timber yard to stock up with more panels of plywood plus a couple of wooden posts as I had spotted a concrete stump sticking out of the grassy verge in the lay-by which did not appear to serve any purpose. I decided to put a claim on this stump and thought that a tall sign on a wooden post attached to it would look quite cool. So for the next two days Lily and I made the new signs in between serving the bewildered customers, under the prying eyes of Beaky.

CHAPTER 7

This was becoming ridiculous. I had to advertise or I would go out of business. Once a month in the Village Hall the Camber Parish Council held a meeting when the local residents could go to air their views or just listen to the current affairs in and around Camber. I decided to attend the next meeting in the hope of getting some support for my café sign problem. There were quite a few people in attendance and the main topic of discussion was the queue of cars that built up to get into the main car-park, which on hot days would cause a traffic jam as far back as Rye and beyond. They then went on to discuss the cars that parked on the pavements and across private driveways and their concern that a fire engine or an ambulance would be unable to reach an emergency along these particular roads. I listened inventively agreeing with the majority in the hope that I would be accepted as one of the whingeing old residents who had nothing better to do than moan. At the very end of the meeting the parish council was open for questions, so I stood up and introduced myself. I felt I was not very popular when I was asked by one of the Councillors if I was that woman who had stuck graffiti all round Camber. I replied that I was possibly that woman and that was the very reason I was attending the meeting. I said that I only wanted to have a sign for my café at the end of my road and that it was causing problems with East Sussex Highways. I suggested an idea I had and that was to place in a central position in the village a signpost giving directions to all the local businesses, and that we could all share the cost in erecting it. The response to my suggestion was that I should ring the Highways in Bexhill with my proposal and a member of the Parish Council would write a letter to them as well. None of the other traders who were at the meeting responded to my idea at all, well why should they, their businesses were along the main road with their A-boards and signs along the pavement and on the telegraph poles and with no harassment from Kilkenny.

The next day I rang the Highways Depot in Bexhill and was passed on to the Licensing and Enforcement Manager. I explained to him that I had been to the Parish Council meeting and how important it was to have signs for my café. I explained my idea for a communal signpost and that the local businesses could fund it, or if not would he permit me to have my own cafe sign at the top of the road. Without even considering my suggestion he spontaneously replied 'NO'. I moved swiftly on and changed tactics trying for a bit of sympathy from him. I told him how Kilkenny was going to wreck my business if he would not let me have my signs at the top of the road. I told him I had advertised my café on the top of the lamppost opposite Pontins as I thought it safe from Kilkenny's reach. He said that Kilkenny had a heart of gold and was a very nice man. I said if I ever saw him taking down my signs I would jump on his back and suffocate him with my 34 DD bosom. He advised me not to do that as Kilkenny had been a paratrooper and went to the gym three times a week. There was nothing to gain talking to this man, - no reasoning or compromise, - so I wished him good-day.

The customers asked why we were making so many café signs and when I explained the reason they offered plenty of good ideas for alternative advertising. A lot of people suggested parking a car on the main road with a sign on top of it or writing Camber Café on it. Apparently there was nothing illegal in parking a car on the highway to advertise on, as long as it had insurance and a valid MOT and besides cars were not council affairs, they would surely be a matter for the police if there was anything untoward. Others thought I should ask the local residents if I might put signs in their gardens or even a blimp which is like a small barrage balloon filled with helium gas and rises up above the business premises on wire. The only problem there was we had a lot of telephone cables around our little area so that could be a possible hazard on a windy day. I had an idea something like that in the sky had to be agreed with Air Traffic Control as well.

I was keen to attach the new sign I had made to my recently acquired stump which I duly did and it looked grand sticking up out of the ground. But right on schedule a few days later some of the signs went missing. The metal cable ties I had so much faith in had let me down. The perpetrator had just cut straight through them with a pair of bolt croppers and left them lying on the ground. I was not sure if Kilkenny was responsible this time as the signs on the BT pole, the one at the top of the lamppost opposite Pontins and the stump sign were all still there. Gone was the sign by the golf course and the signs at the junction on the A259. I did wonder if the grounds man from the golf course had removed the one on the signpost but I dismissed that idea as I could not imagine them bothering to remove the others at the road junction. We replaced them again and now we were getting beeped by well-wishers as they passed us on the road. I don't know what I would have done without Lily helping me; she was great and we laughed so much at what we were doing.

It came to the point where we were always on the lookout for the Highways vans but my plan of meeting up with Kilkenny had so far been fruitless, although friends often reported to us that they had seen Highways vans in Camber. Someone even saw him taking pictures of my café signs on the BT pole; I couldn't imagine what he would want photos of them for.

After Kilkenny had taken about fifteen café signs away I became impatient because I wanted to see him and talk to him. So I made the decision that if he would not come to me

then I would have to go to him and ask for my signs back as
an excuse. It was a lovely sunny afternoon; I had the roof off
the car and The Pogues belting out on my iPod as I drove the
half hour journey to Bexhill Highways Depot. I was excited
that I might be going to see Kilkenny; I presumed that he
finished his working day at four o'clock and would be in his
office. I timed my arrival for a quarter to four in the hope of
catching him as he was leaving. When I got there I did a small
tour of the yard looking for my stolen signs. There were a lot
of lorries and piled up road signs everywhere, and Highways
vans and trucks parked around the yard. I spotted a padlocked
cage full of For Sale signs chucked in a heap; I could not see
any of my café signs though. There was a workman by a large
metal container so I did another tour of the yard and pulled up
next to him and asked him if he had seen my café signs. He
replied that he had not but suggested that I went and asked
Kilkenny for them. I asked him to look inside the container he
was standing next to but he said he did not have the key to get
in; Kilkenny had all the keys to the lock-ups. I parked my car
and went into the shabby building which was really no more
than a glorified shack. I walked through the door into a
corridor and hearing voices which I followed, I entered a
room by the open door to behold several people sitting and
drinking tea; it appeared I had inadvertently walked into the
staff room where a staff meeting was in full swing. I was
challenged by a woman as to how I got to be there and what I
wanted. I explained that my means of entry had been through
the door at the front of the building and I had come to retrieve
my café signs from Kilkenny. I was hastily ushered out of the
building and shown to the main entrance. I did notice a lack of
directional signs to the entrance of the premises, though they
had enough signs in captivity you would have thought they
would realise the necessity to have signs if they did not want
strangers gate-crashing their staff meetings, or at least have a

'No Entry' sign on the door.

I went in the right entrance; it was just a very small reception area. I asked a young girl who was sitting behind the glass partition if I could have my café signs back that Kilkenny had taken. I presumed they were there, although I had not seen them in the yard, as he would surely not have taken them home with him. She replied that Kilkenny was not there and she did not know where my café signs were and that Kilkenny did not always come back to the yard when his day had finished but she would try and get hold of him by phone. About ten minutes later she and her colleague struggled through the door carrying six of my signs. I took a couple from them and they followed me to my car. I asked them where the other ones were and they said that these were all they could find but they would ask Kilkenny where the others were. I put the signs into my car and drove back to Camber. I was disappointed I had not seen Kilkenny and I suspected that he might have been there but was hiding from me.

Three days later I received a phone call from Kilkenny telling me he had not been able to locate my fourteen other signs. I reminded him that he had taken my property and I was entitled to have it back. He told me I was in breach of the 1980's Highway Act and he had the right to take them. He also told me to stop putting my café signs on street furniture. I questioned why he appeared to ignore other signs around Camber but he denied doing that. He said he would continue to remove my signs every time he saw one, and that's what happened. I put them up, he took them down. Alas, I was no nearer to seeing him. I never knew when Kilkenny was coming to Camber, only when he had been, but I knew one thing and that was he came to Camber more than once a week.

Another week went by and on June 17th 2009 the postman delivered a letter from Bexhill. I was hoping it might be a letter from Kilkenny asking me out to discuss the fly-posting issue. Sadly not, it was a letter from his boss formally asking me to cease the practice of placing my 'café signs' on street furniture along the C24 to Camber and within the village. It went on to say that it had been necessary to remove my signs on three previous occasions which I had unlawfully placed and had contravened the 1980's Highways Act and the Town and County Planning Act and the Control of Advertisement Regulations. I had been personally warned by his Inspector Kilkenny and I had blatantly ignored the advice. If further breaches were found then they would consider legal proceedings against me and seek to recover the cost for doing so. Finally if there were any signs attributable to my premises I must have them removed immediately as he was going to arrange checks. He signed it The Tyrannical Clown, Licensing and Enforcement Manager, and added a PS at the bottom saying he had sent a copy of the letter to Rother District Council Planning and Enforcement Team.

Removed on three previous occasions? Maybe Kilkenny had taken the signs home after all as he had far exceeded the three times that The Tyrannical Clown had stated.

I was amused by this letter, but it came as no surprise and I knew my signs around the village were making the place look untidy to say the least, but it was a matter of principle. I believed I had the right to advertise my café and I had only ever wanted the signs at the end of the road to indicate there was a café here. Now I had no choice other than taking them down, but I would leave the two on the BT pole for business reasons and I would not be able to reach the one at the top of the lamppost opposite Pontins. Reluctantly Lily and I went out after work and collected some of the signs. All of a sudden I had an idea. We would write a poem and send a photo of the signs we had taken down just so they knew that we had and also I would have the last word on the matter. We put the signs into the shallow boot of my car and made them into a fan like playing cards. Thank goodness for mobile phones with cameras. I took a few photos of them and some of Lily, she took some of me with a sign in my hand and then we went back to the café and unloaded the car and spent about twenty minutes concocting this poem:

To Kilkenny and The Tyrannical Clown

You'll be happy to know that the boards are now down
So no more moaning and having to frown.
You can come into Camber all happy and gay
And grab some food if you can find your way.
But with no signs to lead you here,
Don't fret, plan B will soon appear.
Upon the fresh tarmac on the C24
The new signs for my café will be sprayed on the floor.
My publicity stunts will never cease
Only now and again to give you some peace,
You must be aware and I feel I must say
I am not a wimp you can frighten away.

We attached a photo of the signs fanned out in the boot of my car and one of me by a lamppost holding a sign in my hands. We emailed it to the Highways contact centre for the attention of Kilkenny and The Tyrannical Clown. I wondered what they would make of that.

So there it was, and I hoped that my signs on the BT pole would stay there. I was of course joking when I told them I would spray café signs on the new tarmac but I wasn't too sure if this particular breed of council employees had much of a sense of humour. I did hope not.

CHAPTER 8

There was no response from the email and photos I had sent to Kilkenny and The Tyrannical Clown but shortly after the sign on the top of the lamppost opposite Pontins disappeared. I would have loved to have seen how it had been removed; Kilkenny was no more than five feet eight inches tall so unless he had used a ladder I could not imagine how he had managed to cut the cable ties and grab the sign at the same time. Perhaps he had a colleague with him who stood on his shoulders. What a funny sight it must have been! More annoyingly the signs on the BT pole had been removed as well.

All the while signs belonging to other businesses in Camber were left alone. I did not put another sign on the lamppost; instead I stood an old lime green A-board on the grass verge and wrote 'Camber Café' Open at 7.30 on it. I also wrote a note on the back as a reminder that this A-board was not attached to any street furniture and was to be left alone.

A local resident offered to make a new A-board with some left over bits of wood he had. When he brought it to me I prepared it as quickly as I could to replace the old one at the top of the road. Everything calmed down for a couple of weeks and I got back into the swing of enjoying the café. Fred and Freda had three chicks this year and had just started to usher them down onto the forecourt to beg for food. Every day we put leftovers in an empty butter box for their dinner and put it out on the patio for them. The chicks would squeak and bob their heads up and down while Fred and Freda gobbled as much food as they could before the onslaught of neighbouring seagulls descended upon the family gathering in the hope of getting a share of the contents in the butter box. When the invasion occurred Fred instinctively protected the family lunch, so with a mighty squawk, wings flapping, a fearful skirmish would ensue while Freda devoured the food as fast as she could. After the last violator had been chased away by Fred, all that remained were a few detached white feathers and several piles of seagull droppings. This daily ritual terrified some of the customers but most of them were fascinated by it and took photos and videos of the spectacle that was going on outside. Fred and his family were the most photographed seagulls in Camber.

It was a month since I had attended the Camber Parish Council meeting at the village hall and another one was imminent so I decided that I would go back to see if there had been any response to the letter from the Highways in Bexhill. I chose not to arrive at the beginning of the meeting as I did not fancy sitting there again agreeing with the ongoing gripes from the locals who had nothing better to do. So I timed my entrance just as the meeting was coming to an end. I could not remember what the person looked like who said he would write the letter so I asked a man who was sitting behind a table with piles of papers in front of him. He said it was not him who had written the letter but pointed out another gentleman saying he thought it might have been him. This was the right man but he said that he had written but to date had not had a reply. So I guessed that was all he could do, he certainly did not offer any encouraging suggestions.

The next day I rang the Highways again just to satisfy my curiosity as to whether the man from the Parish Council had actually written to them. I asked to speak to the Licensing and Enforcement manager. I asked him if he had received a letter from the Parish Council regarding my suggestion for a signpost with directions to local businesses in Camber and he said he had not received any letter and besides he had already told me he would not give his permission for a signpost. He went on to say that because I had put that café sign on top of the lamppost Kilkenny had been forced to break Health and Safety regulations by having to climb up onto the roof of his van to remove it without the protection of a hard hat and if he had fallen off he could have suffered serious injury and because of this he had received a stern talking to. I just roared with laughter at the thought of it and said I would love to have seen him in the act. The Tyrannical Clown did not think it was funny and warned me that to intentionally endanger people's lives was an offence. I replied that I had not intended to endanger Kilkenny's life. However it had been my intention that he would not be able to reach the café sign and I had not forced him to climb up onto the roof of his van; that had been his own choice to endanger his own life. He replied that they took their jobs seriously at East Sussex Highways - so that was that.

I stocked up on lime green paint, cut timber and liquid chalk pens. At every spare moment we were manufacturing new café signs and with all the different coloured chalk pens I was acquiring, and we started to write on them in bright colours. I decided it was time to learn how to make an A-board but first I had to invest in a saw. I copied the A-board the resident had made for me, one meter high and fifty centimetres wide. In fact woodwork turned out to be easier than I thought. I had bought two panels of timber and nine meters of baton which I sawed in half for each panel; one to go across the top and two down either side leaving a couple of inches for the feet. I screwed the batons to the panels using the drill, then I laid them flat and attached the hinges to the inside of the two panels and to my amazement when I had finished making my first A-board it didn't fall apart or rock when I stood it up. I was so pleased with myself, until I realized I had made a slight mistake with the screws. The screws I had used were longer than the width of the timber and I had inadvertently screwed them from the inside of the panel so the sharp ends of the screws were sticking out the other side ready to rip someone's fingers open. Well it was only going to be Kilkenny's, but nevertheless I did write a warning at the top of the A-board. 'Watch your fingers'.

One quiet morning I suddenly had an idea and that was to send Kilkenny and The Tyrannical Clown on a wild goose chase. The idea was to put two café signs miles away from the café in different directions and email them clues in a poem with photos of the café signs. I enjoyed writing silly poems so I got on with that while Lily prepared the café signs.

So the poem was:

Now the summer time is here the boards are going to disappear
But before they're gone for good, we'll have you smiling like you should.
Here's a game for you to play, but you only have one day,
There's two big boards within your reach, I thought you'd like to have one each
We've never travelled out this way so take your lunch to eat midday.
Attached to this email are the clues, if you don't find them then you lose.
This time we've made it easy for you because of your age and the job is new,
Come winter time we'll be back with a bang
So enjoy the peace guys while you can.

That afternoon we drove out of Rye in a northerly direction where we found an isolated sign-post to which we attached one of the signs, and I took a couple of photos. We then drove back into Rye and took the road in the direction of

Winchelsea. We found another sign-post and put the other sign onto it and I took a couple of photos, then we went back to the café to email it all off to Kilkenny and The Tyrannical Clown.

We did not get any response to our challenge. We checked on the signs daily and they stayed there for a week. Then they were gone but we heard nothing. A week later a police car pulled up onto the forecourt, an officer got out and from the back of the car he took out our two café signs. He walked into the café clutching the two large signs, and I laughed at him and asked how he came to be in possession of them and he replied he was bringing them back. I asked him where he had got them from, was it Bexhill or had he removed them off their posts himself? However he had come by them he chose to remain silent, although he did say I was not allowed to attach signs onto street furniture. I asked him if it was permitted to put an A-board on the grass at the top of the road and he said it was.

Over the next two weeks my café signs were going quicker than hot cakes. We put them up one day and they were gone the next, my A-boards were going too and it was hard to keep up with making replacements. I thought about offering Kilkenny a bribe, that's if I ever got to see him again. The Wine Bar signs were still stuck onto the back of the signpost by Pontins and all the businesses in Camber had a multitude of signs and A-boards everywhere; they never got taken. Then I found a new place to put a café sign. There was a fence which ran alongside the pavement in Old Lydd Road; behind the fence there were trees, shrubs and wild rosehip bushes, and thereafter was the bottom of mountainous sand dunes blown by the wind over decades which rose three meters a year. Along this fence other people had attached various advertising signs. There was no reason why I should not put a sign on it as well. I made a new double-sided sign and put it onto a tall thick baton. I had to climb up the bank which was quite steep and awkward to reach the wooden fence. I carried the wooden sign on the baton which was top heavy, the drill, cable ties and copious amounts of loose screws in my pinny pockets. I secured the sign well onto the inside of the fence post with several screws and thick cable ties to make it theft proof not just for Kilkenny but in case any revellers were off to the beach for a barbecue and saw my sign as a convenient piece of firewood.

CHAPTER 9

I received another letter in the middle of July, this time from the Chief Executive's Legal Department in Lewes. It said that several instances of signs advertising my café had been referred to him from the Eastern Highways Department - in particular three instances in May, three in June and further instances in July. I was committing an offence and if I did not cease the infringement of the 1980's Highway Act the County Council would institute legal proceedings without further notice. He added that the matter had been discussed with me by members of staff from Bexhill depot regarding the placement of my café signs. A considerable amount of time and resources were being expended in countering this nuisance and the County Council were not prepared to tolerate any more infringements. He concluded that if any more signs had to be removed they would be destroyed if I did not collect them within seven days.

That was interesting, all the while Kilkenny had been taking my signs I could have got them back, so why had they not told me that I wondered?

I responded to the letter by saying that it was necessary to have a sign for my café at the top of the road because without that, visitors to Camber would not know there was a café in Lydd Road. I did not explain why I had put other signs along the main road because apart from hoping that I would bump into Kilkenny removing them, I had no justification for my actions. I added that I had not damaged the street furniture he had mentioned nor had I drawn graffiti on anything. Also there had been no serious discussions with staff from Bexhill Depot and that although Kilkenny had been here to the cafe I would not be able to recognise him because at the time he was engulfed in high visibility work gear.

On the strength of that letter and in the knowledge that I could retrieve my café signs I drove over to Bexhill after work to do just that. At least I knew the correct way in this time, so I arrived and went into the small reception area and asked for my A-boards and any other signs they might have belonging to me. I was asked to wait and eventually a man appeared through a door and introduced himself as the Licensing and Enforcement manager. He was indeed the infamous Tyrannical Clown. He was not a bad looking man in his early sixties, stocky with crinkly grey hair flattened under a screen of hair cream; he had dark accusing eyes and was about the same height as Kilkenny. He offered me a seat in the tiny reception area, and I showed him the letter I had received from Lewes County Council and pointed to the last paragraph which said I could retrieve my signs within seven days. He took the letter from me and read all of it. He said they only had one A-board as the rest had been destroyed. He proceeded to tell me about fly-posting and Highways Acts and Town and Country Planning Acts on and on. I told him I needed to advertise my café or I would go out of business. I tried to do a deal with him; I said I would take my signs down if he would leave the ones on the BT pole, but he would not agree. I asked him why he did not go after the other businesses and he said they did, so I asked to see the signs of these other businesses they had taken. So he went to fetch my A-board, and after about five minutes he squashed himself and the A-board through the door and handed it to me before we went outside. I handed it back to him and asked him to carry it to my car. I pointed in the direction of where I had parked my car and as he looked over he saw a small Micra parked next to mine. 'Oh' he exclaimed 'that's fine, the back seat goes down in a Micra'. I was furious at the thought of him thinking I would have a stupid little car like that, so I replied indignantly that I would not be seen dead in one of those and my car was the nice little black convertible sports car parked beside it. He passed me the A-board and told me it was better that I put it in the car myself as he did not wish to do any damage thereby possibly being sued by me. So I put the A-board into the front of my car with some difficulty and then I drove home. On the way I remembered he had not shown me the other business signs he had spoken of that he claimed had been removed to their yard so I suspected that he had been lying.

A few days later I had left Lily in the café whilst I went into Rye. On the way back low and behold there was Kilkenny parked up on the side of the road where the sign was on the stump. I pulled up behind him and got out of my car; he had just cut the cable ties and had the sign in both hands about to carry it to his van. I could see instantly that it was not going to fit as it far exceeded the length of the van. He asked me what I wanted so I asked him what he was proposing to do with my sign. At that moment he too realised it was too long to fit into the back of his van. All of a sudden I had an idea; I would offer him a bribe to stop him from taking my café signs away. I had never tried to bribe someone before so I wasn't quite sure how I was meant to go about it and discretion was not one of my best points, so I just came right out with the first thing that came into my head and offered him £2000 cash and a packet of Viagra if he would leave my signs alone. He just stared at me, and for a brief moment I thought he was going to accept my offer, but sadly he informed me he didn't need Viagra so I challenged him to prove it. He said he didn't know how to prove it so I told him I only knew of one way. Sadly it did not work and he chose to ignore my suggestion, and as he opened the back of his van I could see he was trying to work out the problem of fitting the long café sign into it so I said that the sign was not going to fit. He told me not to worry he would make it fit and so he did, he took a saw out of his van and cut the sign in half and threw the two parts into the back. I reminded him that I could have reclaimed it within seven days to which he replied I could not because I was a constant offender. He got back in his van and started the engine. He appeared to be waiting for me. I got into my car and made myself look a complete idiot by accelerating too quickly revving the engine up and not going anywhere; all the while Kilkenny waited for me. We arrived at the next A-board opposite Pontins, Kilkenny got out of his van and I got out of my car. He asked me if I was going to sit on the A-board to prevent him from taking it; I replied I was far too much of a lady to do such a thing. So while he crossed the road to fetch the A-board I tried to open the back of his van to remove what of mine might have been in it. He saw me and shouted across the road that I wouldn't get very far as it was locked, and he was right, it was. When he came back carrying my A-board I asked him to look at my photo I had taken of the signs belonging to the Wine bar showing them stuck on the signpost outside Pontins. First he made a big exaggeration of getting his bunch of keys out of his pocket and jangled them in front of me, then he unlocked the back door and threw the A-board into the back of his van. I showed him the photo on my phone, and he said nothing but went to the front of his van and came back wearing a pair of glasses. He looked at the photo again and asked me where the photo was taken. I told him that he must drive past it every time he came to Camber, but he said he had never seen it. I wasn't going to tell him where it was because he knew where it was. Then he got back in his van and drove off to the BT pole at the top of the road where he turned his van round to face the main road. I pulled up on the opposite side waiting for him to get out of his van to pull my signs down off the BT pole. I waited for a couple of minutes but he didn't get out so I drove back to the café and for some reason, known only to himself, Kilkenny did not take the two signs off the BT pole.

Every year a summer fête was held in the neighbouring village of Iden and each year the signs advertising the fête would be erected along various roads in the area. On the Camber road towards the junction of the A259 there were several small signs in a row running along the side of the road, each sign had one word written on it pertaining to the Iden fête. These signs would go up about one month before the event and come down a week or so after. One day I had an idea, I would make small signs and put them running along the other side of the road opposite the Iden fête ones.

I sawed up four pieces of wood about two feet by eighteen inches. On the first one I wrote 'CAMBER' and then I decided I would add a little rhyme for Kilkenny when he came to take them away. Inspired by seeing him having to saw the stump sign in half I wrote: ' TO STOP YOU FEELING LIKE A TWIT ARE SMALLER BOARDS A BETTER FIT?' On the second sign I wrote 'CAFE' and underneath that one I wrote 'IF YOU TAKE THESE BOARDS AWAY THEN GREAT BIG HUGE ONES WE'LL DISPLAY'. On the third one I wrote 'OPEN' and along the bottom of that one I wrote 'TAKE THESE BOARDS AND YOU'LL BE SORRY NEXT WEEK YOU'LL NEED A 7 TON LORRY'. I just wrote 7.30 on the last one. The plan was to put a short baton on the back of each one and hammer them into the ground, but it was summer and the ground was hard and I couldn't get them in deep enough and they just fell over because the ends were square and I guessed that to hammer them into the ground properly they would need to be pointed. So I took them back to the café and asked a friend to make the batons pointed which he did. I went back to the chosen grass verge on the opposite side of the road to the Iden fete signs and after a lot of exhausting hammering I managed to bash them into the ground and tried to make them stand upright. I was not overly confident that they would stay that way for very long.

CHAPTER 10

The following week I replaced the signs that Kilkenny had taken, including the one on the stump. There were only half a dozen wooden café signs on various bits of street furniture including the two on the BT pole. One evening I pasted half a dozen or so small posters onto bits of old weathered cardboard which had been abandoned long ago and left to rot in various places around the village and beyond. I thought as these old signs had been hanging there for months they had obviously not been a problem to the highway men. I got a bit over zealous with the pot of paste though, I stuck some more of my small leaflets on the bottom corners of the four chevrons on one of the bends on the Camber road. It was blowing a gale that evening and it was really more trouble than it was worth, dipping the brush into the tub of PVA and attempting to transfer it onto the back of a leaflet that was flapping about in the strong wind. I got covered in glue and I lost most of the leaflets and posters I was clutching because they were blown away across the farmers' fields.

Then one lovely hot day in August, the eleventh to be precise, we were sitting outside in the sun and I noticed that the signs were gone off the BT pole, so I walked up the road to check. Indeed they were not there only a small piece of broken café sign remained still attached to the pole with a screw sticking out of it. There was no sign of Kilkenny and his van so I went back to the café, left Lily in charge and asked her to look out for the highway van whilst I went for a drive to see if I could track down Kilkenny and my café signs.

I drove towards Rye and before long I noticed the sign I had put onto the chevron post wasn't there either so I turned round and drove back to the café and got another one and went straight back and replaced it. Then I noticed another one was missing off a lamppost so I replaced that one too. I drove towards Rye, and again there was no sign of highway vans or Kilkenny. The four small signs I had had so much difficulty hammering into the ground were also gone. I wondered if it might have been Donkeykonk, a local man who made a living by selling donkey rides to children on the beach in the summer. I drove back to Camber and blow me down the sign I had just replaced on the chevron had gone again. I wondered who could be so elusive and manage to take all my signs without me seeing them.

I turned into Old Lydd Road and there parked up on double yellow lines was an East Sussex highway van and two highway men standing beside it, one of whom I recognised as The Tyrannical Clown, the other one whom I did not recognise.

I asked The Tyrannical Clown if he had taken my signs. He said he had and he started shouting at me that he was going to get an Anti-Social Behaviour Order against me and I laughed at him and told him he was being ridiculous. He carried on shouting at me about how awful I had made Camber look and his colleague had driven through Camber the other day and had phoned The Tyrannical Clown and asked him if he had seen Camber. The colleague was a long haired, chilled out looking guy and in all probability he didn't care what Camber looked like. I asked him how many signs apart from mine had he taken from the village that morning and I tried peering into the back of their van but he quickly closed the back doors to prevent me from seeing anything, so I guessed he had only taken mine. He asked me if I had known they were in Camber removing my café signs as ten minutes after he had removed one I had replaced it again. I said if I had known they were in Camber I would have waited till they had gone before I went round replacing the signs, not do it while they were still here.

He threatened that if I put any more cafe signs up they would prosecute me. I replied I would stop on the condition that he would treat all businesses within his jurisdiction in same way he treated mine and I gave him three days to remove all business signs in Camber otherwise I was going to replace my signs. They got into their van and drove off. I decided to follow them, so when they pulled off I followed them till the A259 junction and I waited there. They drove a short distance and reversed into a lay-by and for a few moments we stared at each other. I wanted them to think I was up to mischief the moment they had gone. It worked; I turned round on the main road and headed back to Camber. On one of the bends there was an island in the middle of the road with a gap for cyclist to cross to an adjoining cycle path and also for cars to turn round, I drove through the gap and waited in the lay-by there to see if they came back and sure enough a couple of minutes later they went flying past me in the direction of Camber. So I waited there and about ten minutes later they came flying back again in the direction of Bexhill. I did wave at them, and I don't know if they saw me but they didn't wave back.

So that was it, they had taken all my signs, even the one on the fence in Old Lydd Road which wasn't even in their jurisdiction. Nevertheless, taking everything into consideration that had occurred that morning, I would not put my café signs back until I had given The Tyrannical Clown the chance to make everyone else take theirs down.,

That afternoon I drove into Rye to buy some more wood, everywhere was looking rather bare with all my signs gone. The following day I made a new A-board and four more signs in readiness for the inevitable. My woodwork skills had improved tremendously and I could make an A-board in twenty minutes, luckily the blackboard paint dried quickly in the sun but writing on them was the most time consuming.

I stuck to my word; I patiently waited for two days without any café signs. There were customers of course, it was the middle of the summer, most of those had come across the café by chance and nearly all of them asked why I did not advertise it. I was so annoyed; all the other businesses were advertising as usual with their signs out on the pavements and on lampposts, even the Burger van in the lay-by not only had four huge A-boards either side of the road, he had now added red flashing lights to the front and back of his bus.

Three days after The Tyrannical Clown had rid Camber of my café signs, I was overcome with a great sense of urgency to replace them. I took the new A-board and put it at the top of the road, I replaced the sign opposite the caravan park and one opposite Pontins entrance. I replaced the doubled sided sign and baton onto the fence at the bottom of the sand dunes.

Amusingly The Tyrannical Clown had evidently not noticed the large 'fish and chip' sign which was pointing in the direction of the Fish and Chip shop, plus several small signs that were advertising the wine bar which had been nailed at various distances along the entire length of the fence and a huge sign advertising a Circus at Salts Farm at the end of August. So with such an array of signs The Tyrannical Clown and Kilkenny had ignored for so long I had no reason to feel guilty or defiant and I considered my rebellious behaviour utterly justified.

With the signs back out business resumed as normal but sadly was short lived and came to an abrupt end by the middle of the day, when we noticed the new A-board and the sign on the fence had gone, presumably so had the other two. As a matter of routine I periodically checked my emails throughout the day and shortly after noticing the new signs had gone an email arrived in my mail box from East Sussex Highways.

I opened the email with anticipation;

Dear Mrs Pattinson

Request for Interview, Wednesday 19 August 2009

Following the placing of your café signs on street furniture in and around Camber on Tuesday 11th August 2009, I am requesting your attendance at Rye Police Station at 11am on Wednesday 19th August 2009 in order to be interviewed under caution as a precursor to court proceedings. Please be advised that you might wish to consider attending with a solicitor of your choice to be present during that interview. If it is your intention not to attend please let me know as soon as possible and in any event before that date.

Yours sincerely

The Tyrannical Clown
Licensing & Enforcement Manager

I was not surprised at this email request from The Tyrannical Clown. I anticipated that my plan of trying to allure Kilkenny to Camber was in all probability doomed from the start and in hindsight not the best way of going about chatting someone up. I certainly did not want a solicitor present, as I felt sure there would be nothing happening that I could not deal with myself, so I replied asking him who would be there, in the hope he would say Kilkenny. He replied the following day;

Dear Mrs Pattinson

I can confirm that the interview will be with me and a colleague who is also a Licensing and Enforcement Manager for East Sussex Highways.

This interview will be in accordance with the relevant codes of practice contained within the Police and Criminal Evidence Act 1984. I have arranged this interview at Rye Police Station as it is the closest to Camber that is equipped with the

*facilities for recording such interviews. It is for this reason I
need to know whether you will be attending so I can inform
Sussex Police regarding the arrangements for the room. Apart
from the interview being held at the police station the police
are not involved in this case.*

Yours sincerely

The Tyrannical Clown
Licensing and Enforcement Manager

I replied confirming that I would attend Rye Police station
on the 19th August 2009 but that was next week. I had more
pressing things to attend to now so with all the off-cuts of
wood I had acquired I decided to make smaller flat café signs
to put onto the BT pole again, as they took much less wood
than an A-board and were much quicker to prepare. I did the
same for the one opposite the caravan park and on the fence
too. I was not expecting them to stay there for long anyway. I
was eager to know why the burger van got away with four
huge A-boards placed directly on either side of the road. I had
also been driving round Rye to check how other businesses
went about advertising; Rye was awash with A-boards and
signs on the roads and pavements. One restaurant even had
three A-boards in a row straddling the double yellow lines
immediately outside of their establishment. How did they get
away with it or was it within their rights to advertise like that?

Either side of the Camber road the council had dug in
wooden delineator posts to stop cars parking on the grass
verge in hot weather. Prior to this, cars would park crammed
along either side of the road which caused chaos with the
traffic coming into Camber. Donkeykonk had two large fields
off the main road where he kept his five donkeys, and on hot
days he would open up his field as a car park and attach his
'Parking All Day £4' signs to the councils wooden delineator
posts covering the built-in reflectors. He also put a row of

council cones along the route to guide the cars to his field, including two large stolen 'keep left' signs which he had stuck his £4 parking signs on. He would display these signs for days on end in fine weather on street furniture and stolen council property, but nothing ever happened to him for doing it.

There were two fish and chip shops in Camber, one on the main road which did good business with Pontins holiday makers. The other was in Old Lydd Road and I had heard that the jointly owned Café and Fish and Chip shop were to be demolished and replaced by three town houses. That was good news as it would create a fish and chip gap in the market this end of the village, so I thought it would be a good idea for me to fill that gap and stay open in the evenings to sell fish and chips. Although it would mean having to invest in a new double fryer and all the things needed for fish and chips and it would extend my working day by four hours. But this was an opportunity to improve the turnover of the café and not to be missed.

CHAPTER 11

The 19th August dawned, it was a beautiful hot day, not a
cloud in the sky and I was going to Rye Police station to meet
The Tyrannical Clown in a room with a recording kit. But I
did not have to be there till eleven o'clock which meant I had
to go to work first and Lily was going to be in charge whilst I
was away. Lily and I had devised a plan to disrupt the
impending interview; at 11.20am precisely Lily would ring
me to ask for instructions on how she went about cooking
kippers. Appropriately the ring tone on my mobile phone was
a police siren.

I did not dress for the occasion and just wore my working
clothes including my pinny so I could keep my phone, keys
and money in it without having to carry a bag around with me.

I took the roof off the car as it was so hot and I set off in
plenty of time as I liked to be punctual. I parked in the car
park opposite the Police Station and paid and displayed. The
problem of taking the roof off the car meant my parking ticket
was vulnerable and might have been a temptation to others
without change.

I went into the police station and told the guy behind the
counter that I had a date with a couple of highway men. At
that moment The Tyrannical Clown and his colleague
appeared behind the counter. The Tyrannical Clown greeted
me by saying 'Hello Sally' and then introduced his younger
colleague from Ringmer and they both shook my hand. I was
ushered behind the counter and through a door into a room at
the front of the station. The interview room was dark and
dingy with a closed Venetian blind at the window, there were
two tables and three chairs, all very well worked out I thought
and had been placed like scenery on a stage. I was told to sit
on the hard, wooden, armless upright chair in the middle of

the room, opposite me The Tyrannical Clown had a comfortable blue upholstered chair with padded arms beside a table with a pile of papers on it and the colleague from Ringmer had the other blue comfortable chair and table with the recording equipment. I was disappointed, no Kilkenny. The interview room was stuffy so I asked for the window to be opened. The Tyrannical Clown offered me a glass of water which I didn't want so I said it was too hot in there and he reluctantly opened the skylight window and opened the Venetian blind slightly, which allowed a thin trickle of sunshine to glimmer through the gaps of the blind.

The colleague broke the seal of the two cassette tapes and placed them in the tape recorder, which was set into action and the interview began by the colleague from Ringmer introducing himself and stating the rank he held within the Highways Authority at Ringmer, swiftly followed by The Tyrannical Clown introducing himself and stating his position within the Highways Authority in Bexhill. The colleague explained why I was there and that I was not under arrest and I could leave at any time I wished.

The colleague asked me who I was, to which I responded, as he had just called me by my name, why did he want me to say it again? He replied it was for the purpose of the tape. He then asked me for my date of birth so I challenged him to guess it, which clearly annoyed him. He repeated that it was for the tape recording and I was obliged to say it. He continued to tell me that I might end up in Court and it was for that reason he was obliged to caution me, which he did by saying 'You do not have to say anything but it may harm your defence if you do not mention when questioned something you later rely on in court. Anything you say may be given in evidence'. When he had finished the riot act he asked me if I had understood the caution to which I replied I hadn't and please could he repeat it in French. He ignored my request and although I repeated that I had not understood the caution he continued to ask me questions. Firstly the nature of my business and where I operated it from, and how long I had been there. I asked him why he was asking me things he already knew and he said for the purpose of the tape. He asked me if I was aware that I had unlawfully placed signs on the highway. I said I possibly was aware. He asked me in what format I had been made aware. What format? I hadn't a clue what he meant, the only time I had seen the word 'format' was on my computer and I could only think in the stress of the moment he meant what style of writing was used in the letter I had received. So I suggested he asked The Tyrannical Clown as it was his letter. So he immediately said 'then you did receive a letter from The Tyrannical Clown' I had just said I had and took the opportunity to ask him why he had to ask the same question two or three times. He confirmed for the benefit of the tape that the format which made me aware that I was unlawfully placing signs had come in the format of a letter.

So I asked him if that letter was the format he enquired about and why had he not just asked simply instead of using unfamiliar jargon just to confuse me. Having established that I was aware of what I had done unlawfully I guessed in the grand scheme of things it was at this point when I had the opportunity to plead insanity, but knowing Lily's phone call must be imminent I decided to remain sane.

He asked me if I had received a letter from their legal department and to that I replied that I must have received it because I had answered it. He commented that my responses to The Tyrannical Clown and their Legal Department were not an acceptance of the situation and I had just continued to place signs on the highway. I responded by saying it had been necessary. I didn't say the real necessity was to entice Kilkenny to Camber to chat him up.

The Tyrannical Clown produced a book of photos of my cafe signs and stickers, he stood over me turning the pages telling me to look at them and asking if I recognised the signs in the photos. I commented on the stupidity of his question, as the reason I was there in the Police station being interviewed under caution was because of these signs and he had no reason to show me the photos as I had hand-made every sign in his photo album so I obviously knew what the signs looked like and where the photos had been taken because I had put them there.

And then I felt my phone vibrate in my pinny pocket and off went the police siren ring tone, good for Lily right on time.

I answered my phone eagerly and Lily asked me how she should cook kippers as she had never cooked them before. I repeated the 'how to cook kippers' bit so the colleague and The Tyrannical Clown would get the gist of Lily's phone call. I thoroughly explained every detail of how she must prepare, cook, plate-up and present the kippers not forgetting to butter the bread and cut it from corner to corner. The Tyrannical Clown had sat back down on his comfortable chair and was twiddling his thumbs and looking at the ceiling, clearly annoyed at the interruption of his interrogation on his café sign photos. On seeing the peeved expression on his face I repeated again in detail to Lily the process of how to microwave a kipper. The phone call came to an inevitable end and off we went again with the book of photos.

The Tyrannical Clown resumed his domineering stance standing over me again demanding I look through the photos and I purposely looked in the other direction because I didn't want to look at them. He repeated for me to look at them and I carried on looking in the other direction. I repeated that I already knew what they looked like as I had made them myself and put them were I had. I knew everything I needed to know about these signs in his photos. He then asked me if I accepted by looking at these photographs that all these signs were the ones that I myself had placed. I asked him what he did not understand when I said that I recognised them because I had made them and I had placed them where he had found and photographed them. He repeated himself, and was getting on my nerves. If I did not conform to his use of words we would not progress with the interview. He was so childish I thought. So I responded by pointing to each of his photographs and I just repeated 'guilty' to each one. Not content with that he started again and said 'but Sally just look at these photographs and say did you or did you not?' I just said 'yes' he continued 'on every single photo you actually did all this?' I replied 'yes I did' He would not stop and he said 'did you or did you not put every one of these out, every single poster, every single bit of wood?'

He finished that part of his interrogation and announced that he was going to use his collection of photographs as his exhibit. 'Whatever' I said. I was laughing at him; any one would have thought I had murdered someone. He obviously had had practice at this and it did cross my mind that maybe he had been a policeman at some stage in his life.

Back in his seat The Tyrannical Clown put his photo album carefully into a plastic folder and placed it neatly underneath his pile of papers. He then got onto the subject of the café sign on the chevron post which he had removed on 11th August and when he returned ten minutes later it had been replaced with another. I started to laugh again and he said he appreciated my sense of humour but this was a serious matter, so I stopped laughing and tried to look serious. I told him that I had not realised it was him who had taken it and I had blamed Donkeykonk for doing it, then he started to laugh and asked me who did I know with a name like Donkeykonk. I told him he was the man with stolen keep left signs who put parking signs onto the council delineator posts covering up the reflectors and he had numerous stolen traffic cones which he put along both sides of the road not only to direct the cars into his field but to make sure nothing could park on that part of the road or nearby, forcing the motorists into his field whether they wanted to go in or not. All he said to that was he had no interest in things like that. I quickly reminded The Tyrannical Clown that he had threatened me with an ASBO the previous week for my signs on the highway and street furniture but because the colleague from Ringmer was there he had the audacity to say that he had been joking. I then asked when it would be my turn to question them. The colleague said I could ask questions only relating to the offences on 11th August 2009. I felt we had exhausted that topic and I wanted to know why they took no notice of the other signs that were on the highway. I asked The Tyrannical Clown, but as soon as I did so the colleague said that my question did not relate to the offences I had committed on 11th August 2009 and so the interview would be terminated and the tape recorder was switched off at eleven thirty-four.

At this point I was invited by The Tyrannical Clown to repeat my question. I asked him again why he did not pursue other people who put signs on the road and on street furniture, and he replied because he was not dealing with them at this time. He also said that I had driven Kilkenny mad and he no longer would have anything to do with my café signs and from now on I would be dealing with him. I retorted indignantly that he would be dealing with me and he should find something worthwhile to do instead of harassing old ladies. Then all of a sudden The Tyrannical Clown reminded me of my ex-husband sitting there looking smug and arrogant. I started to shout at him about the dreadful time I had in France when my husband had abandoned me and my children and left us bankrupt and homeless and he was just sitting there like a pompous prick making me into a criminal over a few bits of wood. Then my voice rose, I was screaming at him and suddenly I began bombarding him with the contents of my pinny pocket. The first missile that flew in his direction was my mobile phone which broke into three pieces on impact landing at his feet, swiftly followed by my designer glasses which I ripped off my face. Then I hurled a bunch of keys and several dirty tissues and when he saw the second larger bunch of keys in my hand ready to fling at him, he jumped up out of his comfortable chair and dived for cover under the table. When the colleague realised I had nothing else to throw he cautiously got down on his hands and knees and started to gather up my belongings including the dirty tissues and passed them back to me one by one. The Tyrannical Clown emerged from behind the table; he had lost the smug expression he had a few moments ago and was pre- occupied with wiping the blood off his left forearm where the keys had struck him. There followed a deathly silence.

I was expecting the policeman in the reception area to come flying through the door to find out what the commotion was all about, but he didn't. As I regained my composure The Tyrannical Clown, still nursing his injured arm, sat down and started to gather his bits of paper while the colleague put both the tapes into a plastic self -sealing envelope, and told me that I would be sent a copy if they decided to prosecute me.

I politely enquired about the injury I had inflicted upon The Tyrannical Clown's arm, and he said it had felt better before I had thrown my keys at him. I wanted to apologise but before I could do that he said that I was clearly a force to be reckoned with, and on the strength of this observation it seemed pointless to apologise, so I didn't.

The interview came to an end. The Tyrannical Clown opened the door for me and thanked me for coming. I did not want to look at the policeman who was still in the reception area as I was embarrassed at the disturbance I had just created.

I wanted to get out of there back into the sunshine and fresh air.

I got back to my car and the parking ticket was still there. It took me an hour and a half to drive the 3 miles back to Camber as there was a queue of traffic heading for the beach as usual on a hot day. When I eventually arrived in Camber, Donkeykonk had his stolen keep left signs and traffic cones out on the road, so I took photos of them to send to The Tyrannical Clown.

I did not know or care what the outcome of the day's activities would bring; I doubted whether they would prosecute me for a few bits of wood; a more likely reason would be the assault I delivered upon The Tyrannical Clown's arm.

The following day I felt it only right that I should apologise to The Tyrannical Clown for assaulting him with my bunch of keys, so I emailed him an apology and enquired after his injured arm. I told him I would remove the signs I had recently put at the top and bottom of the road and the one opposite the caravan park on the telegraph pole. However, I warned him again if after three days all the other businesses still had their signs displayed around Camber and Rye then I would not hesitate to put mine back again. I also told him I would remove the stickers I had stuck to the chevron signs too. I attached two photos, one of Donkeykonk's stolen keep left signs and the other of his 'Parking £4 a day' signs screwed to the delineator posts. I sent the email, then I reluctantly removed my café signs. It made me feel sick not having any signs out, I worried that people would not find the café and with the threatening onset of a recession I needed to take as much money as I could as, unlike the two previous years, I had not managed to save anywhere near the amount I needed to for the winter months.

CHAPTER 12

Twelve miles west of Camber there is a village accessed by a turn off from the A 259. The village is situated a good mile down a lane where there is a pub, the owner of which had been placing wooden signs on the A259 advertising the pub and the food for years. An A-board stood on the grass island at the junction of the turn off, there were signs screwed onto oak trees opposite the turn off and there were signs attached to street furniture in various places along the lane. Outside the pub and on the opposite side of the lane there was an array of pub signs advertising all kinds of activities and fun day events taking place at the pub. I passed these signs once a week when I went shopping to Sainsbury's and they were always there, the same signs in the same places; they had never been removed, and it was evident the landlord of the pub had the freedom to advertise where it suited him without repercussion from the Highways Inspectors.

It brought into question who did this 1980's Highway Act apply to and who was it enforced upon. Every business needs to advertise and you see signs everywhere - it's a way of life, some businesses would cease to exist without it. Were the actions of The Tyrannical Clown really in the interest of public safety or was he just out to persecute me? Whatever reason he had, it was not going to deter me from advertising my business. In fact I felt pity for The Tyrannical Clown; he might get away with throwing his weight about with other people but this time he had unwisely picked on the wrong woman.

I had started to think seriously about the fish and chips idea. The other fish and chip shop was due to close on 8th September, so it seemed a good idea that Camber Café took over where that one left off. It was onwards and upwards to get it organised. Decision made, the date we would start the fish and chips would be Wednesday 9th September, and we would just sell fish and chips in the evening as there wasn't really enough room in the cooking quarters to do the day time menu and fish and chips at the same time. I needed to buy a new double fryer and make a small alteration in the café to install it, get some fliers printed up to post through the local letter boxes and of course make the inevitable new fish and chip signs to put on the forbidden highway.

Every two or three days my signs would be taken away by highway men. I just carried on making replacements to the point it became a matter of routine. I emailed The Tyrannical Clown and asked him why he had removed my café signs on 11th, 13th ,18th , 26th and 29th August, the latter being a Saturday which is not a normal working day for council workers and then the most recent being September 5th I invited him and Kilkenny to come to the café to explain to me why he persists in removing my signs and I would like to take them on a tour of Camber and Rye to see all the A-boards and signs that other businesses displayed daily. Also I would like them to give me a good valid reason why he did not take the other business signs away. It was unlikely that I would get any sensible answers from him.

When the fliers had been printed, I entrusted a couple of local boys to post one into each and every letter box in the village in the hope that at least half of the residents would receive one. I put a sign on a post outside of the café announcing that fish and chips were starting in the evening of September 9th

The four new signs for the fish and chips were the best we had ever made and very artistic and colourful. I bought all sorts of different coloured chalk pens from eBay as we were using so many for each board. They took ages for us to make and in the end they were ready but I was not going to display them until the evening before we were due to start the fish and chips.

To test out the new menu I had invited a few local friends to come to the café for a fish and chip supper on the evening before we were due to start officially. That morning I had received the tape recording of the 'interview under caution' from The Tyrannical Clown and a short note to tell me to keep it somewhere safe. So that meant my friends would have in-house entertainment by listening to the tape whilst they ate their fish and chips. While I prepared the supper a couple of strong husbands went and put up the new fish and chip signs for me - one on the fence at the bottom of the sand dunes, two on the BT pole at the top of the road and one opposite the caravan park. They used the longest and deadliest screws I had ever seen, they must have been nine inches long and they had small razor sharp blades sticking out of the thread of the screw and they had to use a special drill bit for them. They assured me that nothing would be able to get these signs off the BT poles.

The supper was successful and we all listened to the tape that The Tyrannical Clown had sent me, which was hilarious. It could not possibly be used in a law court and sounded more like a script for a sitcom. After supper I went to admire the new signs. Although the sun was going down I took a couple of photos of them. Our new signs looked so cool and trendy, they were the largest and prettiest we had ever made and what's more they were theft proof too. I went to bed that night full of excitement for the next day and the launch of Camber Café Fish and Chips.

The next morning I was up early. I couldn't sleep as I was excited about the launch of the fish and chips. I went to the shop to buy the daily newspaper and the new signs looked splendid with the early morning sun shining on them.

Lily was coming to work early that day too so we could

prepare for the evening. She arrived at the café at eight o'clock looking puzzled and asked me where the fish and chip signs had gone from the BT pole at the top of the road. I hoped she was joking but she assured me she wasn't. I had to see for myself so I jumped into my car and drove to the bottom of the road first and before I got there I could see that the sign was gone from the fence. I drove back up the road and sure enough the signs had gone from the BT pole too, then I drove up through the village to the far end opposite the caravan park where the fourth sign had been attached and that was also gone. It was barely eight o'clock in the morning and we had only put them there the night before and they were there when I had just been to the shop. I was furious. No one had even had time to see them yet and I thought of all that work and expense making them. I went back to the café and told Lily they had all gone. She was gutted too as she had helped me make them. How had they known they were there, someone must have been spying the night before for them to have been removed so early in the morning. They didn't even start work till eight thirty or nine and the signs had been taken between half past seven and eight o'clock. So much for them being theft proof! I was so fed up and we hadn't seen a highway van or a truck or any other vehicle they drove about in, so who had taken them I wondered. In any event it had to be someone who was mighty strong to have been able to pull the signs down with nine inch theft proof screws through them.

Lily and I had a coffee and suddenly in my fury I sent a text message to Kilkenny, I wrote: *'You arsehole I only just put them up, it's a good job I've got spares'*. Oh how I wished I did have spares, I only had an A-board I could put at the top of the road for now. Whoever had taken them had thankfully left the small fish and chip sign on the pole outside the café. Fuss over, we concentrated on serving the customers and advertised the fish and chips verbally. Later on in the morning we had got over the breakfast rush and we just had three customers left, one of them being the local vicar who had come for a light lunch before going off on her house visits. My phone rang and then stopped again, and when I looked it was from Kilkenny, so I rang him back. He answered his phone but I pretended I didn't know who had rung me and I asked him who he was and why had he drop called me. He said he hadn't rung me but explained that his phone had been lying on the photo copier and the vibration of it whilst printing had made his phone ring my number. What an extraordinary occurrence, a vibrating printer that triggered a mobile phone to ring my number. Anyway, I said I recognised his voice and asked him why he had taken the new signs that morning. He said he had not taken them and that he was not an arsehole. I asked him who had taken them and he replied he did not have anything to do with my café signs and he did not know or care. He went on to say that I had driven him mad with my café signs and if I was a bloke he would come over to Camber and put me flat on my arse, so I invited him to come and do just that, and he said he didn't do that kind of thing to ladies. I said that if he was a man I would put him flat on his arse. All the while the conversation flowed the vicar couldn't help but hear it as she quietly ate her lunch pretending she was not listening. Kilkenny then asked me how I had got his phone number and I said he must have rung me some time, and he replied he had never rung me on his own private mobile phone. I then went off at a tangent and tried to confuse him by asking him something personal that he would have no idea of how I came about knowing such a thing. I asked him if he knew a guy who had a secret kind of government job and obviously he was acquainted with him and he immediately reacted aggressively by accusing this innocent man of giving me his number and before I had the chance to deny it, he was already threatening to go and put him flat on his arse too. I asked him why he was so aggressive but he didn't seem to think he was. I apologised to him for calling him an arsehole but he wouldn't accept my apology, he said that The Tyrannical Clown was going to send me an email imminently and when I had read it I must ring him. So that was that and he rang off.

The email arrived from The Tyrannical Clown at three minutes past one; it said:

Dear Mrs Pattinson
Camber-Café Signs
Thank you for your email of 8th September 2009, the content of which is noted.
Unfortunately legal proceedings have yet to be concluded with regard to the offences of fly posting therefore I am unable to enter into conversations with regard to that case. That said I can assure you East Sussex Highways do have legal powers to remove items from the highway when it comes to safety and obstruction issues. Advertising and the control of such are issues for the District Council planners and I strongly advise that you seek advice from them.
I again reiterate that to place unauthorised signs on the highway or any structure is not permitted and will be dealt with in the appropriate manner. Furthermore it has been necessary on two occasions since 11 August 2009, for our contractors to remove signs pertaining to your café - once on 28 August and again today 9 September 2009. Invoices for the cost of removal will be sent to you in due course but I can say that they to date stand in excess of £300 pounds. In conclusion I urge you not to keep reoffending as the consequences could be expensive.
Yours sincerely

The Tyrannical Clown
Licensing & Enforcement Manager

I read it twice and then rang The Tyrannical Clown as Kilkenny had told me to, and was told that he was unavailable to speak to me and he would ring me back. He rang me back at 13.31 on phone number 01424 724555.

The first question he asked was where I was going to be selling the fish and chips from and I replied it would obviously be from the café. He said I could not sell fish and chips. I asked him why not as I already sold take away chips and baguettes what difference would a bit of battered fish make and he said I did not hold a fish and chip licence. That was ridiculous, if I could sell other take-away food why not fish? He continued to say that if I attempted to sell fish and chips he would have my food licence revoked, and he said he had checked me out and he knew that I held an alcohol licence, a gaming licence and a PRS licence for music, and threatened he would have these revoked as well, so I suggested in that case why did he not revoke my driving and television licences while he was at it.

I asked him what he thought of the photos I had sent him of the stolen keep left signs Donkeykonk was using to advertise parking in his field, but he just said that those things were of no interest to him.

He then said he had reported me to BT for vandalising three BT poles. I asked him how I had damaged them; he said I had made them full of holes which I strongly denied and blamed it onto a flock of woodpeckers. He informed me that my signs were a danger to pedestrians and someone had bashed their head on one of my café signs that had been attached to the BT pole. I said the person should have looked where they were going, and he said the gentleman concerned was blind. Then he said he would pay me one compliment. I braced myself expecting him to pass comment on my determination but he didn't say anything to my appraisal, he just said that I was the most annoying woman he had ever met and he had wasted too much time talking to me and he hung up.

CHAPTER 13

I was unsure if The Tyrannical Clown's threats were real and that he did really intend to have my licences revoked and if he did I would not have a business left. I rang the man at Rother District Council who had dealt with all my licences when I bought the café, and asked him if he knew The Tyrannical Clown and he said he had heard of him. I explained the reason for my phone call and he assured me that as The Tyrannical Clown had not issued me any licences he had no authority to revoke them and secondly it would be the Police who would request for my alcohol licence to be revoked and that would need a valid reason as in serving alcohol to under aged people or complaints about noise and drunken behaviour outside the café, so he told me not to worry.

I was relieved knowing that my licences where safe, but there was no doubt that The Tyrannical Clown's escapade of taking my café signs at every opportunity had become an obsession rather than enforcing Highway Acts.

Despite the absence of the colourful fish and chip signs the evening sales were a great boost to the café's finances. It was a long day but worthwhile. The plan was to sell fish and chips every evening until the end of September and then Thursdays, Fridays and Saturdays in October as the holiday makers started to dwindle once the evenings began to draw in and the Autumnal chill blew over the sand dunes.

The highways continued to take only my signs whilst all the other businesses were hassle free, and one day after all my signs had gone again I emailed The Tyrannical Clown and wrote *'stop being a bully and get a life you saddo'*. The next day they came and took away the replacements, so I emailed him again and this time I just wrote 'so you didn't get a life'.

And then true to his word on 14th September 2009 I received an invoice for £448.04 from The Tyrannical Clown himself for the removal of unauthorised Camber Café signs from the highway on 28th August and the 9th and 10th of September 2009. If I had any enquires regarding this invoice I should contact him. There then followed on the next consecutive Mondays two more invoices one for £418.32 for Camber Café signs removed on the 15th and 16th September and the other one which was dated 28th September for £134.44 for Camber Café signs removed on 18th September 2009. I did not contact The Tyrannical Clown to discuss his invoices. It was easy to see that he had photocopied a blank invoice and filled it out himself. At the top of the page it had in large capital letters INVOICE, Enquires to: Jed Uptland, Business Systems Manager, Heathfield Depot, but in the middle of the invoice he had written in brackets (any enquiries regarding this invoice should be made to The Tyrannical Clown on 0345 6080 193) and there was a paying- in slip at the bottom of the page but no perforated line to tear it off and why would the address be in Heathfield? I was certain that any money owed to the Council would be sent from the Council's Finance Department in Lewes. This was not for his own financial gain but a bully tactic to put pressure on my financial circumstances, and I guessed this Jed Uptland was a friend in another area who he had commandeered into sending him a blank invoice. I was not going to pay them anyway.

Late one Friday afternoon as I was preparing the café in readiness for the fish and chips, a lady came in clutching a bundle of papers, and she asked me if I was Sally to which I replied I was and I enquired who she might be. She said she was from Hastings County Court as she handed me the bundle she was carrying. I looked at her suspiciously and asked her what it was, and she said it was for me to appear at Eastbourne Magistrates Court. I looked at the top page of the bundle which said I had to present myself in Court at 2pm. on Tuesday 29th September 2009.Today was Friday 25th September and as it was the week-end that gave me precisely one day to prepare. They had surely done that on purpose and it was written on the summons that if I failed to turn up the case would carry on without me and the consequences could be serious. It was too late in the day to contact a solicitor which meant I would have to wait till Monday.

Looking at the papers the lady had brought me I was accused twelve times of affixing wooden signs to various structures without the consent of East Sussex County Council as the highway authority without given authorisation or under an enactment or a reasonable excuse in contrary to the section 132 (1) of the Highways Act 1980.

The list was written in twelve separate paragraphs for each offence I had committed, one for a sign on a telegraph pole, three on BT distribution poles, five times on an advanced bend chevron sign, once on an electricity pole number 580108, one on a lamp column and the last one on a structure, the crime being that I had unlawfully affixed wooden signs to various structures. Although some had been leaflets they had nevertheless been described as wooden signs. There were three witness statements, one from The Tyrannical Clown, one from the colleague at the interview under caution at Rye Police station and one from the employee with the long hair who had accompanied The Tyrannical Clown when they invaded Camber. There was the photo album which I had been shown at the police station and a transcript of the tape recording. I had the week-end and one day to organise some kind of legal representation, and I decided that as the magistrates court was in Eastbourne it was probably best to seek legal advice from a solicitor in the same town.

On Monday 28th September I rang a legal firm in Eastbourne I had found on the internet. I spoke directly with the solicitor and explained my predicament, and though it was all very rushed he was able to see me that afternoon. I took the train to Eastbourne for the appointment and I found the solicitor's office quite easily. It was very near to the railway station and it only took a few minutes to walk there. I explained to the solicitor about the fiasco with my café signs and that I had admitted putting them on various objects in and around Camber. He found it all quite amusing as he wrote the statement for my defence. I told him everything and I explained the necessity to advertise, although I did admit that I had been slightly fanatical with my café signs up until 11th August when The Tyrannical Clown had invaded Camber, but despite that I said I did need a sign either end of Lydd Road. I even confessed to throwing the contents of my pinny pocket at The Tyrannical Clown at Rye police station. He said it was a shame but I would most certainly get a fine. I was at the solicitors for about an hour, and paid £450 cash for his fee and whilst I was there he managed to get the court case adjourned to the following Tuesday, October 6th

A couple of days later the solicitor rang me to say that he had not personally dealt with a case like mine before but although he would be at the court case with me, he suggested that his colleague who was a barrister would be better suited to represent me at the Magistrates Court as he had previous experience with the East Sussex Highways and he would know how to deal with them. I said that if the barrister could prove to the magistrate that The Tyrannical Clown appeared to have singled me out whilst letting other businesses advertise, I would gladly have him represent me. He assured me that the barrister, although he would charge an additional fee, would handle my case very well. The additional fee was £300. That was a massive £750 altogether, but if the recommended barrister was going to put a stop to The Tyrannical Clown's shenanigans then it would be money well spent. I felt confident that with the experience of the barrister all would be well.

It was raining the day of my court appearance. I wore black leggings and a soft grey cashmere V neck slouch sweater for my court appearance. I took the train to Eastbourne and decided to get a taxi from the station to the court. No sooner had I sat down in the taxi and told the driver where I wanted to go than I was getting out again, as it only took two minutes to get to the Magistrates Court, but at least I stayed dry. I went into the court, my bag was searched and then I was zapped with a metal detector wand. The solicitor was there waiting for me and he hustled me into a side room. He told me to sit down and asked if I had brought the £300 for the barrister's fee. I had and I gave it to him in cash. He said the barrister would be arriving shortly. After a short while the solicitor excused himself and said he was going to look for the barrister and he got up and left the room. I sat there for ten minutes or more, then the solicitor stuck his head round the door and said he had to go. I was surprised at his rapid departure as he had said in his office he would be in the court room with me, but he said he had to go to collect his child and the barrister would arrive shortly. I sat there for some time, and finally he arrived. He was of Asian origin and well spoken. The solicitor had left a pile of papers on the table, and he picked them up and flicked through them and left the room. I had no idea what was going on. I seemed to have spent an awful long time in the side room on my own, and I thought I would be getting a bit more attention from these people I had paid a £750 fee to.

The barrister eventually returned, and said in a serious tone that he had just found out that I had assaulted The Tyrannical Clown at the police station. As soon as he said it I knew he had not read the notes that the solicitor had written down when I had been in his office and I suddenly got a feeling that this guy was going to be useless. I told him that I had mentioned the mobile phone and key throwing incident to the solicitor when I had made my statement. He did not comment but said we had to go and wait in the foyer, and as we got there The Tyrannical Clown was arriving with two other men. It looked like The Tyrannical Clown was having a bad hair day; his usual carefully groomed hair was a mass of frizz and he was wearing a cream safari suit that was all creased up. One of the men had a pile of folders and files balanced across his forearms so I guessed he was their solicitor and the other guy just looked as if he had come along for the hell of it. They went and stood in the lobby next to the actual court room which had a glass door separating them from me. They looked like the three wise monkeys as they stood in a row leaning against the wall. I was sat in the reception area, the barrister sat on the other side writing things on the papers the solicitor had left for him, then he beckoned me and handed me a form and told me to sign it, so I went back to where I had been sitting and without thinking I bent over and signed it. When I stood up I noticed The Tyrannical Clown had physically moved from leaning on the wall to standing directly opposite me. I realised that he had been looking through the glass petition down the front of my V neck sweater. I couldn't believe he would do such a thing in front of his colleagues and in a magistrate's court too, the audacity of it. No sooner had I handed the form back to the barrister than the court clerk was ushering us into the court room.

The Tyrannical Clown and his chums sat on the left hand side of the court; my barrister and I were sat on the right. No sooner had we sat down than we were told to stand up again for the three magistrates to enter the court room. They were old and impassive and had probably been hand-picked from the local mortuary for the day.

The council's solicitor stood up and proceeded to degrade

me by telling the three defunct magistrates how I had defaced council property and ignored their letters of warning, referring to me as a defiant nuisance. He rambled on and on till he reached the highlight of his speech, telling the magistrates I had written poetry, and he proceeded to read aloud the stupid rhymes that I had written for Kilkenny. He cleared his throat and with vacant tone he spoke; 'take these boards and you'll be sorry, next week you'll need a 7 ton lorry', 'to stop you feeling like a twit are smaller boards a better fit', 'if you take these boards away then great big huge ones we'll display'. There was no expression in his voice when reading my 'poetry,' and the three magistrates stared at him with an equal lack of expression on their wrinkled faces as they listened attentively to the befitting lyrics of my rhymes. I could not contain myself any longer and I just burst out laughing at the scene before me. Was this really how a court case was conducted, it was hilarious. I got a filthy look from my barrister as he stood up to give an account of my side of things, but I quickly regained my composure when I realised the barrister was saying nothing in my defence. He did not have to because I had pleaded guilty to all the charges, so there was nothing for him to defend. He rambled on for a few minutes and I heard him say something about six offences and take another six into consideration, then he lent down and stuck his face right in mine and asked me if he had forgotten anything. Forgotten anything? He had not said one word in my defence, I did not know why he was even there, and I could have defended myself. I wanted to sack him there and then. I was furious as I realised I had been conned by these solicitors. Suddenly it was all over. One of the magistrates asked how much the minimum fine was, and I heard The Tyrannical Clown reply £200 for each offence. We all stood up as they disappeared through the door they had come through earlier and we all sat down again. There was an uncomfortable silence, so I said the first thing that came into my head and asked my barrister if he came here often. In response he grabbed a handful of my nice new cashmere sweater by the shoulder and quickly frog marched me out of the court room saying I needed some fresh air. I did not need fresh air; I did not like being manhandled either. We sat down in the reception area and I ignored him for the duration. I tried to uncrease the shoulder of my new cashmere sweater by ironing it with my hand which also kept me pre-occupied as I did not wish to talk to him, We remained in silence until he announced we had to go back into the court room. Just as we had sat down the three magistrates filed back into the court room, so we stood up again and then were told to sit down. I was clearly guilty, so I was to pay costs of £1500 plus £15 for use of the court and £200 each for six of the signs I had put up. I don't know why I didn't get fined for the other six and neither did I ask. £2715 plus £750 for a useless barrister! I might as well have chucked the money in a bin. I had learned a lesson though; the next time I took a fancy to someone's Irish accent I would use different tactics. The barrister accompanied me out of the Court building and walked with me toward the station, and then suddenly offered me a lift home. I said that was a kind gesture and I would accept it, and he asked me where I lived and when I told him that I lived in Camber his face dropped and he retracted his offer by saying he would walk with me to the station instead and I had best catch the train as he lived in Brighton.

CHAPTER 14

I was so fed up that I had wasted all that money on a useless barrister that I did not go to work the next day as it was pouring with rain with gale force winds. I was disappointed too that The Tyrannical Clown had won, although one consolation was that no one had actually said to me in the courtroom that I must stop putting my signs out. For a while I was sad because I had just spent the last eight years getting back on my feet and it seemed that I was on the verge of losing it all again, because of another man and I didn't even know this one. I decided to go for a walk on the beach and feel sorry for myself and the turbulent weather matched my mood and made an appropriate back-drop to sulk in. I walked all along the beach and got thoroughly soaked to the skin, but I recovered from my miseries and was wishing I was back at home in the warm, so I made my way back along the beach in my sodden duffle coat which now weighed a ton.

As soon as I walked down Old Lydd Road I saw that the café sign had gone from the fence and the one outside the café too, and I knew the Tyrannical Clown would have all my café signs taken away today and having fully recovered from my miseries I was determined I was not going to be defeated. However I was not quite sure what direction I would be going in to advertise the café.

That evening, all of a sudden I had an idea. I thought about asking the occupants of the first and last houses in Camber if they would allow me to put a café sign on their garden walls. I knocked on the door of the first bungalow at the west end of Camber. A retired couple lived there and they invited me into their home. I explained what had happened with the highways and they were happy to let me put a café sign onto their garden wall. The husband told me to bring it to him and he would attach it to his wall himself. I thanked the couple and then drove to the other end of the village and asked the resident who lived in the last house if I might put a sign on her garden wall too, and she was quite happy for me to do that.

The next day I drove to the timber merchants in Rye and bought some more wood panels to make the new signs. I made the three new signs as quickly as I could and because of the new locations I had to write directions to the café on them. I delivered the first one to the husband and he said he would attach it to his garden wall and he would make sure it would be seen by the traffic coming into Camber. The other sign that was going to the far end of Camber would not be facing the traffic but was in good view of the holiday makers going in and out of the caravan park opposite the house. I bought a glue gun and a tube of the strongest grip fill to stick the sign onto the wall so it would be impossible to pull it off.

Half way through the village there was a derelict garage and several caravans surreptitiously hidden behind a very tall hoarding - an ideal structure to stick a café sign on - so I asked the owner of the land if he would put one of my café signs on the hoarding and he said he would. So within a few days of appearing in court I believed I had placed my café signs legally on private property and the highways could do nothing about it. I did however continue to put an A-board at the top of Lydd Road and although it would most likely be swiped by the highway men they were quick to make and easily replaced.

Unfortunately my joy was short lived as two days later the retired resident returned the new café sign because a planning officer from Rother District Council had knocked on his door and told him he had to remove my café sign and if he didn't he would be prosecuted for displaying it without obtaining advertisement consent. He had obviously set out to terrify the poor old guy and had succeeded in doing so. I personally would have refused to remove it and challenged the planning officer but as the wall was not mine there was little I could do. So I thanked the man for offering to help me and I took the sign back off him. Presuming the planning man had paid a visit to the house at the other end of the village too, I went to investigate.

Indeed he had, but the lady who lived there was a harder nut to crack. He had threatened her in the same way he had the older gentleman, warning her about the consequences if she continued to advertise my café, and ordered her to remove the sign. She was having none of it and told him where to go and on his hasty departure he stopped and tried to pull the sign off the wall but of course he could not because it was stuck with the grip fill, so he had taken a photo of it instead.

I did not contact the man who owned the land with the hoarding round it but the sign was still up there and unless the planning officer carried an extendible ladder around with him, that's where it would stay.

One of the members of Camber Parish Council was the caretaker of the Village Hall and as it transpired was the person who had bashed his head on my café sign which had been on the BT pole. I had apologised to him and as he had been having problems with the Highways himself, he invited me to put one of my cafe signs on the wall of the Village Hall. It was not a brilliant place for an advertisement but it could be seen by the people who used the hall. Anyway it didn't matter as a week later he received a letter from Rother District Planning Department telling him to remove it.

In the meantime I heeded The Tyrannical Clown's advice and wrote to East Sussex Highways and Rother District Council to ask who I should apply to for an official sign or a licence for my A-board and how I went about getting advertisement consent. First I emailed the highways directly and asked how I got permission to advertise my café officially. I got a reply the following day which said: 'Signs for advertising businesses were not permitted on the highway and if I wished to erect such signs I needed permission from the Planning Department of Rother District Council and I must get the land owners consent to put signs on private land. Signs are not allowed to be installed or erected on highway land'. This was so unhelpful, when there was a recession looming and I thought councils would want to be helping small businesses, but no, they were more intent of wrecking them it seemed.

I wrote again to the highways and asked them where the highway started and where it ended and if they could suggest an alternative place to advertise my café as they would not allow the A-board at the top of Lydd Road. I wrote to my local MP asking him how I was supposed to run a business without advertising it and I wrote to the planning department asking how I went about getting planning permission to put an A-board at the top of the road.

I wrote to The Tyrannical Clown telling him that I believed the invoices for £1045.00 he had sent me were spurious and I asked for my signs back that he had stolen. Strangely I got a response within the hour saying that The Tyrannical Clown was no longer dealing with the invoices and my query had been passed to a man who worked for a refuse company, so in future I would have to correspond with this person. I was not surprised he had passed his devious doings on to someone else. I knew there was something amiss with those invoices and the way The Tyrannical Clown had presented them to me; surely it was not his job to send bills. It was all too personnel and I believed he had fabricated the costs of the invoices and had done so purely to inflict financial pressure upon me.

The reply to my accusation of the spurious invoices arrived shortly from Jed Uptland, the Business Systems Manager of the refuse company. He had set out a breakdown of the charges:

Invoice 8005024113

This was for the removal of signs on 28 August 2009, 9 September 2009 and 10 September 2009

Contractor's charges for 2 man gang and truck
(3 hours on 28.08.09, 3 hours on 09.09.09 and 1 hour on 10.09.09)
7 hours @ £58.10 per hour - £406.70
Administration charge - £81.34

Total = £488.04

Invoice 8005024265

This was for the removal of signs on 15 September 2009 and 16 September 2009

Contractor's charges for 2 man gang and truck
(3 hours on 15.09.09 and 3 hours on 16.09.09)
6 hours @ £58.10 per hour - £348.60
Administration charge - £69.72

Total = £418.32

Invoice 8005024345

This was for the removal of signs on 18 September 2009

Contractor's charges for 2 man gang and truck
2 hours @ £58.10 per hour - £116.20
Administration charge - £23.24
Total = £139.44

Despite the email from Jed Uptland it had not changed my opinion that the invoices were fraudulent and it was for that reason I would not pay them and as time went on I started to receive regular reminders for the £1045.00. When I did not pay the reminders turned to threats of legal action, but undeterred I emailed Jed Uptland and told him to take legal action against me as that would give me the opportunity to prove that the invoices were fraudulent. At the same time I emailed the Highways Contact Centre as I had been told The Tyrannical Clown was no longer dealing with anything concerning me, asking for the following information:

To Whom it May Concern

I require the following information regarding these invoices-
8005024113 / 8005024265 / 8005024345
Pictures of the cafe signs that were removed on the dates on the invoices.
The name and address of the company who were contracted to remove the signs.
Where the contractors had travelled from on these dates.
Where the contractors were working on those particular days.
The invoices issued from the contractor to ESCC for the removal of the signs.
The receipts for proof of payment from ESCC to the contract.
Thank you

I did not receive an answer to my questions but I did get a reply from Jed Uptland:

Dear Mrs Pattinson,
I am not in position to answer your query regarding complaints received about your café signs. It is something that I do not deal with in the course of my job and I suggest you contact either The Tyrannical Clown or Kilkenny at the Sidley office as they will be able to give you the details you require.
As you can see from my email of 23ʳᵈ October 2009 you have been charged for the removal of unauthorised signs on six

separate occasions. I am told that there have been unauthorised signs removed on other occasions but we have not charged you for these. As you can see from the dates on the invoices you have not been charged for the removal of any signs prior to 11 August 2009, which is the significant date leading to your court appearance on 6th October 2009.
As a consequence of your constant re-offending it was resolved to recover all costs to the council by removing unauthorised signs from the highway by our contractor.
The hourly charge of £58.10 is the rate for 2 men and a truck and is in accordance with East Sussex County Council's current contract with our contractor
In the breakdown of the charges in my email you can see that on four occasions you have been charged for 3 hours and on the other two 1 hour and 2 hours. The difference in the number of hours charged relates to the distance the gang had to travel when they were requested to remove the signs. The gang did not remove the signs we have charged you for without first being instructed by a County Council employee.
It should be pointed out that if the occasion arises we will continue to charge you for the removal of unauthorised signs from the highway.
I hope that this information will be of assistance to you and that you will now be able to settle these invoices without further delay.
Yours sincerely
Jed Uptland

Whether or not Jed Uptland was aware of The Tyrannical Clown's plan to wreck my business I did not know. Someone from the Highways Contact Centre eventually replied to my email regarding the questions about the 2 x gang and a truck saying that it had been passed to Jed Uptland and he would be responding to it. He never did respond to it and despite me sending reminders to the highways no one gave me the information I had asked for which convinced me even more that the invoices were down to The Tyrannical Clown's dirty doings.

CHAPTER 15

On Saturday 31st October 2009 the postman delivered a large white envelope postmarked Lewes and East Sussex County Council. I opened it with anticipation thinking it was something to do with the invoices The Tyrannical Clown had been sending me but it wasn't. Inside there was a letter dated 28th October 2009 and six A3 sized photos of my café signs they had removed on the 7th October, the day after I had been to the Magistrates Court in Eastbourne.

Dear Mrs Pattinson
Unauthorised Signs on the Highway
It has come to the Council's attention that you have continued to place signs advertising your café on the highway despite your recent conviction for similar offences. I enclose two sets of photographs for your attention. The first set labelled 'Set 1' was taken on 22nd October. The second labelled 'Set 2' was taken yesterday. The signs have subsequently been removed. We have reason to believe that these signs have been erected after your conviction on 6th October 2009.

Please refrain from continuing to place signs upon the highway. If you continue in this manner further enforcement action might be undertaken. Consideration will be given to applying to the County Court for an injunction to prevent you acting in this manner. An Anti-Social Behaviour Order might also be considered.
Yours sincerely
Judgement Jones Litigation Solicitor

The photos in 'set 1' were indeed of my café signs but they had removed these on 7th October. The photo of the A-board in 'set 2' was correct; I had replaced yet another A-board on that

Wednesday because they had taken it the day before. I was replacing on average three a week. Having looked at the photos in 'set 1' it was clearly raining the day they were photographed just as it had been on 7th October and as far as I could remember it had not rained since, in fact I remembered the weather on 22nd. October when Judgement Jones said the photos had been taken. It was overcast and a bit windy but it was not raining. A customer confirmed that and added that all that week it had been mild; he kept a diary in which he wrote the weather conditions every day. More to the point, if they had taken these signs on 7th October how had I managed to get them back from Bexhill and erect them in exactly the same places they had been before? It was all very peculiar. Why would they accuse me of doing something they knew I had not done and as for applying to the court for an ASBO, how ridiculous, what was anti -social about advertising a café that was open, on an A-board. The Tyrannical Clown was behaving like a reprobate, so without delay I responded to Judgement Jones accusing and threatening letter. I asked him who had sent the photos to him, I asked for proof of when and by whom had the photos been taken. I agreed I had put the A-board at the top of Lydd Road in the photo in 'set 2'. I also asked him why it was only my signs that were an issue with the Council. I concluded that I looked forward to his explanation of how the café signs had been photographed fifteen days after they had been removed from the highway.

In the meantime I had received another letter from the refuse company threatening legal action. I also received a reply from the highways telling me that the highway started from the middle of the hedgerow across the road to the middle of the hedgerow on the opposite side and a reminder that advertising on the highway was not permitted under any circumstances.

On 3rd November 2009 I received a letter from Rother

District Council in Bexhill. It was from a lady in the planning department who was responding to my email which I had sent asking how I got planning permission to put an A-board at the top of Lydd Road. She said I did not need planning permission to put an A-board at the junction of Lydd Road providing I took it home every night when I closed. I was elated. I knew I could have the A-board there and apart from anything else the café had been here since 1984 and all the previous owners had done exactly the same thing. I couldn't wait to send a copy of the letter to The Tyrannical Clown which I duly did and I asked him to return my property which he had removed unlawfully forthwith or I wanted compensation.

A couple of days later I received another letter from Rother District Council planning department, this one from the Planning Enforcement Officer:

Dear Mrs Pattinson
I believe you are the person responsible for placing signs on three properties in Camber - two on garden walls and one on a hoarding - without consent. You are committing an offence under the provisions of the Town and County Planning (control of advertisements) regulations 2007. Please remove all the signs within 48 hours or I will instruct the Solicitor to the Council to commence legal action without further warning. Please ring if you are unclear about what is required to advertise.
Yours sincerely
C. Pasty. Planning and Enforcement Manager

This man had to be the one who terrorised the man in the bungalow forcing him to remove the sign, but the lady at the other end of the village had not given in and the sign was still securely stuck on her garden wall. I answered the letter from the Planning Enforcement Officer. I said that if the local residents chose to advertise my café on their private property it would be ungrateful to ask them to stop, so I would not be asking them to. I did ask him how I applied for Advertisement consent as he had informed me that it was a legal requirement. I was somewhat confused about which consent I needed as The Tyrannical Clown had advised me to contact the Planning Department to apply for planning permission and since I had been informed I did not need it all of a sudden the requirement had changed to advertisement consent, so I asked him to send me a dozen application forms.

A few days after I had responded to Judgement Jones letter he replied:

Dear Mrs Pattinson
The photos were taken by East Sussex County Council's regular staff.
The A-board in question might not be affixed to anything but it is still obstructing the highway which is a criminal offence.
You must appreciate your boards are distracting to members of the public, especially when driving past in their vehicles. The potential is there for a serious accident, hence the Council's concern over this matter.
As to your final point the Council does not discriminate in its application of the Highways Act and reserves its right to take decisive action against anybody who flagrantly and repeatedly breaches the Act's provisions'.
Yours sincerely
Judgement Jones

He had still not answered my questions, I had asked for proof that the photos had been taken on 22nd October 2009. I knew he could not possibly answer that question because they had taken them on 7th October.

I decided to text Kilkenny to see what he had to say about it. Within minutes of texting him he rang me; he was angry and said I had been told not to contact him on his private mobile phone so I replied that all I wanted was for him to confirm that I had not put the signs in the photos up after 6th October as he knew they had taken them on 7th October. He denied knowing anything about it so I suggested that they were setting me up and asked him to go and look at the photos as he would see they were the ones they had taken on 7th October. He was still cross that I had texted him and said he was going to make an official complaint about me calling him an arsehole and texting him again and he hung up.

Twenty minutes later he rang me back still cross; he said he had looked at the photos and he knew nothing about them and he asked me if I was accusing them of conspiracy. I said I was, as the accusations in Judgement Jones letter were not true. He said if that was the case and the photos were not taken on 22nd October he would report it and order an investigation. I agreed he should. He ended the conversation saying he had reported me to their Legal Department for texting him and calling him an arsehole.

It was obvious that the photos could not have been anything to do with Kilkenny, as he would not be reporting it to have himself investigated, so it had to be down to The Tyrannical Clown again. Just like the invoices he had sent me, it was all lies.

Judgement Jones did not respond to my letter about who had taken the photos on 22nd. Instead he wrote another letter which was headed:

Communications with Council Staff

Dear Mrs Pattinson

It has come to my attention that you have been making several phone calls and sending text messages to a member of staff at the Council, namely Kilkenny, on his private mobile. I must ask that you refrain from contacting Kilkenny at all in future. The Council takes perceived or actual harassment against its staff very seriously. It is simply not permissible to contact Council staff and refer to them as an 'arsehole' and accuse the Council of 'lying and carrying on a conspiracy against you'. I would ask that you do not contact any staff member of the Council and talk to them in this manner, especially on their personal mobile phones. If you have any complaint about the way in which the Council has behaved, I would advise you to write to the customer care manager at Lewes County Hall.

Please note that if you continue to act in this manner the Council will consider seeking a County Court injunction against you to prevent you from acting in this manner. Please note that the breach of such an injunction is an imprisonable offence.

Yours sincerely

Judgement Jones Litigation Solicitor.

If Judgement Jones letter was meant to scare me he had been unsuccessful. In a week I had been threatened from various council departments with one legal action and an ASBO, three County Court proceedings and two injunction orders. Laughably, Judgement Jones had told me they did not discriminate. I was not intimidated by these threats, in fact they had had the opposite effect, and had fuelled my determination to stand up to them. I knew beyond doubt they were liars, so on the grounds that I was dealing with a bunch of overpaid arseholes I prepared to up my game and stand my ground.

A few days later I received a letter and photo of the sign on the garden wall, from Mr Pasty, the Planning and Enforcement Manager at Rother District Council, telling me I had put a sign on the lady's garden wall and I must remove it immediately or they would take legal action against me.

I ignored the letter, but a few days later the section of garden wall where the sign had been was now reduced to a pile of rubble. The lady who lived there told me that she had returned home to find part of her garden wall demolished and my café sign gone. She said she had contacted the council and they had denied any knowledge of what had happened.

There was a building project going on opposite the caravan park just a few metres away from where the lady lived - an extension to a garage with a house being built over the top. The construction had a metal barrier around it to keep people out and the builders sign attached onto it. I asked one of the builders if I might put one of my café signs on the barrier as well, and he agreed, so I made a nice sign indicating that the café was further down the road. The builder attached my sign on the inside of the fence with some cable ties.

CHAPTER 16

I was unable to close the café that winter, as I had not managed to save enough money to take the two months break I had in the previous two years, but it was not a problem as I like working. The only thing was that because the café was only meant to be a seasonal business, sadly there was no heating in it, so with the help of a halogen heater and a ski suit I prepared myself for working in cold uncomfortable conditions for the next five months.

At the beginning of November I received a huge brown envelope with one dozen application forms to apply for Advertisement consent and a complimentary slip from the Planning and Enforcement Manager saying he was looking forward to receiving my applications along with the fee of £90. The questions on the application form were; the applicants name and address, that was easy to answer. Next, the applicant must provide the full postal address of the application site, my answer to that was 'a piece of grass at the top of Lydd Road'. Had I consulted with my neighbours, I wrote yes I had and they were delighted. Then they requested a description of the proposed advertisement, and I wrote an A-board which is the shape of an A. Next question, had I previously sought advice from the local authority about this application? I replied I had and no sooner had I been given authority than it was quickly revoked again. Was the advertisement I was applying for already in place? I answered sometimes it is but often it is not. I said it had been there since 1984 and was frequently being updated. The next question I found very amusing, it asked if the existing advertisement was to be removed and replaced by the advertisement in the proposal. I answered 'it was regularly removed'. I was asked to show the existing sign on an elevation drawing and state the references for the drawing. I did not have a clue what that meant so I drew a highway truck that was being filled up with my A-boards by several little match stick men (being the highway men) who were running round the grassy patch and I drew myself as an exhausted match stick lady lying on my back with my legs up in the air with exhaustion marks above my head. The next question asked me if I had permission from the owners of the land to place my advertisement on it. To that I reminded them that as they owned the piece of land in question only they could answer that themselves and I reminded them this was the reason I was filling out this application form. Finally they wanted details of the advertisement, the type, and height from the ground, dimensions, maximum height, colour, material and the projection. My answers were, it's an A-board, various heights, various widths, one metre high, lime green colour, plywood and it projected upwards. I signed it and sent it back minus the cheque for £90.

Clearly this application form I had filled out was not intended to be used as an application for an A-board; it was most likely used for places that wanted to put large structures on an elevated part of a building.

Three weeks after my café sign had been put on the metal fence where the construction site was opposite the caravan park, one of the builders turned up carrying the café sign. He said he had been told to remove it by the owner of the property as he had received a letter from Rother District Council threatening him with legal action if he did not remove the sign immediately. So it had been brought back.

All the while these threats of legal action and ASBO's kept arriving via email or letter, other people in the area continued to have their signs and A-boards advertising their businesses. I really did not understand why it was only me having all this aggravation.

I wrote a letter to The Tyrannical Clown asking for all of my cafe signs back that they had taken over the last year, and he answered quite quickly saying that it was their policy that if signs removed from the highway had not been claimed after 28 days they would be destroyed and according to his records that time had elapsed. I was getting clever too with my responses to their unjustified actions so I sent him copies of the photos and a letter saying that as according to Judgement Jones the photos had been taken on 22nd October and today was 4th November it was well within the 28 days before my signs would be destroyed so I would like to arrange collection.

He never answered.

Towards the end of November I received a letter from a lady who introduced herself as the Customer Care Manager for East Sussex County Council, informing me that she would be dealing with my advertising issue as The Tyrannical Clown was no longer involved in the matter. She and a colleague who was not involved in this dispute would be coming to Camber within the next two weeks to visit me.

Although I was pleased that at last someone was actually going to come to Camber to see for themselves that the café business would not be viable without advertising on the main road, I was sceptical.

A week passed and I had not heard from the Council, then I received an email from the Customer Care Manager saying although she suggested that we meet to discuss the ongoing dispute she was currently waiting for some information from the Traffic and Licensing team before she could make any further arrangements and hoped to get back to me within the next ten days.

So my gut feeling had been right. I knew The Tyrannical Clown would stop her coming here as he knew she would most likely agree with me for the necessity of the A-board.

After that let down from the Customer Care Manager I decided to contact the Citizens Advice Bureau hoping to get some advice on how to stop The Tyrannical Clown interfering with my business. I told them of my suspicions about the invoices and the photos that Judgement Jones had sent me along with the threats of prison. They advised me to write a letter to the Chief Executive of East Sussex County Council, to send it by registered post and to write private and confidential on the envelope. So that is what I did.

I was not sure how to start a letter to someone in a high and mighty position and I did not know her name either, so I called her Madam. I apologised for bothering her and explained that I had been advised to do so in the hope of keeping my business solvent. I wanted to bring to her attention that certain council employees in Bexhill namely The Tyrannical Clown and Kilkenny had been making things very difficult for me.

I explained I owned a small café which was down a side street and I needed to have an A-board at the top of the road. I told her I had been to Court in October and had received a large fine for unlawfully putting too many café signs on the highway. I also said I had made numerous enquiries on how to advertise my café with approval from the highways authority but I had not had any satisfactory information from them only negative responses and had been threatened with county court procedures, injunction orders, ASBO's and imprisonment.

I said that The Tyrannical Clown had advised me to seek advice from the Planning Department which I had and was told I could place an A-board at the top of Lydd Road without planning permission, but despite sending him a copy of that letter he continued to have my A-boards removed by contractors and had invoiced me for huge amounts of money to pay for their removal. I asked her to please stop The Tyrannical Clown and Kilkenny trying to wreck my business because if I could not have any visible directions to the café I would go bankrupt. I wrote private and confidential on the envelope and sent the letter by registered post on 27th November 2009 and kept the receipt for it.

That done I waited in anticipation for a reply, and in the meantime a friend had offered me his huge Volvo Estate car and suggested I parked it up on the main road outside the church which was opposite Lydd Road. It was a good idea for which I thanked him and so I set about making two huge signs to sit on top of the car. It needed some intense engineering skills to attach it to the roof of the car which I was unable to do, so I commandeered another friend to do the construction work which he did using a massive round central structure to screw the signs onto and then held it secure with ratchet straps that he put through the back windows to attach inside the car. The Volvo was too big for me to drive. I could barely see over the dashboard and with the weight of the signs on top I decided to leave it where it was on the main road.

I expected to hear from the Highways to remove the Volvo and right on schedule on 3rd December 2009 I received a letter not from the highways but from the Planning and Enforcement Manager saying;

Dear Madam

Town & Country Planning (Control of Advertisements) Regulations 2007

Lydd Road, Camber

I note that the above vehicle has been parked on Lydd Road, Camber and that it has advertising for your business on it. The Town and County Planning (Control of Advertisements) (England) Regulations 2007 Schedule 1, class B exempts advertisements displayed on vehicles provided that the vehicle is not used principally for the display of advertisements.

In this particular case I consider that the vehicle is parked for the purpose of advertising your business. Advertisement Consent is required for this vehicle to be displayed in this state and location.

Whilst it is open to you to submit an application to retain it, in my opinion any application would be unlikely to be recommended for approval. The Highway Authority has the final decision on any application. In any case the display of advertisements without deemed consent is an offence, so I suggest that the vehicle or advertisements are removed forthwith

Yours faithfully

C Pasty Planning-Enforcement and Appeals

I had a feeling that Mr Pasty was the third man at the Magistrates Court in Eastbourne. It was strange how he seemed to have taken over from The Tyrannical Clown but whoever he was I was not going to move the Volvo as I could not see over the dashboard. Now I had been sent another lot of conflicting rules and regulations, I emailed Mr Pasty and explained the confusion that surrounded their Advertisement Control Act;

Dear Mr Pasty

On 9th September 2009 The Tyrannical Clown emailed me saying and I quote 'Advertising and the control of such issues are for the District Council planners and I strongly advise that you seek advice from them'. On 27th October 2009 I emailed the planning department and asked how I got permission to stand an A-board at the top of the road. On 3rd November 2009 I was delighted to get a reply from a lady in the Planning-Development Control informing me that I didn't need planning permission to put an A-board at the top of the road.

On 20th November 2009 I wrote again to The Tyrannical Clown enclosing a copy of the letter which stated I did not need planning permission and also asked for him to return at least 8 of my A-boards he had removed from the top of the road as he had done so unlawfully.

On 25th November 2009 the Customer Service Manager replied on behalf of The Tyrannical Clown saying that 'because the signs were continually being placed on a highway maintained at public expense they would not be returned and the District County Planners at Rother do not have any jurisdiction of items being placed upon a highway and therefore their comments did not change his decision'. Rother District Council and the Highways Authority appear to have conflicting policies and procedures. I am trying to comply with the regulations set down for me to follow but they change on a weekly basis and I cannot keep up with them.

To date I have been urged by The Tyrannical Clown to contact the District Planners as advertising is controlled by them. I have been informed that planning permission is not required to place an A-board upon the highway. In response to that information The Tyrannical Clown repudiated his own advice by saying the District Planners did not have any jurisdiction of items placed upon a highway. Now you tell me I need to put in an application form to obtain planning permission for my A-board, albeit irrelevant and furthermore if it were granted The Tyrannical Clown has the final decision and will not authorise it anyway.

Would you be so kind to explain what it all means? All I want to do is to put an A-board at the top of the road. Shall I go and get some advice from the Burger van in the lay-by and ask him what he did to get planning permission for his 4 x A-boards that he places on the highway every day?

Yours sincerely

Sally Pattinson

I doubted that I would get a reply and I still had not heard from the Customer Care Manager or had a response to my letter to the Chief Executive. I was getting fed up with all the contradictions that I was being told to comply with. They did not even know themselves what their own policies were so I wrote again to the Customer Care Manager;

Dear Customer Care Manager
Would you please relate this email to The Tyrannical Clown as I would like him to be aware that since my court case I have tried to deal with the advertising of my cafe in a way that I won't be contemptuous of the law again because I am running out of options here? So far I have asked for permission to put an A-board at the end of this road but his jurisdiction won't let me. I have been refused any kind of council approved sign. I mustn't stick anything on a BT pole although an Open Reach man said I could, I can't stick anything on street furniture and I can't advertise on private property without advertising consent although I asked Mr Pasty for some application forms but never got them. I may not attach a café sign to a fence which is beyond the boundary of the edge of the highway and more than half way through a hedge.
I would like The Tyrannical Clown to be aware that since we went to court in October I have been threatened with 3 x County Court actions, 2 x injunction orders, 4 x legal actions, 2 x ASBO's and 1 threat of imprisonment.
I have been accused of re-offending by putting cafe signs up everywhere which incidentally I hadn't and I have been sent a letter from Judgement Jones saying that I accused Kilkenny of conspiracy, which I hadn't. In fact I had asked Kilkenny if he was setting me up by changing the date that

those photos were taken in 'set 1' because it was not 22nd

*those photos were taken in 'set 1' because it was not 22nd
October but 7th October he had taken them.*

*I was threatened again by Judgement Jones with another
injunction order which if violated would send me off to
prison, this time for texting Kilkenny and calling him an
'arsehole' which, at the time I called him it, he was one in
my opinion. Never mind the day that Kilkenny had rung me
on MY private mobile phone and said that if I was a bloke
he would come over here and put me flat on my arse, well
you tell him from me that if he was a bloke I would take
great pleasure in putting him flat on his arse too and I
could. The Tyrannical Clown also rang me that day and told
me I couldn't sell fish and chips from my café because I
didn't have the appropriate licence, he also said that he was
going to revoke my alcohol and personal licences, my
gaming licence and my licence to sell food, but he would
spare me my TV and driving licence but had reported me to
BT for vandalising 3 BT poles which later it was confirmed
that the holes in the poles had been made by some
woodpeckers and not by me. Don't worry if they had
forgotten about that day they rang me as my mobile phone
has a recorder and those conversations are safe on my
phone that were made on 9th September and are there if I
should ever need them as evidence.*

*I imagine The Tyrannical Clown is fairly intelligent and he
must be aware that much of my revenue comes from passing
trade and therefore he understands the importance of there
being an A-board placed at the top of the road to attract
customers to my cafe and not cause fatal accidents as
Judgement Jones has implied. But instead, for some reason
he sends someone to steal my property on a weekly basis
regardless of the consequences it will have on my business.
Doesn't he care what will happen to me?*

I will not give in to The Tyrannical Clown's obsession of wrecking my business and I have one more idea waiting to be put into action, but he's not going to like it! I hope he knows someone who drives a crane.

But despite all that I am still here and so is my café and so is another A-board sitting up there at the end of the road for another day or so, and I'm still hanging onto my alcohol and personal licences and still selling fish and chips which are the best in Sussex I've been told.

That day The Tyrannical Clown phoned me he gave me one compliment, well I have one for him, he is the funniest man I've ever encountered, he has made me laugh so much with his nasty little habits and his attempts to wreck my business and you can tell him he reminds me of my mother.

So with this amazing achievement on my part for the moment and no doubt to The Tyrannical Clown's dismay, I am now going to conclude this email by suggesting that he shoves his jurisdiction right up his arse and forgets where it is and furthermore I hope The Tyrannical Clown gets a nice gold hat out of his Christmas cracker so he can wear it to work with pride and never take it off as I am sure it will match his character and position in the Highways Authority very well.

Yours sincerely

Sally Pattinson

I also sent a copy of the letter to Judgement Jones and Mr Pasty from the planning, but Christmas was coming and as it was a time for peace and goodwill toward men I thought it would be a nice festive gesture to make The Tyrannical Clown and Kilkenny a Christmas card and stick it somewhere appropriate on the highway for them to see; after all I had only been told I could not advertise the café on street furniture, nothing had been said about Christmas cards. I bought a piece of sturdy wood measuring one meter wide by half a meter in length. I painted it white and although art was not one of my best subjects I practised drawing caricatures of their faces. I painted the wood white and started with Kilkenny on the left hand side of the board. I drew his long narrow face and jaw bone and close set beady eyes, I exaggerated his turned up nose and very small mouth and I gave him a surprised expression and put a green leprechaun's hat on his head so there would be no mistake who he was meant to be. I put The Tyrannical Clown on the right hand side of the board with a large round fat face with dark dead expressionless eyes. I was kind with his nose but gave him a turned down mouth like a wavy M. I did his hair as I remembered on the day at Eastbourne Magistrates Court in October, frizzy and sticking out all over the place, and I stuck a crown on his head. Instead of trying to colour their faces I put make-up on them which gave them a more natural skin colour and I used dark eye shadow on their eyes and blusher on their faces. I drew a holly leaf in the bottom left hand corner and then I wrote them my Christmas message in between their faces; it said; 'Happy Christmas, Peace and Goodwill to the Merchant Bankers from Bexhill' and I screwed the Christmas card to a thick wooden baton.

Early the next morning when it was still dark I drove to the A259 where there was a large signpost on the left hand side with directions to Lydd, Camber and the Beach to the right and Folkestone and Dover straight on. I parked the car up and the ground was frozen solid due to a heavy frost that night but it didn't matter. I had brought a few cable ties with me. I could hardly see what I was doing in the dark and had to wait for cars to come along the road to get any light, but despite the cold I managed to strap the Christmas card to the signpost using the cable ties. It was December 14th and I wondered how long it would remain there and even though it was still dark I took a photo of it for a memento.

CHAPTER 17

Christmas came and went and as the New Year started so did the snow. Although the current A-board had been left in peace since the beginning of December it was the snow that was creating a problem now as it was difficult to take the A-board up and down the road in these weather conditions and though it was in its place the falling snow covered the writing on it. I thought the best thing to do was to commandeer some local children and get them to build a snowman in place of the A-board and I could lean a cafe sign on it. The snowman was a success but in less than twenty four hours some other children had kicked him to death so with some spare wood I had I made two new signs which I intended to zap back onto the BT pole. Kilkenny had not been frequenting Camber lately; probably he was too occupied with weather related issues, so with that in mind I made the new signs but this time, under the Café Open 7.30, I wrote a poem on each one.

On the first sign I wrote:

> *'So here we go another year*
> *I won't give up I have no fear*
> *I won't forget what you have done*
> *So don't assume that you have won.*
> *I will continue wait and see*
> *You will not be one up on me*
> *So when you put these in your bins*
> *Don't forget that who dares wins!'*

And on the second sign I wrote:

> *'Please don't take this board away*

Use your common sense
I have to wait for ad-consent
To stick it on a fence.
I do not want to use this pole
I know that I am bad
But the purpose of me doing it's
To drive you people mad'

I got a tall man to screw them high up onto the BT pole for me and they looked quite grand with the poetry there for all to read and I took the usual photo for the memento.

By the end of the second week in January amazingly the Christmas card to the Merchant Bankers from Bexhill was still attached to the signpost on the A 259. However, I had not received a reply to my letter to the Chief Executive which I had sent nearly two months ago but I had received the information that I had been expecting from the Customer Care manager. It was accompanied by a short note stating they will not compromise on customer safety and therefore it was not viable to have an A-board on the highway and the information provided will clarify what I can and cannot do and what is acceptable from a legal perspective.

All advertisements are controlled by The Town & Country Planning (Control of Advertisements) (England) Regulations 2007.
This legislation splits adverts into 3 types:
· Adverts that require express consent from the Planning Authority
· Adverts that comply with the legislation and thus are understood to have deemed consent from the Planning Authority
· Adverts that are exempt from deemed or express consent
Working in reverse order, adverts that are exempt from

deemed or express consent are:
· *sandwich boards displayed on a person or an animal,*
· *adverts in private land that cannot be seen from the highway*
· *adverts displayed inside a train station or a shopping mall*
· *adverts displayed inside a shop at least 1 metre back from the door or window (non-illuminated)*
· *adverts on a vehicle that is primarily moving such as buses, taxis and commercial vehicles (not parked up as an advert)*
· *traffic signs, brand names on goods for sale, national flags and adverts incised into the fabric of a building are also exempt*

There are 16 classes of adverts that are considered to have 'deemed' consent:
· *Class 1 – local authority signs relating to statutory consultations, public services etc.*
· *Class 2 – signs on premises to advertise what their business, profession or trade is*
· *Class 3 – temporary event signs, estate agent signs, construction site signs and temporary charitable event signs*
· *Class 4 – allows shop signs to be internally illuminated*
· *Class 5 – allows shops and cafés to display adverts on the premises but not on forecourts*
· *Class 6 – allows adverts on forecourts to businesses (petrol forecourts, restaurant terraces but not highway)*
· *Class 7 – allows flag adverts*
· *Class 8 – temporary adverts on hoardings around building sites*
· *Class 9 – allows adverts on structures in the highway such as bus shelters and kiosks if they have been designed for displaying posters*
· *Class 10 – allows Neighbourhood Watch signs*
· *Class 11 – temporary direction signs to new residential developments*

· *Class 12 – adverts in shops within 1 metre of the door or window*
· *Class 13 – adverts that have been displayed in the same site for the proceeding ten years*
· *Class 14 – adverts displayed after expiry of express consent (usually five years)*
· *Class 15 – Adverts on balloons*
· *Class 16 – adverts on telephone kiosks*

All other adverts must have express consent from the local Planning Authority. A planning application will have to be submitted to the local district council. So the conclusion is that unless there is a bus shelter (like adshell) that has been designed to display adverts in Camber, any A-board advert not displayed on the cafe premises will need to have express consent from Rother District Council, the planning Authority to be displayed in the highway.

In considering any planning application for an advertisement in the highway, Rother District Council will consult the Highway Authority to ensure that the proposed location and style of advert will not endanger the public or obstruct their access through the highway.

Prior to 1982 it was not possible to licence objects and adverts to be in the highway as they were considered to be unnecessary obstructions. However the Local Government (Miscellaneous Provisions) Act 1982 amended Section 115E of the Highways Act 1980 to permit the Highway Authority to licence an object or structure for the purpose of advertising in pedestrianized streets or footways and bridleways where vehicular use is prohibited.

The frontages (owners/occupiers of properties adjacent to the highway) and the relevant planning authority need be consulted to obtain 'Walkway consent'. This consultation is intended to address any obstruction concerns of the public and also the issue that the owners of the subsoil beneath the highway have a right to comment.

However, the Highway Authority will not undertake walkway consent consultation unless satisfied that the proposed object is positioned such that it will not interfere with the free passage of traffic through the highway and will not endanger the public.

Consequently, when proposing locations for an advertising structure, the following points should be considered:
· No structures placed within 60 metres of a junction with a principal road or in visibility splays at minor junctions or bends
· No structures placed so as to obscure or interfere with the visibility of traffic signs
· No advert to mimic traffic signs and give traffic directions to motorists
· No structures to be placed within 450mm of the edge of the carriageway
· Where adjacent to roads that are 40mph or above, signs must be passively safe (that is readily collapsible if struck by a vehicle)
· No object placed to obstruct passage through the highway
· No object placed so as to interfere with access and egress from private premises adjoining the highway
· No structure placed so as to interfere or damage utility apparatus
· Public liability insurance for £10million to indemnify the highway authority against any claim associated with the structure

This list had been sent to me supposedly to assist in the advertising of the café; all the options they had given me were useless apart from putting a sandwich board on an animal.

There were no shopping malls, railway stations or adshel bus stops in Camber. I could put a sign on private land as long as it could not be seen from the highway; I could put a sign on the forecourt providing it was not a forecourt for a café and finally I could put a sign on a car but only if it was moving.

There was one chance though where they had tripped themselves up. Class 13 stated that a sign which had been in the same place for longer than ten years was considered to have deemed consent, and as the café had been in existence since 1984 and all the previous owners had put A-boards and signs at the top of the road, my A-board must surely have this Deemed Consent. This was their document and their legislation and it appeared I had finally found something official to use in defence of my controversial A-board.

It was two months now since I had written to the Chief Executive of East Sussex County Council, and I had not had any confirmation or response regarding my letter, so I decided to phone the Customer Care Manager to see if she could put some light on the matter. I had the direct number to her office as it was on the emails she had sent me, so I rang it. She answered the phone but when I told her who I was she seemed to be taken aback and surprised that I had contacted her. I got straight to the purpose of my call and asked her why I had not had a reply or confirmation of my letter. I could hear by her voice that my question had made her uncomfortable; she kept repeating herself by saying ermm, ermm, obviously trying to think of something constructive to say. I tried to make it simpler for her so I asked if the Chief Executive had actually been given my letter. She replied that it had come to the office, so I asked again if the Chief Executive had seen it, and she said the letter was no longer there. I wanted to know where it was or if it had been thrown away. She told me that the letter had gone to Bexhill. Had it been given to The Tyrannical Clown I asked and she repeated that it had been passed to Bexhill. I admired her for her honesty, but I was furious that the Chief Executive had not had the chance to read it; I knew that when that letter was delivered it would have been signed for as I had sent it by recorded delivery and anyway someone would definitely have sent confirmation of it telling me someone would respond within ten days, that was the normal procedure.

Although I was annoyed that my letter had ended up in Bexhill in The Tyrannical Clown's pocket he had only demonstrated what a cowardly arsehole he truly was, so with that comforting thought I was more determined than ever in my quest to fight for my A-board's rights to stand on the grass patch at the top of the road.

CHAPTER 18

I continued to get reminders from the refuse company for The Tyrannical Clown's fraudulent invoices. I had ignored all of the reminders and threats of legal action but eventually I decided to email them and explain why I was not going to pay as I believed they were not genuine and besides I had no money. A couple of days later I received another letter from the refuse company asking me to send proof of my finances which was to include my outgoings, income and bank statements. I rang them and asked why they wished to know about my personal finances and I was told that a woman from the Accounts Department in East Sussex County Council was going to assess my financial situation so she could decide how much money I could pay the council in monthly instalments for the money owing on the invoices. I asked for the woman's name and address so I could send them directly to her. Maybe it was a good idea to let the council see how hard up I was. So that's what I did, I sent off my accounts for the last two years; twelve months of bank statements, a list of expenses and other outgoings and everything I thought she would need to know, not that I had any intention whatsoever of paying them a penny. I enclosed a short letter asking her to confirm when she had received my papers and I requested that she did not share any of my private documents with The Tyrannical Clown.

In the meantime as I had not received answers I re-sent the email to the highways contact centre regarding the invoices for the removal of my café signs.

To Whom it May Concern

I require the following information regarding these invoices -
8005024113 / 8005024265 / 8005024345
Pictures of the café signs that were removed on the said
dates.
The name and address of the company which was contracted
to remove the signs.
Where the contractors had travelled from on the said dates.
Where the contractors were working on those particular days.
The invoices issued from the contractor to ESCC for the
removal of the signs.
The receipts for proof of payment from ESCC to the contract

I received a reply from them within twenty four hours. It said that my queries had been forwarded to the Business Systems Manager at the refuse company for a response. Him again, I had already spoken to this man on the phone some weeks beforehand and he made it quite clear he was just there to collect the money, so how was he supposed to provide answers to these questions he knew nothing about?

On the last Thursday in January, I had spotted Kilkenny in his Highway van driving around Camber, but he had either not seen or had chosen to leave my signs on the BT pole. I wondered if he had seen the Christmas card attached to the signpost on the A259, so when I finished work I drove to see if it was still there and much to my amazement it was.

The next morning I needed to go into Rye to buy some bread before the café opened. I left early around a quarter past seven and as I turned onto the A259 I saw immediately that the Christmas card had gone, I could see the wooden baton I had screwed it to was broken in half, obviously by someone strong as the baton was quite thick. It was inevitable that it would not be there for ever and I was astounded that it had survived for seven weeks.

There had been quite a lot of snow again and the roads were dangerous with ice on them and the gritters were few and far between, so I was worried about the Volvo with the café sign on it, as I didn't want a car skidding on the ice and crashing into it. The roads were hazardous enough without me adding to the danger with that huge car, so I told my friend he could have it back. Besides I had my poetic signs on the BT pole.

Now that Kilkenny knew I had put new signs back onto the BT pole I decided I would attempt to get written permission from 'Open Reach' the telecommunications network. There were Open Reach engineers in Camber almost every day so spotting one was not going to be difficult. In no time at all I saw an Open Reach van parked at the top of the road near to the BT pole with my signs attached. I went up to speak to him hoping that he would be nice. I asked him if it was all right to have the signs on the pole and he said it would be because there was only one phone line attached to it, so the chances of it needing to be repaired were minimal and they would only have to remove the signs if they restricted their access. He said that people were always putting signs on BT poles; they were even used as bus stops. He was a nice man and I explained to him why I needed to have permission in writing to put my signs on it, which he thought was ridiculous, especially as the poles were BT property. I gave him the café address and he said he would see what he could do. I was so pleased, that would be one in the eye for The Tyrannical Clown if I had written permission from OpenReach.

Needless to say my jubilations came to an abrupt end when days later I received a letter from the Operations Manager from Open Reach saying that he sympathised with my problem with the local authority but their concerns were that unauthorised signs or attachments of any kind on BT apparatus, in particular poles, might cause damage or impede access to climb and maintain. Only attachments that had been formally agreed with them were allowed, anything else could be removed by them and they were entitled to charge for removal costs. He concluded that they do not allow non BT attachments but they will allow certain things but only if they go through the proper process and achieve local approval. Drilling holes in poles was not allowed. He gave me till 18th February to remove them.

I was not going take no for an answer so I compiled a pleading letter to the Operations Manager. I explained again that I had to advertise the café or I would not have enough customers to keep the business solvent. I asked him why he should not formally agree to me putting my signs on his pole as he had mentioned in his letter that it was possible if there was an agreement. I asked him to reconsider as my livelihood depended on his benevolence. I offered to fill the holes in the poles with poly grip and use glue and not screws to attach the signs.

I sent the email and waited in anticipation for a response. I waited two days and I heard nothing and as the deadline of 18th February rapidly approached I could wait no longer so I rang him. I did not speak to the Operations Manager but to one of his colleagues who left me hanging on for ages while he checked to see if there had been a change of heart. Eventually he came back to the phone and explained that one of the engineers had visited the site and in his opinion saw no reason why I could not put my café signs on the pole. I was so pleased and thanked him profusely but I needed to have their consent in writing so I asked very nicely if he was able to verify the permission in writing and he agreed.

I was getting so exasperated with the behaviour of the council I decided to ridicule The Tyrannical Clown and expose him for looking down my jumper at Eastbourne Magistrates Court. I composed a short rhyme called "The

Tyrannical Clown":

The tale I am going to expose will keep this tyrant on his toes
He is an evil looking clown and on his head he wears a crown
He thinks he is a hard old nut but he is just a saddo slut
He likes to look down ladies tops a pair of tits to see
The next time I will break his neck if he does that again to me.

I took a photo of the first drawing of The Tyrannical Clown I had made when I was practising for the Christmas card and attached it to the rhyme in the hope that he and all of the Contact Centre staff at East Sussex County Council would recognise and ridicule him. I did not send it from my normal email address, but made another one and called myself Agatha Crunchbucket and I sent it to the Highways Contact Centre in Lewes.

I had not heard back from the Accounts Manager from East Sussex County Council Finance Department even though I had sent all the requested information over a week ago. I considered it would have been courteous of her to have sent a quick email just to confirm receipt of the papers I had sent her by recorded delivery, but she had not and I wondered if the whole lot had been for the Tyrannical Clown to look at. I emailed her and asked why she had not contacted me when I had asked for conformation on the receipt of my papers and I reminded her of my request not to disclose my personal information to The Tyrannical Clown.

She did not respond to my email and neither did Jed Uptland the Business Systems Manager who was meant to be answering my questions regarding the invoices within ten days. The more they evaded answering my reasonable request for simple information the more convinced I was that the invoices were faked by The Tyrannical Clown. I wanted my stuff back from the Accounts Manager so I emailed her again asking her why she had not answered my previous email. This time she replied almost immediately and explained she had been on holiday but regarding my questions she had forwarded them on to the Highways team in Bexhill, and she suggested I should pay the council £300 a month to pay off the invoices.

I got my papers back from the Accounts Manager but I never had any response from the Business Systems Manager regarding the detailed information I had requested about The Tyrannical Clown's invoices and neither did the Highways Contact Centre make any reference to it. The Customer Care Manager never came to visit Camber and I had no response to the application form I had sent to the planning department applying for advertisement consent and I did not send one penny to pay the outstanding debt from The Tyrannical Clown's fraudulent invoices.

For a short while the harassment ceased, the café signs on the BT pole were left to do what they were there for and the poems on them were frequently read and photographed. Even the signs on the sand dunes fence were left in peace.

One day two guys came into the café for their breakfast, they were doing some outside work at the caravan park. We got chatting about the fuss over my café signs with the council and all of a sudden I had an idea. If I could concrete a scaffold pole into the ground opposite the caravan park I would no longer have to screw my signs to the telegraph pole. I was glad I mentioned my idea as the two men kindly offered me a bucket of ready-made concrete which I gratefully accepted and offered a breakfast in part exchange. Before they left I gave them a large black bucket to fill up and bring back with them the following day. I went into Rye after I closed the café and bought a twelve foot long scaffold pole for £20, which was awkward to transport because it was longer than the interior of my car. The next morning the guys came back with the black bucket full to the brim with ready-made concrete which weighed a ton. I could barely lift it and I had to keep it cold so it would not set before I used it. That afternoon I set off to the other end of the village equipped with the scaffold pole and the bucket of ready-made concrete. I did not own a spade so I had to improvise with a soup ladle and a fish slice.

It was not easy digging a hole with a soup ladle as the ground was still quite hard from the winter frosts, but I persevered and finally with the help of the fish slice had made a hole barely big enough to put a golf ball in. I tried to get the attention of the builders who were still building the extension and eventually one of them came and dug a deep hole with a proper spade. I held the scaffold pole while he poured the concrete in. Job done, I held onto the pole for five minutes more to make sure it stayed up straight while the concrete set.

Having read The Town & Country Planning (Control of Advertisements) (England) Regulations 2007 sent to me by the complaints manager, I found a possible solution for advertising the café without having to apply for all the different types of consent which they had been demanding. Class 3 stated that temporary signs were considered to have deemed consent and did not require planning or advertisement consent. This gave me the bright idea to make one large café sign plus two smaller signs that could be attached across the top of the larger one, each of them advertising a different temporary event which I would alternate every two or three weeks, that way I would be well within my rights to advertise as these temporary events would be taking place in my café and I had to make any potential visitors aware of the location of the event. So for the first temporary event sign I wrote

'Temporary Event.' 'Home Grown Pot' 'Plant Exhibition'.
For the second sign I wrote 'Temporary Event' 'Local Art
Exhibition'. I had already prepared the sign for the scaffold
pole and it took no time at all to make the two temporary
event signs. The first temporary event was the 'Home Grown
Pot' 'Plant Exhibition'. I put the signs onto the scaffold pole
and was proud of my first attempt at creating my very own
piece of street furniture.

CHAPTER 19

I had seen Kilkenny driving round Camber in his highway van
on a couple of occasions recently and someone else had seen
him taking photos of my café signs on the BT pole, but for
whatever reason, the café signs were still on the pole and the
temporary event sign on the scaffold pole was also still there.

I knew the lack of activity would not last long and I was
right. Just as I was getting ready to close in the afternoon on
Friday 12th March 2010 a lady walked into the café carrying a
bundle of papers. I recognised her straight away; she was the
same lady who had come from Hastings County Court last
October who had delivered the bundle for the court case in
Eastbourne. I welcomed her back and offered her a cup of tea
but she declined my offer. Instead she placed the bundle of
papers directly into my hands. I said that I didn't expect
another court case quite so soon and when I looked to see
when it was taking place I couldn't believe it, Wednesday 17th
March, just five days away. The lady left and I read the front
page of the bundle of evidence. This bundle was quite a lot
thicker than the previous one for the Eastbourne court case.

The application had been prepared by Judgement Jones the
Council's solicitor asking the court for an injunction order

forbidding me whether by myself or instructing or encouraging or permitting any other person from placing any signs, posters or structures on the highway or which abut the highway without the express written consent of the claimant as the highway authority and that I shall not use foul, abusive or defamatory language or engage in threatening behaviour towards any member of the claimant's staff. The application included written evidence from The Tyrannical Clown which was sworn on 6th January 2010 and Kilkenny's sworn on 23rd February 2010.

I was completely puzzled why they needed to give me an injunction order for using foul and abusive language. Surely that was not for calling Kilkenny an 'arsehole'. I had never sworn at any of them and I had no idea where the threatening behaviour bit had come from. I hadn't threatened any of them either, although I had hurled projectiles from my pinny pocket at The Tyrannical Clown at the police station seven months previously, I had not threatened him, it was a spur of the moment reaction and as it took place in the police station he had every opportunity to have me arrested and charged with GBH but he had not.

No matter what evidence they were going to produce, I could and would deal with it myself, especially after the encounter I had with the incompetent barrister in Eastbourne, and in any case I didn't have any money to pay for another one. I knew that I would have to prepare my own evidence in triplicate, one for the court, one for Judgement Jones and one for myself, and I only had the week-end to do it as it would have to be posted on Monday for them to receive it in time for the hearing on Wednesday. It was quite obvious that the court summons had deliberately been delivered at the last moment to give me as little time as possible to prepare my case. Going by the dates on the witness statements they had evidently been planning this case for some time, so there was no reason why

I had been given such short notice. The last time they had done exactly the same thing but the solicitor in Eastbourne got the case adjourned for one week. I was undeterred and rose once again to the challenge of preparing my own evidence and in the very short time they had given me to do it. I would prepare my bundle and they would receive it on Tuesday morning.

That evening I started to gather all the evidence I could, emails, letters and photos. I thought about how to write my statement, the easiest way was to copy the lay-out of The Tyrannical Clown's. After the initial who I was and what my business was I wrote that since my court case in Eastbourne five months previously I had on several occasions written and asked the Highways and Planning Department of East Sussex County Council and Rother District Council how I could attain authorisation to advertise my cafe. I said I had received a letter from the Planning Department stating that planning permission for an A-board was not required and no sooner had I got it than the permission had been revoked.

I made comments regarding The Tyrannical Clown's statement. I said that I felt I was being bullied by the claimant's staff, the reason being I had on several occasions been threatened with legal action, injunction orders, an ASBO and imprisonment. I said in my opinion The Tyrannical Clown's motives were too personal and had become out of control, unprofessional and not befitting an employee with management status. It had been for that reason I had written to his superior to complain about his behaviour to which I had not had any response and I believed my letter had been handled by a devious member of staff who, having received my letter, had warned The Tyrannical Clown and had been told to send it directly to him. Lastly I said that I had requested reasonable information regarding the invoices I had been sent but as yet no one had been able to provide me with answers.

Then I responded to The Tyrannical Clown's witness statement. He claimed that despite my conviction at Eastbourne Magistrates Court on 6th October 2009 I was constantly placing signs upon the highway which had to be removed by their contractors and the cost to the council was considerable, currently amounting to one thousand pounds and rising, this being both an inconvenience and a financial drain on the council.

To that I could only say that the reason I had to constantly put signs on the highway was because they constantly removed them and I had to advertise my café somehow.

Then he had made an example of one of my signs by producing a photo of it. This photo was presented as his exhibit 1 and was the Christmas card I had attached to the signpost on the A259. I chose not to make any comment about that.

Then he said although he had not seen me since the court case in Eastbourne I had sent him several offensive emails and these emails were collectively his exhibit 2. He had chosen a paragraph from one of the emails saying it was dated 29th November 2009 and I had sent it in response to a letter sent by the council's legal department threatening me with injunction proceedings if I did not desist in placing signs on the highway and sending abusive emails. He quoted my email '...no doubt to The Tyrannical Clown's dismay, I am now going to conclude this email by suggesting that he shoves his jurisdiction up his arse and forgets where it is'.

The second email in his exhibit 2 was written on 12th January 2010 and he said in a comment he believed to be directed towards himself asks the council to tell '...that bumptious old fart to hurry up'.

The third email dated 18th February 2010 he said was sent to the Highways Contact Centre for circulation. This email clearly referred to himself in what he considered to be a most offensive manner which he believed had been sent by me (the Defendant) but I had used a different email address referring to myself as Agatha Crunchbucket. He believed the poem referred to him as 'The Tyrannical Clown' and I had described him amongst other things as an 'evil looking clown' and a 'saddo slut' and he felt intimidated as the poem threatened physical violence against him. As well as the email he had produced a photo copy of the rhyme and his portrait I had sent with it.

My answer to this section was I had sent the emails because I felt I was being bullied by The Tyrannical Clown because of the frequent threats of legal action, ASBO and imprisonment and the reason I made the personal remarks was that I felt I knew him in a bad way and I had stooped to his level of understanding.

This was the email with the poem that threatened physical violence to The Tyrannical Clown if he dared to look down my jumper again. I admitted writing but I denied all knowledge of how it had been sent to the Contact Centre.

I also added to my defence that I had been sent a list of ways I could legally advertise my café but apart from an A-board draped over the back of a donkey there was nothing positive that would benefit my predicament.

Finally in response to the invoices I had not paid, I wrote that I had requested reasonable information regarding them which had been ignored and until it was provided I would not pay.

Then I made copies of the emails and letters I had sent asking for permission to advertise my café and copies of the negative answers I had received. I included Judgement Jones letter accusing me of putting café signs up after 6th October 2009 plus the photos and dates as recorded on my mobile phone of when I had really put them up last summer as the

sky was blue and flowers were in full bloom in the
background. I made copies of the fraudulent invoices and the
other letter from Judgement Jones about communications with
council staff and accusing them of lying and conspiracy. I
copied letters and emails I had sent asking for the return of my
café signs that they had taken over the last year and The
Tyrannical Clown's answers.

I included in my bundle of evidence:
The letter from the planning department which stated I did not
need planning permission.
A copy of the Town and Country Planning (Control of
Advertisements) 2007 Regulations they had sent me.
The three invoices from The Tyrannical Clown.
Five local residents who had lived in Camber for longer than
twenty years had written statements for my evidence
confirming that all the previous owners of Camber Café had
placed A-boards at the junction of Lydd Road and had never
had been asked to remove them.

Finally at the end of my bundle I put in my ace card, the
chain of emails between the BT engineer and his site manager
discussing whether or not I could have written permission to
use the BT pole and there the last email said 'I can confirm
permission has been given for these signs. I visited the site
and saw the signs in question and I can see no problem
attaching these signs and issuing a permit to the owner of the
café. There is only one D/W off the pole in question and we
would require a hoist to work off the D/P anyhow'.

I included twenty-eight photos I had taken of other
people's business signs, mainly A-boards that were on and
abutting the highway around Camber and Rye. I enclosed one
photo advertising my cafe which was the one of the snowman.

It took the whole week-end to prepare my evidence, in-
between working in the café and running home to do the
bundle. Lily kept the café going in my absence. After I had

completed all the paperwork I had to make triplicate photo copies of it all and divide it into three bundles, and when I had finished I had to use a hole- puncture to tie it all together and all I could find was some white ribbon with little red hearts on it. So I threaded each bundle together with the ribbon, addressed the large brown envelopes I had bought and placed a bundle in each one.

I had done it, with hours of searching through letters and emails, typing and printing. I'd show them what I was capable of doing. The whole case was ridiculous anyway. The Tyrannical Clown was trying to evoke pity from the judge whingeing about names I had called him. How could a reputable judge look at his evidence and sympathise with him. I felt sure it would all be chucked out of court and it was all such a waste of time and money.

On the Monday morning I sent the bundles by recorded delivery; one to Hastings County Court and the other to Judgement Jones at County Hall, Lewes.

CHAPTER 20

I arrived at Hastings County Court at 10 o'clock with my bundle in my bag. Both I and my bag were searched on entry to the court and I was zapped with the metal detecting wand.

I was told to report to the check- in desk which was manned by two policemen and a security guard. I told them who I was and they asked me why I was there. I told them I had been summoned there by East Sussex County Council because I had called a highways inspector an 'arsehole'. They found it quite amusing and told me to go up some stairs to check in with the clerk of the court.

As I mounted the wide staircase I saw Judgement Jones and The Tyrannical Clown sitting next to each other in the reception area. I smiled and said hello to them and plonked myself down next to Judgement Jones. The Tyrannical Clown asked me what I was going to throw at him today and I replied I had brought eggs but I would save them till later. I also warned them that they would be dealing with me today as I was representing myself. I knew Judgement Jones had had dealings with that barrister before, the solicitor in Eastbourne had told me that a company had not paid the licence fee for their skips they had put on the highway and had duly been fined for the offence. I said to Judgement Jones that I imagined he had been delighted when he had seen the barrister I had to defend me at Eastbourne Magistrates Court knowing he was useless, but before he could answer The Tyrannical Clown warned him to be careful what he said, so he said nothing.

Judgement Jones had an air of arrogance about him; his voice was quiet, expressionless and nasal. I asked Judgement Jones if he was intending to read my poetry again to the judge and if he was would he have the courtesy to put some expression into what he was reading or it would lose the poetical rhythm I had intended for it. At that moment we were ushered into the court room. Judgement Jones went first with his bundle of papers balanced across his forearms again, then to my amazement The Tyrannical Clown held the door and told me to go in front of him. I asked him why, but he did not answer, instead he shoved me into the court room.

It was just a room with a large table and several chairs round it and the judge sat at the top of the table behind a desk at the far end of the room. She was a lady, small and very attractive and was wearing normal clothes and no gown or wig. The Tyrannical Clown and Judgement Jones sat to her right and I sat opposite them to her left. When we were all settled Judgement Jones stood up and proceeded to tell her all about my misdemeanours with my café signs and the guilty verdict and fines imposed upon me at Eastbourne Magistrates Court and how since then I had continued to place my signs on the highway which were potentially dangerous to motorists and furthermore I had sent several abusive and threatening emails and poems which were written deliberately to intimidate council staff.

He made it sound so dramatic and spoke about me as if I were some deranged miscreant; he was literally making a mountain out of a molehill. When he had finished he asked the judge to grant an injunction order ordering me not to place any signs on or abutting the highway and not to use foul or abusive language or threatening behaviour towards council staff.

The judge asked me if I had prepared a bundle of my evidence for her. I explained that I had despite the short notice given to me by Judgement Jones and I said I had sent it on Monday. She was fine about it and asked to borrow Judgement Jones bundle and just as she started to look through my evidence a lady came into the room carrying the other bundle I had sent to the court. The judge looked at the ribbon holding it all together and commented how pretty it was. She spent a few minutes looking through it whilst we all sat there looking at her. When she got to the photos of all the business signs she commented on my snowman photo saying what a lovely snowman he was. When she reached the email from OpenReach giving me permission to put my signs on the BT pole she questioned Judgement Jones that if I had permission from BT then that was surely acceptable. It was obvious that neither Judgement Jones nor The Tyrannical Clown had actually read any of my evidence and this devastating news landed like a lead balloon in their laps. Judgement Jones quickly flicked through the bundle looking for the email in question. He was clearly flustered as the pages were rustled back and forth until he found what he was looking for. He was clearly embarrassed and when The Tyrannical Clown asked him if he had known about this email he sheepishly had to reply he had not. I was delighted to see their reaction and I hoped they were going to have an argument over it in front of the judge. The Tyrannical Clown was so outraged it looked as if he was on the verge of bursting all the blood vessels in his forehead, and all I wanted to do was to laugh at them, but I dared not as things seemed to be going in my favour. Sadly there was no argument and shortly they both regained their composure.

After the judge had finished reading my evidence she closed it and looking at The Tyrannical Clown and Judgement Jones said she would not grant an injunction against me. It would have to go to trial but in the meantime I would have to agree to an undertaking of not using abusive language or threatening behaviour towards council staff. I agreed. She said to Judgement Jones she would expect him to prepare my bundle for me. What her reason was for that I do not know, maybe because he had given me such short notice to prepare my bundle of evidence which I had tied together with a white ribbon with little red hearts on it. She suggested that the three of us should go into one of the side rooms of the court and reach a compromise.

Their faces were like thunder and they were furious. The Tyrannical Clown stood up and raised his voice to the judge and shouted at her that I had nine miles of café signs along the highway. I looked at her and shook my head and said to her calmly that I had not and that The Tyrannical Clown was exaggerating. Whilst Judgement Jones gathered up all his bits of paper The Tyrannical Clown was ranting and raving at the poor judge like a spoilt child having a tantrum. He was obviously used to getting his own way. All the while the judge had been writing and ignoring the commotion The Tyrannical Clown was causing, and she handed me the document for the undertaking and the consequences if I breached it; I read it and signed it.

They started to leave the room and I thanked the judge and she smiled kindly at me. I followed the two angry men into a side room where we all grabbed a seat. 'So let's compromise' I suggested and The Tyrannical Clown replied aggressively that he was not going to compromise with any one, least of all me. I asked him if he had ever been a policeman and he said that he had, so I questioned what rank he had held, he arrogantly replied that he had been a Detective Chief Inspector. I did not believe he was intelligent enough to hold such a rank so I retorted that I did not care if he had been Father Christmas. So The Tyrannical Clown and I talked rubbish for the entire duration and not once did he cast his eye down upon my ample bosom. All the while Judgement Jones had remained silent until all of a sudden he started waving his arms about saying this conversation was going nowhere and it was time to go. I agreed, and as we prepared to leave I

politely went to shake Judgement Jones hand, but as I took
hold of it, it felt floppy and detached, and I thought I had
pulled a false hand off the end of his arm and my reaction was
to catch it as it fell but I realised it was still attached and was
nothing more than a limp wrist with a severe lack of grip that
had given the impression of his hand separating from the rest
of his arm. Then I shook hands with The Tyrannical Clown,
he took my hand and squeezed it violently, blocking the blood
circulation to my fingers. I said 'ouch you're hurting me ' but
he did not release his grip until he was satisfied he had
inflicted maximum pain upon my hand which was by now
white and numb with imprints of my rings embedded in my
fingers, and it remained like that for a few moments until the
blood flowed back into my hand.

We left the building and they walked off towards the town
and I heard The Tyrannical Clown say 'let's go and have some
lunch'. I went back to my car and back to the café.

CHAPTER 21

The following week I received an email from Judgement Jones which said:

Dear Mrs Hutchinson,
I will send you a composite bundle in due course and if you have any objections to it, please let me know.
Just as an aside, can you not ask a local farmer or other private landowner if you can put one of your signs on their private property? They will charge for it, but if it provides you with lots of customers, isn't it worth it? The Council is only concerned with maintaining the highway. If you leave the highway alone, we won't bother you anymore and this whole matter can be dropped.
Yours sincerely
Judgement Jones

What a cheek! Who was Mrs Hutchinson and what was he talking about? I had already put my signs on private property and been threatened with legal action within two days. I replied to his email telling him so and added that putting a café sign three miles down the road in a field where it must not been seen from the highway was of no significance or benefit to my business, but I said that as I had written permission from BT I had no intention of removing my signs off the BT pole. However, if he reimbursed me the cost of all my A-boards, the £2715.00 fine, compensation for the inconvenience in having to defend my livelihood and an apology from the Highways staff, then I would agree to him dropping the case.

He replied almost instantly by asking if he might call me Sally and saying I had misunderstood him. They would only consider dropping the case if I gave a legally binding undertaking to permanently cease advertising my café on the highway.

Why would I agree to that and how could he even have expected me to? Maybe as the judge had refused to grant the injunction this time he thought that the next court case would also be unsuccessful. Well he knew what he could do with his suggestion. I answered 'see you in court'. I did not get a reply.

A few days later I received a letter from the court informing me of the date of the next court case which was at 10.30 on 9th April 2010 at Hastings County Court. It only mentioned the claimants request for an injunction order to forbid me from using foul and abusive language and threatening behaviour toward the claimant's staff as the highway authority. I wondered if it was possible that maybe they had actually given up on my café signs and were not going to bother trying to stop me anymore, but I wasn't going to get too excited. The duration of the court case was going to take half a day which seemed a mighty long time to decide if I could call the council staff names or not.

The judge had told Judgement Jones to prepare my bundle for me, but I needed to add some more evidence to it so I attached photos and a copy of the breakdown of the invoices sent by Jed Uptland from the refuse company and forwarded them to Judgement Jones. At the same time I asked him to provide a written statement from the Senior Highways Technician who had reportedly taken the photos of my café signs on 22nd October 2009.

The next day I sent him another email, I said:

Thank you for preparing my bundle. Did you get the photos? I take it you have dropped the café sign charges as it is not mentioned in the letter I received from the court yesterday.

Although half a day is quite a long time to decide if I can refer to council staff as a ' trou de cou' et puis les 'branleur'.
Regards Sally

I had chosen to write the offending words in French as I knew if I wrote them in English they would have twisted it and say I had breached the undertaking I had signed in the court.

I was emailing stuff for my new evidence and it was becoming quite tiresome as I worried that there would not be a lot of thought for my evidence and it would all be put in the wrong order; I would have much preferred to have prepared it myself. A couple of hours later another email arrived from Judgement Jones, it said:

Sally
I did get the photos thank you but I disagree with your statement that 'I take it you have dropped the café sign charges'. I presume you are referring to the Court Order. First of all, these are civil injunction proceedings so there are no 'charges' as such. Secondly, the Court did not make an interim injunction order and instead you undertook not to use foul, abusive or defamatory language towards ESCC staff. The Council's application for a full injunction has not yet been determined and so our application stands. We still intend to apply for a full injunction against the unauthorised placing of signs on the highway as well as the abusive language towards Council staff.
Judgement Jones

For goodness sake! I had only asked a question, why did he make such dramas out of every little thing I said? I just emailed him back ignoring all the legalities and I thanked him for doing my bundle for me.

I did not want to hear back from him anymore but unfortunately that evening after he had finished work I got another email:

Sally

I must remind you of the terms of your undertaking. Please do not refer to Council staff as 'arseholes' and 'wankers', even if it is in the French language!

He was getting on my nerves. He knew I had only been making reference to the letter I had received from the court; I had not written anything that suggested they were, not that time anyway.

My bundle of evidence arrived by attachment for my approval. I checked that everything I had sent to Judgement Jones was all present and in the right order of events.

I had included the letters and emails I had sent requesting permission to advertise my café, the fraudulent invoices from The Tyrannical Clown and the breakdown of them from the refuse company's business systems manager, my reasonable request for information regarding the collection of my café signs by the council's contractors, to date ignored, my request for service ticket 58061 with the alleged complaint about my café signs on 17th November 2008, to date ignored, the photos of my café signs allegedly taken on 22nd October 2009, the email I had sent requesting a written statement from the Senior Highways Technician who had removed and photographed the signs on 22nd October 2009, to date ignored.

I included a copy of the letter I had sent five months previously to the Chief Executive complaining about The Tyrannical Clown, to date unanswered.

An added extra that Judgement Jones had inadvertently sent me, was thirty-one photographs of my café signs which had surely been taken by Kilkenny as his Highway van was visible in most of them. I asked Judgement Jones to remove them as they served no purpose in amongst my bundle.

I believe the Council had no credible evidence to support their claims and accusations regarding certain matters, and that was surely the reason they had ignored my many requests for proof because there was no proof.

After I had thanked Judgement Jones again for preparing my bundle of evidence he sent me theirs. I was absolutely shocked by what Judgement Jones had done, the rotter had written to the OpenReach site manager who had given me permission to put my café signs on the BT pole enclosing a copy of the letter I had presented as part of my evidence at the last court hearing and his letter to Open Reach:

Dear Sirs
Re: East Sussex County Council-v- Sally-Ann Pattinson
Unauthorised Attachment to BT Pole at Lydd Road, Camber, East Sussex
I enclose copies of correspondence sent by yourselves to Mrs Pattinson 3rd February and 15th March 2010. Mrs Pattinson has been convicted of several counts of attaching unauthorised signs to the highway, contrary to s132 of the Highways Act 1980. Since her conviction last October she has continued to offend and is currently subject to injunction proceedings in Hastings County Court. As I am sure you are aware, it is a criminal offence to attach signs to street furniture or other signage on the highway, regardless of whether or not the owner of the furniture consents to it.
At the interim injunction hearing last week, the Court declined to grant an interim injunction in the Council's favour. The decision was partly based on your email to Sally Pattinson of 15th March which she used in her defence.

I write to express on behalf of my client the Council's dismay that its attempt to enforce its legal rights has been in part thwarted by BT. In fact it is arguable that by permitting Mrs Pattinson to attach signs to one of your poles, that you are in fact aiding and abetting a criminal offence. I'm sure that neither of these is your intention, but I would ask you to rescind any consents you have given to Mrs Pattinson and confirm that consent will not be given in the future.

The Council as the Highway Authority is using the civil process in order to enforce its rights against a persistent offender. I would be grateful if BT would assist, rather than undermine my client in this process. I look forward to hearing from you as a matter of some urgency.

Yours sincerely

Judgement Jones Solicitor for Director of Law

CHAPTER 22

Recently a single decker bus converted into a burger van called AJ's had been pitching up in the lay-by by the lakes and Golf course on the road into Camber. The guy who owned the burger van business had made himself famous by taking a photo of Cherie Blair when she had something stuck up her nose, but now he had retired from the paparazzi and had set up his burger bus for something to do. He had four huge A-boards both sides of the Camber road and I asked him if he had ever been told he could not put them there, and he said he had not.

As soon as I knew that, I emailed The Tyrannical Clown and asked him why he had not told AJ to take his A-boards off the main road. He did not answer, but a couple of days later they had gone from the main road and now one was placed on the grass next to a broken barbed-wire fence just off the road and there was another at the top of the lay-by where the burger van was parked. The other two A-boards were nowhere to be seen. I felt mean reporting him, but Kilkenny must have seen the huge A-boards as he passed them every time he came to Camber.

I sent my friend Jenny from Love Lane to have a cup of coffee at AJ's to have a friendly chat and try and find out if he had got permission from the council to put his A-boards on the side of the road. He told Jenny everything I wanted to know. He had been told by the Planning Department at Rother that he did not need planning permission for his A-boards.

There was no difference to where AJ put his A-boards on Council land to where I had put mine. I emailed Judgement Jones and I said:

Judgement Jones

I understand that AJ's burger van has been told by the
planning department that he may put his A-boards in the field
by the main road which can be seen from the highway. He
was not asked to put in a planning application.
So how come this is possible for him but not me?
Sally

His reply was brief:

Sally
The field is privately owned by the golf course who have given
him permission. It's not on the highway so it's no concern of
the Council's.
Regards
Judgement Jones

It was time for my third court case within six months, starting at 10.00 am, and I arrived alone in plenty of time. My bag was searched and I was zapped with the metal detecting wand. I reported to the check-in desk and I was told to wait in the main reception area and not at the top of the stairs as I had the previous time. I went and sat down trying discretely to look out for the foe, I was not nervous or frightened, I was ready and quite excited about this new experience that was about to take place. Then suddenly I saw them as they filed out of a side room. The Tyrannical Clown appeared first, he was not wearing his creased up safari suit today, he was better dressed in casual clothing. I could see he was looking to see if I had turned up. Kilkenny followed and he looked like he was going to a funeral, dressed all in black. There was no sign of Judgement Jones but there were two other men in tow whom I did not recognise. The taller man came over to me and addressed me by name, introducing himself as Counsel for the claimant. He asked me if I had any legal representation to which I replied I had not, and he said he wanted to ask me some questions and I told him I would not answer them. I took an instant dislike to this man, who looked like a Puffer fish, and he said if that was my wish and he sauntered off to join the others where they had gathered at the far end of the hall.

I sat there minding my own business until the Clerk to the Court came and ushered me down a long flight of stairs to the lowest depth of the County Court. As I arrived in the small waiting area I heard The Tyrannical Clown say that he had not known this part of the building existed. As we were waiting they chatted amongst themselves ignoring me although I did say hello to them. The new kid on the block was strangely the same height as Kilkenny and The Tyrannical Clown although he was a good twenty years younger than they were. He had a round podgy face and his neck hung over his shirt collar and his forehead was covered in beads of perspiration. He wore a double breasted blazer and casual trousers and I noticed that he was wearing winkle pickers with worn down soles which made me laugh. Anyway I did not recognise him and then he came over to me, his eyes blinking rapidly as he spoke and he informed me that if they lost this case they would appeal against the decision. I pacified him replying he must do what he felt necessary. I asked him who he was, and he told me his name was Rag-Eme-Kale. I recognised that name on some emails that had been sent to me and it was his name that had been put on the last of the spurious invoices. I was wondering why he should say that. Maybe they were expecting to lose, so I told him that if I lost I would also appeal against the decision.

Just at that moment we were ushered into the court room, and I was told to go and sit on the far side of the court and their barrister, now wearing his gown and wig, sat on the left side. The Tyrannical Clown, Kilkenny and Rag-Eme-Kale sat behind us. We were told to stand up when the judge came in and then we all sat down again. The judge was a six foot tall blond, large boned woman with a deep voice wearing all her court swagger and I did not like her.

The barrister stood up and bowed to the judge and proceeded to tell her how I was in contempt of the law, I had no consideration for the public, I was abusive, threatening and a financial drain on the Council's resources. I had sent abusive emails to employees of the Highways Department and written threatening and intimidating poems. I had also threatened physical violence to The Tyrannical Clown and had ridiculed him by sending abusive emails for circulation to his place of work and beyond. He told the judge I had appeared at Eastbourne Magistrates Court on 6th October 2009 and received a fine of £2700 which I had refused to pay. The claimant therefore was asking the court to grant an injunction order for the duration of three years forbidding me from placing signs on or abutting the highway without the written consent of the claimant as the authority and furthermore to forbid me using foul and abusive language and threatening behaviour towards council staff.

The judge listened attentively, nodding her head periodically in agreement as the barrister described me as a contemptuous persistent offender who believed I could do what I wanted when I wanted and where I wanted and I had to be stopped.

I could hardly believe that the barrister was talking about me. How dare they accuse me of refusing to pay that fine. I had initially paid £1000 and then set up a direct debit and paid £50 a month to the fines office in Brighton. Judgement Jones had never mentioned it and he surely would have done if I had paid nothing in six months. If they had included that accusation in their bundle I could have taken my bank statements with me as proof I had been paying it.

I was honest and a law abiding citizen, and this barrister was deliberately twisting and exaggerating everything to make it sound far worse than it really was. I wondered how they could possibly believe that a silly rhyme threatening to break someone's neck for looking at a pair of tits could be taken so seriously to the point of believing it could be a real threat of physical violence. I hoped the judge would see it that way but the formidable expression on her face implied that she believed the barrister. The judge appeared to be shocked at the thought of me threatening The Tyrannical Clown with physical violence. She would surely realise if she had any intelligence that it was not written to be taken seriously but because it rhymed with the line before. I was suspicious of her to the point I wondered if in fact she was a judge at all.

The Tyrannical Clown was called to the witness box and with the bible held high in his hand he swore by Almighty God to tell the truth the whole truth and nothing but the truth, and stated his name and rank within the highways authority. He then proceeded to tell the judge how I persistently flouted the law by placing signs upon the highway, and portrayed in a pitiful tone the financial drain the removal of my signs from the highway was having on the council's resources. He continued by saying that I had bombarded him and council staff with abusive and threatening emails, and referred to his exhibits, an email to the Complaints Manager when I had suggested that 'he' (which he believed to be himself) 'shoves his jurisdiction up his arse and forgets where it is' and another when I had referred to him as 'that bumptious old fart'. He said I had refused to pay the fine which I received at Eastbourne Magistrates Court in October. He went on and on, he told her that I had been sent invoices for the removal of my café signs which I had also refused to pay, then he arrived on the subject of the Christmas card attached to street furniture on the A259. At that moment the barrister jumped up bowing like crazy to the judge offering to assist by reciting the Christmas message I had written on the card. The judge nodded in approval, and in his glee the barrister appeared to curtsey rather than bow and read aloud to the judge, 'Happy Christmas Peace and Goodwill to the Merchant Bankers from Bexhill'. The judge, looking puzzled, asked the barrister the meaning of 'merchant bankers'. Bowing and calling her 'madam' he said that he was grateful she had asked him that and he explained to her that a 'merchant banker' was cockney rhyming slang for a 'wanker'. She readily accepted his interpretation which made me wonder how she could be so unfamiliar with a 'merchant banker' but appeared familiar with a wanker. She asked me what I had to say about it and I denied all knowledge of it and said I was not an artist and besides, I said I would have called them 'tossers'. She asked me if I had commissioned someone else to paint the picture and I asked her how anyone else would know what The Tyrannical Clown and Kilkenny would look like. She did not believe that I had not made the card and she said so too and she had no doubt it was me who had painted the picture and attached it to street furniture on the A 259. At that point I heard Kilkenny sniggering behind me; I turned around and frowned at him.

I needed to say something but I did not know how to address the judge. I couldn't call her Mi' Lord, so I stood up and asked for permission to speak which she granted and I told her that I had been paying the fine that I had just been wrongly accused of refusing to pay. As if he had not heard me she turned to The Tyrannical Clown and repeated that I had said I had paid the fine, again he said I had refused to pay it. I explained that I had paid £1000 off the fine within a couple of days of the court case and then I had set up a direct debit to pay £50 a month to the fines office in Brighton which was paid on the 25th of each month The judge repeated it all to The Tyrannical Clown again and he said unashamedly that I had refused to pay it.

I could not believe he had said that, as someone on the council must have known I had been paying it or I would surely have received some kind of reminder, but before I could open my mouth to say anything else the judge quickly moved on to the next subject of the phone call The Tyrannical Clown had made to me on 9th September 2009. She looked at him and asked him if he had made the phone call. He deliberately avoided eye contact with her and looking at the floor he said he had not. The judge knew he was lying but she did not give me the opportunity to contest his denial or question him; instead she said she had no reason to disbelieve him as he was an ex-policeman. Well that came as no surprise but no one had mentioned he had been a policeman till then, and the judge must have known him which explained why this whole court case was such a farce. The Tyrannical Clown might have been an ex-policeman but at this moment he was a perjurer and what was more disturbing the judge knew he was and she ignored it.

I wanted to object to the lies he had just told but again we were rushed on to the next offence I had committed. The barrister stood up and did the bowing and 'madam if I may', and told her of the undertaking I had agreed to on 17th March 2010 not to use foul and abusive language toward council's staff and that on 26th March 2010 I was in breach of the agreement by writing an email to the council's legal department stating that half a day was a long time to decide if I could refer to council staff as 'trou de cou' and 'branleur'. The Tyrannical Clown butted in and said he had been reliably informed that the English translation was 'arse-holes' and 'wankers' and said that the reason I wrote the abusive words in French was because I thought I would be exempt by doing so. I stood up and told the judge that Judgement Jones had misinterpreted my email and I was making reference to the letter I had received from the court, I was not making any aspersions about the council's staff. I asked her to look at the email I had sent Judgement Jones in response to his accusation so she could read my explanation but she said it was not necessary. My bundle of papers in front of me was in such a muddle I could not find my copy of the email to show her.

The Tyrannical Clown then referred to the email I had received from the OpenReach manager giving his consent to me to attach my café signs on the BT pole. He said despite this authorisation from BT I was still committing an offence under section s132 if the 1980's Highway Act because I did not have the consent of the local highway authority regardless of whether or not BT or any other organisation agreed to it. Their department had written to BT who had cooperated by writing to the defendant and had rescinded the consent they had granted previously. He brought to the attention of the judge to look at his exhibit of the letter and the response he had received from OpenReach in his bundle and she did look at his evidence after refusing to look at my email to Judgement Jones.

He then said they had gone out of their way to help me by sending me a lengthy letter informing me of all the ways I could advertise my business legitimately and he referred to another of his exhibits which was a copy of the list of nonsense they had sent me whereby the only option was advertising on an animal. He stressed that despite the time they had spent in assisting me I had continued to persistently offend and I wrongly believed I was being unfairly treated by way of my signs being removed from the highway. So to prove that I was not being singled out The Tyrannical Clown had exhibited three photo copies of unauthorised signs that had been removed from the highway, so he claimed. These photos, like everything else had been exhibited solely to demonstrate integrity on his part to impress the judge. The first photo was of a pile of Estate Agents 'For Sale' or 'Sale Agreed' signs which were not illegal anyway and came under Class 3 of the Town and Country Planning Act which was part of the section with deemed consent. The second one was of a pile of temporary event signs for several 'Halloween Parties' and 'Bonfire Nights' which were one day event signs and did not require consent and most probably had been collected long after the event had been and gone. The third photo was taken in a room I expected was at the highways office building and was of several neat piles of brand new directional signs for housing developments, caravan parks and 'Farm Watch' signs waiting to be erected. I looked at the photos and I said that the signs in one of the photos were temporary event signs and none of them were pertaining to any businesses. The judge pointed out that there was one for a farm shop and I suggested that the farm shop was most probably a side line to the farm. There were no signs in that photo that someone's livelihood depended on. The 'For Sale' signs were not illegal and the brand new signs which were all piled up on a table in an office ready to go were also legal. I could not believe the judge did not say anything; it was so blatantly obvious that the photos had been exhibited only to mislead the judge and were not what The Tyrannical Clown had claimed them to be.

Then The Tyrannical Clown read from his bundle that 'On Tuesday 30 March 2010 contractors employed by the Claimant took photographs of several signs advertising the Defendant's Café that were found to be within the highway boundary. The photographs had been passed to him and he had exhibited them in his witness statement. He said one of the photographs exhibited contained a board photographed by Kilkenny on 1st of February and which could be found in the Court Bundle. During these proceedings, the board has been removed and put up again. The board contained a message that was both menacing and threatening towards the Claimant in its tone. The fact that the Defendant had seen fit to reinstate this board and keep it in place on the highway during these proceedings is a clear example of her flagrant and repeated breaches of the law and clearly indicates the contempt in which she holds the legal process.'

I was getting infuriated with all his lying, he was talking about the time the OpenReach manager had told me to take the signs down which I had and then they had changed their minds and told me I could have them on the BT pole, so on the strength of that I had put them back up again.

Then he continued his evidence by trying to give the impression he was concerned for my wellbeing and he said he would like to point out that neither he nor his colleagues wished to disrupt my business nor did they wish me any ill will and that their only concern was to ensure that the highways were free from commercial advertising and obstructions and if they allowed me to place my signs on the highway then other commercial advertisers would follow suit which would lead to a serious health and safety hazard. He said if I complied with the Highways Act by not placing signs on the highway or on Council property then neither he nor other officers of the Council would need to have any contact with me. I suddenly remembered the morning he had been driving around Camber in the fog and I asked for permission to speak and I said to the judge that I had been trying to apply for written express consent but apparently there is no such form, I said that my friend had tried to get an application form for it too, and immediately The Tyrannical Clown asked if that was 'Love Lane'. I said it was and asked him if he had been checking her out that same morning I had seen him driving a highway van at 7.15 in Camber in the fog, but he did not answer me and neither did the judge make any comment or query on how I could go about seeking 'written express consent'. Instead she asked him if he would like to add anything else to his evidence. He declined the offer saying he had covered everything, and she told him he could leave the witness box.

I had not had my turn in questioning him yet, so I quickly stood up before he could get away and said I would like to ask him some questions. The judge told me I had had the opportunity to do that when The Tyrannical Clown was in the witness box, but it was too late now. I asked her what she meant: 'when had I been offered a chance to question him? I thought the chance was now'. She retorted that if I had questions to ask it should have been at the relevant time during the procedures. I asked why nobody had told me that. I should have been informed of the procedure of a court case. You cannot argue with a judge and with a smug expression on his face The Tyrannical Clown stood up, left the witness box and returned to his seat.

CHAPTER 23

I was outnumbered five to one. I had no legal representation which they were clearly taking advantage of. I realised if I was going to get my turn in questioning the witness I would have to say what I had to say at the precise moment the witness had stopped speaking. So I prepared myself ready to butt in to quiz and question Kilkenny at the first opportunity with or without the judge's permission to speak.

Kilkenny took the witness stand and he too solemnly swore to tell the truth the whole truth and nothing but the truth. The barrister spoke for him and said there had been a complaint about my café signs in November 2008 and Kilkenny had dealt with the complaint. Before anything else could be said on the matter I butted in and I looked directly at Kilkenny and I suggested he had not had a complaint about my café signs but only the signs relating to the wine bar. He asked me how I had reached that conclusion and I said that I had been advised that he had written a letter to the wine bar informing them that a complaint had been received regarding their signs and they had eight days to remove them. He answered that by saying he did not write letters. He was being facetious, so I suggested that someone, possibly a secretary had written the letter on his behalf. I said that I had not received such a letter and therefore I knew that the complaint did not refer to my café signs as if there had been a complaint about them the normal procedure should have been carried out which was to inform the establishment in writing prior to taking any action. To my astonishment he agreed with me, so I asked him in that case why he had removed my signs when nobody had complained about them. I was even more amazed at his second reply. He said it would not have been fair to remove the wine bar's signs and leave mine on the pole. I waited a moment for the judge to register what he had just admitted or at least question that in his witness statement he clearly wrote that he had had a complaint about my café signs and he had even included the number of the complaint ticket. He had just admitted he had not had a complaint about my café signs but even now when the judge could damn him to hell for committing perjury she looked at me and said 'there you are, it wouldn't have been fair to take theirs and leave yours on the pole'.

What unbelievable injustice against me! Kilkenny had just admitted lying in his witness statement, the judge knew he had lied and evidently condoned it and accepted his reasons for doing so. I was convinced that she was as corrupt as they were. She could not possibly be a bona-fide judge, and I did not even believe she had bothered looking at my evidence.

The barrister stood up and bowed again to the judge and told her that on 1st February 2010 Kilkenny had been requested to go to Camber and photograph two signs which had been attached to a telegraph pole located at the junction of Lydd Road in Camber and these photographs he had produced as an exhibit marked KK/1.

At this point the judge asked Kilkenny to continue in his own words and he could remain seated. He shuffled around on his chair and cleared his throat and said the boards he had photographed were relating to Camber Café and did not have the authorisation of the claimant as the highway authority; thereby I was breaking the law. He said that furthermore these signs presented a distraction to passing motorists because they were designed to be read. Up jumped the barrister bowing to the judge and asked that if madam wished he would read aloud the offending parts of the poems I had written on the signs. She did wish and he told her that they had been written purposely to provoke the claimant, and he read:

'I do not want to use this pole
I know that it is bad
But the purpose of me doing it's
To drive you people mad',

And the second one he told the judge had been menacing and threatening to the claimant. He read;

'So here we go another year
I won't give up I have no fear
I won't forget what you have done
So don't presume that you have won'.

The barrister told the judge that the messages on the boards went beyond simple advertising of the café and had been written purely to harass the council's staff. He continued by showing her exhibit 7 which was a photograph of my café sign opposite the caravan park which he said was attached to street furniture, and written on the sign was 'Temporary Event' 'Home Grown Pot' ' Plant Exhibits'. I so much wanted to tell them that it was not their street furniture it was my scaffold pole which I had put there myself but I dared not for fear of them going there and pulling it up out of the ground. Exhibit 8 was a photo of my sign on the fence at the bottom of the sand dunes which was nothing to do with them either as it was not on the highway, and that part of Camber was Rother District Council's anyway. The barrister told the judge that was the end of Kilkenny's evidence and she told him he could leave the witness box.

I had enclosed two photographs of Lydd Road in my bundle, taken either end of the road for her to see that without any sign to indicate a café existed down Lydd Road it was impossible to know one was there. Six residents who had

lived in Camber for longer than twenty years had each written
a statement confirming that there had always been an A-board
advertising Camber Café placed at the top of Lydd Road.

She asked me if I had anything to say but my mind had
gone blank, most of my paperwork was on the floor and
whatever I had wanted to ask had totally gone out of my head,
but I did say that I would appreciate it if she would look at the
two photos in my bundle which showed that there was no
evidence of my café without a sign and she must consider the
necessity of my café having an A-board at the top of the road,
She did not answer me and gave the impression that she had
not heard me. Instead she said that this problem had gone on
for long enough and had to be resolved, that she would give
careful consideration to the evidence but she had no reason to
disbelieve The Tyrannical Clown or Kilkenny as they were
both ex-policemen. I wanted to say that was the very reason
not to believe them but I was in a compromising situation so I
had to stay quiet.

The barrister did his summing up speech saying I had no
respect for the law and that my actions had been a huge drain
on Council resources and I had to be stopped. Then he likened
me to some man who had committed some terrible crime in
1603 and had been executed for his misdemeanour. What a
cheek insulting me like that, I was not the criminal here and
they knew that. They had lied and committed perjury and to
my mind they were no better than the counsellors who were
mixed up in the Donnygate corruption scandal of the mid-
nineties producing false documents.

When he had finished the judge stood up and so did
everyone else, and the barrister was bowing to her and she
adjourned the court for one hour so she could consider the
evidence.

When she had left the clerk came over to me and told me
to leave my papers as they were. I asked him if I could pick

them up off the floor and he said I had to leave everything where it was. I was the last one to leave the court room and they were all huddled together smiling and chatting. I was not looking forward to having to pass them but I did not wish to stay there with them either.

I left the building and went and sat in my car for warmth and comfort. I wondered if the judge was really considering the evidence, but I doubted if she would look at any of mine let alone consider it.

She had declared she had no reason to disbelieve The Tyrannical Clown or Kilkenny, in which case she was not going to believe me. I expected she was probably having her lunch in the Judges Restaurant chatting to her colleagues, as her mind had been made up before she adjourned for lunch.

I thought about driving off and not going back in there, and wondered what they would think. I imagined their faces if I disappeared and the barrister bowing to 'madam' telling her the defendant had absconded. There were ten minutes to go so I got out of my car and went back into the court.

Bag searched again, down the stairs and they were still chatting together. They ignored me and I sat down and waited to be ushered into the court room to hear my fate.

CHAPTER 24

Back in the court room my papers were still strewn all around were I had been sitting. The judge came back into the court room with the same old palaver and we all stood up and she bowed her head, the barrister was grateful and we all sat down. She said she had considered all the evidence carefully and told the claimants that they should be mindful that there were four of them and one of me and that was most likely quite daunting for me and as I had chosen not to have legal representation it would have been difficult for me to understand the process of the day's hearing. Nevertheless that was no excuse for my ignorance of the judicial system, however she realised that running a business in these difficult times was not easy. She added that she had no reason to disbelieve The Tyrannical Clown and Kilkenny's evidence. I wanted to tell her to stop patronising me, as I was not daunted by this preposterous farce, it was the East Sussex Highways staff who were the real criminals here and they had given a splendid demonstration of corruption and perjury in her court room and she knew it.

What she did not know was how to manage a business in a recession and at the same time be harassed by a bunch of cretins. Of this she had no idea and what's more she was totally unperturbed that she was just about to condemn mine to ruination. She continued that I thought that I could do what I wanted and say what I wanted and I had to be stopped, so she would grant in favour of the claimant and issue an injunction order for one year. She said I would have to pay a contribution of £1500 towards their costs and a further £1000 for the removal of my café signs which I had refused to pay. The barrister stood up bowing and told her he was grateful that she had seen in his client's favour and that his client was delighted by her decision and they were relieved as it was imperative to eradicate this nuisance. However they would prefer a three year injunction. The judge said she did not think that a three year injunction order was necessary and looking at me she said that if I breached the injunction within that time I would risk a heavy fine or imprisonment or both. I succeeded in pulling a defiant face which showed no emotion to the judge's decision. I knew that any fine or costs I was ordered to pay were irrelevant. They would not redeem their costs from me as I had no money, so I did not care whether they wanted £10 or a million, it made no difference to me. She told us to leave the courtroom while she concluded her paperwork. We all stood up as she swept out of the courtroom and we filed out into the waiting area.

The Tyrannical Clown had a jubilant smirk on his face, so I went up to him and I warned him that if his lies resulted in me losing my business I knew where he lived and I would pitch a tent up in his garden and live in it. My threat amused Kilkenny and he laughed out loud so I told him that I also knew where he lived.

I then approached Rag-Eme-Kale and asked him his position within the Highways. He told me he worked in the Ringmer office and he was The Team Manager for Traffic and Licensing. I asked him if he was familiar with The Town & Country Planning Control of Advertisements Regulations 2007 and he said he was and that it had been sent to me to help me understand where I could advertise my business legally. I said to him in that case I would put an A-board at the junction of Lydd Road as it had 'deemed consent' as the café had been advertising on an A-board at the top of the road for the last 26 years. He said straight away 'I think you'll find that 'deemed consent' only applies to signs on the actual business premises'. That was a deliberate lie. I knew there was another clause that permitted 'forecourt' advertising, but he went back to his colleagues before I could answer. I thought from his remark that he must be regularly up-dated with my activities in Camber.

The barrister was all smiles chatting to his clients and they were congratulating him on the grand job he had done. They made me feel sick and were nothing but a bunch of immoral low-lives. I was a decent honest person and they had discredited me and lied to the judge who was surely acquainted with The Tyrannical Clown and Kilkenny.

We were soon called back into the court room and as we went in the barrister made a bee line to the judge saying I had just 'threatened' The Tyrannical Clown that I would put a tent in his garden. She really was not interested in the barrister's tittle-tattle and told him so. We all sat down but just as I started my sitting manoeuvre the judge told me to remain standing so I stood up again. She told me that the injunction order was forbidding me from placing signs, posters and other structures on or abutting the highway without the express consent of the claimant as the highway authority and I shall not use foul or abusive language or engage in threatening behaviour towards any member of the claimant's staff. She asked me if I had understood the terms of the order and I answered that I thought so. She also said I was ordered to pay £1500 costs to the claimant and £1000 for the collection of the signs, and again she asked me if I had understood and I replied I had understood but I was not going to pay any of it especially for the removal of the signs.

I don't know if she heard my remark or not but she made no comment to it. With that the clerk handed me my injunction order and everyone stood up as the judge bowed and the barrister did his final sweeping bow, muttering that he was eternally grateful and she left the court room.

I gathered my papers from the floor and the ones on the table and stuffed them back into the carrier bag, I had been there for four and a half hours and I wanted to go home.

I left the court and went to my car and as I drove away from the car park I saw The Tyrannical Clown and his entourage leaving the court together smiling and chattering to each other. I chuckled to myself for if they were thinking that an injunction order was going to stop me advertising my café they didn't know what was coming. A-boards might be banned for the moment but on the way back to Camber I was thinking of lots of other ways I could advertise the café. Time was of the essence and I had to do something fast.

I decided the quickest way was to put a car on the main road with a sign on it again. I could not imagine that the council would be bothered to have a car towed away and besides as long it was taxed, insured and had an up to date MOT they could not do anything about it.

The next day I asked everyone who came into the café if they knew of a cheap car for sale in the immediate vicinity, and soon after, a local couple said they had just bought a new car and they wanted to sell their old Peugeot 106 which was taxed and had an MOT for a couple of months, £150. Perfect! Just what I needed. Deal done, I made a new sign for it and instead of it being the usual lime green I changed it to a white background and shocking pink writing outlined in black. One of my regular customers drilled holes through the roof of the car and attached two brackets to hold the café sign in place. In less than forty-eight hours of being given an injunction order forbidding me from placing anything on the highway, I had a car parked on the main road with a sign on it far bigger than an A-board and I was quite confident they could not do anything about it.

As my temporary pot plant exhibition sign had been removed from my scaffold pole opposite the caravan park, my thoughts turned to how I could advertise on the scaffold pole without attaching a sign to it. As I contemplated, a local child pulled up at the café on his bike, and there was my answer. I asked the young man if any of his friends had an old bike they would want to sell for £10, and without hesitation he replied that he wanted to sell his bike. It looked a lovely bike to me and far too good to use for putting a café sign on and I told him so, but he insisted that it would be OK. I suggested that he should go and check with his parents first. Off he skedaddled and within minutes he was back saying that his mother had said it was his bike and he could do what he wanted with it. I gave him the £10 note and he headed off in the direction of the corner shop BJ's On the Beach. What I planned to do was to chain the bike to the scaffold pole and then attach a café sign to the bike like the old fashioned butchers bikes, so the sign would be on the bike and not on the pole. I would not be in breach of the injunction order as it did not forbid me from chaining a bike to a scaffold pole.

Ten minutes after I had paid the young man £10 for his bike he came walking back past the café with two carrier bags stuffed with sweets, crisps and fizzy drinks. I asked him if he had spent the whole £10 on sweets and he said he had, and I was quite shocked that he had spent so much money on so much rubbish. Goodness knows what his parents would have to say.

I made a new café sign for the bike, purchased three meters of heavy chain and a sturdy padlock to attach the bike to the scaffold pole. 'Frosty' my neighbour transported the bike to the scaffold pole opposite the caravan park in the back of his van for me and I followed on in my car with the sign, chain and padlock. I leant the saddle of the bike against the scaffold pole and threaded the chain in and out of the wheels and round the handle bars and I wrapped the rest of the chain several times round the scaffold pole. I attached the sign to the cross bar of the bike and secured it with thick cable ties. I rested the bottom part of the sign on the pedal so it was a good twelve inches from the ground.

So even with an injunction order I had managed to promote Camber Café twice on large signs neither of which were on or abutting the highway.

CHAPTER 25

I wanted to know what this 'written express consent' was so I checked it out on line, and it was not difficult to find and the definition was:

'If an advertisement you want to display is not excluded from control and does not benefit from any of the provisions for deemed consent, you need the planning authority's express consent before you can display it. Some frequently displayed types of advertisement for which you need planning are;
Virtually all posters
Some illuminated signs
Fascia signs and projecting signs on shop fronts or business premises where the top edge of the sign is more than 4.6 metres above ground level
Most advertisements on gable ends.'

There was nothing there about A-boards and of course there would not be because there was no government legislation to control an A-board.

However, I needed at least to make an attempt to get this 'express consent' as that was the order from the court. I knew I would never be granted it because I did not need it. Clearly by the definition alone 'express consent' was for large advertising structures to be erected onto buildings. They had done this on purpose because they knew I could not possibly pay the fees and what Rag-Eme-Kale had indicated was that I could only have a structure, not an A-board. I needed to locate the person who was responsible for granting 'express consent' so I could start the procedure of applying for it. On the Monday morning 19th April I rang the Highways office, and spoke to a man who told me he would email me the appropriate application form later that day. I thanked him and told him that having asked several times already how I went about applying for this form he was the only person that knew what it was. I spent the next three hours waiting for his email to arrive. It came at lunchtime with two attachments, one for a poster licence application which I had not asked for and one for an object application.

He said in his email that he had sent me the forms I had requested, the latter of the two forms being the one I had referred him to regarding an application form for 'express consent', and he said that even if agreed by the highways authority I would still have to seek permission from the District Planning Authority for the object or structures to be placed on the highway. If I required further information I should contact him.

This is what I had been waiting for, at last an application form to place my A-board at the top of Lydd Road, I eagerly opened the attachment, which set out their conditions, costs and requirements.

The first part covered their policies and basic requirements to place an object on purpose built walk ways and pedestrianized areas.

A non-refundable fee was required in order to process the application whether it was successful or not. I needed to satisfy myself that no further permissions were required as in Health and Safety issues.
I had to describe briefly the nature and dimensions of the structure, if the structure was on part of council land where the highways owned the sub-soil, a fee would be payable. The structure had to be protected by a hard continuous physical barrier featuring a tapping hand rail.

The fee was paid in two parts, the initial fee £300 which covered costs up to the point where a decision is made whether or not a permit might be offered. This fee was non-refundable whether the permit was actually offered or not. The second part of the fee became payable if and when the permit was offered. The administration fee was £205.

If it transpired that the Highways Authority owned the topsoil, it would have a significant effect on the cost, since a rent might also be involved. Applicants were strongly advised to check before submitting an application.

The applicant shall provide at his own expense five copies of a plan to a scale of not less than 1/500 showing the proposals. Marked on the plan shall be a line showing the area within which the obstruction shall be contained.

No permit shall be issued where it is deemed likely by the Highway Authority that the activity, advertisement or people attracted to view or attend it would be likely to spill onto a carriageway, or cause passing pedestrians to spill onto a carriageway.

I could not believe this was an application form for an A-board. It was crazy, as it was not going to be a permanent structure, and they knew I would only put it there during the day when the café was open. As for the point made that I would need to apply to the District Planning Authority, I had already done that and been told I did not need planning permission for an A-board.

I decided to reply to the man who had sent me the application form. I told him I had read the guidance notes which stated that an object may be placed on a purpose built foot-way or pedestrianized area, and I explained that I only wanted to place an A-board on a piece of grass which was not mentioned in the guidance notes. I asked him if he had sent me the wrong application form as it stated that the object must be protected by a hard, continuous physical barrier featuring a tapping hand rail, but if that was the case then my A-board would be hidden on all sides and not be seen. The A-board was to advertise my café, that was the reason I wanted the application form, but the application form had nothing pertaining to an A-board and that was the reason I thought he had sent me the wrong thing.

I did not get a reply to my email so I sent another one a couple of days later. I asked him if he was sure that the application form he had sent me was for placing an A-board on a small area of grass and not an application for building an advertising structure.

He did reply this time, saying that prior to sending me the forms he had conferred with Rag-Eme-Kale, Traffic and Licensing Team Manager, on the correct forms for my request. So given my assessment of the forms he had sent me, he had passed my enquiry to Rag-Eme-Kale for him to respond to, which would be within the next ten days.

Over the next two weeks there followed a succession of emails exchanged between myself and Rag-Eme-Kale - he giving me good reason why he would not give me his permission to place an A-board at the top of Lydd Road and me giving him every good reason why he should.

I received the first of the spate of emails from Rag-Eme-Kale with the Town and Country 2007 Advertising Act, informing me where I could advertise my café, the same list I had already been sent in January from the complaints department telling me I could put a sign on an animal, in a shopping mall, a railway station, an Adshel bus shelter and a farmer's field providing it could not be seen. He knew I had already been sent this form because he mentioned it at the court hearing. As well as the Town and County Advertising Act he had written;

Our policy permits A-frames to be considered in the highway only outside the shop. Where there is a desire to place an advertisement in a location away from the shop, or in your case, café, then I have to be satisfied on behalf of the Highway Authority that the structure is made of materials and constructed in such a fashion that it will be safe to leave unattended in the public highway. This means that the advertisement will have to be securely fixed to the highway as a structure so that it will not only withstand windy conditions, but is also robust enough to cope with some interference or vandalism without becoming a danger to users of the highway.

In your submission for a licence to place a remote advertising structure in the highway you will need to consider (or obtain advice from a consulting engineer) the size and materials of the advert and how it is to be secured. For example, if you make the sign too big, then the wind load it has to withstand increases and the supports have to become thicker and have to be buried deeper in the ground. Previous case law has placed a liability on highway authorities relating to passive safety. That is to say, when motorists have accidentally collided with large motorway signs, they have successfully sued the highway authority for not designing a sign that would crumple on impact, absorbing some of the energy of the collision and improving the chances of the survival of the driver. This has led to many signs being supported on 'lattice' type posts on higher speed roads. Any new sign in East Sussex that is on a road faster than 40mph will have to be 'passively safe'.

All adverts must have express consent from the local Planning Authority. A planning application would have to be submitted to the local district council. As I understand it you wish to put an advert which is not on the café premises but in the highway and that does not fall into the 'deemed consent' category and

would need to have 'express consent' from Rother District Council. That is to say, Rother District Planning Authority will wish to consider the proposed advertisement and assess its impact on the environment of Camber. In considering any planning application for an advertisement in the highway, Rother District Council would consult with the Highway Authority to ensure that the proposed location and style of advert will not endanger the public or obstruct their access through the highway.
I hope that the information I have given is helpful to you.
Rag-Eme-Kale

It was not helpful at all; in fact an A-board would be ideal for a car to smash into as it would fall over. I did not wish to put my A-board on a motorway either. The Injunction order forbade me from placing structures on or abutting the highway without the written express consent from the Highway Authority. Rag-Eme-Kale was now saying the express consent had to come from Rother District Council, who had already told me I did not need planning permission to place an A-board on the grass at the top of Lydd Road.

All of a sudden I had an idea, I was going to play these people at their own game and now it was my turn. I emailed back to Rag-Eme-Kale:

Dear Rag-Eme-Kale
I have some good news; someone has offered me a Llama called Alma to put up the top of the road wearing a sandwich board across its back. Can I tie it to the signpost up there? And I won't need planning permission, advertisement consent or express consent, will I?
It's coming next week so I need to know please.
Sally

An hour later I got a reply:

Dear Sally Pattinson
Thank you for your email. While I understand that planning
permission is not required for an advertisement on a person
or an animal, because they are moving and not affixed in the
highway, I certainly would not wish to encourage you to leave
a llama unattended in the public highway. I would not consent
to you tethering a llama to any street furniture or signposts.
The posts have been designed to support our signage and are
not expected to withstand the lateral loading that a tethered
animal could exert when pulling on the rope. In addition, the
paint or protective coating intended to protect the post from
rusting would be abraded by such an action.

Aside from section 155 of the Highways Act 1980 which deals
with penalties in connection with straying animals on the
highway, you would need to be mindful of other legislation
concerning the welfare of the animal and the deposition of
faeces and urine in the public highway. These are offences
under environmental legislations and certainly, if the animal
is unattended no-one will be 'poop-scooping'. Effectively, the
highway is there to pass and repass. Unless this verge is
registered as Common Land, you do not have the right to
graze cattle on it. (There is a register of Common Land
available for inspection on the internet as a result of
legislation introduced in 1962).

The signs that have been previously removed by this authority
are not suitable to be licenced as a structure in the highway,
so please do not submit plywood signs cable-tied to street
furniture as your permanent advertising structure as they will
not be given approval. Poster licences are only for temporary
events, and are not suitable for advertising your café.

Planning permission application charges are set by the Local
District Authority. 'A frame' charges in the highway have

been set by the County council. They are different authorities charging for different activities. However, you may be aware from the guidelines to the application that an A frame will only be permitted adjacent to the shop. I understand that you have an A frame outside your café already. The issue is that another A frame left unattended at a road junction is not permissible under the A frame policy and consequently, a licence for a structure is the only way forward. Licences for advertising structures in the highway may not be granted in a carriageway. Therefore they can only be considered in pedestrianized roads, wider footways, bridleways and grass verges. As all of these parts of the highway might be walked over by the public, care must be taken concerning obstruction and safety...
Rag-Eme-Kale

I could not believe Rag-Eme-Kale had bothered to answer in such detail reasons not to tether an imaginary llama to a signpost. Now he was telling me that I could not put an A-board on a llama on the grass at the top of Lydd Road and the only way forward was a licence for a structure although licences for structures in the highway may not be granted in a carriage way. What was the difference between a highway and a carriage way I wondered and what the hell was an A-frame policy? If A-frames were not allowed on highways why would they need a policy? It was ridiculous; I had no doubt they were determined to stop me advertising my business. They knew I had no money to pay application fees and even if I had I would not be applying for licences because I did not need one. They had tried to stop me in every way I had advertised the café so far, even telling BT they were aiding and abetting in a criminal offence, and now 'Alma' had also got the knock-back. Now I had another idea; I would buy a Gorilla costume from a fancy dress shop on eBay and someone could dress up in it and stand at the end of the road wearing a sandwich board terrifying everyone.

I realised why Rag-Eme-Kale had been at the court case. He had been commandeered to deal with me in a more technical manner than The Tyrannical Clown was capable of doing. Rag-Eme-Kale had a degree and the letters MCIHT after his name, and was therefore qualified in road and transport issues, but that did not mean he was a better liar than the other two. Rag-Eme-Kale was a good twenty years younger than Kilkenny and The Tyrannical Clown so I reckoned he would have to be very shrewd if he was going to keep up The Tyrannical Clown's charade. From the brief meeting I had with Rag-Eme-Kale at the court I could tell he was a weak character who would think twice about putting his well-paid job on the line. However he was evidently quite devious, so I expected to have a more astute conflict with him rather than a common brawl like I had with Kilkenny and The Tyrannical Clown.

I hoped my personality was stronger than Rag-Eme-Kale's but would that be enough to outwit him. I wrote back to Rag-Eme-Kale;

Dear Rag-Eme-Kale
Thank you for your email
What is it you do not understand when I repeatedly tell you that I only want to put an A-board at the top of the road in the morning and fetch it back when I close the café? At the moment I only seem get a day off when I am sitting in a court room with your colleagues, maybe I might have a real day off soon and if I had a permanent structure people might think I am open when I will be closed . How do you know that a temporary event sign is not suitable for my café? You don't know what goes on inside my café, and you don't even know what goes on outside of it either.

I think the only way forward is to consent to me zapping my café signs back onto the BT pole which were never complained about as you heard yourself from Kilkenny in the court and they will not be colliding with traffic or blowing over or being bumped into. If you do this I will be able to resume my happy, tranquil life which I was enjoying before The Tyrannical Clown and Kilkenny barged into it.

Please hurry up as I am losing business and need to get my café signs put up somewhere soon. And by the way I think you should check with the County Planners about your charges of £505 application and administration fee (page 5 box 2 relating to Advance signs which are not situated or visible from the site directing the public to the premises). I have seen the application fees and you should be asking for £95 at the most, it only costs £335 for a planning application per dwelling on a development of a maximum of 50 houses.

So what the heck are you talking about Rag-Eme-Kale?

And I wouldn't let him influence you too much in case you end up as corrupt as he is not to mention un voleur et un sale menteur.

I see Donkeykonk is still using his stolen keep left signs which you were going to do something about.

I look forward to hearing from you

Sally

CHAPTER 26

The gorilla outfit arrived and I was disappointed with it as only the head mask, hands and feet were hairy, while the body was just a brown pair of elasticated trousers with elasticated ankles and the top was just a top with long sleeves. No one wanted to wear it anyway and stand at the top of the road wearing a sandwich board so it was put back into the bag it came in for the time being.

I had been driving around the local area taking photos of signs and A-boards which were remote from the businesses they were advertising. The first two signs were only five hundred yards along the main road from my A-board; they were made of metal about three feet high and two and half feet wide, and they advertised hot food and drinks on one and fish and chips on the other. The business they were advertising operated from within the Western Car Park in a building which was rented from Rother District Council. The two signs flanked either side of the entrance to the car park and were placed at the edge of the curb on the main road. The owner of the business claimed he had never had any problem with placing his signs on the highway and the reason for that was because he paid a substantial rent to the council. That assertion was rubbish of course, as section 132 of the 1980 highways act did not make exceptions for council tenants. The real reason he had never had a problem was because he was not doing anything wrong.

In Rye town there were A-boards and signs everywhere. One pub, besides having an adequately sized forecourt with tables and chairs and a decorative chain across the front, also had three A-boards straddling the double yellow lines that were directly adjacent to the business premises. It looked fine and never as far as I knew had caused problems to the public, just as my single A-board on a piece of grass hadn't.

The remote village off the A 259 always had an A-board displayed on the island one mile away from the pub. There were farm shops, pubs and cafés, all with remote signs. I took photos of all of them.

A couple of days later Rag-Eme-Kale emailed me again.

Dear Ms Pattinson

Thank you for your email of 26 April 2010. Please understand that any application for a free standing A-board style advert in the highway, left unattended and remote from the café will be refused.

In our previous correspondence I have given guidance on the need to ensure that the advert you wish to place in the highway for your benefit does not endanger or obstruct users of the highway. I am not satisfied that an A-frame will be safe. As you wish to display this advert frequently, almost permanently, then it is reasonable that you undertake to provide a sensible design. You may wish to consider that the proposed sign has a lockable cover to it so that you can remove your advert from the sign on the days that you are closed.

Temporary event signage is permitted for charitable events and other infrequent local community events. They are licenced by me on behalf of this highway authority. It is quite correct that I do not know what goes on in your café. Any application you make for a temporary event sign will need to be supported by evidence that the event is predominantly for a charitable cause, and not an attempt to advertise your business. If you place such signs in the highway, they will be unlicensed and you will be in breach of the injunction placed on you by the court.

With regard to the fees charged by the Planning Authority, Rother District Council, please be advised that this is a

*different authority to East Sussex County Council and that the
fees applicable to a planning application are not the same as
the fees applicable to a structure licence application.
However, as you will be aware from our previous
correspondence, you will need to secure planning permission
(express consent) from Rother District Council for this advert
if your formal application to place the structure in the
highway is successful.
I do not appreciate comments concerning corruption and I
would be grateful if you would submit your application
together with a location plan and a scale drawing of your
proposed advertisement for my consideration....*
Rag-Eme-Kale

I had no idea what a structure was meant to look like. All I
could imagine was the 'Statue of Liberty' and I couldn't put
one of them up there. How did he expect me to do a scale
drawing in the first place of something I hadn't a clue what it
was meant to be a scale drawing of and what's more I did not
even know what a scale drawing was, I just imagined a picture
of the 'scales of justice'. I believed they were trying to put so
much pressure on me hoping that I would give up and
eventually render myself insolvent, but they had another think
coming and all of a sudden I had an idea for a structure. I
would have to spend time and money on this one. I did not
respond to Rag-Eme-Kale but concentrated on finding my
mega-structure instead.

Sadly one Monday morning only three weeks after buying
the little red Peugeot, it was vandalised, every window was
smashed and the body work had been kicked and dented, so
the road and seats were covered in shattered glass, but the sign
on the roof was still intact. Luckily, I had become acquainted
with the bin-boys by giving them a mug of tea every day.
Their job was to empty the local council bins and clear the

beach of rubbish on a daily basis. They had seen the glass all over the road and offered to sweep it up. One of them wanted to buy the car off me to go banger racing in so I sold it to him for £50, but as boys can be boys I made him sign the log book before I handed over the keys, which was a good job as the next day the police turned up and said they had found my car abandoned and smashed in a road in Little Common. I explained what had happened to the car and that I had sold it as seen to the bin-boy. I had sent the log book to the DVLA the previous day but it had obviously not yet been processed. I said I believed the young man lived in Little Common.

So here I was with no car and no A-board; things were in a precarious situation. I needed to buy another car and I also needed to buy my mega-structure, but I had no spare cash to buy either.

I was quite surprised when, as I was sitting outside having a coffee, Bodger came out and told me that when he and Beaky the old Hag had the café he put a large Volvo car on the main road with an illuminated flashing 'Café Open' sign in the rear window and one day someone had smashed the window of the car and stolen the sign. He said he didn't put a car there after that. I didn't care what he had to say to me, so I just listened and pulled agreeable faces at him till he went away.

The next few days were pretty grim. Visitors in Camber were not aware that there was a café in Lydd Road. We did have customers of course but the lack of advertising for the café was having an effect on the takings.

A few days after the little red Peugeot had been vandalised another friend phoned me to say he had a white Peugeot 205 automatic for sale with a year's MOT but no tax and he wanted £500 for it. I said it was too expensive but he agreed to let me pay for it in instalments. He delivered the car and Frosty the neighbour screwed the cafe sign onto the roof and I sent off for a new tax disc. Next I drove the car up onto the main road; I would not leave it there all the time after what happened to the other car.

I drove into Rye and as I drove over the bridge I saw that the fish shop, which also had an A-board on the pavement at the entrance of its parking area, now had a large sign advertising Fresh Seafood, Cockles, Jellied Eels, Whelks, Mussels and Prawns, which was hanging from a bracket attached by two metal clips to a lamp post. I pulled up on the double yellow lines to quickly take a photo of the sign. This one I was going to send to Rag-Eme-Kale to see what he had to say about it.

When I got home I wrote a short email to Rag-Eme-Kale and attached the photo of the fish sign. I said I was sending him the photo of the fish shop sign which was attached to a lamp post so I presumed he must have given his permission for it to be there, so on the strength of that and to show that he was not discriminating against me I was going to put my signs back onto the BT pole.

It was 4.30pm when I sent that email to Rag-Eme-Kale. Ten minutes later I got a reply. He said:

'This does not have permission from me. If you have the name of the street, I will ask that the site is inspected and action taken as appropriate'.

As he had not said I might not reattach my signs to the BT pole I sent a quick reply saying;

'Is that a yes then? That place is on the A259 in the direction of Camber just before the bridge on the right. They've got A-boards on the pavement as well, like everyone else has in Rye'.

Five minutes later another email arrived;

That is not a 'yes'.
This appears to be another unauthorised advert on the
highway and it will also need to be removed, and the owner
advised of the law.
As you will be aware from our previous correspondence, A-
boards immediately adjacent to the premises might be
tolerated, as yours is outside your café. Remote A-boards and
structure need to be removed unless they are licensed. The
procedure to obtain a licence has been discussed between us
at length
Please do give consideration to my previous suggestion that
you secure the services of a professional sign manufacturer to
help you submit your application.

Kilkenny must have passed this fish sign hundreds of times
but he had chosen to ignore it as he had all the other signs in
Rye and Camber. It would be interesting to see if anything
would transpire from my email. I did not wish to cause
trouble for the owner of the fish shop, I just wanted to see if
Rag-Eme-Kale actually would do something about it.

It was 1ˢᵗ May and a lovely warm sunny morning when a
lady came into the café and I recognised her as the lady who
had brought the court summons, but she had not brought one
with her today, instead it was a copy of the injunction order
with a letter from Judgement Jones stapled to it.

Dear Sally,
Enclosed is a copy of the Injunction Order made against you
at the hearing on 9ᵗʰ April 2010.

Please ensure that you read and pay attention to the terms contained therein. Breach of the Order is a serious offence which can result in a sentence of immediate imprisonment.
Yours sincerely
Judgement Jones (Solicitor)

I asked the lady from the court if she would like a cup of tea but she said she had to go. I was quite amused at Judgement Jones familiarity, calling me by my first name like he was writing to an old friend. I was quite proud of my injunction order so I laminated it and stuck it onto the back of the hot drinks machine on the counter so all the customers could read it whilst waiting to give their orders.

CHAPTER 27

Rag-Eme-Kale's demands were becoming tiresome and repetitive. This had all begun with a fictitious complaint about my two café signs that I had permission to put on a BT pole. I was told I had to acquire planning permission, then I was told I didn't need it, then it was advertisement consent, then it was walkway consent and now written express consent, all for putting an A-board on a piece of grass which had been used for the same purpose for the last twenty-six years. Rag-Eme-Kale was now telling me he would never give me permission to put an A-board which was remote from my café and if I wanted to advertise my café legally it would have to be on a structure. I emailed back to him;

Dear Rag-Eme-Kale
I want to put my café signs back on the BT pole. Give me one reason why I can't. They were safe, no one complained or hurt themselves and BT didn't mind.
I don't know how to submit a plan for something I have no knowledge of; I don't know what you want it to be like. Do you remember I took a photo of a 'hot food' sign for the pub, which is just a piece of plywood on a triangle of grass at the junction on the A259 at the top of the lane that goes to a remote village? That sign has been there for years and is over a mile from the pub, so why is that acceptable to you?
Why was I told I needed an application form for Advertisement Consent for an A-board when now you are asking for something else and telling me I can't have an A-board? Why did the lady from Rother District Council tell me that planning permission is not required for an A-board? How can something change so often?
Can I also nick a keep left sign to advertise my café on? The

*Tyrannical Clown said Donkeykonk's were OK including the
fact he had nicked them.
I am in the process of planning a charitable event which will
be permanently raising money, and no it's not to pay my fines
with!
As for the corruption bit, I didn't like hearing lies being told
about me and I did not get the opportunity to prove that The
Tyrannical Clown was making things up and denying things
he'd said. And as for me being in contempt of the law, I have
never even had a parking ticket, that's how bad I am. I have
just been trying to run my business that's all.
One last thing; when I launch my charity event do you need to
be told and are you going to make a donation?
Sally*

I received a lengthy reply saying;

*Dear Ms Pattinson
If you erect signs on the BT pole in the highway you will be in
breach of the injunction handed down to you by the judge in
Hastings County Court. With regard to your email of 28 April
2010, I will not condone the replacement of the advertising
sign on the BT pole for the following reasons; this pole is an
asset belonging to BT. It has been designed to carry the
telecommunication wires that form part of their
communications network. It is unclear if the timber pole is
capable of accommodating the additional weight of the timber
sign that you wish to affix to it. No calculations have been
undertaken to consider the wind loading that a flat sign board
will impose on the BT pole. The fixings (nails or screws
driven into the BT pole) have no calculations or guarantee by
you or your agent that they are adequate and that the sign
will not come loose in high winds and injure a user of the
highway. Similarly, such holes driven into the timber pole*

through the treated outer layers might expose the core of the pole to rot or insect attack. This can lead to a reduction in the life of BT's asset and I cannot give you permission to display your signs at their expense. You have not express consent from the Planning Authority for this advertisement. You do not have public liability insurance for this sign. You might not have the background and experience to submit an application for a permanent structure in the highway and I would advise you to approach a sign contractor to help with designing the sign structure, undertaking the calculations and creating the scale drawings. If you sincerely wish to have a lawful advertising sign in the highway, remote from your business, then I would recommend that you consider securing professional advice. It is likely to be helpful when you approach your insurance provider to discuss public liability cover for the structure. Certainly, you will need to employ a contractor who holds the relevant accreditation and liability insurance to work in the public highway.

With regards to your comments concerning A-boards, you already have an A-board outside your café. This has never been removed and I would refer you to my previous comments concerning signs adjacent to your premises and signs erected and left unattended in the highway, remote from your premises. I cannot condone any intention for you to acquire a 'keep left' sign and adapt it for an unlawful use. Concerning your proposed charitable event please be aware that you still require licences for the temporary event signs. I shall not compromise the validity of our policy concerning charitable event posters by permitting you to use it as a vehicle to place unlawful adverts in the highway for your own business. To this end, I will be requesting the charity registration number of the charity that your proposed event supports. Please note, a 'permanent' charitable event sign will not be permitted.

I would be grateful if you would submit your application together with a location plan and a scale drawing of your proposed advertisement for my consideration. Guidance notes were attached to the application for the structure and I attach them again for your convenience. In addition, I can send you a scale extract of our highway terrier map so that you may indicate the proposed location of your advertisement sign (please be mindful of the proximity to junctions and obstruction issues).
Regards
Rag-Eme-Kale

This whole thing had been blown right out of proportion. I wanted a sign just to indicate there was a café down a side street. My café was offering a public service not only to holiday makers but to travellers and workmen passing through Camber. Rag-Eme-Kale was expecting me to employ a contractor and consider amongst other things wind, weight and sub-soil. No other small businesses that I knew of had ever been told to apply for any consent to put an A-board near or far from the premises. I felt sure they were harassing me just for the hell of it. Well they could try, but I would rise to the challenge and get my own mega-structure on my credit card.

I got straight onto eBay to find the mega-structure I had decided to buy. It was expensive at £450 but it would be worth it and there was nothing that they could do about this one either. So mega-structure ordered, delivery date confirmed, I wrote a disparaging but decisive email to Rag-Eme-Kale.

Dear Rag-Eme-Kale,
You know as well as I do that I have no intention of submitting anything that involves giving money to you or any other

department of ESCC.
*However, I am pleased to inform you and your colleagues that
I have got my own mega-structure arriving next Tuesday to
advertise my café on the highway and furthermore it does not
require your consent or your permission or a procedure to
follow or any suggestion of yours you have advised me to
consider....*
So brace yourselves boys, it's huge.........haha!!!
Have a nice day!
Sally Pattinson

In the meantime I had decided on a subject for a temporary
event. I would hold a weekly raffle for all the holiday makers
and the prize would be one free breakfast a day for the
duration of the winner's stay. I thought that was quite
reasonable and I would sell the tickets at £1 a strip of five and
all the money would go to the Fire Brigade.

All the firemen in Rye were volunteers and several of them
worked together at Rye Hire, so I went there and made my
proposal and in due course I was supplied with the charity
registration number and collecting box for the fire service.

At last I was in a position to fill out the application form
for a temporary event. I answered the questions diligently. For
the name of the event I wrote 'a very good cause' because if I
had put a raffle I was sure that would give Rag-Eme-Kale an
excuse to refuse my application. I put the name of the charity,
the venue and location. Then it wanted dates so I put 'on a
weekly basis for the duration of three years'. I was not sure
how that would go down but that was how I wanted it to be.

I had to put the location of the posters I intended to
display, but I was not quite sure where he would let me put
them so my answer was 'all over Camber'.

I signed the application form and noticed the small print at
the bottom of the page;

'The permitted location of the posters will be specified on the licence if granted and authorised ESCC stickers will be sent to attach to the back of each poster. Two Posters only will be allowed on each approach road to the event and must not be erected within 60m (200 feet) of a road junction or roundabout or fixed to any street furniture.
A minimum of £5 million Public Liability insurance is required'.

I sent the application form to Rag-Eme-Kale at Ringmer near Lewes and I wondered how many people who held jumble sales and craft fairs and similar events actually applied for this temporary event application as well as holding a £5 million liability insurance. I had often read posters advertising events but I could not recall ever seeing Rag-Eme-Kale stickers stuck on any of them. Anyway, Rag-Eme-Kale did not acknowledge or respond to my request to hold a fund raising event at my café and when I still had not heard back I emailed him again asking him where my 'stickers' had got to. He did reply saying;

Thank you for your email of 27 May 2010.
I have seen your event poster application form. I will not approve posters for an event that lasts for 3 years at a location ''all over Camber'.
You will be aware from our previous correspondence that charitable events are such things as church bazaars, school fêtes or local jumble sales. I would expect an application for an event to be on a certain date. Temporary event posters may then be permitted to be displayed for up to five days in advance of that event and would be limited to only two posters in the highway on each approach to the event venue.

Your application appears to be deliberately vague and does not have my approval. I have previously explained our policy on event posters, but you persist in sending emails that do not attempt to comply with the policy in a reasonable or professional manner. Please be aware that to display your event posters as a way of advertising your café would be in contradiction to the injunction placed on you by the county court and you would be liable to further prosecution and penalties.
Regards
Rag-Eme-Kale

I knew he was not going to let me have my temporary posters. He was giving reason after reason why he should not. I answered him;

Rag-Eme-Kale,
Of course I'm being vague because if I tell you exactly what I'm going to do you are going to say 'No'.
I am not going to do the things you suggested, as a café is not a suitable place to hold a jumble sale and what's more I do not want old women's smelly drawers in here as it would become a health issue, so I am going to do something more hygienic than that and will offer my customers a reward for their donation.
It will be something that I will do on a weekly basis and all the proceeds will go to the charity, therefore I will be giving something to the charity every week too.
I would like to stick posters in a few places, one opposite the caravan park and one either end of this road, that's all.
There, is that less vague? Maybe mine is a more modern way of raising money as people do like to get something for nothing. And by the way, the sea food sign is still hanging off the lamp post.

Regards, Sally

CHAPTER 28

I drove into Rye that afternoon to buy an extension cable for my mega-structure; I saw that the fish sign was still attached to the lamp post. On my way back I wondered how long Rag-Eme-Kale would take to answer my email informing him of the imminent arrival of my mega-structure. Needless to say when I arrived home he had already replied;

Dear Ms Pattinson
Thank you for your email of 14 May 2010.
I note that you do not intend to submit a formal application to place a structure in the highway. With this in mind, please re-read the terms of the Court injunction and carefully consider how it applies to your mega-structure.
With regards to your email of 12 May 2010, I am pleased to inform you that we have been in contact with the individual that attached the sign to the lamppost in Rye and it has been removed.
Yours sincerely
Rag-Eme-Kale

Before I answered Rag-Eme-Kale's email for a brief moment I carefully considered if my mega-structure would be in breach of the terms of the Court injunction I had received on 6thApril.

Dear Rag-Eme-Kale
I have re-read that injunction order and guess what? It doesn't! (apply to my mega-structure). I might have to borrow

a couple of bollards from Donkeykonk though, he has an
abundance of stolen ones in his field, in fact guess what
again? They are all yours!!!!
And incidentally the fish shop sign is still hanging from the
lamp post ...
Regards
Sally Pattinson
PS. please refrain from referring to me as Ms as I am not a
lesbian and before you call me Mrs I am happily divorced...

So all we had to do now was to wait for the mega-structure
to arrive. Sadly it was not delivered on the Tuesday as we had
expected and even sadder for the highway inspectors as they
were out in full force on the Wednesday in their entire fleet of
highway vans driving in all directions round Camber in search
of my mega-structure,
To put them out of their misery I emailed Rag-Eme-Kale;

Hi there Rag-Eme-Kale
Sorry your inspectors had a wasted journey today. There was
a delay in the delivery of my 'mega-structure' as it needed a
wide load escort and is coming from the north east of
England. Indeed, it is comparable to the 'Angel of the North'.
So they will have to come tomorrow to attempt to remove it!
Sally

The next day my long awaited mega-structure arrived; a
large box delivered by DHL. Christine was working with me
that day as Lily was at school. We struggled to get the heavy
fan out of the box and struggled even more trying to fit the
long red tube over the top of it and press it onto the Velcro to
secure the tube to the fan, but we managed. We placed the
mega-structure about six feet from the edge of the road. I

unwound the extension cable and plugged it in, having made sure that the cable would not pose a hazard to my customers. I went back to the mega-structure, pressed the 'on' button and as the air bellowed into the tube up it went, wow! 'Tall Paul' was launched into orbit, all twenty feet of him. He was an inflatable red tube with 'Café Open' sewn onto his front. He stood tall and erect, his long arms with white tassels billowing from the ends of them were sticking straight out just like the Angel of the North. He had long white tassels blowing out of the top of his head and a big smiling face beaming down onto the café forecourt. We were delighted at the Camber Café mega-structure. The only down side was the noise the fan made, which was more of a roar than a hum, but never mind, only a small price to pay compared to the costs I might have had to pay for one of Rag-Eme-Kale's structure applications.

On the Friday morning 'Tall Paul' was standing proud and erect on the forecourt and who should turn up at the café but the Health and Hygiene inspector from Rother District Council. She said she had received a complaint about a large red inflatable and she had come to inspect it. I pointed to 'Tall Paul' and asked if it was him someone had complained about but she had already spotted the extension cable which ran from the side door in front of the patio door and which I had tucked under the bottom part of the step and then it went right up against the neighbouring wall and behind the bins to where the fan was standing. She said the cable was dangerous where I had put it, but I told her that as it was right up against the wall and running down by the side of the two picnic tables so I could not see anything dangerous. She disagreed with me, saying that if someone was wearing stiletto heels they might put the heel through the cable and electrocute themselves. I thought she was joking but when I looked at her she clearly was not, so I agreed with her and apologised for thinking that most people went to the beach in flip-flops or flat sandals. I had forgotten that the majority climbed up the steep sand dunes to spend the day on the beach in stiletto heels. With that I lifted the cable from along the bottom of the wall and put it on the other side in the neighbour's garden, I reassured the Health Inspector that it was now safe from the risk of a stiletto heel going through it resulting in electrocution. As I stood there looking smug an untimely gust of wind came along which caused Tall Paul's top half to bend into the road right in front of her. I stood there as if nothing had happened, but the Health Inspector was overjoyed at the spectacle of Tall Paul bent over with his head lying on the road as it justified her visit. She claimed he was a potential danger to the public. I quickly grabbed his arm and pulled him back up, I dragged the fan further back onto the forecourt and put the big rubbish bin between him and the road so as to prevent him bending over into the road and reassured her that I would not let it happen again. Having got over that she asked me if I had a cut-out switch to plug the extension cable into, which I hadn't, but I said I would go that afternoon and buy one; she left without condemning Tall Paul back to the box he had arrived in.

When I got home later a piece of paper had been stuffed through my letter box, from Beaky the old hag upstairs. She had written a note telling me I could not change the café advertisement without her consent and if I did not stop the 'noisy red thing' she would go to her solicitor. She had not even put her note in an envelope and I did not care if she went to her solicitor anyway.

The following morning Tall Paul looked proud and domineering, and there was not much of a breeze but I put the bin in front of him just in case, as I did not want him to be a danger to anyone. I put him further in on the forecourt too. I just wanted him to be seen from the main road. I left Lily in charge while I drove up to check on the bike opposite the caravan park and that was all intact. I was still waiting for my temporary event stickers from Rag-Eme-Kale so I sent him a reminder:

Morning Rag-Eme-Kale
This is to let you know that as you haven't sent me my stickers I am going to start my charity event on Monday anyway. OK?

He replied almost immediately;

Dear Sally Pattinson,
Regrettably I cannot process deliberately vague applications. The fund-raising you describe is not an event by the very definition that you intend to do it every week.
With regards to the sea food sign, I attach a photograph from a different angle to the one you provided. In this photograph it can be clearly seen that the sign is on a wooden post in the property of the retail outlet, not attached to the lamp column at all.
Regards
Rag-Eme-Kale

It was true I could see by the photo that the fish sign had been moved onto a pole running vertically next to the lamp post.

Tall Paul was quite an attraction and was getting us customers, and though he was vulnerable to gusts of wind which sent him in all directions, it only took a tug of his arm to pull him back up straight again.

The following Tuesday the nice lady from the court turned up again. I said hello to her and offered her a cup of tea before she was able to explain why she was there. She had a large white envelope in her hand and she must have read my thoughts as she said 'don't worry it's not a court summons, it's a letter'. She declined the offer of a cup of tea and said she would like a bacon sandwich but she dare not as she was here on a mission; I said she was quite welcome to have one, but again she said no and left.

I opened the letter which was from Judgement Jones and was stapled to another copy of the injunction order, the third copy I had been given.

Re; Injunction Order 9/4/10

Dear Sally,

You have of course been served with a copy of the above Injunction. A copy is once again attached. The order compels you to pay the Council's costs to the sum of £1500 by 23rd April. It also compels you to pay a further sum of £1000 in damages to cover the cost of removing the signs. The total sum of £2500 is to be paid direct to the Council. No such sum has been received by the Council.

I would be grateful if you could send me a cheque made payable to East Sussex County Council by 5pm on 2nd June so that this part of the order can be fulfilled.

Please note that the sum of £2500 is not optional. It is an order of the court and failure to comply with it is contempt of court. You did not appeal this decision and so it stands.

If I do not hear from you with the cheque for the full sum or your alternative proposals to satisfy the debt by 5pm on 2nd June, enforcement action will be taken to recoup the monies owed. This will include instructing bailiffs.

I look forward to hearing from you

Yours sincerely

Judgement Jones

That was a surprise, as I thought that the new lot of fines and costs would have been added on to the last one that I paid by direct debit to the fines office in Brighton. No one had said in the court that I had to pay these new costs and fine directly to the Council. I quickly sent an email to Judgement Jones saying;

Dear Judgement Jones

I just got your letter and you have made a mistake. I am paying the last lot of fines including the £1000 for my café signs being nicked, to some place in Brighton and your court costs I pay to that place as well. You say you want it paid by 5pm. on 2nd June, but the only way to accomplish your demand is that I swamp Camber with café signs in the hope of getting an abundance of customers! Otherwise I'm afraid that you'll have to wait.
Sally

Judgement Jones answered immediately;

Sally
Don't forget there are two sets of court costs:
1. £1500 costs re: the criminal case. These are to be paid to the place in Brighton and are then reimbursed to the Council;
2. £2500 costs in connection with the injunction. As this is a civil order, these costs are owed directly to the Council and should be paid to us. You are out of time to appeal the decision, unless you are given special permission. In any event, the costs order still stands.
I am sure we can come to some arrangement if you are unable to pay the sum in full, but it is unacceptable not to pay any of it over one month after the deadline!
I look forward to hearing from you.
Judgement Jones

He did not have to wait long to hear from me as I replied directly. I also noticed he had dropped the 'dear'; maybe this was reflecting his mood;

Judgement Jones
That's your fault because that lady did not deliver your letter and a copy of that blimmin injunction order until 1st May. OK, in that case I propose that I pay you £1 a month for 2500 months by which time I will be dead and as I have bequeathed my café to The Tyrannical Clown in the event of my death he will have to pay what's owing. If I can't have a few café signs up in Camber I can only pay 50p a month by which time everyone will be dead!
I look forward to your reply
Sally

Judgement Jones did not respond to my suggestion, so I put £20 in an envelope and sent it to him at County Hall, Lewes. Whether it was going to stop him sending the bailiffs or not only time would tell; that was all he was going to get for now.

CHAPTER 29

As The Tyrannical Clown's inspectors only appeared to have time to remove my café signs, I thought it would be a nice gesture on my part to give them a helping hand by collecting other business signs they had not had time to remove from the highway. So under cover of darkness Lily and I started to go out and about in my car collecting all the remote signs we could find. When we had collected seven or eight signs we waited till late into the night before driving to Bexhill to the Highways Depot where we stood all the signs up in a line outside their office building, not forgetting to take a couple of pictures for memento. We went on our filching expeditions on a regular basis, ridding the countryside of business signs and depositing them outside the Highways office in Bexhill. The landlord from the remote village pub must have wondered what the heck was going on, as he had been putting his signs there for years and now they were disappearing at a rate of knots, but like me he replaced them.

The elections had just taken place and the Labour MP for Hastings and Rye had lost his seat. He must have cleared out his office as he returned all the paperwork and letters to me from when I had initially contacted him. Amongst the papers was a copy of a letter he had written on my behalf to the Director of Economy, Transport and Environment at East Sussex County Council. I decided to write to this Director and tell him that the Highways staff at the Bexhill depot were trying to wreck my business.

Dear Sir
My name is Sally Pattinson and I have received a copy of the letter that my local MP wrote to you. It was not my intention to break any laws but to keep my business going and it is

*imperative that I have an A-board at the top of Lydd Road for
potential customers to find the café as it is down a side street.
Kilkenny is adamant there has been a complaint about my
café signs on the BT pole, I am adamant that there has not.
For the last twenty six years all the owners of the café have
put an A-board or some kind of advertisement at the top of the
road.*

*Please consider the effect on my business by not having an A-
board and that combined with the current recession you must
surely realise how extremely difficult it is to try to stay
solvent, but if you cannot, at least try and imagine.*

*75% of my business comes from passing people who have
seen my sign on the main road, and if I did not have a café
sign there I would very quickly become insolvent. None of the
other businesses in and around the area had ever had any
problems with advertising or been harassed by highway men.
David Cameron has pledged in his election speech that
Councils should be helping small businesses in difficulty due
to the recession, but contrary to this East Sussex County
Council are going out of their way to destroy mine.*

*I am not going to stop advertising my café as my livelihood
depends on my business.*

Yours sincerely
Sally Pattinson

I did not expect a reply from him. I emailed Judgement
Jones and asked him if he had received the £20 I had sent him
on the previous Friday and would he please confirm when he
did. I also asked him if the £1350 I had paid off the first fine
had materialised yet since he accused me of not paying it.

I was surprised to receive a reply from the Director of the
Highways only two days after writing to him, as I thought he
would have been too busy or not interested in my grievance,

but he was evidently a courteous man and had taken the time to respond to me. He said;

Dear Mrs Pattinson

Thank you for your email of 24 May 2010.

I understand a structure application has been emailed to you so that you may apply to place the object in the highway. In this way, we will know and can agree the location of the sign, we'll know who is responsible for its maintenance and who is liable should a third party claim come in against the object. We will be able to consider passive safety issues (will the sign collapse if a vehicle hits it) and we can be sure that access to statutory services is not obstructed.

You will be expected to pay a licence fee of £300 to cover the work. You will also have to employ a sign maker to make the permanent sign and it will have to be installed in the highway by contractors with public liability insurance and NRSWA accreditation. This sign and its location could then be considered by the planning authority from an amenity angle.

I understand that the judge at the recent court hearing informed you that you should not place unlawful signs in the highway and must formally apply to the County Council to place an object in the highway. The judge also informed you that you need to pay the fines and our costs.

To date, I understand no formal application has been received and no payment received by the Court for the fines imposed. I know you are rightly passionate about your business and I want to ensure we resolve this situation. I think we can, given the above.

Yours sincerely

Well it was very nice of him to answer my email but regardless of his optimism the situation was not going to be resolved given the above. He could not force me to fill out a structure application form I did not need. Had my café been part of a chain of fast food empires I could understand it if I needed to put a dirty great sign at the top of the road, but I just wanted my A-board.

I replied to the Director of the Highways:

Dear Sir

Thank you for your email. I forgot to mention that I did go to Camber parish council and I was given their permission to zap a café sign onto the village hall which I did, but guess what, four weeks later it was ordered to be removed !!!!!

So with the written permission I got to put my A-board up the road by the lady from the planning department, written permission from BT to use their pole and permission from the parish council, someone stopped it.

I thought that the last lot of costs would be added onto the ones at that place in Brighton and that's why I haven't paid anything. So when I received Judgement Jones letter yesterday I made a proposition to pay £1 a month for 2500 months, but I haven't heard back from him.

I'm trying to do a lengthy charitable event not only to raise money for a charity but to help my business too, but Rag-Eme-Kale wants me to have a jumble sale. I don't want old women's drawers in my café, and I've got a much better idea. So maybe you could ask him to hurry up and send me my stickers.

I have no money so I cannot even think about council approved structures being erected.

Indeed, I would like this situation to be resolved too and it will be, but it's going to be my way, because I can't afford yours.......

Regards

Sally

CHAPTER 30

A few days after I had another email from the Director of Transport and Environment. I was surprised to hear from him again:

Dear Mrs Pattinson

Thank you for your email. As I am sure you can appreciate, the Council, like all public bodies, has a duty to ensure that the law is followed. There are set procedures in place which involve applications and the payment of a fee. The fact that you feel you are unable to financially afford to go through this process is not our concern. With respect, you do not have a fundamental right to advertise your business at the expense of the law, simply because existing legislation and procedures are inconvenient for you. If the Council feels that a law has been broken, we will take any action that we consider necessary.

I would comment that it was the Council's lawyer Judgement Jones who wrote to BT informing them that they were in possible breach of the law by allowing one of your signs to be attached to a BT pole on the highway and not The Tyrannical Clown.

Judgement Jones has already explained to you that the costs due in relation to the injunction are completely separate to those ordered during the criminal trial. The terms of the order and the costs due were read out to you in court on 9th April and a copy of the Order was personally served on you the 1st of May. Your offer to repay the costs at a rate of £1 a month is not acceptable. I look forward to your proposals for an alternative offer. It is noted that you paid the fine to the court

*of £1200 relatively promptly after you received your criminal
conviction, yet you have paid none of the costs in either the
criminal or civil proceedings. Enforcement action is being
actively considered should the costs remain outstanding.*

*The Council has no wish to prevent you from advertising your
business, but procedures have to be followed and the law has
to be obeyed. Any application you make to the Council will be
given the same consideration as an application made by
anybody else.*

I look forward to hearing from you.

Yours sincerely

I would like to have known who was informing this
Director with the wrong information; I guessed it was most
likely Judgement Jones. I did not understand why if they truly
believed that I had not been paying the fine it had not been
mentioned prior to the court case, or why had someone not
contacted the fines office in Brighton to clarify their
accusations.

I checked my bank statements and on the 25th of each
month £50 had been paid by Direct Debit to the fines office in
Brighton. I decided to phone HMCT to find out for myself if
the money had actually been paid to the council. I spoke to a
young man who checked the payments and he assured me that
all the money I had paid to date had been forwarded to the
council. He also explained to me that the money for the
council's costs gets paid before any money is paid off the fine.
I understood what he meant and I was satisfied that my money
had without doubt been paid to the council.

So now I had this unequivocal evidence I once again
emailed the Director of Transport and Environment

Thank you for your email.

I can only tell you that to date I have paid £1350 towards the council's costs of the first court case, so why don't you believe me?

I have sent Judgement Jones £20 today, which is all I can afford as I have had to buy some stock for this week-end, but I will try to send some more soon. I can't write a cheque as it will bounce and I don't want any bank charges.

There are many 'remote' advertising boards in this area and I have asked the owners if they have had to go through any procedures to display their boards and none of them have, so why is it just me? I have asked Rag-Eme-Kale to tell me where I can go and see a structure similar to the one he wants me to have but he can't tell me because no one else has one.

I'm confused why I cannot display an A-board at the top of this road without breaking the law but if I give the council 100's of pounds it's OK. Why not just charge a reasonable rent for the small space it would be occupying.

I know it was Judgement Jones who wrote the letter to BT. You asked me to approach the Parish Council which I did and I told you what happened and that was the Tyrannical Clown's doing as was the letter I got from the planning department telling me I did not need permission to place an A-board at the top of Lydd Road, which he also contradicted that.

I will tell you again that I didn't realise that I had to pay this lot of costs directly to the Council; I thought they would be added onto the last lot.

Why don't you offer me an official 'brown sign' and that would solve everything!

Regards
Sally

So that was that for the time being. Lily and I continued our late night life of pillaging other people's signs. We went as far as Bexhill via country villages where there was always an abundance of remote signs. We took them all and then deposited them in neat rows outside the Highways office in Bexhill.

We were adapting well to our new lives of crime and were becoming more brazen as to what we would steal and dump outside the Highways office next. We decided we were going to steal Donkeykonk's stolen 'keep-left' signs and return them to the place from whence they had come. He kept them in his field along with his six donkeys and several dozen stolen traffic cones. As the keep-left signs were rather bulky and had very large thick Perspex signs stuck on them we used the white Peugeot as the getaway car and as a precaution I removed the large café sign from the roof. So in the dead of night we drove to Donkeykonk's field, we climbed over the wooden gate, where we could see the keep left signs in the light of the street lamp. We carried each one between us as quickly and quietly as we could, and chucked each one and then ourselves back over the gate. We struggled to push the stolen goods onto the back seat of the car, and the '£4 a day parking' signs were extremely awkward but we forced them and managed to close the doors. Off we went to Bexhill. We drove down the track to the highways office and parked in the usual place. At the last minute we decided to remove the notices off the keep-left signs in case they guessed it was us. Lily climbed into the back of the car with the signs, she had a hell of a job trying to break the thick Perspex as it had been stuck on with super glue, I assisted from the outside but we were only able to break it off in chunks. Finally we had removed all of the plastic from the keep-left signs, Lily crawled out of the back of the car exhausted and put one of the signs one side of the entrance to the highways office and I put one the other side. The super glue had left a visible square mark where the parking signs had been stuck onto the front of the keep-left signs. It felt like we had been there for ages but it was really only a matter of minutes. We jumped back into the car and drove away quickly but we needed to dispose of all the broken plastic which was now all over the car. On route back to Camber there was a lay-by flanked by a tall hedge that was in full leaf. I pulled into the lay-by and as Lily grabbed all the broken plastic I chucked it as high as I could over the hedge, some bits didn't quite make it to the top and fell into the hedge but must have stayed balanced on the branches as none of it fell back down to earth

I received another email from the Director of the Highways. I had even seen him on television recently so at least I knew who I was corresponding with

Dear Mrs Pattinson
Thank you for your email. I can confirm that you have paid £1350 in respect of your criminal conviction. However, please note that this only covers your sentence, which was a fine of £1200 owed to the court. You were also ordered to pay the Council's costs to the sum of £1500 of which you have paid £150. In addition, the County Court separately ordered you to pay a further £2500 direct to the Council, of which you have paid £20. In total, therefore, the Council is still owed a total of £3830. In eight months, you have paid the Council a total of £170. This is not acceptable and I would be grateful to receive your revised proposals for satisfying the Council's debt.
In relation to the other matters you raise, if you would like to apply for an official 'brown sign', you will need to contact the Council's Traffic and Safety Manager, Sidley Depot, Bexhill on Sea.

You comment also that you believe you are being unfairly targeted in relation to your advertising boards in comparison with other people. I would point out the Council's Highways Team cannot, as I am sure you appreciate, monitor every part of the highway on a round-the-clock basis. Temporary boards at the edge of the highway are sometimes tolerated unless a complaint has been made. The difference is that you wish to advertise on a permanent basis for which a formal application needs to be made. The rules are the same for everybody in your position.

This is also true in relation to the proposed 'A-board' at the top of your road. I note your comment about paying a rental sum. The Council has sympathy with your suggestion, but I am afraid that we cannot comply with it because it is against the law. There has to be a formal application and approval process, with a fee paid. Again, this is the law and it is the same for everybody.

Yours sincerely

I had had enough of these false accusations of refusing to pay the fines and costs. I rang the fines office again and I spoke to the same man as before. I read the email to him and again he checked that the payments had been paid to the council. I asked him how I could prove that I had been paying the money to them. He told me to suggest that they call him and they should ask to speak to 'the only Rob in the office'.

So that is what I did and once again I emailed the Director of the Environment and Transport;

Thank you for your email.

I am going to tell you for the last time that I have paid to your COUNCIL via that place in Brighton £1350 off the first lot of costs, I have NOT yet paid anything off the fine, someone is misinforming you. Will you please phone 01273 811670 and

ask to speak to 'the only Rob in the office' and he will tell you that I am right and you are wrong. I realise it is not your fault if council staff are not giving you the right information.
I disagree with you that I am not being targeted by those highway men in Bexhill, maybe that's something else you have been misinformed about. Had you been present at the court case you would have heard The Tyrannical Clown and Kilkenny lying to the point of committing perjury.
Maybe you would be so kind as to tell me what is happening with the 'enquiry' which Kilkenny was arranging regarding me being falsely accused of putting signs around Camber after 6th October 2009.

Regards
Sally

CHAPTER 31

I had laminated the injunction order I had been given at Hastings County Court and stuck it onto the back of the hot drinks machine for my customers to read while they were waiting to give their orders and in the hope that one day someone would come into the café and save me. One day a jolly middle aged and chubby little man came into the café and was reading my injunction order in more detail than others had. From what he was saying I got the impression that he was a solicitor, and he asked me how I had ended up with this injunction order. I told him as much as I could in a short time and I explained that I felt I was being victimised by The Tyrannical Clown and Kilkenny and that they were determined to wreck my business. I explained to him that I felt sure that they would be taking me to court again before long as Kilkenny was still taking photos and was often seen driving around Camber. The guy's name was Kerry and he was sympathetic about the situation and he asked if he could take all the paperwork home with him to read and the bundles from previous court cases. He was a kind genuine man and this was who I had been waiting for to save me. I happily handed over all the paperwork that had accrued over the last eighteen months. I was so relieved that at last someone was actually going to help me. He gave me his business card and took my stuff with him and said he would read it that week and then come back and see me. I thanked him and looking at the card I saw he worked for solicitors in Folkestone.

That same day the fire officer had delivered the collection box, posters and all the stuff for fund raising on behalf of the Fire Service so as soon as he had gone I emailed Rag-Eme-Kale:

Dear Rag-Eme-Kale
I now have all the promotion stuff from the Fire Brigade for
the fund raising I am going to do for them, all I need now is
your permission to advertise it. I sent you another
application form. Will you please give your consent so I can
get on with it?
I look forward to hearing from you soon
Sally

He replied half an hour later:

Dear Sally Pattinson,

Thank you for your email. I am in receipt of your
application of 9 June 2010. I regret that a 'Speculative
Commercial Venture' is not a charitable event. Also you
have not specified the date of the event. You have completed
the application to indicate that your commercial venture
shall start on the 30 June 2010 and continues indefinitely.
With regards to where charitable posters can be erected, the
policy provides for two posters on each main approach to
the event. I suggest that this would be a total of four posters
in the main Lydd Road, two posters in the verge, spaced 50
metres or so apart, on each side of the junction with your
road. They may be erected 5 days in advance of the event
and must be removed within 2 days after the event. There is
to be no commercial advertising on the posters other than a
direct reference to the event. Therefore, while Camber Café
is the venue on the posters, the main heading has to be the
event. I suggest that 'Speculative Commercial Venture' is
not the caption you intend to use on your charitable event
poster. Please can you be more specific about this event. In
what way is it supporting the East Sussex Fire & Rescue

Service? What day is it occurring on? Until I have this more specific information, I shall not issue a licence.
Yours sincerely
Rag-Eme-Kale

I replied immediately

Dear Rag-Eme-Kale
Blimey, you are making this hard work.
All the money I am going to attempt to raise is ALL going to be donated to the Fire Brigade. I am NOT taking anything from it.
My application form was meant to be just for the 30th June, but if I can do it for a longer period I would like to, as it gives me more time and because of the promise I have made to the Fire Brigade one day is not going to raise much money.
How will anyone know where to go if I can't put Camber Café on the signs?
As you appear to believe that a 'speculative commercial venture' does not exist then I have invented it and it will be the very first one and you never know, maybe it will catch on and lots of places will want to do one.
I look forward to hearing from you soon
Sally

What was wrong with Rag-Eme-Kale? He really did not want to issue me with a temporary event licence and that was if they even existed, but I would continue to send him application forms till I got what I wanted. Again he replied shortly after I had sent him the email;

Dear Sally Pattinson,

What is the event please?

I had to tell him, so I reluctantly answered;
A RAFFLE.....

Needless to say he answered within the hour;

Dear Sally Pattinson
I do not issue event poster licences for raffles. Raffles are
most frequently a side-line to the main event and are covered
by the Gambling Act 2005. There is a Code of Practice to help
guide you on this fund-raising venture, and I attach a link:
www.institute-of-fundraising.org.uk
You will note from section 2.1 of the Code of Practice that the
law requires you to sell the tickets at the fund raising event,
and that the draw must happen at the event. There is guidance
on the value of the prize.
However, may I suggest that you consider the fund-raising
event to be a 'Baked Bean eating competition', or something
similar? This would be the fund-raising event in the Camber
café at which you could sell the raffle tickets and comply with
the Gambling Act 2005.
Yours sincerely
Rag-Eme-Kale

A baked bean eating competition! How did he expect me
to do that and what's more who would want to participate in
such a ridiculous activity. What a stupid man to even suggest
such a thing. There was nothing wrong in having a weekly
raffle.

Dear Rag-Eme-Kale
In that case I don't need your consent....

*When I worked at the 'New Beach Club' in Pett Level where I
was the steward I did raffles every week to help pay for the
entertainment I booked and to buy prizes. My café is no
different from that really, apart from you don't have to be a
member to come in here, and for your information I have a
gambling licence still as The Tyrannical Clown did not
succeed in getting it revoked.*
*You are wrong saying it's not an event. An event is something
that happens and my fund-raising is going to happen. I can't
see what your problem is with it apart from you don't want me
advertising my café.*
*So as I still have my gambling licence I can go ahead with it,
can I?*
*I looked at the link you sent me but couldn't find what you
were referring to.*
Anyway, you don't know what I'm raffling do you!!!!!
*Would you like to buy some raffle tickets and then in the
unlikely event of you holding the winning ticket you will find
out!*
Sally

He did not answer. So I gave in to his suggestion and wrote
back to him saying;

Dear Rag-Eme-Kale
*OK we'll do a baked bean eating competition as you
suggested. And you won't be able to refuse as it was your
idea!*
So can we get on with it now please?????????
Sally

I did not care about Rag-Eme-Kale's temporary event
licence or his stupid stickers, I started to sell the raffle tickets

from the café anyway and I made sure the proceeds were put into the collecting box by the purchaser.

The prize was only a breakfast but people liked to donate to the fire service. I had provided everything Rag-Eme-Kale had demanded, I had provided him with the number of the registered charity organisation and I had sent him two application forms. There was nothing wrong in holding a raffle; he was just being cantankerous, determined not to let me have any signs anywhere.

I had no acknowledgement from Rag-Eme-Kale regarding his ridiculous proposal of a 'bean eating competition' and I had no intention of doing one anyway.

And then that evening I was watching the local Meridian news and saw a story about a charity event involving Sixty Scarecrows that were going to be popping up all over the town of Battle in East Sussex from 5th-25th July.

A three week fund raising event with sixty scarecrows embellishing Battle? I wondered how these scarecrows would be displayed and if the correct procedure had been carried out and been given Rag-Eme-Kale's blessing and temporary event stickers. There was only one way to find out.

Dear Rag-Eme-Kale
Did you tell me that temporary events can only last for one day? Because I was watching the local news last night and the town of Battle is holding a fund raising event between 5th-25th July and 60 scarecrows are going to be popping up all over the town. Has the correct procedure been followed for this event and have you issued the 60 scarecrows with your stickers?
I look forward to hearing from you
Sally

He replied the next day;

Dear Sally Pattinson

I am not aware of the event in Battle that you refer to. There are many private forecourts in front of the shops on which the proprietor might place a scarecrow without it being on the highway. However, if they begin to appear at junctions, left unattended or strapped to street lights, then they shall be removed.

Yours sincerely

Rag-Eme-Kale

CHAPTER 32

I did not receive a reply to my last email to the Director of Transport and Environment. Instead I got an email from Judgement Jones saying;

Dear Sally,

I have been asked to respond to your email to the Director of Transport and Environment. You raise a number of points in your correspondence of that date, and I will respond to them in turn:

1. I have spoken to The Tyrannical Clown and I presume that you are referring to an email the complaints manager sent you on 25th November 2009. The Tyrannical Clown did not email the Parish Council in respect of this. I understand that the lady from the planning department of the District Council informed you that signs advertising a business do not always need planning permission but where the sign is on the highway the consent of the highway is needed. This has always been the position, and you have been aware of it for rather a long time!

2. Accusing two Council employees of perjuring themselves in court is a clear breach of your injunction which forbids you to 'use foul, abusive or defamatory language' towards ESCC staff. Alleging that someone has lied on oath in a court room is clearly defamatory. I must ask you not to use that language in future. Further breaches of the injunction will result in the Council taking this matter to court, which could result in you receiving a sentence of imprisonment.

3. You refer in your letter to an 'enquiry'. Having spoken to Kilkenny, I understand this relates to an incident on 10th October last year whereupon you accused the Council of falsifying photographs and even deliberately changing the dates on the photographs. If you believed this to the case, I suggest that you make an official complaint, stressing your allegations, with evidence, and an independent enquiry can deal with it if you wish. Clearly, if you are making allegations that are this serious in nature, they need to be substantiated and you need evidence to back up your claims 4. The Injunction Proceedings are of course separate to the criminal proceedings. I understand that you are paying £50 a month in order to cover the Council's costs in the criminal case and have so far paid £1350, thus leaving £150 outstanding. However, in the injunction proceedings you were ordered to pay £2500 by 23rd April. You have so far only paid £20 in two months. If you can pay Brighton fines office in £50 a month instalments, can you please do the same for the County Court costs? I look forward to hearing from you.

Regards

Judgement Jones

Someone had obviously spoken to 'the only Rob in the office' as Judgement Jones had finally acknowledged that I had been paying the fine but not even offered me an apology despite the fact they had made that allegation in the court on 15th April. He had threatened me with a sentence of imprisonment for accusing council workers of perjuring themselves. I was given that injunction order on the strength of two council employees' lies and now I was being threatened with imprisonment because I had complained to their superior about it.

I was glad that at last Judgement Jones had mentioned the 'enquiry' Kilkenny had proposed nine months ago and I did have proof of when I had put those signs up.

I had to answer his letter with extreme caution as I did not want to end up in prison for telling the truth, as it would be portrayed as defamatory language and in breach of the injunction order.

I wrote:

Dear Judgement Jones

Thank you for your letter, although I realise I must be very careful how I answer it.

Surely I would only be in breach of that injunction order if I was using defamatory language by making false accusations, which incidentally I wasn't.

Presuming you still have a copy of the bundle from 9th April I will only make reference to written statements as you have once again threatened me with imprisonment and I do not want to be in prison just as the season is about to start.

Please look at Kilkenny's statement and read section 2. I had previously asked to see a copy of service ticket number 58061 which presumably was the complaint, but I wasn't sent it. In the court I asked Kilkenny why the wine bar had received a letter from the Highways asking them to remove their signs following a complaint about them and I hadn't been sent a letter. I then suggested that the reason I hadn't had a letter was because no one had complained about my café signs, to which Kilkenny agreed. I then asked him why in that case had he removed my café signs and he replied that it wouldn't have been fair to take the wine bar's signs down and leave mine up. The judge looked at me and said 'there you are then it wouldn't have been fair'.

I have no idea of an incident you refer to occurring on 10th October 2009. The first time I was aware of allegations made against me after 6th October 2009 regarding unauthorised signs on the highway was when I received a letter from you written on 28th October 2009 threatening me with an ASBO. I agreed that I had put the A-board in 'set 2' at the top of Lydd Road. The point here is you accused me of putting up café signs after 6th October 2009 and I had not. The photos in my *bundle clearly show when I had put them up and the photos from you were taken on 7th October 2009. I have said nothing about the dates on your photos being false.*

Now read section 8 in Kilkenny's statement.

In my bundle read page 40 and then look at pages 41, 42 and 43 which are photos of when I put up the café signs in question, including the dates. I took the photos with my mobile phone which automatically puts the date onto the photo, but you must know that.

I know for a fact that the photos you sent me were taken on 7th October 2009. Indeed, I certainly do request an inquiry. Who do I contact?

I presume the other bit of 'defamatory language' you are referring to is the telephone conversation I had with The Tyrannical Clown on the 9th September 2009 at 13.31, I don't know why he denied having that conversation with me that day and actually just before that I had been speaking to Kilkenny on the phone and he told me that The Tyrannical Clown was sending me an email and after I had read it I had to phone back, which I did, but he was unavailable and I was told he would ring me back, which he did.

The only part of that conversation I did not include in that letter was that he said he would pay me one compliment, that being I was one of the most annoying women he had ever known and he had wasted too much time talking to me.

You now accept that I have paid the council £1350, but maybe you should have checked prior to accusing me of refusing to pay it in front of the judge.

I am not committing myself to pay £50 a month to you. However, I will send you as much as I can.

From Sally

I was keen to know how the investigation would be carried out and I was sure that it would be so easy to prove that their allegations were false it should not take very long and I had all my evidence ready for when it would be required. Five days after I had sent my cautious letter I received the reply along with three photos attached, from Judgement Jones;

Dear Sally

Thank you for your email dated 11th of June.

In response to the points raised:

1. You did not appeal against the Injunction made against you and, in any event, you are out of time to do so. The decision therefore still stands. The judge clearly accepted the evidence given therein by The Tyrannical Clown and Kilkenny. If you are suggesting that both the Council's employees deliberately lied on oath, with the intention of lowering your reputation, that is a very serious allegation. If you persist in making these allegations, you risk being prosecuted for breaching your injunction;

2. The Council will not accede to your request for an inquiry as we fail to see what purpose will be achieved by one. Even if, which is not accepted, the photos to which you refer were taken on 7th October 2009, and the signs were erected before your first court appearance, you would still be breaking the law after your conviction. In any event, the main reasons why the Council brought the injunction were because of your persistent abusive emails and, in particular, your sign on the highway which referred to The Tyrannical Clown and Kilkenny as 'the merchant bankers from Bexhill'. Both incidents happened after 6th October 2009.

3. The 'photos' incident makes no material difference to the granting of the injunction and I think it unlikely that the court would have come to a different result. If you are accusing The Tyrannical Clown and Kilkenny of lying on oath, why did you not bring this to the judge's attention in court? You had ample opportunity to raise your arguments. The appropriate forum for dealing with these matters is the court. You had the right to appeal against the judge's decision. The Council cannot be blamed if you did not avail yourself of that right;

4. I enclose a photograph recently taken in relation to your café. As you can see, there is an advertising board clearly on the highway outside the café and the giant inflatable man has clearly blown onto the highway as well. These are causing obstructions and are impeding free passage of the highway. Please ensure that both structures are kept clear of the highway. This is a breach of the first terms of your injunction which prevent you from 'placing any signs, posters, street furniture or other structures on the highway or which abut the highway without the express written consent of the claimant as the highway authority'.

5. Enclosed is a further photo of a sign attached to a bike which is further attached to a pole, namely street furniture. I understand that this bike is permanently attached to the pole which is of course against the law and I would ask you to remove it.

6. Please pay attention to the terms of your injunction or you will find yourself in court if you continue in this manner and might end up serving a sentence of imprisonment.

Yours faithfully,

Judgement Jones Assistant Director for Legal & Democratic Service

No enquiry! I knew why too, he had realised that my evidence was far too damning to be anything other than the truth. The more familiar I became with the likes of Judgement Jones and The Tyrannical Clown the more I realised that they were devoid of all morals and conformity.

Dear Judgement Jones,

I didn't appeal against the court's decision as I didn't know I could, but when I did know I asked for an appeal form and it was too complicated to fill out so I didn't bother.

You don't need to worry about my reputation being 'lowered'. However, I said Kilkenny wrote in his statement that he had a complaint about my café signs on 17th November 2008, and in the court room he admitted that he had not. Why don't you ask him yourself? And The Tyrannical Clown denied the phone call and the things he had threatened me with on the 9th September 2009.

When I sent you that email on 29th November 2009 regarding that phone call, you didn't write to me then and tell me it was not true and that I was defamorating The Tyrannical Clown's reputation. A bit like those café sign photos taken after 6th October, it 'makes no material difference'. It still happened. Why am I in breach of the injunction order for telling the truth? Are you suggesting I am fabricating this information? Furthermore the judge did hear what I said to Kilkenny and I told you what she said to me, so she clearly wasn't concerned by what he had written in his statement and what he said being contradictory. I was wrongly accused by your barrister and The Tyrannical Clown of refusing to pay the first lot of court costs. I said twice that I was paying £50 a month to that place in Brighton and twice The Tyrannical Clown insisted that I had refused to pay it. So although the judge heard what I said she chose to believe your clients because she had no reason to disbelieve them she said, as they had both been policemen. Maybe I should have told her that I was a very sexy cabaret dancer and belly dancer when I was in my twenties; she might have had no reason to disbelieve me then. Would you like a photo of me in my dancing days to add to the Sally folder?

The judge also said to them that it was probably a bit daunting for me as there were four of them and one of me. Not true, I wouldn't have cared if there had been four hundred of them; I will not be intimidated by anyone and the more someone tries to intimidate me the more it fuels my determination.

Of course you won't accede to an inquiry into you accusing me of putting up café signs after 6th October because you know I am telling the truth. So in section 8 of Kilkenny's statement he says that the allegations were serious and 'if the allegations were true it would amount to the council conspiring against her' and he would request an investigation. That sounds quite drastic to me. So how can you come to the conclusion that something so serious has no purpose and doesn't warrant an inquiry?

Well, I will find someone who does take these allegations seriously. And it's nothing to do with any injunction I've got, it's the fact that I have been wrongly accused again of something I didn't do.

I don't know why you have the impression that I had ample opportunity to raise arguments, one you weren't there and two every time I attempted to say anything contrary to their account of things we moved swiftly on to the next issue.

Rag-Eme-Kale informed me that A-boards outside premises are tolerated. As for the bike, I got legal advice before I put the board on it and technically the board is not on the highway and the pole is not yours. I can't help which way the wind blows. Maybe you can arrange for a set of traffic lights to be installed outside my café so the traffic stays on the other side of the road when the wind is blowing in an easterly direction. Anyway, I don't stick 'Tall Paul' out there in adverse weather as I don't want him to rip.

I see the old hag Beaky from upstairs has joined in now; the photo of Tall Paul bending in the breeze was clearly taken from her living room above the café.
Sally

CHAPTER 33

I sent Judgement Jones £30 towards their costs and I
reminded him that I couldn't afford to send him my hard
earned cash so I asked if I could work off the costs by doing
community service. I could collect unauthorised remote signs
and temporary event signs as there were loads of unlawful
signs about and obviously Kilkenny had not the time to
collect them all as if he had they wouldn't be there.

Then I sent one more email to Rag-Eme-Kale on the
subject of temporary events;

Dear Rag-Eme-Kale
You have told me that temporary events can only last for one
day, now looking at the evidence which was on Meridian
News they can last for up to three weeks if it is for a
scarecrow event in Battle. I would like to know how you are
going to supervise the scarecrows and have you provided the
participants with your stickers and does this event have your
approval?
Assuming that this event will take place with or without your
stickers I too am going to run my temporary event for three
weeks.
Sally

His answer was;

Dear Mrs Pattinson
I will not sign a licence for a three week long raffle. I do not
consider that this is an event, but rather you are intending to
advertise your business by means of the charitable poster
licence policy.

Regards
Rag-Eme-Kale

So no temporary event, but it really didn't matter. I had bought a loud hailer anyway and in the afternoons I drove up and down the main road and Lily shouted to all the holiday makers through it that Camber Café was just around the corner; it was ok but became a bit monotonous after a while so we gave up on that idea.

'Tall Paul' had been in service for three weeks and already we had a visit from the Health and Safety department and a complaint from Beaky the old hag when a letter arrived from the Planning Enforcement and Appeals, Mr Pasty

Dear Madam
Town and Planning (Control of Advertisements) Regulations 2007
Re: Inflatable Character Advertisement-Camber Café
The above has recently been displayed. My records indicate that advertisement consent had not been granted. Whilst you may apply for express consent, it is in my opinion that an application is unlikely to be recommended for approval.
I must draw to your attention to the fact that it is an offence under the provisions of the advertisement regulations to display a sign without consent. If the advertisement is not removed in the near future, the Council's Solicitor will be asked to commence legal proceedings.
I would appreciate receiving conformation of how you intend to deal with this matter within 7 days from the date of this letter.
Yours faithfully
Planning Enforcement

I did not intend to do anything with Tall Paul. I had just

paid £450 for him and besides other businesses advertised with Air Dancers, as that was the whole point of them and they would be illegal otherwise. I rang the Planning Enforcement Manager and he did not sound to me as if he was capable of enforcing anything, in fact he sounded quite timid. I asked him what the problem was with Tall Paul and he wanted to know how tall 'Tall Paul' was, so I asked if that would be on or off his fan, and he said on. He was making me laugh already so I asked him why he wanted to know and at a guess he was roughly 20ft high, so then he wanted to know where I had bought it. I was surprised and I asked him if he wanted to buy one too, and told him I had bought it from a seller on eBay and told him the company name and he asked for the phone number. Nevertheless he told me I could not display Tall Paul. The reason I had bought it was to advertise the café and at this moment in time that was the way forward.

One week later I received another letter from Mr Pasty

Dear Madam
INFLATABLE CHARACTACTER ADVERSTISEMENT-
'CAFÉ OPEN'
I refer to my letter dated 14th June 2010.
I believe that you are the person responsible for the display of the above advertisement.
This advertisement requires Advertisement Consent but no such consent has been granted and you have already been informed that it should be removed.
An inspection of the site made on Friday 18th June 2010 at 3pm showed that the advertisement was still in place.
Therefore you have committed an offence under Section 224 (3) of the Town and Country Planning Act 1990.
Under the circumstances, I am writing to you to obtain further information regarding this matter. Before asking you any questions I should advise you that you may, if you wish, seek

*independent legal advice before answering the questions in
part two of this letter. I should advise you that, if you prefer,
you may give the answers to the questions in an interview at
the Town Hall Bexhill. If you wish to do this, please contact
me as soon as possible on the above telephone number.
Should you need anything in the letter explained, please
contact me as soon as possible.
Yours faithfully
Mr Pasty*

I looked at Part 2:

Please read the following caution carefully.

*You do not have to say anything but it may harm your defence
if you do not mention when questioned something which you
later rely on in Court. Anything you do say may be given in
evidence.*

*I draw your attention to the provisions of section 34 of the
Criminal Justice and Public Order Act 1994, which allows a
court to draw proper inference from your failure or refusal to
account for the facts about which you are being questioned.*

*I request that you reply to this letter, in writing, within 7 days
as a decision will be made whether to prosecute you for this
offence. If your reply is not received within that period it will
be assumed that you have declined to reply.*

*If you find it hard to read English you should take this letter
to a Citizens Advice Bureau or a Solicitor who will be able to
help you.*

PART 2
*What is your full name?
What is your address?*

Do you have any interest in the site where the advertisement is being displayed? If so, what?

Does the advertisement give publicity to your goods, trade, business or other concern?

Are you the person responsible for displaying the above advertisement?

Are you jointly responsible for the display of the advertisement with another person/s?

Does any consent apply to the advertisement? If so, what is the reference?

If you are not responsible for the display of the advertisement who is?

If you are not responsible for the display of the advertisement, please give any information which might help clarify how or why you have no involvement.

Are you able to remove the advertisement?

When was the advertisement first displayed?

Do you have any explanation for failing to comply with the Council's request to remove the advertisement?

Signed

Print Name

Date

There was not one question there that Mr Pasty could not have answered himself. What was the purpose of sending me a questionnaire with the riot act for me to read to myself? I was not going to fill it out and I thought it would be quite entertaining to go to Bexhill and face Mr Pasty in the flesh. I rang him and told him I would rather deal with his request directly with him, and I told him that I would go to Bexhill so he could interview me there. He said that they currently did not have a spare interviewing room and he would let me know when there was one available.

Every three months I took the four filters above the griddle and fryers into Rye to be steam cleaned by a haulage company. The filters would get in a disgusting greasy state and I did not like removing them from the wooden hood where they were placed. That morning I decided to take the filters to Rye to be cleaned. I did not want to have them in my little black car but at the same time I did not want to be without a café sign either, so I put an old A-board in the boot of my car and drove to the top of the road, parked up and placed the A board on the grass where it used to be before I was given an injunction order forbidding me from putting it there;, after all I was only going to be twenty minutes and if a highways inspector was on his way to Camber I would pass him on route so I could phone Lily who would rush to the top of the road and move the A-board quickly. I swapped the two cars over and drove back to the café in the Peugeot. Lily helped me put the greasy filters into bin liners and we put them in the boot of the car. Off I drove surrounded by the scarecrows and I got quite a few strange looks on my short journey into Rye. I left the greasy filters at the haulage yard and drove back to Camber. I swapped the cars over again picked up the A board and drove back to the café. Lily was sitting outside and I could see by her face she was eager to tell me something. She said that soon after I had left to go into Rye, Bodger had appeared from behind the gates with a bicycle never seen before, and Lily, being suspicious of what he was up to, had said good morning to him and commented that it was a lovely day for a bike ride. She watched him ride up to the top of the road where he had stopped and she saw him taking photos. She said he returned after just a few minutes with his bike in tow and disappeared behind the gates to their flat. I said he would probably send his evidence to The Tyrannical Clown, but anyway I did not care what he did with them.

Lily and I were both keen to take a look at the scarecrow event in Battle, so early that evening we left Camber to go and check out these scarecrows. On the way there we noticed two rickety old signs displayed either side of a road junction attached to two equally rickety old wooden posts advertising a Farm Shop ½ a mile down the lane with directional arrows. I had been told numerous times by Rag-Eme-Kale that remote signs are unlawful unless they had been designed by a professional structural engineer. I decided to stop the car and take a closer look at these signs. Surely they must have Rag-Eme-Kale's approval or they would have been removed long ago and looking at the state of them they must have been there for years. I took photos of them to send to Rag-Eme-Kale and ask him if this was his idea of a structurally sound advertising sign for if it was I could design and make them myself without having to employ a structural engineer to do it for me.

As we approached Battle town the first exhibits we saw were standing attached to garden gates of the residents' homes but as we got nearer to the town centre there were scarecrows everywhere placed in front of shops, along the High Street and around the large parking area just outside of the Abbey. Some were indeed propped up against lamp posts and signposts, certainly not causing an obstruction but more of a distraction to motorists. Some of the scarecrows were well made and others were more like someone's dress on a hanger with a hat stuck on top. As we were driving home I had an idea. We would make our own scarecrow and if Rag-Eme-Kale was not aware of the Battle Scarecrows I would make sure that he was aware of ours. The next day we put our plan into action but neither I nor Lily had any idea how to make a scarecrow. We looked on YouTube and sure enough there was an American lady called Monkey Sue giving very good instruction on how to make a scarecrow which we watched and were then ready to make our own. We needed hay, a pair of tights and a ball of strong string. The tights would be stuffed with hay and would be the arms and head and the rest of the body would also be stuffed with hay. I drove into Rye to buy the things we needed. When I returned we filled the tights with hay but as we stuffed the hay into the legs they became longer and longer and were about ten feet long, so we pushed the hay further back up the legs and tied knots half way up to make them shorter. Once we had put enough hay in for its head we tied a knot at the top. We put a long sleeved green t-shirt on it and stuffed the torso with hay. I got an old pair of leggings which we stuffed and used for its legs and tied the ends in knots. During the construction of our scarecrow the old Hag Beaky stuck her head out of her window and asked us what we were doing. Lily, on the ball as usual, told her we were making it for her nephew for a school fête but she still continued staring at us for some time and we ignored her. After we had stuffed the leggings we put an old pair of trousers on it and then we had to attach the top half to the bottom half which was a lot easier said than done. It was a matter of threading the string through the belt loops several revolutions and then up and over its shoulders to hold it together like a pair of braces, and we had to be careful not to pull the string too tight because everything just scrunched up together. Eventually we finished its body and made its face out of a paper plate by drawing droopy eyes on it. I cut about half a centimetre off the bottom of a polystyrene take-away cup for the nose and used a red straw to make its mouth, and a string mop head on it for its hair. We stuck all the extra bits on with super glue. For a joke we put a pair of my old green French lace knickers over the top of the trousers. One of Lily's friends donated a high-vis jacket and we tied a black scarf round its head like a bandanna with the stringy hair sticking out over the top and the front bit as a fringe. We pushed its ankles into a pair of my old boots and pushed the ends of its arms into a pair of yellow rubber gloves held on by elastic bands. So there he was, a life size effigy of 'Rag-Eme-Kale'! He was splendid and Lily and I were very pleased with our creation. As my car was so small we had to transport him in the Peugeot so I had to remove the sign off the roof again for discretion. The plan was to take 'Rag-Eme-Kale' to the Highways depot in Bexhill that night, but it was raining hard and we didn't want him to get drenched and fall to bits or get ravished by a fox, so we got up at five o'clock the next morning and loaded Rag-Eme-Kale into the back of the Peugeot and took an old IKEA stool for him to sit on. It had stopped raining and the morning was bright and fresh as we drove to Bexhill. Lily was worried in case we were stopped by the police or worse still we were caught putting Rag-Eme-Kale outside the Highways office. I assured her it would be most unlikely that we would have any encounters with the police at that time of the morning. We arrived and chose the place to put Rag-Eme-Kale on the stool. We had to carry him between us in case he fell in half, luckily he stayed together and we sat him on the stool but he slumped forward so we moved him and the stool further back so he could lean on a sapling. Now he was in place we wanted to get away quickly. It was nearly six o'clock and people would be getting up. I took a photo of him and noticed his knees were bent in the wrong direction, but we left him in that position. He looked so funny sitting in the damp grass on an IKEA stool; I wondered what the highway men would make of him or even wonder where he had come from. We drove back to Camber and opened the café early.

Later that day I composed a letter to Rag-Eme-Kale about the rickety old Farm Shop signs we had seen on our way to Battle:

Dear Rag-Eme-Kale

If these signs at the junction of Crowhurst Road and Queensway have been designed by a structural engineer and have been approved by you, then you must have been having a laugh with me regarding all that rigmarole you tried to get me to comply with. Not only are these signs made of crap material, they are only a midges-dick away from the junction of a main road with a 60 mph speed limit, they are remote as well. In fact they are everything you told me I couldn't do. This is what you sent me remember?

Consequently, when proposing locations for an advertising structure, the following points should be considered

☐No structures placed within 60 metres of a junction with a principal road or in visibility splays at minor junctions or bends

☐No advert to mimic traffic signs and give traffic directions to motorists

☐Where adjacent to roads that are 40mph or above, signs must be passively safe (that is readily collapsible if struck by a vehicle)

So were these advertisements designed undertaking calculations and scale drawings by a structural engineer? Did the contractor who erected them hold the relevant accreditation and liability insurance to work on the highway? If so, they are the worst examples I have ever seen in my life of Council approved structures.

These signs have been there for several years so you must have given them your approval or as your inspectors come to Camber at least once a week they must have passed them loads of times and surely would have removed them if you had not given your consent for them to be there.

Sally

I printed the photos of the Farm Shop signs clearly showing the proximity with the main road and junction. I put it all in a large envelope, addressed it to Rag-Eme-Kale at the Highways Authority in Ringmer near Lewes and to make certain Rag-Eme-Kale received it I sent it by recorded delivery.

CHAPTER 34

Two weeks had passed since I had received the questionnaire from Mr Pasty and he had not contacted me to make arrangements to interview me, so I rang him. He was clearly flustered when I asked him if there was an interviewing room available yet. He said that his manager was going to interview me but he was on holiday and he would contact me on his return.

I doubted that there was going to be an interview with Mr Pasty; he was clearly acting on The Tyrannical Clown's instructions to try and frighten me, but in this instance I think it was I who had frightened him. So Tall Paul survived the Council's attempts to make him redundant and remained tall and proud on the forecourt when it was not windy but when the wind blew then he was bent and proud.

The recession was certainly showing in the takings of the café and apart from a week of hot weather in May the sun had not really shone since.

One morning the nice Beach Ranger Simon who had given me permission to put my café signs on the fence at the edge of the sand dunes at the bottom of the road came to the door carrying the café sign still screwed to the drain pipe. He explained that he had received a phone call from Rag-Eme-Kale who had told him that if he did not want to put his job in jeopardy he must remove and return my café sign to me and rescind the permission he had previously given. I asked him how Rag-Eme-Kale had known he had given me permission and how had he managed to contact him. Simon answered that it had taken many phone calls and finally he had got Simon's number from his boss. So in other words if he did not obey Rag-Eme-Kale's orders he would risk losing his job over my café signs. Simon said he would not tell me again to remove the café sign and if he saw it there again it would stay there because he knew I would always replace it.

I had been sending Judgement Jones £20 pounds a month towards the court costs but I knew I would not be able to afford to give him anything through the winter months so I sent him a letter enclosing another £20 and asked him to hang on to it until the following January as I knew I would not have any money to make payments through the winter. It seemed quite a reasonable request and to protect myself from more accusations that I was refusing to pay anything.

Judgement Jones replied to my letter;

Sally,

Thank you for the £20 cash. However, you have told me the money is 'not to be put into your account until January 2011'. With all due respect, why wouldn't you want me to do this? The £20 is of no use to you or me otherwise. It's not like a postal order or cheque that can be stopped. You have already withdrawn the money and given it to me. I might as well give it to finance and use them to pay off some of your debt. If it's left languishing in my file, it might get stolen. Wouldn't you rather it was put to the use for which it was intended?
Regards Judgement Jones

I was quite amused that Judgement Jones he had implied that his colleagues were thieves. Friends had leased a local farm just before Camber village, which had a vast amount of land and two large fishing lakes The house was built of stone and set at the top of a long drive way, and was idyllic. Some of the land ran alongside the Camber Road, and Emily, the beautiful and feisty daughter of the family leasing the farm, was sympathetic to my predicament and invited me to put a large advert for my café on their land beside the road. I was delighted at the prospect of a huge café sign on private land which I had been advised to do by Judgement Jones. I happily accepted Emily's kind offer but before I put any construction in place I needed to check with the Planning Department at Rother District Council. I took two photos of the land which ran parallel with the footpath alongside it, one photo from the west side and one from the east. I printed the photos and onto each one I painted the front view and then the back view of the proposed café sign which I was going to erect in my friend's field. When I had finished I photographed them again and it looked quite impressive. My large café sign on legs in a field not more than a few hundred yards from where the burger van had his, except mine would be on private land. I emailed Mr Pasty the Planning Enforcement Officer attaching the photos of my proposed sign and told him of my intention.

Dear Mr Pasty
I have attached two pictures of the location plus a front and back view of the café sign I am intending to stick in this field. If you are going to tell me that I need some kind of consent I am not going to believe you as AJ's burger van sign is on the golf course just down the road from this location and when I asked Judgement Jones why that was ok he sent me this answer which I have included;
'Because the field is privately owned by the golf course who have given him permission. It's not on the highway so is no concern of the Council's.'
Sally

Mr Pasty replied:

Advertisement consent will be required for your proposal. I suggest that you ask the landowner to contact me so that I can clarify the matter.

This was just going to be another chain of inconclusive emails. I wrote back to him explaining that I could not contact the landowner as he was currently living abroad. I also asked him why Judgement Jones had told me that if I advertised my café on private land they would not bother me anymore. I asked him if he would clarify exactly which part of their legislation applied to me and which part applied to AJ's Burger Van.

His answer to that was:

The sign will require advertisement consent. If you place the sign without consent, the landowner will also be open to prosecution. With regard to AJ's burger van sign I understand this is on the highway and the responsibility of East Sussex Highways.
Regards
C Pasty

So Judgement Jones had said that AJ's signs were on private land and that was the responsibility of the planning department at Rother District Council and Mr Pasty the Planning Enforcement Officer had said that AJ's signs were on the highway and the responsibility of East Sussex Highways.

Someone was lying; I would put my money on Judgement Jones from my previous experience of his devious doings. There was only one way to find out, I copied the two contradicting emails and sent them to Judgement Jones for an explanation;

Dear Judgement Jones
I asked you and Mr Pasty the Planning Enforcement Officer the same question, I have attached two emails one is from you and one is from Mr Pasty. You have both given contradictory

replies. Which one of you is telling the truth please? Clearly
one of you isn't.
Sally

He replied;

Sally
'AJ did have some signs on the highway but they were
removed. We gave him some advice which he listened to. As a
result, the sign he currently displays is on privately owned
land and not on the highway.'
Judgement Jones

Gave him advice? They never told him to do anything;

Dear Judgement Jones
Will you please tell the Planning Enforcement Officer that
then because I am going to put a café sign on private land and
he says I have to get consent? One of you is lying, why? AJ
never had to get consent did he?
Sally

I had got him in a corner that he could not wriggle out of
without exposing himself or Mr Pasty as a liar.

Sally
May I remind you that the terms of your injunction preclude
you from using foul or abusive language when communicating
with employees of East Sussex County Council and also from
using defamatory language? Accusing me of being a liar is
such a breach. The Council has the right to apply to have you
sent to prison for breaching your injunction. The judge can
sentence you for up to two years' imprisonment. I suggest you

stop putting signs on the highway and using foul language to myself or any other Council employees or you will be sent to prison.
Judgement Jones

Every time I presented Judgement Jones with a situation he could not answer he used my injunction order like a shield to protect himself and threatened me with imprisonment. Going by his response I guessed he was the liar. I had not directly accused him of lying, only asked which of them was lying. To be certain, I emailed the Enforcement Planning Officer again to verify;

Dear Mr Pasty
Somewhere along the line your planning permission policies have gone awry. You may understand AJ's sign is on the highway but the highway men do not understand it is on the highway, they understand it's on the golf course. Judgement Jones understands it's on the golf course too. Can I stick my new café signs on the golf course which is neither on nor off the highway or on the highway which is neither on nor off the golf course?
Wherever AJ's board is, it still needs consent from you and you haven't given it.
I'll stick mine beside his then or even I could stick a car in the lay-by next to AJ's van.
Yes. I'm going to do that. Tomorrow.
Sally

I did wonder if these guys actually checked with each other what they were putting in their correspondence and if one of them was genuinely honest what was his opinion of his colleague who was not, and did they really expect me to

accept their explanations on the authenticity of AJ's A-boards.
It was time to answer Judgement Jones threatening letter.

Thank you for your email Judgement Jones
I don't think I understand the meaning of the word
'defamatory'. My definition of 'defamatory' is for example;
to accuse somebody of doing something after a certain date
that they had not done or accuse someone of refusing to pay
a debt when they had paid it or someone who has received a
threatening phone call when the caller denies making it,
therefore insinuating that the recipient of the phone call has
lied. So yes.... to make a person's character appear bad
when it is not. I didn't realise 'defamatory' meant to ask a
question.
I did not directly accuse you of lying, I sent you the emails
from yourself and the Planning Enforcement Officer for you
to read and it is not my fault if you have both given me
conflicting answers to my one question. After all it was you
who suggested I ask a farmer if I can advertise my café on
their private land and I took your advice and asked one and
he said yes I can and as big as I want it to be.
Will you please explain to me exactly the meaning of
'defamatory' so I don't do it again?
Thank you
Sally

Judgement Jones answer was;

''Defamatory'' means that you have published a statement
about me which would cause a reasonable person to think
worse of me. The statement can be expressed or implied.
Your statement implied that I was lying when, acting upon
my client's advice, I informed you that AJ's Burger Van sign
was on privately owned land. As I am bound by Rules of

*Conduct, implying that I deliberately told you an untruth is
an accusation of professional misconduct, which most
'reasonable people' would consider defamatory.*

I answered him;

Dear Judgement Jones
Thank you for your email.
*I did not write 'you have' or 'Judgement Jones has', you had a
choice of answering and it was a question not an accusation.
You could have said 'It's not me'. I did not publish or send
that email to any other person apart from yourself so nobody
will think you have acted unprofessionally apart from me. I
had not intended to ruin your reputation. I don't think my
question implied you were being unprofessional.*
*I have been 'wrongly accused' loads of times during the last
20 months by your clients, but I don't worry about it. Maybe
your clients don't understand the meaning of 'defamatory'
either, so you could tell them too.*
*Anyway, I am going to put my new café sign on huge wheels
so it won't need consent from the Planning Enforcement
Officer, The Tyrannical Clown, Rag-Eme-Kale or anyone
else!*
Sally

Sadly I never did get to put my huge sign in the field as my
friends decided to leave the farm shortly after. Neither did I
hear any more from the Enforcement Planning Officer or
Judgement Jones on the controversial subject of highways and
private land. It did not matter anyway, as I already had
another idea.

CHAPTER 35

The white Peugeot was regularly photographed by the
highway men in high-visibility jackets. In fact a neighbour
had seen a man with a clip board walking round the car
checking the wheels and looking through the windows. I
decided it was time to take action and give them something
else to take photos of. We had plenty of hay left from when
we had made Rag-Eme-Kale and we had the empty body of
the gorilla so Lily and I set about making our second
scarecrow, this one was attributed to Kilkenny and we were
going to sit him on the back seat of the car to scare off any
predators and to smile into the cameras as they snapped
photos of him. We made Kilkenny much quicker than we did
Rag-Eme-Kale and he had a ready-made face. We soon
stuffed the hay into the tights and an old pair of leggings; we
dressed him in a purple and red stripy jumper with a green t-
shirt over the top and black trousers, and stuck an old green
Leprechaun hat, with a black band and yellow buckle just
above the brim, on his head. The costume had come with
hairy hands and feet and we put a scarf round his neck to hide
all the bad bits. As the Rag-Eme-Kale scarecrow had been
quite floppy we gave Kilkenny a spine by pushing a length of
wooden baton up his back so he was able to sit up straight. All
the while we were making Kilkenny outside we sensed Beaky
the old Hag was watching us through her blind.

We carefully carried Kilkenny to the car and sat him on a
couple of bits of wood to make him taller on the back seat,
strapped him in with the seat belt and turned his head slightly
to be looking out of the window ferociously and ready to
scare off those highway men. After a few days he was
beginning to look quite lonely sitting there in the back of the
car all on his own, so I decided we would make effigies of all

the council meanies who had given me grief and they could sit in the car all together.

I bought plenty of hay, pairs of tights and wooden spines to shove down their necks, and we got plenty of stuffing for their bodies. I looked on eBay for suitable masks for them. Finding a mask for The Tyrannical Clown was easy, a lovely mask of an ugly clown with frizzy yellow and orange hair sticking up all over the place just like it had been on his bad hair day at Eastbourne Magistrates Court. Its huge mouth stretched from ear to ear with big brown teeth exposed, it had yellow eyes, one looking up and the other looking out, and it was a perfect likeness to The Tyrannical Clown. Then we found Judgement Jones a mask, which was also a clown with a purple open mouth and black gums exposing grey teeth, brown eyes, a big purple nose and a bald head. I checked out accessories for the effigies and for The Tyrannical Clown I bought a crown and for Judgement Jones I bought a judge's wig and a large red bow tie with white spots. We dressed The Tyrannical Clown in a shirt and tie and some old trousers and stuffed the fingers of a pair of rubber gloves and pushed them onto the ends of his arms and wrapped elastic bands round the wrists to hold them in place. I had plenty of old boots to push their footless legs into. We dressed Judgement Jones in a pair of old trousers and a red and grey hoodie and put the judge's wig on his head, topped off with a PVC leather-look Village People biker hat with a chain across the brim. When they were finished we sat Judgement Jones in the middle next to Kilkenny and also needed to raise him up on bits of wood and beside him The Tyrannical Clown placing one rubber hand in his crotch as if he were adjusting his appendage and the other arm resting along the bottom of the window.

So there were the three baddies sitting in the back of the car. We wondered what people would make of them. The one thing that did concern me was that the car had to be parked outside the church and there was the play school held there every day and I did not want to scare the children with the effigies, so I turned The Tyrannical Clown's head slightly looking straight ahead and not out of the window.

The car and its occupants did bring quite a few curious customers to the café wanting to know what were those ugly things sitting in the car. I explained they were effigies of two corrupt highway men and the council solicitor and that they were trying to wreck my business. Some people even recognised them as council employees as it transpired that these types of corrupt council employees could be found all over the country apparently.

There was still an empty seat in the front of the car and recently we had been listening to the American rapper Eminem. I quite liked some of his music and Lily knew every word to every track he had ever made but there was one song in particular I liked called 'Big Weenie' which was about jealousy of Eminem's success. The gist of the song was that the jealous party should look in a mirror, put on a pair of sunglasses and ask himself what he saw, and the answer was 'a frog, green with envy, wearing sunglasses'. I could relate to the lyrics in this song as they were quite appropriate to The Tyrannical Clown. I felt he was possibly jealous of me as I did my own thing without compulsion whereas his career had been governed by rules and regulations and his achievement of power which he had used and abused beyond belief. So we decided to make the front passenger a frog who Lily aptly named 'Defrogatory' as I had been forbidden to use 'defamatory' language. We made one more scarecrow, bought a frog mask and a huge pair of sunglasses, dressed him in black trousers and a white shirt, Lily's old school tie, a leather jacket and a pair of old slippers for feet. We sat him in the front passenger seat looking in the mirror of the sun visa and in case there was any doubt as to the identification of

Defrogatory we copied the song 'Big Weenie' onto a CD and sent it to The Tyrannical Clown at his office at the Highways Depot in Bexhill so he would know that the frog was himself.

Explaining to curious customers what the ugly things in the car were day after day became rather repetitive so I decided I would write a poem explaining who they were and what they were trying to do to my business. It did not take very long to write it and I wanted to incorporate East Sussex County Council initials into the title...

EXTREME SADDOS COCK-UP CAFES

Those saddos who we know so well it's time to tell their story
They think they're high and mighty and they wallow in their glory.
But the truth is far from that you know they're really cruel and wicked
So much so in fact you'll see their minds are quite insipid.
They prey on single ladies because they think we're meek and mild
Once they did just that and picked on a lady who was wild.
They did not know what they had done to the rebel that would unfold
This time they'd met their match ha ha....., for she was very bold.

The leader of the saddos' club was that infamous Tyrannical Clown
He was the meanest man of all and he wore a stupid crown.
He abused the power of his job and pretended he was tough

But really he was just a coward and full of straw and fluff.
Once he did a manly thing, just to get his kicks,
While the lady signed a form in court he moved to see her tits.
Kilkenny was the next in charge he was a bloody liar
He nicked her boards, denied it, then burnt them on a fire.
Judgement Jones who was skin and bones did threaten her with jail
Not just once or twice, oh no, it was weekly without fail.
And then there is Defrogatry, who the hell is he?
Don't know what he's doing here or where he's meant to be
He's green and has a sickly smirk and a very wrinkled frown
Is he that tyrant in disguise that crown adorning clown?

They tried to close her café down by taking all her signs
And when she put them back again she was given great big fines.
They took her to the county court an injunction was imposed
'You must not be abusive to these men who are your foes'
The judge continued hard and mean and then went on to say
'You must not put your café signs in or abutting the highway'
The lady sighed this was not good how will she survive?
If no one knows my café's here my business will not thrive.
So the choice I have is not so good and this is what is given
I end up going bankrupt or I serve a term in prison.

The lady asked how she could place a sign with their approval

The terms and conditions to do that were provided by a noodle.
To ask for application fees so huge it was a joke
How could that lady pay so much to that seemingly nice bloke?
So that idea was ditched alas, were they being straight?
The fee's the same if you want to build a fifty house estate.
And if indeed it was agreed and they allowed a sign of steel
If turned down by planning it could then go to appeal,
And that would cost another load of cash she hadn't got
It's never going to happen, at least not with this lot.

The lady thought of other ways how she could advertise
She wasn't really all that young but experience had made her wise.
A car would be a good idea with a sign on top
An arrow pointing down the road could lead people to her shop.
It wasn't really obvious that a café was down there
So she needed something else to make the people stop and stare.
A mega-structure that would be a very prominent sign
So a 20 foot air dancer was ordered then on line.

With 'CAFE OPEN' sewn up its front it was very very tall
And it was named after someone short that's why he's called 'Tall Paul'
To stand on the café's forecourt you'd think would be ok
Not a chance of that oh no, the threats arrived next day.
You cannot have that structure there it has a noisy fan

So with your A-board and that man they'll cause a traffic jam.
If someone in stiletto heels stamps their foot in anger
It could slice through the cable and blow up half of Camber.
It's far too high you need consent to advertise it there
And if you don't cooperate you'd better be aware
That off to court you'll go again to a prosecution charge
Remove the blow-up man right now you know he is too large.

One day soon a photo came of Paul flopped on the road
His arm and head were lying there that's what the photo showed
Spotted there from her upstairs we call her' that old hag'.
She's always spying down on us, I hate that sad old bag.
She only took a photo of the momentary lapse
When an untimely gust of wind had caused 'Tall Paul' to collapse.
The hag had sent the photo to that nasty bunch of men
In the hope that they will order her to go to court again!
She'll surely go to prison now she'd been told it very often,
If she does, I really hope that she'll never be forgotten.

So the moral of this story is do not dare loose heart
Face adversity full on and do it from the start.
Do not let the bullies win be firm and stand your ground
Keep on laughing all the time and happiness will abound.
If you find you're sad and down give yourself some time
Just think of them and what they've done and write it in a rhyme.

Don't give up, believe in you, this is all you need
Remember it's your life you live and you really can succeed.

I hastily added at the bottom of the page 'All the characters in this rhyme including myself are a figment of my imagination and do not relate to anyone we might know....apart from a various bunch of dodgy employees from East Sussex Highways Department both past and present....'

I printed the four pages, laminated them and spread them out on the parcel shelf in the back of the Peugeot to make sure every word was visible for anyone to read.

CHAPTER 36

The solicitor from Folkestone had not been in contact since he took my stuff to read but there was a huge amount of reading and like all my paperwork it was all in a muddle. I emailed him and asked him if he had had a chance to read any of it. He did reply saying he had not forgotten me but he had been busy with work as he was often called to the police station to deal with criminals who had been taken into custody, but he would read it by the end of the week and then come and see me. Kerry did not come to the café by the end of that week nor the end of the following week either so I forgot about him for the time being.

Despite Kilkenny claiming to have ceased any connection with my café signs since July 2009, a year on he was regularly seen taking photos of the car and the sign on the bike opposite the caravan park. Someone had even written on the large signpost at the top of Lydd road 'CAFE' with a large arrow pointing towards my café in black chalk pen and Kilkenny was seen photographing that as well!

Six weeks after I had received the letter from Mr Pasty the Planning- Enforcement Officer I still had not heard back from him to tell me when I was to go to the Town Hall in Bexhill to be interviewed on the legalities of 'Tall Paul', so I rang him again and asked when the interview was going to take place and he told me that his manager was still on holiday and would deal with it when he returned. Having sent me the riot act via a letter, and despite his concerns that I had committed an offence so serious the legal team were going to deal with it, his enthusiasm to do away with 'Tall Paul' appeared to have waned as he made one excuse after another that the interview he had requested with me was becoming more of an inconvenience than an urgent requisite.

So on good days Tall Paul was outside on the forecourt billowing in all directions surrounded by all our rubbish bins to stop him from bending into the road, probably to Beaky the old Hag's annoyance as I was sure she would be at the ready with her camera concealed behind the blind waiting for him to perform an inadvertent incline in the direction of the road.

August should have been the best month of the year for weather and business and despite all our efforts overcoming the restrictions forced upon me by the injunction order, we had managed to advertise the café without placing anything on or abutting the highway.

That entire summer holiday Camber was shrouded in a blanket of grey cloud, the sun never shone and most of the time we sat in the café twiddling our thumbs. Out of boredom I started to write poems about the Council employees, one of which was about the day I was interviewed under caution at Rye Police Station;

INTERVIEW UNDER CAUTION

It was in the Rye Police Station, a momentous hour and a half
I was summoned there by email from the nasty Highways staff
For the day they raided Camber which was a real shame
Of the twenty boards they found, it was me who got the blame.
Perhaps as they were all lime green and directing to Lydd Road
The perpetrator I encountered was ready to explode.
You know who I'm referring to he's prime subject in this book
And when you're bending over he moves to have a look.

On that day in August when I caught him in the act
He shouted and did threaten me with an ASBO, that's a fact.
So there I was in this room with a tape recorder going
I admitted that the boards were mine in the photos they
were showing,
I didn't think to deny it as I don't like telling lies
But he is not a friendly man and is one that I despise.
All of a sudden he made me cross; my hand went in my
pocket
In his direction missiles flew as fast as any rocket
Bunches of keys and dirty tissues my specs and mobile
phone
A deathly silence then ensued which was followed by a
groan,
He dived for cover behind his chair while his friend picked
up the mess
My mobile phone was in three bits and I don't know about
the rest.
His arm was bleeding, goodness me whatever had I done
I wondered momentarily if I should quickly run.
I told him I would throw no more he was safe to come back
out
But then I feared for my own life if he gave me a clout.
Afterwards the din died down and I apologised
He told me my behaviour should be analysed.
When I'd left the building and normality had returned
He was speaking to a copper, who had been quite
concerned,
He'd told him that he really had been fearful for his life
The copper reassured him and said 'she could have had a
knife'

And being as he was ok he surely should forgive
But he replied insisting I was a force to reckon with
Time passed on, the boards went up and quickly they were
taken
I didn't put so many out so some signage was forsaken.
Then one day an envelope came from Judgement Jones to
me
This could only mean one thing, a summons probably
Yes it was and yes I went to answer allegations
To three old wrinkled women who looked like dead
crustaceans.
I lost was fined and got their costs and was found
completely guilty
The only word that rhymes with that I can't write as it's
filthy!

Then I metamorphosed Rag-Eme-Kale's email justifying why I should not screw a café sign onto a BT pole.

REASONS NOT TO USE BT POLES

BT poles are assets which belong to Open Reach
Designed to carry wires on which enable us to speak
To one another on our phones or on the internet
To replace a cafe sign on one will not be happening yet.
Because;
It isn't very clear if the extra weight will hinder
The tall and fragile state of the type of BT timber
And also undertaking to consider the wind load
A flat board being secured by me might fall into the road.
The fixings as in nails or screws which have no calculations

Or guarantee to keep at bay an invasion of infestations.
Also holes in timber poles could damage treated layers
On the outside of the pole which would burden the defrayers.
So if a cafe sign was zapped back onto this structure
The shape and weight and screw size could cause a massive rupture.
So BT's finest asset will have no 'café open' board
Unless there's some progression of reaching an accord,
Like express consent from them and my liability insurance
And even if I had all that there would be no assurance
That I could zap my café signs back on that BT pole,
So I'll buy some concrete, get a spade and dig my own damn hole
And plant a scaffold pole myself to attach my café sign
In bright lime green as usual so people know they're mine.
I did have BT's permission in writing for my defence
Guess who sent a letter saying they were committing an offence!

Lily and I continued our night time excursions collecting remote business signs that Kilkenny had missed. In all we must have deposited at least thirty-five more signs outside of the highway depot in batches of seven in Bexhill. Did they know it was us I wondered and did they return them to their rightful owners? We were always taking the remote pub signs and quite often they were identical to some we had already taken to the highways depot. Despite me sending photos of the pub signs to Rag-Eme-Kale he took no notice and he ignored the two signs up the road advertising fish and chips and hot food from the kiosk in the council car park.

Things were getting so difficult it gave me a good excuse

why I could not send much money to Judgement Jones so I told him;

Dear Judgement Jones
I'm sorry but I can only send you a fiver this month as I have more money going out than has come into my business. I have to give the council £70 to pay for my alcohol licence this month so with that and £80 for my business rates and another £80 for my domestic rates I will actually be giving the council £235 so you can't moan about that.
The weather is crap, Camber is empty and so is my cafe. Instead of trying to close businesses down why doesn't the council try and do something constructive to give the tourist trade a boost in Camber? No chance of that happening of course, that would be too sensible.
If business doesn't improve soon, the rate I'm paying off this blimmin' debt, your colleagues will be residing in nursing homes wearing bibs and incontinence pads before I've finished paying it!!
Imagine that......... Ha-ha!!!!
Sally

Needless to say I received a letter from Judgement Jones in response to the menial £5 I had sent him, he said;

Dear Sally,
Re: Injunction Order dated 1st April 2010
Thank you for your letter. My understanding is that you only have £50 to pay towards the costs of the criminal proceedings. In respect of the costs owed to the Council from the civil injunction action, you have so far paid £100 and a further £2400 is outstanding. This is not satisfactory because

of the current rate of progress it will take you six years to comply with the order.

I am informed by the Brighton Fines Office that you have an instalment plan in operation whereby you make regular payments of £50 a month The last payment is due this month If you are able to conform to this arrangement, why can you not treat the Council in the same way?

Can I suggest that as from September, you agree to an instalment plan whereby you pay the Council £100 a month until the sum is fully repaid? After the end of August, you will have an extra £50 to add to the civil debt.

This matter is not going to go away, and the Council reserves the right to take legal action to enforce the debt. I look forward to hearing your revised plans for paying off your debt.

Yours sincerely

Judgement Jones

The hypocrisy of it, he had contacted the fines office in Brighton and was now telling me that I had been paying £50 a month regularly after accusing me at the court case in April of refusing to pay it despite me saying three times that I had been paying it, and by direct debit.

I answered his letter;

Dear Judgement Jones

Thank you for your letter.

I never got an injunction order on April 1st 2010, I suggest that you get your facts right first, it was 14th April.

Well I may only have £50 left to pay towards the costs of the criminal proceedings but unfortunately I then have to pay a blimmin fine of £1200 at £50 a month which is going to take another two years.

If you wanted your costs to be paid quickly you should have

picked on someone with no financial difficulties and not an impoverished, timid and defenceless single old lady like myself. I have a right to earn a living and because of what you people are doing to my financial situation you will have to wait your turn before I can even consider paying you any more than I am at the moment....
I note that you have been in contact with that place in Brighton. It's a shame you did not take the initiative to contact them prior to my court case so you could have been aware of the amount I had paid off your costs instead of accusing me of refusing to pay anything.
So I will not be able to accede to your request. You can enforce legal action if you have to but it won't make me any richer any quicker. Besides I now have to start saving for the rent for next January and if I manage that, I have to save for the rent for October which is only two months away....
So the answer to your question is that you are going to have to wait......a long time
Sally

September was as bad as August and I could only manage to send £10 to Judgement Jones,

Dear Judgement Jones
Here is £10 for you to put towards my debt but not till December 2010. It will all be downhill now as the season that never started has come to an abrupt end. From now on I will only be able to send you not much. But if I get through this winter in about 7 months from now it will be April and I can hopefully resume advertising my cafe properly again without it being cocked-up for me.
Has Kilkenny been prosecuted yet for wilfully stating evidence about my cafe signs which he knew to be false? Does the

Head of Highways know about Kilkenny's false statement? He should do.
When I have paid you £1500 will you tell me please because until I have had proof and the answers to my questions about the invoices The Tyrannical Clown sent me for removing my cafe signs I'm not going to pay the £1000 which, if were true, should be £1045!
Have a nice day
Sally

The Head of Highways name had popped up on all the court bundles that I had received and from what it appeared, they had to request his permission to prosecute me which he had obviously given. I wanted to know if he was aware that Kilkenny had written falsifications in his witness statement and maybe he should give his permission for Kilkenny to be prosecuted for perjury, although the way these people conducted themselves I expected this guy's morals were no different from the others.

I had been looking to see if I could find any of the ESCC employees on Facebook, a universal social networking site, subscribe to by millions of people. In fact I found quite a few names I recognised. Sometimes people left their face book pages wide open for all to see including the Head of Highways. As I read his posts and looked at his photos it soon became clear he was arrogant and self-centred; his life was all about him, what he ate, where and when he went shopping, what he bought himself. He had posted a photo of a brand new car stating that he had only gone to the garage to buy a windscreen wiper and had come out with a brand new car. He spent his winter holiday skiing in the Alps. He had gone to a leaving do for a colleague and referred to the older members of staff as 'old crusties'. He sounded a horrible man full of his own self-importance. I already disliked him but after reading his Facebook I disliked him intensely and now I had seen what he looked like I had an idea for another effigy to put in the car with the other nasties, but I had no name for him nor had I ever had contact with him, as he had not attended any of the court cases he had given his permission for. I kept a close watch on his Facebook page to see what he got up to.

CHAPTER 37

The summer holiday was coming to an end and there was nothing much going on in the café and so I suddenly had an idea. It was time to make another effigy to go in the Peugeot and this time it would be female. We modelled Highway Hen on me; she had the head of a rooster with white spiky hair, a pink leotard to hold her body together and a 34 DD bra stuffed with newspaper to give her a voluptuous buxomness. She wore a little red rah-rah skirt with a pair of black French knickers underneath, round her shoulders she wore an orange cape with a high collar made of orange feathers and we wrapped a yellow feather boa round her neck. I had to go to the harbour in Rye to find her legs which was a sixteen foot length of thick rope threaded through the crutch of her knickers with big fluffy yellow mop heads for feet. She was a right cracker and sat majestically in the driver's seat of the Peugeot.

Lily had gone back to school and I was working on my own again. The café was still quiet and not likely to pick up now, so with the winter fast approaching I did not hold out much hope of the business surviving through to the following year. I carried on regardless, juggling the little bit of money the café was taking to pay the bills. The rent was the biggest commitment; it was so much money to find but I had agreed to it in 2007 so I had to honour that agreement. As the bills stacked up, the turnover went down and I was starting to feel dejected until one morning the lady from Hastings County Court walked in with another letter from Judgement Jones. I wanted to know why he could not send his letters in the normal way, why did his correspondence have to be hand-delivered? I liked the lady from the Court and I offered her a cup of tea. She said she would like a bacon sandwich as well but she dared not under the circumstances in that she was delivering Judgement Jones letter. She did not stay long, just enough time to put the large white envelope into my hand, and after she had left I opened the letter;

Dear Miss Pattinson
Injunction Order dated 9th April 2010,
It has come to the Councils attention that you have repeatedly breached the terms of your injunction that forbids you from placing unauthorised signs on the highway and from using foul or abusive language or threatening or defamatory behaviour towards Council staff.
If you continually breach the terms of your injunction, the Council will have no option but to apply to the court to have you committed to prison for the contempt you have shown the court. The judge has the power to sentence you to a term of immediate imprisonment.
In order to avoid this I will ask you to do the following:
Stop placing signs on the highway without Council consent.
Stop sending abusive emails to Council staff.
Remove any signs you still have placed on the highway. This includes, but is not limited to the bike, the sign outside your café (placed on the road) and Tall Paul. As long as all these signs are clearly removed from the highway, no further action will be taken.
I hope we can avoid making a court application, but one further breach of your Order and we will have no hesitation in applying for your committal to prison.
Yours sincerely
Judgement Jones

That raised my spirits, so on the strength of Judgement Jones threatening letter I decided it was time to give Kerry a ring. I told him of the letter I had just received from

Judgement Jones and he said he would come and see me before the end of the week. This time he kept to his word and two days later he came to see me in the café. He had lost a huge amount of weight and I hardly recognised him. I mentioned about his weight loss and he opened his jacket and tugged on the surplus fabric of his shirt and said he had lost three stone. He did return all my paperwork and said he had read all of the documentation, letters and emails and he would write to Judgement Jones and ask for the information that I had previously requested regarding the initial complaint service ticket, the name of the person who had supposedly taken photos of my café signs on 7th October 2009 and the information I had asked for several times about The Tyrannical Clown's spurious invoices. He said he would take photos of other business signs and send them to Judgement Jones and ask him to explain why these businesses had not been ordered to apply for advertisement consent.

I felt a great sense of relief that at last someone actually believed that I was being unfairly treated by the Council and it appeared that Kerry was going to deal with them and hopefully put a stop to the harassment towards me.

A couple of days later he emailed drafts of the letters he had prepared - two for me, one of which confirmed that I had instructed his company to assist me in the capacity of 'business consultants'. I noticed that Kerry referred to himself as 'we', and thought it was a bit strange as the heading on his writing paper appeared to be his private home address and he had told me he worked in a solicitor's in Folkestone. There was also a copy of their Terms of Business and drafted letter for Judgement Jones for my approval. He said he intended coming to Camber later that day at 14.00 to prepare a full proof of evidence to include photographing other offending signs in support of my dispute.

He strongly advised me not to correspond with any persons

involved in this dispute during their tenure. He reminded me that there was a Court Order in place and if I breached the contents of that order I might find myself back in Court 'to show cause' why I should not go to prison.

He ended the draft letter by telling me he would see me later that day.

I read the short draft letter he had written to Judgement Jones;

Dear Sir

We have been instructed to act in the capacity of 'Business Consultants' and enclose herewith a Letter of Authority confirming our appointment.

We have read a copy of your letter dated 6th September 2010 and request that you suspend any further action until we have had the opportunity of taking our client's further instructions.

Yours sincerely

Kerry arrived at 2pm as he said he would, and I was pleased to see him as I felt I had been rescued. He was kind and caring and I trusted him. We discussed a lot of the current issues and the most recent letter that Judgement Jones had sent me, and after we had talked for about an hour we went out in my car for Kerry to take photos of other business signs. I knew all the places where the signs were located and I drove from Camber through remote villages as far as St. Leonards and back through Fairlight and Winchelsea Beach. Kerry must have taken at least twenty-five to thirty photos of all the business signs I showed him which were on the highway and outside of the businesses. All the signs Kerry took photos of were on or abutting the highway. Some were remote and some were attached to street furniture, all in similar situations that the Council had forbidden me to place mine.

We arrived back in Camber a good hour and a half later,

and Kerry promised me that he would send the photos he had taken as soon as he could and then he would set about compiling a file of evidence to make a formal complaint against The Tyrannical Clown, Kilkenny and Judgement Jones.

The next day I received an email from Kerry;

We write further to our meeting on the 14th September 2010. We suggest that you do not place any advertising boards, save for the vehicle, on the public highway for the time being, especially while we are requesting information from Judgement Jones.

As you will see by our letters, we intend to investigate this matter in depth, we have requested he suspend any action, but he will sense that we are probing for information to support a complaint and/or to challenge the authenticity of the injunction and/or costs awarded against you at Court.

We look forward to seeing you later today.

Yours truly,

He had attached two more draft letters for Judgement Jones; the first one asked;

Dear Sir

Would you please disclose the details of the persons who took the pictures on the 27th October 2009 (set 2) as we cannot ascertain with any accuracy by the court documents who supported this evidence during the Court hearing.

We can confirm that the Letter of Authority has been sent to you by first class post, please confirm receipt.

Yours faithfully,

And the second letter asked;

Dear Sir

Would you please supply a breakdown of the invoices which you relied upon at Court when a successful application for costs was sought?

We would like disclosure of the contractors' name, sight of time sheets and/or any other recorded information/documentation which assisted the preparation of the invoices. We understand that the client has made previous requests for this information without any success.

We can confirm that the Letter of Authority has been sent to you by first class post, please confirm receipt.

Yours sincerely

The next day I received another email with attachments from Kerry;

We refer to our meeting on the 14th September 2010 and confirm our next appointment is on the 15th September 2010 at 14.00 hrs as arranged.

In relation to our meeting on the 14th, we enclose herewith a copy of the proof for your perusal and signature. You will appreciate that this document needs to be expanded in due course; however, we feel that we should exhaust all the issues raised first before any further instructions are obtained from you.

The issues that have been raised so far.........

Letter from Landlady Beaky the old Hag – need to see copy of lease.

Obtain evidence that Beaky the old Hag placed an A-board on the road for many years

Obtain a statement from the previous lease holder also confirming she placed an A-board on the road for many years.

Request further and better details from Judgement Jones in relation to invoices.
Need confirmation from Judgement Jones to confirm who actually took set 1 of the pictures which was mentioned during the court hearing.
Obtain the Court notes from the hearing for the injunctions. In relation to 1. above, the writer has seen a copy of the previous tenants lease and there is a clause therein which states that permission has to be obtained by the Landlord for any advertisement boards on the front, but refusal has to be in reasonable circumstances, it is the writers opinion that she would win any fight due to the noise and size of the Tall Man; we suggest that we ignore her letter for the time being. We have sent another letter to Judgement Jones, copy attached for your consideration, let's see if he replies? Once we have dealt with the above matters, we can then expand the Proof. We look forward to seeing you later today.

His last attachment to me was for the costs for the visit he had made the previous day and the attached correspondence; Attendance, travel, mileage and letters that he had told me to print and send to Judgement Jones by recorded delivery amounted to £366 for 5 hours work, although I had to pay the cost of the postage. I did not know where I was going to find the money to pay Kerry. I had told him that I did not have any money but he had said not to worry about it but I did not want to end up with a huge bill. I had been saving the rent as usual so I would have to take some money from that to pay him something. I decided I would give him £200 to start with.

I did not want him involving that old Hag and I certainly did not expect her to give me any support so he could forget that particular line of enquiry. I was not really happy with him contacting the lady I had bought the café from either. I had already produced witness statements from various residents in

Camber who knew that there had always been signs at the top of Lydd Road, so I did not know why he needed to involve any other people especially as the Judge had not even bothered looking at them.

I was quite impressed with Kerry's determination though and I was confident that he would right the wrong-doings of the Council's employees; he had a very low opinion of Judgement Jones and claimed he could get him the sack. I was not sure that I wanted him to get the sack; I was not out for revenge, I just wanted to be able to advertise my café without all the aggravation, although Kilkenny and The Tyrannical Clown probably deserved some kind of retribution for the perjury they had committed and lies they had told.

Kerry did pop into the café later that day with three letters for me to address and send to Judgement Jones. I offered Kerry a cup tea and just as I had made it his phone rang and after a few moments he said he had to rush off to Folkestone Police station as there had been a murder and he was needed at the station as the duty solicitor. So off he went saying he would be sending me a portfolio of the photos he had taken the other day and we would send them to Judgement Jones.

That evening I watched the local news on television intensively to hear about the murder Kerry had gone off to in such a hurry, but nothing was mentioned about it that evening or the next.

CHAPTER 38

Jenny, my friend from Rye who had tried to acquire an 'Express Consent' form from The Tyrannical Clown a few months previously, had a friend called Lesley who I had occasion to meet when she and Jenny had come for the evening at The New Beach Club when I worked there. Jenny had told me that Lesley had grave concerns about a woman who had been appointed as executor to Lesley's Auntie's estate but Lesley had reason to believe that this woman was involved deviously with the acting solicitor for her Auntie's Will and they had both committed serious professional misconduct. After three years Lesley was still waiting for the 'Probate' to be finalised and she had also discovered that there were huge amounts of shares that the solicitor had failed to disclose. Kerry had told me that he had in the past practised private investigations so Lesley thought it might be a good idea to talk to him about the possibility of him investigating this woman, so on Kerry's next visit I explained to him that Lesley would like to speak with him and gave him Lesley's phone number for him to contact her, which he did, and they discussed the possibilities of seeking the information that Lesley required.

Kerry worked some very strange hours. When he emailed me it was always between three and four o'clock in the morning. The day after he had come to the café and rushed off again, he emailed me an itemised list of things he intended to do to gather evidence against the council.

Firstly he wanted to interview the lady I had bought the lease from and obtain a statement from her.

I did not want to involve her as she had sold the lease to me because she wanted to get away from the café, so I did not imagine she would be willing to give a statement to Kerry, but

I did not know where she lived so I was hoping that Kerry would not go looking for her.

He would write to Hastings County Court and asked to see the Court notes from the Court case on April 9th 2010, and contact The Tyrannical Clown's employers about the phone call he made to me on 9th September 2009.

He needed to read all the paperwork and provide an evidence analysis report, and interview and obtain formal statements from all the witnesses who had already supplied them for me at the Court hearing to confirm that a café sign had been at the top of the road since the café first opened in 1984.

He said that there was a lot of work to be done and so before we progressed the case any further it was best to cover all the issues highlighted before addressing any other new issues at this stage.

What I did not like was he strongly advised me not to display any advertisement boards that would breach the injunction as I was risking being committed to custody and he urged me to remove the bike opposite the caravan park, but I did not want to as the sign was on the bike, not on or abutting the highway.

He said he was going to investigate the matter thoroughly with the view to seeing whether they could file a formal complaint in relation to Judgement Jones, The Tyrannical Clown, Rag-Eme-Kale and Kilkenny and to see whether there were any grounds to overturn the injunction and to evaluate whether the actions of all parties amounted to victimisation or harassment by bullying.

He warned me that all the work to be done would be a time consuming exercise and through taking court action, I would incur costs which might not be recoverable.

Then, as if he had had an afterthought, there was another email referring to his visit of the previous day saying he had uploaded images of the business signs to the computer, copied the set of original images to 2 CD's and sent me a copy via email to index.

He had re-sent the letter to Judgement Jones requesting information about the photos they claimed were taken on 22nd 2009.

He made reference to issues raised during our meeting on the 14th which included writing a letter to the landlady Beaky the old Hag because he needed to see a copy of the lease and obtain evidence that she also placed an A-board on the road for the eleven years she ran the café.

He had already written two letters to Judgement Jones but to date he had not replied, so Kerry said he was going to write again requesting better details in relation to the spurious invoices from The Tyrannical Clown and he needed confirmation from Judgement Jones as to who actually took the photos taken on 22nd September 2009 in 'set 1'.

Finally he would obtain the Court notes from the hearing for the injunctions.

He said that in relation to our meeting on 15th September 2010, save for the pictures taken, these issues would be dealt with later.

I was very impressed with everything Kerry was doing to help me, though I was worrying how much it was all going to cost. I had given him another £200 which made £400 altogether. He was coming to see me two or three times a week, but quite often during his visits he spent a lot of the time on his mobile phone or using my computer for his other job. He explained that his own company dealt with matters like mine and investigations were done in his spare time and were not part of his full time job, so he had to juggle his time between the two.

After he had written again to Judgement Jones he received a reply:

Dear Sir

Thank you for your letters. Firstly my clients are not prepared to suspend further action. My colleagues have had to endure weekly emails and letters from your client which were constantly abusive and have accused me of being a liar and have described my colleagues of being corrupt and in one case a thief and a liar. In the ten days since your client received my letter she has accused a member of Council's staff of falsifying a statement and asking for him to be prosecuted. In addition an effigy of a lawyer and Council staff had been constructed which have been found in the back of a car on which one of her café signs has been placed. So as I am sure you can appreciate that it would not be appropriate to suspend any action in these circumstances.

In relation to your second letter, I do not intend to supply you with the invoices you have requested. The money to which you refer was subject to a Court Order. The Court had ordered your client to pay the Council £2500 and this supersedes any invoices, and as your client did not appeal or challenge the Court Order she is committing contempt of court by not complying with it.

The Council therefore is perfectly entitled to enter judgement against her and instruct bailiffs to seize her goods if considered appropriate. Your client always insists that she is too poor financially to satisfy the debt and is only able to pay the Council around £10 a month The fact that presumably she has sufficient funds to pay for your services is something that the Council will take into consideration when considering what action to take.

Yours faithfully

Judgement Jones

Kerry responded to Judgement Jones letter;

Dear Sir

We thank you for your 'cogent' letter dated the 17 September 2010.

We are trying to placate the situation, and have been reassured by our client that no correspondence has been sent to you, your clients and/or your colleagues since our intervention on 14th September 2010. We therefore repeat our request and ask that you stay any action for the time being; if you ignore this genuine plea to avert costs then this letter will be adduced at court. While on the subject, should it be necessary, the writer will be applying to the court to act as her 'McKenzie Friend'.

We fully understand the powers of an injunction and/or an order imposed by a Court, and the appeal procedure. We fully appreciate that the client has made various admissions to various allegations in various courts in the past and we do not seek to defend her actions thus far as lawful, in your own words 'superseded by an Injunction'.

That said, we are commissioned, inter alia, to thoroughly investigate the whole affair as the client feels that, at the very least, she has been victimised and that certain parties may have failed in their Duty of Care. We cannot comment on any of the client's actions prior to 14th September 2010. What we can say is, the client does have certain rights whether convicted or not?

It is noteworthy, that at no time in your letters to the client did you ever advise her to seek independent legal advice on a matter that is so serious she could be incarcerated. To suggest that the client should not ask for help for financial reasons is wrong.

We will write to you in the next few days requesting information to assist our enquiries. Should you continue to refuse then we will consider other options to obtain disclosure.
Yours faithfully

What was a Mackenzie friend?

I phoned Kerry and asked him what he had meant by saying he would be my 'Mackenzie Friend'. He explained that as Judgement Jones had mentioned that I was always pleading poverty it would appear in my favour if he came to court with me as my Mackenzie Friend as it would not cost me anything. He would do that free of charge as there was no fee for that service, but if he came to court as my lawyer then that could be quite costly. I asked him how therefore I was meant to present the evidence he had been gathering, and he assured me that he would be whispering to me telling me what I should be doing. The situation was becoming slightly discouraging. I thought Kerry was going to make meat-balls of Judgement Jones and his clients but it now appeared that I would be having to do it on the strength of Kerry's evidence and whispers, but on the other hand I knew I could not afford solicitors fees as well as pay for the investigation Kerry was doing, so maybe it was for the best.

A couple of days later I received another email from Kerry with attached statements and covering letters from various residents he had interviewed in Camber. He told me to print them and get the appropriate people to sign and date the documents. He also said he was preparing an album of photos for Judgement Jones and his clients to comment on. He had written a letter to Hastings County Court as well.

24 September 2010
Dear Sirs,

RE:East Sussex County Council v Sally Ann-Pattinson – OHS00231

We act in the capacity of 'Business Consultants' and enclose herewith a letter of authority confirming the appointment.

Would you please supply us, on behalf of the defendant, the judges notes, and/or open correspondence (letters) from Judgement Jones Litigant Solicitor for the Claimant's which relate to the hearing adjourned on 15th March 2010, and the hearing on the 9th April 2010 when the court considered the application.
Yours truly,

Over the next two weeks Kerry arranged to meet and interview the people who had provided statements for me when I had gone to court earlier in April. I did not really see the point of him doing that as I already had statements from them and annoyingly he had managed to locate the lady I had bought the lease from. I so did not want to involve her in this matter but Kerry did and he got a statement from her too saying that she had placed an A-board at the top of Lydd Road when she had occupied the café as had Beaky the old Hag and Bodger.

Kerry also had a reply from Hastings County Court saying they would not allow him the information he had asked for, and he said he thought that Judgement Jones had something to do with their response.

Against my better judgement Kerry eventually persuaded me to remove the bike from opposite the caravan park. I did not want to because in my opinion the café sign was on the bike it was not on or abutting the highway. The bike was not even on the highway as it was more than a metre away from the curb, but I did remove it and I knew that I would lose business through it not being there. As soon as I told Kerry the bike was no longer attached to the scaffold pole he wrote to

Judgement Jones to tell him. I got the feeling that Kerry just wanted to appear to have some kind of influence over me and show that he had succeeded where the Council had failed. He wrote:

Dear Sir
We write further to our letter dated 18th September 2010.
We have been instructed by our client that she has removed the bicycle and board attached thereto.
We aver that this action demonstrates a turning point in this whole catastrophic breakdown.
This letter remains open in relation to costs and mitigation should an application for an order of committal be sought by your clients.
Yours faithfully

He also sent a letter and several photos of signs attached to other BT poles to the Central Operations Manager who had given me permission to attach my café signs onto the BT pole and then rescinded his permission after Judgement Jones had terrified him by threatening legal action for aiding and abetting in a criminal offence. He wrote:

Dear Sir
We act in the capacity of business consultant for our client Sally-Ann Pattinson and enclose herewith a letter of authority.
We have also read a copy of your email to our client dated 30th March 2010 – 16.57hrs.
We enclose herewith a selection of pictures taken on the 20th September 2010 by the writer in the East Sussex jurisdiction.
Would you please advise why these signs have approval as opposed to our client's sign which has been refused and

removed at her cost, notwithstanding the fact that you gave
her full permission?
This letter has been sent by first class post with a copy of the
letter of authority.
Yours truly

The Operations Manager did not respond to Kerry's letter and I was really not surprised as he must have had far more important issues to deal with than having to answer to Kerry why I could not stick my café signs on his pole.

CHAPTER 39

In due course Kerry received another letter from Judgement
Jones:

Dear Sir

*Please will you confirm the basis on which you are acting on
behalf of your client? When court proceedings eventually take
place I presume you are aware of the limitations of acting as
a 'McKenzie Friend' that is assuming the court even grants
your application. You would not be entitled to act on Sally's
behalf, address the court or examine any witnesses.
Furthermore you are forbidden from managing her case or
acting as her agent. Your letters appear to be effectively
constructing a case which you are not entitled to do, you will
be restricted to 'quietly' giving advice on points of the law and
providing assistance only.*

*Although confirming that the bike has been removed there are
various other advertising boards still in place. As a result of
these continuing and flagrant breaches of the injunction, the
Council will be issuing proceedings very shortly. I anticipate
that your client will be receiving a court summons to answer
an application for committal to prison very shortly.*

Yours sincerely

Judgement Jones

I was beginning to have doubts about Kerry's status in the
legal system. I had believed he was a lawyer but now I was
not so sure as Judgement Jones letter implied he was not. I
was becoming quite concerned with the impending prospect
of being slung into prison and as it looked at the moment I

had no one to represent me.

Kerry turned up with an album of the photos he had taken of other business signs and told me to send it to Judgement Jones by recorded delivery. He said I needed to find a solicitor quickly, and when I told him I could not afford one he said he would find a solicitor and I could apply for legal aid or possibly my café insurance might cover legal costs, so I could claim the money back. I asked him why he had changed his mind about representing me and was it because of my lack of finances? He surprised me by saying it was not the usual thing he dealt with as he worked as a duty solicitor at the Police station and was more suited to dealing with murderers than fly-posters, but he assured me he would accompany me to the first appointment with the solicitor to present his evidence against the Council and he could work alongside the solicitor to a certain extent.

I searched on the internet for solicitors in the area whilst Kerry was ringing them on my mobile phone but none were prepared to take any case involving legal aid. Eventually there was one solicitor in Tunbridge Wells who agreed to take on my case, so an appointment was made. Kerry had said before that he would come with me to the solicitors with the evidence he had prepared, and I wanted to ask him if we would travel to Tunbridge Wells in my car or his, but he left before I had a chance to ask him.

I got a text from Kerry the next day saying he would not be able to come over as he was in the Police Station and had been there all night with a client who had been charged with murder. I understood that, and that evening I watched the local news to hear about the murder in Folkestone but there was no mention of it that night or the next or ever.

Kerry did email me the copy of a letter he had written to Judgement Jones;

Dear Sir,

We write further to our letter dated 1ˢᵗ October 2010.

We urgently need your direction in relation to whom we send correspondence to in the future?

In the meantime we have sent to you an album of pictures and statements in support of deemed consent, both under separate cover.

We make it abundantly clear that this correspondence is in support of our appointment as business consultants to re-establish the client's fundamental right to advertise, the pictures and/or the statements are in no way connected with any Court proceedings or indeed constructing a case in those proceedings; we are not attempting to act as solicitors, agents or legal representatives, we act as business consultants and lead by way of correspondence on behalf of the client – no more and no less.

Yours sincerely

He also sent me an email;

Dear Sally,

I write further to our meeting last week when I attended on a pro bona basis. As you are aware the purpose of my visit was to explain my theory about the injunction.

Ironically, Judgement Jones did advise you by email that committal papers have been lodged with the Hastings County Court so you should expect service shortly.

In the meantime I have hopefully secured the services of a solicitor in Tunbridge Wells; I have sent him an email outlining the case. I will endeavour to return your original papers in the next few days as I am sure he will need to see them.

It is imperative that you are legally represented at court.

Please pursue the insurance option just in case there are

problems with Legal Aid. I have considered being your Mackenzie Friend as the last resort; however, it is very limited as to what involvement or role I can play so it is important that you have a solicitor on the day.

I strongly recommend that you remove any advertising signs which are unlawful at this stage and do not correspond (only via your solicitors) with Judgement Jones and/or any staff member now that formal proceedings have been filed.

I am going to be out of action for the rest of the week, but keep me informed by text or email; we can meet after the committal hearing has been dealt with to see if you still wish me to act for you as a business consultant with the view to secure you lawful advertisings rights and to see whether it is worth pursuing any formal complaints

I will prepare an interim bill at some stage, but I fully understand your position at the moment in regards to payment. What is more important is that you are legally represented at Court even if you have to pay by credit card.

Yours truly,

After reading that and looking up what *'pro bona'* meant (free of charge) I had a feeling the rest of it might have to be *'pro bona'*

CHAPTER 40

Kerry did return my paperwork which he had sorted and put neatly into a folder for the solicitor but annoyingly he had highlighted some bits of it in fluorescent yellow and written really unimportant stuff in between the paragraphs like 'made a confession' or 'admission' unnecessary remarks which had just defaced the paper and I would have preferred it if he had not written on it at all. He apologised for not being able to accompany me but he was needed at the police station as there had been yet another murder.

I left Lily to run the café for me the day I went to Tunbridge Wells to see the solicitor. It took roughly three quarters of an hour to get there and I parked in the main car park at the top of a steep hill right in the town centre. Just as I was getting out of my car Lily rang me to say that the lady from the court had turned up with a court bundle for me and she wanted to know what time I'd be back in Camber. I asked why the lady could not leave it with Lily in the café to save her having to come back again, Lily asked her but the reply was she had to physically put the bundle into my hands. I told Lily to tell her to come back at six o'clock as I should be home by then.

My appointment was for three o'clock. I walked the short distance to the solicitor's office and arrived in good time. I had to climb five flights of stairs to reach his office. He had received an email from Kerry explaining the situation. Before anything was to be discussed I had to fill in the application form for legal aid, as there was no point in going into great depths of what had been going on until the solicitor was certain he was going to be paid for his services. So the free hour the solicitor had kindly offered me was spent answering questions about my financial circumstances, and he said there was no point in him keeping the paperwork Kerry had prepared which I had brought for him as there would be no point at this stage looking at it until I was guaranteed legal aid. I quite understood, but he did want me to send a copy of the Court bundle. I left the solicitors and drove back home none the wiser than when I had arrived there.

When I got home Lily had closed the café and gone home, and as I drove into Denham Way the lady from the court was waiting for me in her car. I parked up and went over to her, and apologised for her having to come to Camber twice that day but she said it didn't matter. She handed me the huge bundle. I was amazed at the volume of it, and when I got indoors I made myself a cup of tea and sat down to read it.

On the front page was the Application Notice to the court and it had been requested by Judgement Jones, Solicitor representing East Sussex County Council.

Judgement Jones had written;

ON 9TH APRIL 2010 AN INJUNCTION ORDER WAS MADE AGAINST THE DEFENDANT. IT WAS PERSONALLY SERVED ON HER ON THE FIRST OF MAY. A COPY OF THE ORDER AND STATEMENT OF PERSONAL SERVICE IS AFFIXED TO RAG-EME-KALE'S AFFIDAVIT AFFIXED HERETO.

THE DEFENDANT HAS REPEATEDLY BREACHED THE TERMS OF THE ORDER. THE ORDER MAKES IT CLEAR IF SHE DOES NOT OBEY THE ORDER SHE WILL BE GUILTY OF CONTEMPT OF COURT AND MAY BE SENT TO PRISON. THE CLAIMANT THEREFORE APPLIES TO HAVE HER COMMITTED TO PRISON.

The hearing was to last the entire day before a Circuit

Judge on 14th December 2010.

The bundle consisted of 137 pages, and included witness statements from Rag-Eme-Kale, Kilkenny, Judgement Jones, a Senior Maintenance Technician, Beaky the old hag and Bodger They had each made separate statements. There was no statement I noticed from The Tyrannical Clown which did not surprise me after the perjury he had committed the last time. I expect he had been told to keep a low profile.

It beggars belief that Beaky and Bodger had each written witness statements against me. I had paid them thousands of pounds in rent, providing them with their income, and spent a lot of money improving the café, yet they had the audacity to try and assist East Sussex County Council in committing me to prison.

I quickly rang Kerry and told him the date of the Court hearing and that the bundle had arrived. He said in that case he would write to the court telling them not to provide him with the information he had asked for. I did not see the purpose of him writing to the Court as they had already refused his request.

In the meantime I started to read the evidence against me. Bodger's statement was first;

He said I was arrogant in the way I flouted the law and he wanted to know how I was allowed to park a dirty car with a large sign on the roof which was clearly a distraction to motorists and in a dangerous position. The dirty car was parked there daily from 7.30am till 8pm. Furthermore there was a large sign attached to a bike opposite the caravan park at the other end of the village and further café signs outside the café which impede traffic.

On 27th July he had witnessed me put an A-board in the boot of my car and I had driven off, he pursued on his push bike to the junction of Lydd Road where he had seen that very same sign that he had seen me putting in the boot of my car now displayed on the grass at the road junction with the arrow pointing in the direction of the café. He took two photographs on that date, one which shows the A-board resting on the grass at the junction and the other of the black car which the defendant had used to transport the A-board and which was now parked in the place where the dirty car with a café sign on the roof was usually parked. The A-board is clearly on the Highway land and these two photographs he produced as his evidence B/1 and B/2.

Unfortunately he was going abroad on 14th September and would be unavailable to attend court for my committal to prison.

I did not know what to make of Bodger's statement, which was like evidence for a murder case, the A-board being the proverbial weapon and me being the main suspect unless he was confessing to being a stalker. If the council needed that kind of evidence to commit me to prison their evidence was going to have to be a darn sight better than Bodger's. I moved excitedly on to Beaky the old Hag's witness statement.

She claimed to have endured three years of inconveniences caused by me including the continual placing of A-boards outside the cafe on the forecourt which she had to move to get in and out of her premises. This she said had come to a head when the Defendant acquired a large red blow up figure which was operated by a fan and was located in the café car park below her window. She believed that the blow up man had been named after one of the managers in the Highways Department and called 'Tall Paul' and she estimated it was 15' high. The noise from the fan was constantly in operation all day long which prevented her from being able to open her windows.

By 2nd June 2010 she had had enough and made a complaint to Rother District Council. She had seen 'Tall Paul' on numerous occasions bend over into the road and that along with my A-board was making a hazard for the cars on the road. She followed up her action with a complaint to the Claimant and produced, signed and dated by herself, Exhibit BTOH/1, a photograph of 'Tall Paul' taken on 2nd June 2010 showing it bending into the road with the A-board clearly placed on the road.

She then produced signed and dated by herself Exhibits BTOH/ 2, 3 and 4, a further 3 photographs taken on 3rd June 2010 which clearly showed the A-board on the inside of the double yellow lines, but despite the evidence in her own photographs, she claimed that the A-board was on the road and of the difficulty experienced by cars when attempting to pass this obstruction.

She produced another Exhibit BTOH/5, a photo of 'Tall Paul' blowing in the wind on 14th June 2010.

She said she had made several complaints to Rother District Council but she had received no satisfaction. Again she contacted the Claimant and demanded that they or someone from Rother District should take action and responsibility for the removal of 'Tall Paul' and the A-board.

She produced Exhibits BTOH/6 and 7 again of 'Tall Paul' dancing in the wind.

She too mentioned my dirty car and the bike chained to a pole opposite the caravan park. She said she had been continually complaining to Rother District Planning Department and the Highways Department demanding that action must be taken against the Defendant. She produced more exhibits signed and dated by herself BTOH/8, 9 and 10, more photos of 'Tall Paul' in various positions.

On July 27th she witnessed the Defendant putting a colourful A-board with 'Camber Café Open' and a red arrow painted on it into the boot of her car, the Defendant drove off towards the junction and Mr Bodger followed in pursuit on his bicycle.

She produced signed and dated Exhibit BTOH/11 a photograph of an A-board outside the café blocking her access.

She also was not available to go to Court due to her vacation.

I hoped the judge would really pay attention to Beaky the old Hag's evidence. She claimed 'Tall Paul' was under her window but she also claimed he was in the road and he could not be in both places at the same time. The photos she produced showed the front of the forecourt including their access was at least 40 feet in width; she could easily get in and out of the premises. I laughed at the thought of Beaky the old Hag driving the Council mad with her phone calls and emails complaining about me.

Served them right!

The next witness statement was Rag-Eme-Kale's - a Highway Manager employed by the Claimant in the Transport and Environment Department. He reminded the judge that on April 9th 2010 an injunction order was made against me the Defendant. One of the conditions was that Sally-Ann Pattinson shall not use foul, abusive or defamatory language or engage in threatening behaviour towards any member of the Claimant's staff.

He said that from 9th April he had received regular emails from the Defendant on a variety of issues commencing on the 26th April 2010 when he received an email from the Defendant requesting to put the A-board back at the junction of Lydd Road and to re-attach signs to a telegraph pole. At the end of the email on 26th April at 09.09 the Defendant comments 'I wouldn't let him influence you too much as you might end up as corrupt as he is, not to mention 'un voleur et un sale menteur.'

He understood the French part of the sentence translates as

'a thief and a dirty liar'. The implication behind the sentence is that he will end up as corrupt as The Tyrannical Clown who is an employee of ESCC and he would argue that the statement is a breach of the injunction. The Defendant has a tendency to use abusive language in French.

He then produced his first exhibit, signed and dated by himself REK/1a, an email dated 26th March 2010 and sent to the Claimant's solicitor Judgement Jones in which she comments that 'half a day is quite a long time to decide if I can refer to council staff as a 'trou de cou et puis les sale branleur' which he believed translates into English as 'arseholes' and 'dirty wankers'.

He responded to the Defendant on the 28th April and she responded the same day at 19.29 which form part of his next exhibit REK/1. Most of the Defendants email regularly complains about The Tyrannical Clown. She effectively accuses him of lying on oath during the injunction proceedings and says the judge did not give her the chance to rebut his allegations. She comments that she did not like hearing lies being told about herself nor was she given the opportunity to prove that The Tyrannical Clown was lying and denying things he had previously said.

He then submitted that what I had written was defamatory language against The Tyrannical Clown which is in breach of the injunction.

He produced another exhibit, signed and dated REK/2, an email which makes it clear that the defendant has no intention of complying with the law if it involves submitting a fee to the Claimant. It is also provocative in that she intends to install a 'mega-structure' which she claims she does not need permission for. She comments 'so brace yourselves boys, it's huge ….ha-ha'. The mega-structure to which she refers is a giant inflatable structure which was erected outside her café shortly after this email was sent. The structure is named 'Tall

Paul' after one of the Claimants staff, The Tyrannical Clown.

The third signed and dated exhibit, REK/3, he produced was a chain of email correspondence from the Defendant to himself on 27th May. The Defendant had applied for a licence to erect a temporary poster to advertise a charitable event but he submitted that she was being deliberately vexatious by suggesting that the temporary event would last for three years. In an email sent at 11.42, the Defendant states 'Of course I'm being vague because if I tell you exactly what I am going to do you are going to say No'.

His signed and dated exhibit REK/4, a chain of emails on the 12th May which demonstrates that the Defendant is being vexatious by sending misleading information to the authority that is intended to waste their time and ratepayer's money. On 12th May the Defendant sent a photograph claiming that it was a sign attached to a highway street lighting column, but when the Licensing and Enforcement Officer (The Tyrannical Clown) had driven to the site, it was clearly demonstrated by the photograph that he took from a different angle that the sign was erected on a post in private land beyond the highway boundary.

He also produced exhibit REK/5, a letter from the Defendant sent to the East Sussex County Council's Transport and Environment's Complaints department on 10th August. In this letter addressed to himself the Defendant presumes he had acted unprofessionally stating 'you must have been having a laugh with me regarding that rigmarole you tried to get me to comply with' and then she proceeds to use foul language when describing other unlawful signs placed in the highway as 'made of crap material' and 'only a midges-dick from the road junction'. The Defendant ends her letter requesting to put a sign back onto the BT pole that had previously been refused.

His final exhibit REK/6, signed and dated by himself, was a chain of emails sent to their Legal Services Department where the Defendant implies that the Claimant's Solicitor is lying in relation to an email he had sent her which appeared to contradict advice given by the District Council. The Claimant's solicitor responded by warning the Defendant that an application to commit her to prison will be made if her behaviour continues. The Defendant's response triggers a debate over the meaning of the word 'defamatory' and concludes in a defiant and unapologetic tone. Therefore implying the Council's solicitor is lying is defamatory and a breach of the injunction.

The next witness statement was a mystery; it was from a man I was unfamiliar with whose name was Peter Plonker and his job title 'Senior Maintenance Technician, Reactive Maintenance, based at Sidley Depot, Bexhill and his area covers Camber East Sussex.

On Friday 10th September 2010 Peter Plonker was in Camber and photographed the following;

A motor vehicle with a café sign on top, this photograph produced as an exhibit PP1.

A rear view of the same motor vehicle showing the sign and the caricatures inside the car, this photograph produced as an exhibit PP2.

Further views of the caricatures in the car marked PP3.

A photograph of the board attached to a bicycle which is attached to street furniture is produced PP4.

A photograph of the café frontage showing the inflatable 'Tall Paul' and the A-board on the carriageway, this photograph is produced marked PP5.

Following on from Peter Plonker the Senior Maintenance Technician, there was a copy of the injunction order provided as part of Rag-Eme-Kale's Affidavit and a statement from the nice lady from the Court who had delivered the summons and letters from Judgement Jones. A copy of the letter Judgement Jones had sent me via the nice lady from the court and another statement from her saying she had delivered it.

Then there was Kilkenny's witness statement which contained exhibit after exhibit of emails and recorded telephone complaints from Beaky the old Hag and Bodger about a 'large tubular thing which is blown by wind and sticks into the sky and a café sign blocking her entrance.

Kilkenny had emailed the team of highways staff and the Council's solicitor to ask who was responsible for dealing with the 'blow up'. Judgement Jones had informed Kilkenny it was his responsibility but it did not answer the question of which way the 'blow up' might end up.

Another email suggesting that Judgement Jones wrote to me to remind me of the conditions of the injunction and the ramifications of breaching it.

Email after email, some from Beaky the old Hag and some from Bodger. Eventually Bodger had got a response from Kilkenny assuring him that at present they were doing everything in their power to put an end to this continual problem.

Beaky the old Hag had contacted them as a matter of urgency as she could not understand why she was not getting any assistance from the council. She was advised to seek legal advice.

Then Bodger had sent them multiple photos of the bicycle opposite the caravan park and the car being used to advertise Camber Café.

More complaining emails from Beaky the old Hag asking why my car and bicycle were still advertising Camber Café.

The complaint records from Beaky and Bodger to the Highways were made on a daily basis for weeks. Then one of the records said Bodger was prepared to give a statement to assist the Council in committing me to prison and he would attend the court if necessary.

Then Kilkenny had produced, signed and dated by himself,

exhibits KK1 to KK13, photos of my car, the bike and Tall Paul.

Beaky the old Hag and Bodger had produced photographic exhibits BTOH 1-11 and B 1-2.

Getting towards the end of the bundle were all of Rag-Eme-Kale's exhibits of my emails and letter and his responses and photographs.

Finally Peter Plonker, the Senior Maintenance Technician's photographs of the car, the effigies and the bike.

CHAPTER 41

One of the photos Beaky the old Hag had provided in her statement was that of two cars passing one another outside the café one day when Tall Paul was billowing in the wind. She claimed that one of the two cars had to stop to allow the other one to pass. I knew this was not the case and a photograph would only portray a static scene anyway, so her photo did not prove that either vehicle had to stop to give way to the other. As luck would have it one of the vehicles in the photo was the regular postman's van so at the soonest opportunity I was able to show him the photo and ask if Beaky the old Hag's account was correct. It was not and the postman told me that the narrowest part of Lydd Road was outside number 19 about 100 yards up the road where there was a telegraph pole on the edge of the road where it was narrower than any other part. He said he would write a witness statement that his car was not stationery at the time the photo was taken.

I was insulted by Rag-Eme-Kale's accusation saying I had purposely taken the photo of the fish sign at a certain angle to make it appear to be attached to the lamp post. Only The Tyrannical Clown would be devious enough to suggest that is what I had done. I knew that the sign had been attached to the lamp post and I wanted to go to the owner of the shop and ask him to make a witness statement to confirm this, but I was apprehensive as to how he would react when I would have to confess that it was me who brought it to the Council's attention in the first place. He used to have an A-board on the pavement but when I asked The Tyrannical Clown why he had not asked the fish shop owner to remove it Kilkenny had been sent to deal with it and it was after that visit the sign was put onto the lamp post.

After work the next day I went into Rye to have the bundle

photocopied to send to the solicitors in Tunbridge Wells but first I went to Lesley's to show her the bundle, and she was shocked and appalled at the amount of time the Council were wasting on such a trivial affair as a sign on a bike and a sign on a car when her road was full of neglected pot holes.

I asked her if she had got any further with her investigation into her Auntie's Will, and she said after sending Kerry a cheque for £50 he had got back to her giving her information that she already knew so it had been a total waste of time and money. I felt embarrassed as I had told her he would be able to help her but unfortunately I was wrong. I also realised although Kerry had written letters and taken photos and asked for statements he had actually not achieved anything I did not already have. He appeared to be more of a con man than a solicitor.

I collected the photocopied bundle for the solicitor and sent it by recorded delivery. It cost a fortune as it was so heavy, but I still did not think it would be looked at until the guarantee of legal aid had been confirmed.

It was imperative that I got a written statement from the owner of the fish shop and the only way I was going to achieve it was by going there and asking him to provide one for me. He was a jolly nice man and I explained why I had mentioned his A-board to the Highways and I had not complained about it I had just asked why it had been all right for his sign to be on the highway but it was not all right for mine. I apologised if I had caused him grief and assured him I had not intended to make any trouble for him. He said he remembered a Highways Inspector coming to his fish shop in May that year and telling him he must remove the A-board from its current position. That was the reason for attaching the new sign to the lamp post until the Highway Inspector returned and told him he could not have the sign on the lamp post either, so then they changed it to its current position.

I explained to him that I had to go to Court for committal to prison and I told him that Rag-Eme-Kale had accused me of taking the photo at an angle to make the sign appear to be attached to the lamp post. I asked him to write a statement as it would be vital evidence that they were lying and if I could prove at least one lie then maybe the judge would consider the possibility that the rest of their evidence might also be flawed. He told me to write the statement and he would sign it. I was so grateful to him; I thanked him and said I would come back in a few days with the statement ready for him to sign.

I was pleased that I was getting evidence from people who could prove that the accusations from Rag-Eme-Kale and Beaky the old Hag were false. I had got witness statements from residents who had lived in Camber for years who had remembered the previous owners having signs on the main road, then the postman and now the fish shop owner.

I emailed Kerry with the news that I had got a statement from the Fish shop owner, and he replied with a bizarre suggestion;

Hi Sally,
Well done - have you been granted Legal Aid yet?
I'm just about to order something using a credit card value
£295.00 if you paid for it I would knock double off your bill
i.e. £600.00
Food for thought.
Kerry

I told Kerry I was not in a position to use my credit card so I was not able to pay for his goods in lieu of part payment of his bill.

The next day I received another email from Kerry with two letters attached, one was to Judgement Jones;

Dear Sir,

We understand that an application for Civil Contempt of Court has been filed with the Hastings County Court. In those circumstances we suspend any requests for information until the hearing has been heard by a Circuit Judge. This will ensure that there is no misunderstanding in relation to our locus standi.

We are pleased to learn that proceedings have now been re-opened and a hearing has been listed for14th December 2010. This will afford the client the opportunity for disclosure under the CCR rules as there are various aspects of this case that need bringing to the Court's attention by her acting solicitors.

Yours sincerely

And the second attachment was to Hastings County Court;

Dear Sir,

We thank you for your compliment slip reply to our letter dated 4th October 2010.

We understand that there has been an application filed by the Claimant's Solicitor for Contempt of Court and a date has been listed. In those circumstances we feel it right and proper to withdrawn our request.

We have been instructed by Sally-Ann Pattinson as Business Consultants for the sole purpose of assisting the client in relation to advertising which obviously inter alia did link our duties to part of the Injunction order. We formally commenced working on behalf of the client on the 14th September 2010 and we are confident that the client did not infringe and/or breach any terms under the injunction since we were appointed.

We wrote to Judgement Jones Solicitor for the East Sussex County Council, making it clear to him from the outset our locus standi. We made it abundantly clear that we needed

time to absorb the facts and asked that he suspend any action whilst we attempt to resolve various issues. We ask for various items to be disclosed, but to-date we have not received any assistance from Judgement Jones save for a 'bully boy' approach accusing us of acting as her solicitors. We fully appreciate that the claimant is entitled to bring any breach to the Courts notice, however we would like this letter placed before the Circuit Judge on the day for consideration, if only to show that Sally-Ann Pattinson was addressing the problem on or after 14th September 2010.
Yours truly,

I no longer wanted Kerry writing these embarrassing letters that were getting me nowhere. The one and only time I was grateful to Judgement Jones was for making it abundantly clear that Kerry was neither Solicitor nor Mackenzie Friend. I did not understand why he had written to the Court asking for private information. Of course they were not going to give confidential information when he did not have any legal standing. Lesley had serious doubts about Kerry. We did wonder if he might have once been a solicitor and been struck off, as he was quite knowledgeable of the laws of the land. Lesley decided to check up on him to see if his name was on a list of struck off solicitors in 'Solicitors from Hell'. His name was not on the list but then she did see his name on a list of 'Solicitors Clerks from Hell'. It was him, and someone had written:

'Do not use this Clerk from Hell in Folkestone, I had all the evidence to prove my innocence and he did not use any of it and I lost my case thanks to this jerk.'

When she told me of her findings I was not surprised at all. The letters, photos and interviews Kerry had carried out had only been to impress and to justify his charges. I had given him £600, copious mugs of tea, toast and Kit-Kats, and let him use my mobile phone and computer for doing little more than I had already done myself.

CHAPTER 42

Winter arrived with a vengeance at the end of November 2010, with freezing conditions and snow, the like of which had not been seen since the severe winter of 1963. The café had no heating as it was only meant to be open in the summer months, I was freezing and the customers were very few and far between. The roads were not gritted in Camber as it was remote and unimportant, and the workmen I relied on so much during the winter months were unable to work in such bitterly cold weather, so for the next few weeks I was giving away more hot drinks to cold people outside than selling any to people that braved it inside. There was no comfort in the café and I never took my coat off as the temperature hardly changed between outside and inside and when I did get a customer I had to keep my gloves on to stop my hands from going numb. It was misery for everyone who had to struggle to work in the freezing ice and snow that seemed to go on forever.

It was 29th November and I had not heard from the solicitor as to whether I had been granted Legal Aid. Time had nearly run out and the Court case was two weeks away. I did not fancy spending Christmas in prison and the solicitor had said that the case would cost £3000 if I was unsuccessful with my application for legal aid I had applied for. I had no spare money to pay him for I had been saving the rent which was due on 16th January. That same day I was sent an email from the solicitors telling me I had been unsuccessful with the application for legal aid and if I sent them £30 they would return the court bundle. What was I to do? Just as I was wondering, who should turn up but Kerry! I thought he had come in search of his money he thought he was going to get, but in fact he had come to find out what was happening with the court case and if I had been granted legal aid. When I told him I had not he was surprised and said he would find me a barrister in his circle of legal friends who he had worked with over the years. I explained to him I had no money to pay for a barrister and that I still owed him money. He said he was going to make a purchase that afternoon which was going to cost £400 and if I paid for it on my credit card it would reduce his bill. I told him I was not in a position to be using my credit card because I did not have one.

He spoke with a couple of his colleagues and one of them agreed to take my case on for an all-in fee of £1000 and he would meet me only once to give him the bundle and then he would attend the Court case. His name was Gary and he was a barrister from London. Kerry had finally done something worthwhile.

Time was of the essence and I had to wait for Gary to contact me to make arrangements to meet him. I did not fancy the idea of having to go to London as I always got lost every time I went there. When I was an eleven year old Girl Guide I had gone to London on a day trip with my fellow Guides, and we were walking in pairs in a crocodile along Oxford Street. I was in awe of all the street traders selling amazing things. A stall of bouncy black fluffy spiders with pipe cleaner legs had taken my fancy, a bargain at sixpence. I stopped to admire all the spiders bouncing up and down on elastic in front of me. You never got things like that in Bexhill-on-sea and this was probably my one and only chance to own one. After a few moments the street trader asked if I wanted to buy one and I did so want one of these spiders, so I said I did and I paid my sixpence which was half of my spending money and I was overjoyed with my purchase, as I had my very own black fluffy spider on elastic. However, when I turned round to re-join the other Guides there was not one in sight and they had all disappeared, so I found myself alone and lost in Oxford Street and it was beginning to get dark. Eventually I presented myself to a policeman who was on duty in Oxford Street and told him I was lost, and he said he would take me back to the Police Station. I went with him and when we turned into a dark road I suddenly didn't want to be there and I told him my mummy said I was not allowed to go with strangers. He must have put my mind at rest because I did end up in the Police Station and was given some apple pie while the Police Force were out in search of a group of Girl Guides from Bexhill-on-Sea who were eventually traced to Victoria Station were the Captain and Company of Girl Guides were sitting on the train waiting for me to be reunited with them so the delayed train could finally depart on its journey. It transpired that the Girl Guides had all gone into Lyons Corner House for tea whilst I was being distracted by fluffy spiders, but it was an adventure being driven through London in a Police car with the siren going and no doubt a relief to all the commuters who had been delayed for a good half hour by me and my fluffy spider.

Anyway, I need not have worried as Gary rang me the next day and arranged to meet me at the Road Chef Service Station at Maidstone just off Junction 8 of the M20 at 10am on 13th December, the day before the court case was to take place. In the meantime I would await the return of the bundle from the solicitors in Tunbridge Wells to take with me and pass it over to Gary.

I had not been looking forward to driving to Maidstone in the snow and ice but the road conditions had improved greatly and the drive to Maidstone only took 40 minutes. I went into the cafeteria to wait for Gary, but I had not a clue what he looked like so I sat near the entrance with my pile of papers and folders exposed on the table top so he would hopefully recognise his client. I also made the mistake of buying myself a large coffee which was served in a receptacle that resembled a Victorian Chamber Pot, heavy and filled to the brim with the most disgusting strong coffee I had ever tasted.

I eyed every man that walked through the door, looking for someone who would be carrying a brief case, but none came. I decided to change tables so I got up and moved towards the centre of the cafeteria and I spotted a gorgeous looking man sitting by the window alone at a table typing something onto his laptop. He was so handsome I was going to ask him if I had an appointment with him and whether he was Gary or not and as I approached the table he looked up at me and yes he was my man. Oh joy! What luck that this handsome man was going to fight my case for me, and I thought of the Council's ugly barrister. We introduced ourselves politely and I sat down with all my stuff. I knew that before long my paperwork would be strewn all over the cafeteria so firstly I handed him the envelope with his £1000 cash which I had taken from the rent I had been saving, as I did not want him to be anxious as to whether he would be getting paid or not.

I quickly realised that I was not there to talk but to listen to what Gary had to say and answer only when he asked me a question. He went through each of the eleven breaches and told me his opinion as to whether I was guilty or innocent of breaching the injunction order. Each time Gary said that it was his opinion that I had breached the injunction order I tried to convince him I had not. I had been accused of placing my A-board on the highway directly outside of the café on 3rd June and 7th and 8th July. I rummaged quickly through my papers and showed him two emails I had received from Rag-Eme-

Kale stating 'you already have an A-board outside the café that has never been removed' and 'A-boards immediately adjacent to the premises might be tolerated, as yours is outside your café'. I asked Gary how I could have breached the injunction order when I believed from the emails that Rag-Eme-Kale had sent me he had permitted me to place my A-board directly outside of the café.

Then the allegation and photo from Bodger saying he pursued me on his bike and saw the A-board on the grass at the top of Lydd Road. I looked Gary straight in the eye and I told him I had placed the A-board over the fence which surrounded the children's play park area and it was my belief Bodger realising I had swapped my cars around and that I was not in the vicinity, had purposely removed the A-board from the fence and placed it on the grass and taken a photo of it with the intention of discrediting me to the Council.

I told him regarding the sign on the car, it was my opinion that the car was on the highway and the sign was on the car and therefore I had not breached the injunction order and the same for the sign on the bike - it was my opinion that only the bike was on the highway but the sign was on the bike.

He did not question my explanation, but noted my opinions onto his laptop.

Regarding the defamatory language I had used in my emails, I said that I believed what I had written was true, I did believe The Tyrannical Clown was corrupt and I did not accuse Judgement Jones of being a liar.

After an hour the interview was over, the conversation changed to the following day. Gary asked me to collect him from Hastings Station in the morning at 9am so we would have another hour to discuss the case at Hastings County Court and he said he would email me a draft statement later that day. I bade him farewell as he packed all his stuff away into his brief case and I stuffed mine back into the carrier bag and left for Camber. I was looking forward to the court case the next day seeing my gorgeous barrister standing next to the Council's ugly one.

I did not go straight home, but drove to Lesley's and over a cup of tea I described the gorgeous Gary to her in every detail. She said she had wanted to come to my court case anyway but now she definitely did and so did Jenny. We discussed how we hoped the case would go and if I would end up in prison for Christmas, then my phone rang and it was the listings officer from Hastings County Court to tell me my case had been adjourned for the time being and he would let me know when another date had been arranged. I asked him if he had any idea how long it would be and he said not before March 2011 as the court was too busy. Lesley was gutted and so was I; what a disappointment! I rang Gary immediately and told him that the court case had been temporarily adjourned. He appreciated me letting him know and said he would email me the next day with details of how he would proceed with my defence.

Disappointing as it was, I was not going to spend Christmas in prison after all and as it had been so rushed it was probably for the best.

The next day I received the promised email from Gary saying he would in due course send me the details of our meeting from the previous day and the advice he had recommended. I would then agree in writing what the appropriate course would be, and he would then send our case to the Court and the other side.

A week later Gary emailed me with his proposals in response to each of the allegations made against me by East Sussex Highways Authority.

He agreed that I had not breached the injunction order on 3rd June, 7th and 8th July by placing an A-board outside my café because on the 12th May 2010 I had been given permission by Rag-Eme-Kale to put the A-board outside of the café and it therefore did not constitute a breach.

27th July he believed the A-board which I placed over the fence was a breach.

11th August he believed I had placed the bike deliberately in order to affix a sign to it. The bike which is on the verge to which the public have the right of passage it is on the highway and it was his view that because the bike has only been placed there to put the sign on it was a breach.

10th September it was his view that I had parked the car legally but the car had been parked on the highway for the same reasons as the bike and that was to place a café sign on it which he considered to be a breach.

26th April it was his view that I had breached the order by describing The Tyrannical Clown as being corrupt and was also defamatory towards Rag-Eme-Kale because what is being said is that he will be corrupt if he takes notice of what I had suggested.

28th and 26th April 2010. I did not accuse Judgement Jones of lying so this was not a breach.

10th August the email to Rag-Eme-Kale implying he discriminates against me was not a breach.

20th August 2010: I had simply pointed out that I had been given two pieces of conflicting information and in my view one of them is false. Not a breach.

So that was the response to the accusations. Gary had then set out how he would proceed.

It was Gary's view that I had breached the injunction on four occasions and not the eleven asserted by the County Council.

He said if I agreed with him then there would be nothing to be served by putting the County Council to the expense of a fully contested hearing with witnesses. This would just increase my costs.

It was Gary's view that we should write to the County Council setting out what we accept and deny and see if they would be prepared to accept that and then there is no need for the judge to decide whether or not I had in fact breached the order or the extent to which I had. The advantage of this would be that it would undoubtedly count in my favour when the judge decides what action to take.

We could still serve a statement from me and a bundle of material in which we would set out our case. He advised that in doing this we should be simply trying to explain why the order was breached rather than denying it.

The choice was ultimately a matter for me to decide. Contrary to Gary's views, I did not believe I had breached the injunction order at all, so as it was ultimately my decision. I replied to his email with my opinion of his recommendations.

Dear Gary,
Thank you for your email and here is my response.
3rd June. The inflatable structure was sold to me with a BSS guarantee they are sold to advertise and promote businesses and there are many on display between Bexhill and here and in rural villages. If they cannot be displayed on the highway, which is understandable or on private forecourts what would be the purpose of them? Judgement Jones wrote to me in June and asked me to put it in a bit more he never asked me to remove it. I am telling you this in case they say something about it.
27th July I put the A-board hanging over the fence; the fence belongs to the Parish Council and surrounds a field and a play area. The board was not touching the ground and in my opinion was not abutting the highway when I left it there. So even if they can prove that it was, they could only say half of it was near the highway.
11th August The bike was attached to a pole which was put

there by some workman who were building a house next to it, they said I could use it to put the bike onto, the pole is not placed to obstruct the passage way as no one would need to walk there. I would argue with the council that the pole is not on the highway as it is behind the bus stop, the board on it was facing the entrance to the caravan park so as to be seen by the holiday people it was not put there to draw attention from the passing traffic. I asked the council last year where the highway started and ended. I can produce an email which tells me the highway starts from half way through a hedge row over the road to half way through the hedgerow the other side. So if there was a hedgerow here then the bike would be beyond half of it and in any event I believe that the sign on the bike was not abutting the highway.

10th September: Regardless of the previous two cars I had here which have never been mentioned or removed by the council or indeed the present car which was never mentioned until the bundle arrived, the highway is there to pass and re-pass and the car is legally parked as you said but I can't see how the board on it can prevent any one passing or re-passing the highway. There are many vehicles placed in lay-byes, farmers' fields and on highways as in the photo I took in Bexhill with adverts on them and I believe this is a common form of advertising.

I do not agree that the order applies to advertising 'indirectly'. If they wanted there to be no trace of my café should they not have said 'no signs anywhere'.

26th April I was giving Rag-Eme-Kale some advice in the hope that he doesn't end up corrupt like The Tyrannical Clown.

I realise that from your professional opinion I should agree to your advice but if I do that I truly believe that I will be admitting to something I am not guilty of.

I hope you won't be offended by what I have written as I have

*not entirely agreed with you, but I have only responded as I
see the situation.*
*Alternatively will I only get the opportunity to prove they have
lied by admitting that I have breached the order?*
Regards
Sally

So that was my response to Gary and I emailed it to him
directly and looked forward to hearing what he had to say
about it.

CHAPTER 43

Lesley was incensed with the way the Highways department were wasting so much time and money on me and my café signs so on 10th December 2010 she wrote to The Tyrannical Clown complaining about the neglected snow and ice on the pavements and roads in Rye town centre and especially the Green Grocer who's Christmas trees were tied to the signposts and lamp posts along the street outside and beyond his shop so that it was impossible to walk along the pavement with all the trees there and the only way to get down the street was to walk on the road which was especially dangerous for mothers with pushchairs. She had not received a response so she wrote again on 14th January 2011;

Dear Sirs
I first complained about A-boards all along Cinque Port
Street in Dec 2010. No immediate response which was, at that
time, urgent as the pavements and roads were icy and the
local Council had done nothing at all to clear them.
The green grocery shop is actually trading and their goods
are displayed right across the pavement leaving
approximately 18inches for pedestrians on the pavement.
Nobody could push a pushchair along here without having to
get onto the road or the pull-in right outside there.
IT IS DANGEROUS! All the shop premises are on a retail
highway and they can be clearly seen from the pavement by
potential customers and also from the highway. Why do they
need additional boards? Why are they allowed to use the
pavement for trading and are they paying to do so?
Regards
Lesley

A response was promised within 10 days. Seven weeks later she got a reply from The Tyrannical Clown:

Dear Lesley
I can confirm that following your complaint of 16 December
2010 the street was visited on 23 December 2010 by Kilkenny
of my department and matters within our powers were dealt
with. It was not possible for Kilkenny to contact you to exactly
establish your concerns as no contact phone number was
given in your email. The problem with that street is that there
are private forecourt areas and not all of the paved area is
highway. This allows some premises to place out items at the
front of their shops
Advertising of premises is a matter for Rother District
Council, not the County Council. Obstruction of footways can
be dealt with by the police; highways have very limited
powers to do so. The police do patrol Rye, our Inspectors do
not. They only inspect the condition of the highway on a cyclic
rota and react to emergences.
I hope this helps you to determine what further action is
required, if any. Finally I am sorry that you did not get an
earlier response but I am sure you can appreciate that our
priorities have been directed at weather related and ongoing
resultant problems.
Yours sincerely
The Tyrannical Clown

Lesley was furious at The Tyrannical Clowns response, how could he have the cheek to say that obstructions were a matter for the police when he himself had been removing my café signs regularly for the last two years. Now they had upset Lesley they would be on the receiving end of her wrath which she demonstrated in her reply to The Tyrannical Clown;

Tyrannical Clown

*I did leave my telephone number and address with the
receptionist when I initially telephoned you.*

*I do find it difficult to understand why you do not deal with
the matters of A-boards along Cinque Port Street Rye as you
do seem to deal with them in Camber and this I understand
comes within your jurisdiction, also section 132 of the 1980s
highways act seems to imply that this is your responsibility.
Are you aware of this Act?*

*When I called your office I was obliged to listen to a recorded
message for people to be mindful that if drains are
overflowing it is because it is raining hard! No surely not!
Surely the whole reason for their design is to take away
excess surface water is it not? If they were cleaned out from
time to time they might well manage to do the job they were
designed for. The ones outside my home are half full of paper
and dirt where a road sweeper comes by and pushes it down
them. THEY DO NEED CLEANING OUT FROM TIME TO
TIME! I had to insist this was done a couple of years ago
when the drains could not cope with a heavy rainfall because
they were full of paper and dirt and the water came in under
my door. When I asked for sandbags I was told to go to B &
Q! If this happens again I will sue for damages as the drains
are now in need of another clear out. You also request that we
inform you of dangerous pothole and poor surface conditions
on the roads. Where do you want me to start? The whole of
the length of Rope Walk Rye might be a good place to start.*

*I take it from your emails that you do not intend to do
anything about my enquiry at all despite the fact that you say
I was not the only person to complain. What do you deal with,
if the roads are running with water because the drains are
never cleaned out, the road is full of potholes because they*

are never kept in repair and you cannot restrict A-boards on narrow icy pavements? You say that you could not reply sooner to my enquiry because of weather conditions. As you could not cope with clearing ice and snow from the roads or pathways of Rye and surrounding area and then could not cope with the rainfall because drains were never cleaned out, what was keeping you so busy?
Could it be that you were concentrating, from what I hear and should it be true, on matters concerning an A-board and a vehicle in Camber? Is this preferential treatment?
Yours sincerely
Lesley

Again she received no reply from The Tyrannical Clown and infuriated by it she wrote again;

Tyrannical Clown
I enquired way back in Dec 2010 about the conditions of the Cinque Ports St, Rye, pavements and A-boards thereon. Also the restriction along these dangerous icy pavements due to the fact that Xmas Trees were being tied to Street Furniture. Following that you advised me that this was not your concern. However, you appear very concerned with some in Camber and are spending an undue amount of time pursuing these despite the fact that THEY ARE NOT YOUR CONCERN! Please explain why you cannot deal with Rye ones but you can those in Camber. The signs in Camber appear to be legal according to the information you have given me. I AM VERY CONFUSED NOW.
Do you or do you not deal with signs on pavements and street furniture? If yes, why do you choose to pursue only specific persons that do so? Is this discrimination? Or will you pursue ALL complaints?

Whilst trying to contact your Office by telephone, unsurprisingly my call was not answered and I was subjected to a taped recording regarding overflowing drains and potholes in roads. You asked that we report the potholes and ignored the drains as it was due to heavy rain.
1. The potholes have been reported in Rope Walk, but NOT attended to, therefore ignored.
2. The drains in Rope Walk should have been designed to take excess water away not bubble over! The drains in Rope Walk are not cleaned out regularly and therefore they overflow because they are full of dirt and rubbish from the Market and cannot take away heavy rain for which they were designed. Perhaps you should spend some time cleaning these and not rushing around Camber doing a job you are apparently not supposed to be doing.
You appear to give contradicting advice - you tell me that you do not have jurisdictional to remove items from street furniture in Cinque Ports Street, Rye but I gather you do in Camber. Section 132 of 1980s Highways Act does appear to give you this authority and I am led to believe this is part of your job.
Surely you should not be seen to enforce your duties in one area (Camber) but appear to totally ignore it in another (Rye).

Needless to say, again Lesley did not hear back from The Tyrannical Clown.

CHAPTER 44

Another year had passed and my dispute with the Council had been going on for more than two years. I was not going to give up my fight for my café signs.

As usual for this time of the year I was absolutely skint. I had borrowed £2000 from a friend to make up the short fall of the rent which was imminent as I had taken £1000 from the saved rent to pay Gary the Barrister. I decided I would write a begging email to Judgement Jones to explain my financial difficulties;

Morning Judgement Jones
On July 6th 2010 I sent you £20 for you to keep in your folder till January 2011, do you recall that?
Well I am wondering if I could have it back please as my rent is due on Sunday and once again I don't have enough money for it. If you do let me have it I will pay it back next month as there is a sci-fi weekend at Pontius on 3rd February and I did quite well from that last year.
Please Judgement Jones?
Sally

There was nothing to do in the café; customers were few and far between, so to liven up the day I thought I would see how many East Sussex County Council employees I could find on Facebook, a social networking website. I started to search; I hoped that once I found one employee I could most likely locate others by looking at their list of friends. I found a colleague of Rag-Eme-Kale's, a fellow engineer called Erma Horse; she was quite a boring type according to her Facebook page, but looking down her list of 'About' at the bottom of the page she had written 'I've paid my car tax, now mend the fucking pot-holes', which was all very amusing as that was a major issue with the roads in East Sussex, but I wondered why Rag-Eme-Kale had made such a fuss and appeared to be so offended by my description of the 'Farm Shop' sign which I had described as 'being made of crap material and only a midges dick from the road junction' and yet he worked alongside this woman who obviously had a foul mouth using that kind of language. I took a screen print of the page for future reference if needed.

Continuing my search of Council employees on Facebook, I was scrolling down the list of Erma Horse's friends looking for names and profile photos to see if there was any one I recognised and all of a sudden I thought I spied our scarecrow 'Rag-Eme-Kale 'that Lily and I had left sitting outside the Highway office in Sidley early one morning in July. I quickly scrolled up again to take a closer look and yes it was our scarecrow sitting on the stool, but he had been put in a different position, the scarf had been put around his neck and the hood had been pulled up over his head and his legs were crossed. I was amazed to see he had become the profile photo of an employee called Lexi Goodfellow who worked in the complaints department at the Council Offices in Lewes Goodness, how did that come about I wondered. I guessed that when he had been found he had caused much amusement and been subject to a photo shoot which must have been circulated round the Council's internal computing system for all the employees to see and had ended up as a profile photo. That was so funny; Lily and I laughed so much at seeing our creation being innocently exhibited on Facebook. The exhibitor was most probably totally oblivious as to how and why Rag-Eme-Kale the scarecrow had come to be sitting on a stool in the bushes at the Highway Depot in Sidley. I took a screen print of the profile photo.

Two days after writing to Judgement Jones I received a short sharp reply regarding the £20 I had asked him to temporarily give me back:

Sally,
No, you can't have it back! It's already been paid and you owe the Council thousands of pounds!
Judgement Jones

How could he say I owed the Council thousands of pounds when I did not? Anyway I did not care how much I owed; Judgement Jones was not going to be getting any more payments from me till the weather improved so he would have to wait.

The Head of the Highways department was probably unaware that his Facebook account was open for all and sundry to read. He was the man who had given his permission for me to be prosecuted each time The Tyrannical Clown had requested it. Oh my, what a revelation from a man who was of the opinion that I had used defamatory language toward his colleagues. Besides referring to his older fellow work mates as 'incontinent old crusties', on Sunday 19th December 2010, in the middle of the big freeze, he had been obliged to work but he claimed to have nothing to do and he had posted to Erma Horse his foul-mouthed colleague who had paid her road tax that *'Rag-Eme-Kale was running around like a demented thing, where as he was just swanning around his office looking cool'*. What a disgrace, this man who's job title was 'Head of Highways Operations' with the job description 'Responsible for all areas of highway maintenance operations including structures, planned works, reactive works and winter emergency service' had publicly and proudly announced that he was just swanning around his office looking cool.

I decided he could swan around my white Peugeot with his incontinent crusty old friends as there was still space for another effigy. I called him 'Swanoff Swanker' as a tribute to this Head of Highways Operations. The mask was an evil eagle which I stuffed with newspaper and stuck on the end of a broom handle pushed down a one legged pair of leggings stuffed with straw and taped with gaffer tape to hold it all together. I put it right next to the window in the front passenger seat next to Defrogatory.

I learnt a lot about Swanoff Swanker by his Facebook posts. It was clear from the response to his posts that his 'friends' were only his friends because he was the boss and they were bootlickers.

Council employees were such hypocrites, they used foul and defamatory language when it suited them and the likes of Judgement Jones, The Tyrannical Clown, Swanoff Swanker and Rag-Eme-Kale considered themselves superior by overestimating their intelligence and abilities whilst they had unjustly discrediting mine.

Kilkenny was not over intelligent; I could only accredit him with being a compulsive liar.

I was often being asked who the creatures were in the car, so the best thing to do was to print a picture of each of them with their names and character descriptions and stick them inside of the car windows.

The Tyrannical Clown -The Perpetrator and Perjurer.
Judgement Jones - The Overseer
Kilkenny - The Liar
Swanoff Swanker - The Ultimate Narcissistic
Defrogatry - The Coward
Highway Hen -The Intrepid Victim

CHAPTER 45

As the cold winter days dragged on and the customers were few and far between I still saw Kilkenny and his colleagues driving by the café, their faces turned in our direction trying to have a quick glance. One day I was so bored I decided to expose Swanoff Swanker's defamatory remark about Rag-Eme-Kale and the foul mouthed Erma Horse, Rag-Eme-Kale's colleague.

I attached the screen print of the Erma Horse's remark - first I wrote;

Dear Rag-Eme-Kale
If you think my language is bad what do you think of your colleague's language in this attachment? A fine example of East Sussex County Council staff.
Take note of the comment she makes at the bottom of the page....
Sally

It did not take long for Rag-Eme-Kale to answer, he wrote;

Dear Sally Pattinson
Thank you for bringing this to my attention. I have spoken to my colleague and asked her to be mindful of the groups on Facebook that she joins, particularly if they have ironical themes such as 'I've paid my car tax, fix some..... potholes'. In this instance it is clear that this comment is not about any one individual person, whereas defamatory comments aimed at individuals published on Facebook or twitter would be considered as slander.
Yours sincerely

Rag-Eme-Kale

That was the best answer I could have ever hoped for and now it was my turn to produce evidence of slanderous defamatory language so I attached the next screen print and wrote;

Dear Rag-Eme-Kale
It is my opinion that what is written is 'bad language' and very unprofessional for someone who works for a County Council. I did not say it is defamatory language.
*However, it **is** my opinion that in the attachment I have sent you this time, defamatory language is being used, towards you.....3rd. paragraph. This statement might make a reasonable person think worse of you because of what it implies. And a disgraceful example of the person who wrote it as he appears to have nothing better to do whilst you were running around like a demented thing.*
Sally

I did not get a reply from Rag-Eme-Kale but the next time I went to see what Swanoff Swanker had to say on his Facebook page, curiously it was no longer open for all and sundry to read.

I had not heard from the listings man from Hastings County Court, so I rang him to ask if he had a date for me yet and he said they were very busy but he could arrange the hearing to be at Brighton County Court. Otherwise I would have to wait until after March. This was going on forever, so I said I'd think about it and let Judgement Jones know my decision, as apparently I had the final choice if the hearing was held anywhere other than in my own area. I did think about it; Brighton was quite far and if I did go to prison what would happen to my car? It would get clamped if it was left somewhere for two years and then if I took a train that would be expensive and I might not get the opportunity to use the return ticket. So I decided that I would turn down the listing man's offer.

I emailed Judgement Jones and made the excuse that I could not go to Brighton as I did not know where Brighton was.

He replied by saying he did not think it was an excuse that I could not go to Brighton because 'I didn't know where it was'. He said there is a direct train from Hastings to Brighton which can be cheap if I booked it far in advance. Also the problem was because there was the possibility of me receiving a custodial sentence, the Council's application has to be heard by a Circuit Judge (i.e. a senior County Court Judge). Unfortunately, there was only one Circuit Judge in the Hastings/Eastbourne area and he was the one who was booked up till Easter time!

He thought it was in both our interests to try and get the matter resolved as it had been dragging on for months. He said Brighton was only another 40 minutes from Eastbourne and the court was a gentle 10 minute stroll from the train station with picturesque views of the splendid Royal Pavilion.

Judgement Jones information was all very well but nevertheless Brighton was still a long way to go. I emailed Judgement Jones to make him a proposition. I asked him how he thought I could possibly book a train ticket far in advance to Brighton if no one had a clue when the hearing was taking place so I proposed that I would go to Brighton if I could cadge a lift with Kilkenny.

I was impatient to get a response from Judgement Jones so I emailed him again the next day and asked him if Kilkenny was prepared to give me a lift to Brighton.

He replied:

Sally,

I didn't ask if Kilkenny would give you a lift for two reasons:
a. I know the answer will be 'no';
b. It would be contempt of court if he gave you a lift bearing
in mind that he is giving evidence against you!
Judgement Jones

So I replied;

I don't mind if he is giving evidence against me, I don't mind
anyone who is giving evidence against me. All I want is a lift.
Anyway you're not giving evidence against me so can you give
me a lift please Judgement Jones? I will give you the petrol
money....
How can giving someone a lift to a court hearing be contempt
of court, are you sure you have got your facts right Judgement
Jones? I promise I will sit in the back and I won't speak to
you, I will look at the picturesque scenery as it flies by... will
that be ok?
Sally

I had one more short email from Judgement Jones;

Sally,
Sadly I don't own a car.
I can't even drive.

CHAPTER 46

A month had passed since I had responded to Gary's proposals
for the court hearing and I was becoming concerned that I had
not heard back from him but I did not want to bother him with
my business as I felt sure he had far more important things to
deal with. Then I received an email from him reminding me he
had sent me a letter before Christmas setting out in detail his
advice about my case. He asked if I had decided which way I
wanted him to proceed as the sooner we decide what we were
going to do the more time we would have to prepare. Would I
let him know as soon as possible how I wished to proceed? I
had answered his proposals within two days of receiving his
email and it must have been delivered somewhere because it
had not been returned to my mail box. I quickly rang Gary's
office and explained to the clerk that I had already answered
Gary's email and I had been waiting to hear from him. He said
he would ask Gary to phone me when he had finished talking
to a client. Later that day Gary rang me back and I apologised
that he had not received my email sent in December. I checked
his email address with him to be sure I had it correctly and
said I would resend it immediately and I asked him to confirm
when it had arrived. I sent it again, after half an hour Gary
rang me and asked if I had sent the email yet and I said I had
but again he had not received it. Giving up on my capability of
sending an email, Gary said he would send me an email to be
sure I would send my response to his correct address, and
when the email arrived, I realised that I had used the wrong
casing for his initials. I quickly pasted my original response to
his email and returned it, and after a moment he sent me a
reply saying he had at last received it.

I remembered the fuss Judgement Jones had made over the
controversial A-board advertising AJ's burger van as to

whether it was on or off Council land. He had accused me of publishing defamatory language about him by suggesting he was a liar which could make a reasonable person think less of him. I decided to send him the screen print of Swanoff Swanker's remarks about Rag-Eme-Kale being a demented thing.

Dear Judgement Jones
I would like you to tell me if the attached published statement regarding Rag-Eme-Kale is true and if so is it a permanent condition or just a temporary one caused by circumstantial pressure of the day? Because of this published statement which implies that Rag-Eme-Kale is a demented thing, I am concerned that being a reasonable person myself, should I think less of Rag-Eme-Kale or if I should feel sorry for him. The author of this published statement boasts of doing nothing apart from swanning around his office looking cool. If he had so little to do why was he not assisting Rag-Eme-Kale knowing he was in a state of dementia instead of wasting tax payer's money being at work doing nothing apart from publishing defamatory remarks about his colleagues? But on the other hand, if this published statement was true and the condition to which it refers is permanent, I really do not think it appropriate for Rag-Eme-Kale to be giving sworn evidence under the influence of dementia when my liberty is at stake and could well be taken away from me if I am incarcerated for two years on the strength of a deranged witness.
Sally

I did not get a reply for two weeks;

Sally
Apologies for the late reply. I've been on holiday in Kuala Lumpur for the last two weeks

I believe Rag-Eme-Kale has already dealt with your concern in my absence. As part of your injunction nearly a year ago, you were ordered to pay £2500 in costs in total. In the space of 11 months, you have only paid £275 and therefore still owe £2225.
Judgement Jones

I had no money to give to the Council and I had no intention of giving them anymore. I wrote another email to Judgement Jones.

Dear Judgement Jones
As I am unable to pay you any money for the moment, I have decided that in fairness to me you can ask The Tyrannical Clown to give you the cost of my A-boards and Café signs which he had removed from their various locations in and around Camber.
The wood, paint, writing equipment and my labour in making them amounts to £1950 Inc. VAT so therefore I would only owe you £265.....
I hope you will find this arrangement satisfactory.
Sally,

Sally
I do not find this arrangement satisfactory. The full debt remains owing and enforcement action may be taken if you do not pay the full sum forthwith The Tyrannical Clown was simply doing his job in removing the signs which were placed illegally. This involves a considerable amount of time and expense on behalf of the client. To expect reimbursement is therefore inappropriate. With all due respect, if you continue to treat the legal system in this manner, you risk serving a lengthy custodial sentence!

Judgement Jones

I was slowly gathering contradictory evidence that I could and would use when the need arose, this was one of those occasions to do just that. I replied;

Judgment Jones

How am I meant to find the money Judgment Jones? I suppose I could try selling my body, and even in the unlikely event that I did have any clients they would surely demand a refund.......
Why should I serve a lengthy custodial sentence for not having any money is that a crime now 'to be skint'? Anyway Judgment Jones, even if I do go to prison it won't be for very long because I have watched 'Colditz' and I know how to escape and I will.
And one more thing, are you sure The Tyrannical Clown was only doing his job, as this email to Lesley would contradict that? He claims in response to her email that advertising of premises is a matter for the police and Rother District Council and nothing to do with the County Council. If that is the case he had no right to take my cafe signs so why did he? Therefore I would like them back.....

Dear Lesley

'I can confirm that following your complaint of 16 December 2010 the street was visited on 23 December by Kilkenny of my department and matters within our powers were dealt with. It was not possible for Kilkenny to contact you to exactly establish your concerns as no contact phone number was given in your email. The problem with that street is that there are private forecourt areas and not all of the paved area is highway. This allows some premises to place out items at the front of their shops.

Advertising of premises is a matter for Rother District Council, not the County Council. Obstruction of footways can be dealt with by the police, highways have very limited powers to do so. The police do patrol Rye our Inspectors do not. They only inspect the condition of the highway on a cyclic rota and react to emergences.

I hope this helps you to determine what further action is required, if any. Finally I am sorry that you did not get an earlier response but I am sure you can appreciate that our priorities have been directed at weather related and ongoing resultant problems'.

Yours sincerely
The Tyrannical Clown
Licensing & Enforcement Manager
East Sussex Highways

Predictably, he ignored my email.

CHAPTER 47

The draft copy of my witness statement arrived via email from Gary for me to read and approve, wow it was amazing. Gary had written it in a way that although I agreed I had carried out each of the accusations I had not breached the injunction whilst doing so.

DRAFT WITNESS STATEMENT OF SALLY-ANN PATTINSON

I, SALLY ANN PATTINSON, of 15 Lydd Road, Camber, East Sussex, TN31 7RJ, say as follows:

1. The Claimant has applied for an order that I should be committed to prison for disobeying the injunction order made by the Hastings County Court on 9th April 2010.

2. I do not accept that I have disobeyed the injunction order let alone that I have done so persistently. I have done all that I possibly can do in order to advertise my café in a way which I believed was consistent with the terms of the order. I have to advertise my café because otherwise I will simply go out of business. I have tried to communicate with the applicant's employees in a way that will enable me to understand how I can go about advertising my business and what I can and cannot do. I have tried where appropriate to seek clarification to avoid breaching the terms of the injunction.

3. I will deal with the specific allegation of breaches in the order with which they appear on the application notice.

4. On 3ʳᵈ June 2010 an A-board was placed on the road immediately outside my premises by me. I did this because Rag-Eme-Kale had told me in writing that I could do so. I exhibit a copy of the communication from him sent on 12ᵗʰ May 2010 at my exhibit SAP1. It can be seen that in the letter he says that A-boards immediately adjacent to the premises may be tolerated, as yours is outside your café. I understood this to be express written consent by the East Sussex County Council that I could place an A-board immediately outside my café and that is what I did.

5. I accept that I also placed the A-board outside my premises on both 7ᵗʰ July and 8ᵗʰ July 2010. I did so however for the same reasons as on 3ʳᵈ June 2010, namely that I understood that I had express written consent from East Sussex County Council.

6. In relation to 27ᵗʰ July 2010 I placed the A-board hanging over a fence by the field. The fence belongs to the Parish Council and surrounds a field and a play area. The board was not touching the ground and in my opinion was not abutting the highway when I left it there. I returned about 20 minutes later and found the A-board sitting on the grass. I brought the A-board back in the boot of my car. I did not see who moved my A-board off the fence and onto the grass. I believe it was Mr Bodger based principally on information provided to me by others. I do not believe that by placing the A-board above the ground in the way that I did I had breached the order. I deliberately did this in order to avoid breaching the order.

7. I agree that in respect of 11th August 2010 I did place a flat piece of wood containing an advertisement for my café on the bike. The bike however was attached to a pole which had been put there by the workmen who were building a house next to it. I was told by them that I could attach the bike to the pole. The pole does not obstruct the passage way as no one would ever need to walk there. I would argue with the council that the pole is not on the highway as it is behind the bus stop, the board on it was facing the entrance to the caravan park so as to be seen by the holiday people, and it was not put there to draw attention to the passing traffic. I asked the Council last year where the highway started and ended. I produce an email which I exhibit as my SAP/2 which tells me the highway starts from half way through a hedgerow over the road to half way through the hedgerow the other side. So if there was a hedgerow here the bike would be beyond half of it and in any event I believe that the sign on the bike was not abutting the highway. It is my belief that the sign was on the bike and not on the highway. The order does not prevent me from placing a sign on a bike. I had taken legal advice from the Citizen's Advice Bureau prior to doing this and was of the firm belief that I was not breaching the order

8. On 10th September 2010 I agree that I placed the sign on the car. The car was legally parked. It did not prevent any member of the public from moving along the highway. There are many vehicles placed in lay-byes, farmer's fields and on highways as in the photo I took in Bexhill with adverts on them which is my exhibit SAP/3 and I believe this is a common form of advertising. The order does not cover placing a car on the highway. I believed that I placed the sign on the car and not on the highway. I do not believe that this is a breach of the injunction and again I did it this way in order *to advertise my business in a way which avoided me breaching the injunction.*

9. *I accept that in a communication dated 26th April 2010 I said to Rag-Eme-Kale that he should not allow himself to be influenced by The Tyrannical Clown or he might end up as corrupt as he is not to mention un voleur et un sale menteur (a thief and a liar). I am of the opinion that what I said was accurate and truthful. I believe I am entitled to express my opinion. The order prevents me from using foul, abusive or defamatory language or engaging in threatening behaviour towards any member of the applicant's staff. The order does not prevent me from using foul, abusive, or defamatory language about a member of the applicant's staff. I was not communicating with The Tyrannical Clown but with Rag-Eme-Kale. I did not swear or use insulting language towards Rag-Eme-Kale.*

10. *I accept that on 28 April 2010 I compiled the emails contained within exhibit REK/1. I did write that I did not like hearing lies being told about me and I did not get the opportunity to prove that a certain person was making things up and denying things he'd said. It is my view that I am simply explaining the comment I made on 26th April 2010. I am not using foul, abusive or defamatory language towards The Tyrannical Clown and I am not even communicating with him. I would also like to point out that the order refers to defamatory language it does not refer to the language being either express or implicit. I did not understand that any implied comment could constitute a breach of the order. I did not understand at any time that by expressing my opinion in this way I was breaching the order. I am still of the view that I was not.*

*11. In relation to 10th August 2010 I am not able to locate the
precise letter that I am alleged to have written. The
application asserts that I implied Rag-Eme-Kale
discriminates against me by approving application for signs
on the highways from other business. I do not agree that I
wrote that, I do recall asking him if it depended on who
someone was as to whether he allowed them to place a sign
on the highway but I have not been able to locate the
document where I made that comment. In any event none of
the local businesses that I have asked have been requested to
apply for any consent. I have a copy of a letter dated 7th
August 2010 written by me which I exhibit as my exhibit
SAP/4. If this is the letter that forms the basis for the alleged
breach then it can easily be seen that I have not used any
language that is defamatory. It is my view that I have not
breached the order by writing this letter or at all.*

*12. On 20th August 2010 I accept that I wrote the sentence
'Will you please tell Mr Pasty The Planning Enforcement
Officer that then because I am going to put a café sign on
private land and he says I have to get consent. One of you is
lying, why?' I do not accept that this is using defamatory
language towards a member of the applicant's staff. This
comment follows on from emails sent by me before the grant
of the injunction in which I observed the difference in the
information with which I was being provided. I exhibit these
emails as my exhibit SAP/5. The comment simply highlights
the fact that I had received two pieces of conflicting
information. I did not call Judgement Jones a liar I pointed
out that they both could not be correct. The Planning-
Enforcement Officer is not a member of the applicant's staff.
He works for the Rother District Council. It is my view that
this is not a case of me using language that is expressly
defamatory. It can be seen that my understanding of what I*

*was doing is displayed in subsequent emails where I wrote
(see applicant's bundle 131)*

*'I did not realise that defamatory meant do not ask a question.
I did not directly accuse you of lying' I sent you the emails
from yourself and Mr Pasty for you to read and it is not my
fault it you have both given me conflicting answers to my one
question.'*

*I conclude that email by asking Judgement Jones to explain
to me exactly the meaning of defamatory so I don't do it
again. The response I received at page 130 of the applicant's
bundle was as follows:*

*'Defamatory means that you have published a statement
about me which would cause a reasonable person to think
worse of me'*

*If this definition is correct then I do not believe that a private
email conversation between Judgement Jones and me can
possibly cause anyone else to think worse of him. This
conversation was not published by me.*

13. *I accept that on 6th September 2010 I made the following
statement in a letter to Judgement Jones. 'Has Kilkenny been
prosecuted yet for wilfully stating evidence about my café
signs which he knew to be false? Does Swanoff Swanker know
about Kilkenny's false statement? He should do.' This
statement concerns the previous court proceedings and a
statement made by Kilkenny. I would like to make similar
observations in relation to this comment as some of the
previous comments. The first observation is that this statement*

is not made to Kilkenny but to Judgement Jones. The second is that I have merely asked a question about whether or not he has been prosecuted and whether Swanoff Swanker knows. I have not said that Kilkenny is a liar and I do not accept that I have even implied that he is a liar but even if I have I do not believe that the injunction covers implicit remarks.

14. I do not believe that my conduct has breached the injunction order on any of the occasions asserted by the applicant. I have done my best to avoid breaching the order as I understood the terms to be.

I believe that the facts contained within this statement are true.

So that was my witness statement. I wondered what Judgement Jones and the ugly barrister would make of it. I suspected they would both be extremely miffed this time as I actually had a decent barrister to defend me, unlike previous court hearings when I had stood alone apart from the first time with that incompetent barrister from Eastbourne.

I sent the witness statement off to Lesley to read as I knew she would be delighted by it.

So all we needed now was a date. I had been given the Council's bundle for my committal to prison at the beginning of October and it was now the beginning of February. I had everything I needed to face them in court. I was totally confident that Gary would do a grand job; he was in a totally different league to any Council Solicitor and the barristers they employed. I supposed that in an incident like this because the Council had such self-righteous opinions of themselves they had little need of employing a good barrister as in any event they would be believed for the very reason they were the Council. I had a pleasant feeling that the overconfident Judgement Jones and his clients were in for a shock this time.

CHAPTER 48

I printed my three page witness statement and five exhibits and eagerly posted them off to Judgement Jones at County Hall in Lewes. My whole bundle was a mere eight pages compared to the Council's bundle which was a massive 164 pages.

In the meantime Lesley was becoming more irritated by the lack of respect to her and the lack of response to her emails from The Tyrannical Clown, but despite the Council's customary practise to ignore issues if it suited them, she was determined to get the answers to her questions and so she wrote an email to Judgement Jones.

Dear Judgement Jones

I believe Sally Pattison of Camber Café has forwarded you an email sent to me by The Tyrannical Clown sometime in Dec /Jan. Having spoken to Sally I now realise the reason why The Tyrannical Clown did not take my query seriously. I had a real complaint about a real problem and The Tyrannical Clown even acknowledged this by saying that I was not the only one with a complaint about this matter. However, he said that he had no power to do anything about it. I learned of Sally's situation and have put two and two together. I obviously did not get taken seriously because he felt I was supporting Sally. If you care to look back into your records you will see that I had occasion to call about another problem in the Rope Walk outside my house several years ago, long before I met Sally. Furthermore, I have as much right as anyone to make a complaint and for that to be investigated. I also should be able to see that the reason for not doing anything about it is justified. It does not appear to be justified in the light of Sally's plight. I had put off my complaint several times about the restriction to the pavement along Cinque Port Street, Rye until it became extremely dangerous in the snow, which yet again the Council decided to do absolutely nothing about this year.

It is clear to me from the above and I am of the opinion, having spoken to Sally that you are discriminating and victimising this lady. She has reiterated her story to me and whilst there are always two sides to a story and Sally has a unique way of responding to problems in her life, it is still very clear to my eyes that this is a case of victimisation. You appear to have singled her out as an easy target as she is single, and a woman of very little means. Sally has fortunately a sunny outgoing personality and despite problems in her life overcomes them with determination and fortitude. However, it seems very heavy handed to treat this lady in the way in which you have but then turn around and not deal with similar problems in the area as they might be a lot trickier to handle and they might actually have the funds to defend themselves.

Since speaking to Sally I have noticed many more flagrant breaches of signs on the highways and, yet again, no action taken by you. This is either favouritism or you are singling Sally out as an easy target. Sally is trying to make a living without redress to Social Services as many others in her position would have done. Your persistent intention to take away her chance of earning a modest living is causing her great hardship although she would never let you know that. I have seen emails from yourselves that threaten her with long prison sentences. This must surely come under the description of threatening and harassing behaviour. It appears that you have taken away her boards, to indicate her Café is open, in numerous amounts not only depriving her of income due to lack of customers as they cannot see that she is there but also the cost of the boards which eat into her small profits and to add insult to injury you have charged her for doing this at extortionate rates. It would appear that you are deliberately trying to put this lady out of business. On driving to Camber yesterday I passed a burger van who was actually pulled into a lay-by on the highway and clearly was using this lay-by to put an A-board upon - THIS IS ON THE HIGHWAY! Furthermore he has red flashing lights on the front of a van on the oncoming side of the road - very distracting to a driver. I have no wish to deprive this man of his living either but why the obvious favouritism to this individual?

I cannot help but see all around the Rye and surrounding area exactly the same breaches (if that is what you would call them) that Sally is making and no action is being taken against any of these people - why? Surely if the rules are there they are there for all not certain individuals that you choose to pick upon.

Sally's car and board are in no way as big a distraction as the burger van and certainly do not produce the dangers to pedestrians that the Cinque Port Street situation does, so other than the reasons I have concluded, what is the reason for pursuing this lady in such an aggressive way?

I wonder if the local press would like to hear of this story.

Sincerely

Lesley

She did receive a reply from Judgement Jones albeit only to inform her that he had passed her grievance onto Rag-Eme-Kale,

Lesley,

Thank you for your email. I am sorry that you feel the Council is 'discriminating and victimising' Sally-Ann Pattinson.

However, as the solicitor dealing with the case, my role is to act on my client's behalf and deal with the process of bringing this matter to court. Your queries relate more to matters of policy and enforcement. These are best dealt with by my client. I have therefore copied in Rag-Eme-Kale who is the Team Manager at Inspection and Enforcement in the Highways department to your email. He will investigate your concerns and respond in full in due course.

Yours sincerely,

Judgement Jones

After more than two weeks since Lesley had written to Judgement Jones she eventually received a reply from Rag-Eme-Kale, he wrote;

Lesley

Thank you for your email of 9 March 2011 to Judgement Jones concerning A-boards and your concerns for Sally Pattinson. I apologise for the delay in my response. You will appreciate that I cannot disclose to you our correspondence with Sally Pattinson in detail, as that is information personal to her. Our policy permits A frames to be considered in the highway only outside the retail outlet, and this is dependent upon available space remaining for users of the highway to pass by. Where there is a desire to place an advertisement in a location away from the shop, then I have to be satisfied on behalf of the Highway Authority that the structure is made of materials and constructed in such a fashion that it will be safe to leave unattended in the public highway. This means that the advertisement will have to be securely fixed to the highway as a structure so that it will not only withstand windy conditions, but is also robust enough to cope with some interference or vandalism without becoming a danger to users of the highway. Remote and unattended advertisements such as this require planning permission from the District Council.

The A-board outside the Camber Café has not been removed as it can be seen from the premises and could be stood up if blown over. Our action to date has been to try and regulate the large timber structures that were erected in the highway at various remote locations, sometimes nailed onto BT telegraph poles at height. It is a matter of public record that the judge required formal application be made to erect remote advertising signage so that the safety of users of the highway is not compromised by individual commercial gain.

Regarding the burger van in the lay by, I agree that flashing lights are an unacceptable distraction to motorists and I shall ask that they be removed from the highway.

Yours sincerely

Rag-Eme-Kale

Team Manager, Inspection & Enforcement

EAST SUSSEX COUNTY COUNCIL

Lesley was not satisfied with Rag-Eme-Kale's answer to her email and she was not going to desist pestering them until she had been given an intelligent and plausible explanation as to why they were wasting so much time harassing me while they were neglecting far more important issues like the pot holes and overflowing drains in her road. It was so reassuring having Lesley's support, as she had been the only person who had not suggested that I should forsake my café signs, whereas most of the people in Camber had urged me to give up as it was their opinion that I would never beat the Council. Never would I give in to those obnoxious, corrupt individuals to whom we paid our council tax, and their comments just fuelled my determination to rise to the challenge.

Lesley replied:

Thank you for your response. I am afraid that I still find that you are prepared to hassle this lady as opposed to others. You do seem to be targeting her and making small things an issue that you will ignore elsewhere. This must surely be defined as discrimination.

The A-boards in Cinque Port St, I am bound to say, are much more of a hazard to both pedestrians and traffic than that which is outside the Camber café which is in a side road of little and slow moving traffic and few pedestrians. During high winds the boards from the Cinque Ports Public House right along that road can be found flat across the pavement causing pedestrians to walk out into the very busy and dangerous road. Not to mention should they go into the road. I am pleased that you will be doing something about the flashing lights on the burger van. His A-board was down and broken and abutting the highway not so long ago too! Surely this would cause a BIG problem if it were to blow into the already busy and dangerous Camber Rd - particularly in Summer months when car loads of children are being ferried down to the coast. This board again presents a much greater hazard on the busy main road to the coast than the Camber Café which as I mentioned before is in a remote side street of little traffic and that which is there is slow moving.

I just do not see your logic at all. Surely the rules are for ALL not JUST FOR ONE.

If you care to check the pavement outside the Green Grocery in Cinque Port Street there was less than 18' space the other day. Would it not be a good idea to remove the lay-by and use this as pavement if you wish them to use the pavement?
Lesley

There was no response from Rag-Eme-Kale.

CHAPTER 49

At 11.59pm on 9th April 2011 the injunction order bestowed upon me one year previously expired and I became a liberated woman once more, free to use foul, abusive and defamatory language and place signs on or abutting the highway, if I chose to of course.

The following day I received a phone call from Hastings County Court informing me that a date had been set for the hearing for my committal to prison, that being 15th April 2011. Straight away I contacted Gary to tell him the long awaited news and also to be sure he was able to attend the court on that day. He was available and he told me to meet him at the court at 9am sharp to discuss the procedure. I did get the feeling that my crimes were rather petty compared to the usual criminals Gary had to defend, but I was confident he would win the day.

Later that morning I received an email from Judgement Jones:

Sally,

Back in February, you sent me some defence evidence which consisted of your statement and three exhibits. Is this all the evidence you will be relying on? Who is representing you at the hearing?

Rag-Eme-Kale and Peter Plonker are sending new statements and exhibits and I will forward these to you by the end of the week.

.

For a start I had sent five exhibits not three and the fact that Rag-Eme-Kale and Peter Plonker had written more statements convinced me they were worried about the way Gary had responded to the allegations.

Judgement Jones,
I sent you five exhibits which two have you lost?
Please will you email me the new statements before you send
them as I will have to decide if it is necessary for me to
respond? You haven't given me much time again have you?
Sally

He replied saying he had found the missing exhibits and he was anxious to know if I had someone to represent me at the Court hearing the following week and if I had would I tell him as soon as possible.

I told him if I had any news on the matter he would be the first to know. It was not long before he emailed me:

Sally
At next week's hearing we will also apply for a new two year
injunction against you. My application and a statement
supporting it are attached.

I opened the attachments and read the contents.

The first was a copy of the application applying to the Court for another injunction order for two years. As I read it, it became clear that because of the way Gary had written my defence in respect to their allegations against me they had sought to change the wording on the new Injunction Order for which they were applying. Whereas the first time I was 'forbidden to use foul, abusive or defamatory language or engage in threatening behaviour <u>towards </u>any member of the applicants staff' it had now been re-worded to '<u>towards or about</u>'. That sounded to me as if all the allegations made regarding that part of the breach had failed hopelessly; why else would they want to change it?

WITNESS STATEMENT OF JUDGEMENT JONES

I, JUDGEMENT JONES, of Lewes County Council

1. *I am a Solicitor of the Supreme Court employed by the Applicant authority, and have supervision of this matter on its behalf.*

2. *I make this statement in relation to the Applicant's application for an order for committal to prison in respect of the Respondent, and, more particularly, in relation to the Applicant's application for the Order made on 9th April 2010 ('the Order') to be re-imposed.*

Background

4. *The Order was granted by this Honourable Court following a hearing at the conclusion of which it was found that the Respondent had, on numerous occasions, placed signs on or abutting the Highway. This had repeatedly been done, despite the Applicant's attempts to engage with the Respondent. The Order, which contained a penal notice, was thus very much a last resort.*

5. *The second limb of the Order prevented the Respondent from using foul, abusive or defamatory language, or threatening behaviour, towards the Applicant's staff. This was imposed because, when the Applicant attempted to engage with the Respondent, their staff was usually met with such behaviour on the part of the Respondent*

6. *As a result, the Order was granted, for a term of 1 year, expiring on 9ʰ April 2011.*

7. *Unfortunately, the Applicant says that the Respondent's behaviour persisted. As a result, on 14ʰ September 2010, the Applicant issued an Application for committal. This was listed for hearing on 14ʰ December 2010 but that hearing was adjourned due to difficulties with listing.*

8. *The hearing has been re-listed for 15ʰ April 2011*

9. *The Applicant will say that, at the time of making the Application for committal, the   Respondent had on numerous occasions breached the Order by, for example:-*

i   Placing an inflatable doll by the side of the Highway, nicknamed 'Tall Paul' on 15th May 2010 which blows over into the Highway and has generated complaints from the public;

ii   Placing a sign on the Highway on 7th July 2010;

iii   Placing a sign on the Highway on 8th July 2010;

iv   Placing a sign on the Highway on 27th July 2010;

v   Chaining a bicycle to a pole situated on or abutting the Highway on 11th August 2010;

vi   Placing a sign on the roof of a parked car on the highway on 10th September 2010.

10. *These steps have been taken by the Respondent despite warnings about her behaviour from the Applicant. In particular, on 6ʰ September 2010, the Applicant wrote to the Respondent warning her that the repeated breaches of the Order could result in her imprisonment.*

11. *The Applicant will also say that the Respondent has continued to abuse the Applicants Staff in breach of the Order.*

The Position Now

The position as set out above was how matters stood when the Application for committal was made last year. Since that hearing was adjourned, the position has changed.

The Respondent has served upon the Applicant a witness statement, dated 21ˢᵗ January 2011, in which she denies breaching the Order. However, she accepts placing an A-board outside her premises on numerous occasions between June and July 2010, placing an advertisement on the bicycle aforesaid, and placing a sign on the roof of her car, which she maintains she then 'legally parked' on the Highway.

1. The Respondent also accepts corresponding with the Applicant last year, in the course of which she, inter alia, called a member of the Applicant's staff a thief and liar in French, and alleged that the Applicant's staff had lied about her.

2. The Applicant will thus say that, by the Respondent's own admission, she has breached the Order.

3. Since December, however, the Respondent does appear to have taken down most of the signs she had placed on or abutting the Highway. As a result, since the start of this year, the Applicant has found the following:-

i. Defacement of the existing Highway directional signage by adding the word 'Café', photographed by the Applicant on 14ᵗʰ May 2010 and seemingly still in place on 29ᵗʰ March 2011. The Applicant alleges that the Respondent is responsible for this;

ii. The Respondent's car was, on 30th March 2011, found parked on the C24 New Lydd Road, near the junction with Lydd Road, with the advertisement in situ.

1. Whilst the Respondent is silent on the first point above (the defacement of signage) she does accept that she has parked her car as alleged.

2. However, the Applicant in turn, would accept that the position as it now stands is a marked improvement from where matters stood at the time that the Order for Committal was applied for last year. The Applicant accepts that the Court might well wish to extend every opportunity to the Respondent to avoid a prison sentence.

3. Certainly, from the Applicant's view point, the priority is not to send the Respondent to prison; the priority is to avoid hazard to users of the Highway – particularly such hazards as the use of the signage and the inflatable doll 'Tall Paul' represents.

What the Applicant Seeks

4. If the Order has had the effect of reining in the Respondent's behaviour, and controlling the situation, then the Applicant is delighted. It is public money well spent.

5. However, what concerns the Applicant is that the Order will, by the time of the re-listed hearing, have expired. The Respondent will be free of any checks and controls upon her behaviour. And that behaviour has only recently improved and, to some extent, continues.

6. *Moreover, the Applicant is concerned that the behaviour might start all over again.*

7. Exhibited hereto as GJ/1 are the following:-
i. E-mail received from the Respondent dated 24th January 2011;
ii. E-mail received from the Respondent dated 7th March 2011;

1.In the e-mail of 24th January 2011 the Respondent asks whether, upon the expiry of the Order, she can 'rip it up and toss it the bin [sic] or do what I do with it, like give it back to you, and does it mean I am free to resume my freedom of doing things like I was before?'

2. On 7th March the Applicant received an e-mail from the Respondent saying 'only 33 days to go!' – A clear reference to the expiry of the Order.

3. Effectively, of course, once the Order expires the Applicant is free to go back to doing what she was doing before. This concerns the Applicant because:-

i. In her witness statement, the Respondent accepts the behaviour alleged but denies breaching the Order. She seems to think she has done nothing wrong;
ii. The Respondent continues to have a presence on the Highway;
iii. The Respondent seems to suggest, in the e-mails exhibited hereto and referred to above, that she will return to her previous behaviour once the Order expires.

1. Further, and or alternatively, the Applicant will of course say that the sending of such e-mails is in itself threatening and in breach of the Order.

2. The Applicant thus seeks a renewal of the Order, to run for a period of two years.

3. The Applicant accepts that, in applying for a renewal of the Order, and asking that application to be dealt with at the next hearing, matters are at something of a late stage. However, the Applicant would respectfully submit that:-

i. The position now is different to that in place at the time the Application was made last year;

ii. The Applicant wished carefully to consider its options before becoming embroiled in further litigation;

iii. Developments in March (the continuing use by the Respondent of her car and the e-mail of 7th March both referred to above) have forced the Applicant's hand;

iv. There is no prejudice to the Respondent thereby; her behaviour does seem to have improved, but it is clear on her own admission that it has not resolved, and she continues to threaten that it will worsen.

Summary

1. The Applicant is less concerned with punitive measures, and more concerned with preventative ones. The Applicant does not of course wish to usurp the functions or authority of this Honourable Court.

2. Thus, whilst the Applicant contends that breaches of the Order occurred last year, and continue this year, although on a lesser scale, the Applicant's main concern is to secure a further Order.

3. It is on that basis that this witness statement is made, and I would respectfully submit that a further Order is a necessity in order to prevent a recurrence of the behaviour that caused the Order to be made in the first place.

*4. I would seek the same wording as in the existing injunction, save that the phrase 'foul or abusive language or defamatory behaviour....**towards** any member of the Claimant's staff' be replaced with '**towards or about** any member of the Claimant's staff:*

So that was Judgement Jones witness statement. He seemed to be asking the court not to commit me to prison after all but to issue me with a new injunction order to last for two years. How condescending, I thought, when it had been his main objective for the last twelve months to have me incarcerated. This court case was his ultimate chance in achieving it and it seemed that he had changed his mind. It must have been something to do with my three page witness statement.

I printed the statement to take to Lesley but as it came to the end of Judgement Jones statement it just carried on printing. I could see that something else was being printed. When it stopped I took the papers and put them into the correct order. I soon realised there was more there than just Judgement Jones witness statement and as I started to read the extra printout, I could not believe what Judgement Jones had accidently sent me. It was from the ugly barrister advising Judgement Jones clients of the way he was going to advise

Judgement Jones and assist him in writing his witness statement.

How could Judgement Jones be so incompetent by sending this private document which was all about me to me?

I read the surprise document; it was so exciting knowing that it had not been intended for me. It was from the ugly barrister to the Highways and for the attention of Judgement Jones;

I have recently discussed this matter at some length with my Instructing Solicitor, following updated witness statements obtained by him – with his usual efficiency – from his clients. I am concerned about the prospects of obtaining a prison sentence, or even suspended sentence, at the hearing on 15th April 2011 as, from what I can see, the Respondent's behaviour currently boils down to (1) defacement of a sign that cannot be proved to have been her responsibility and which cannot be dated, as I read the position, and (2) the continuing presence of her parked car with an A-board on the roof.

This is a markedly improved position over that which prevailed when the original application for committal was framed.

Moreover, the Order of 9th April 2010 expires tomorrow. Thus I suspect that the Court will extend sympathy to the Respondent.

However, the risk is that her behaviour immediately resumes once the Order ceases – and her e-mails of this year seem to imply that this is a possibility.

I understand that the Applicant's primary aim is to protect the position to stop the behaviour resuming. To that end, I would suggest shifting the focus of the coming hearing away from the punitive measures associated with breaching the Order, and instead focusing on renewing the Order itself.

To that end, I have drafted a witness statement for my Instructing Solicitor to review and, if he is content, sign. The e-mails mentioned therein will need to be exhibited as REK/1. I would strongly suggest issuing a new Application Notice to accompany it, so that the Respondent and Court are on notice that the Applicant will apply to renew the Order.

Turning to the content of the Application Notice, Form N244 can be used. The Order the Applicant is asking the Court to make can I think be described as 'An Order that the Injunction Order granted on 9th April 2010 shall resume in the same terms as before for a further 2 years'.

The second page can be filled out merely by ticking the box marked 'the attached witness statement' and, in the box below, writing 'Please see attached witness statement'.

In terms of running the hearing on 15th April I would suggest softening the stance away from the breaches of last year. It is likely that those breaches can be established, but they are now somewhat historical.

The Court may wish to punish them in any event. However, I would suggest that the Applicant's focus should be on renewing the Order.

As the Application for renewal of the Order is being made at a late stage there is the risk that it is not heard at the next hearing. I think that unlikely, however. Should it arise, it might be possible to persuade the Court to grant an interim Order.

I would suggest serving the statement and Application Notice as a matter of urgency. In the covering letter to the Respondent I would suggest stressing that this is an additional step to the application currently before the Court.

Hopefully the position is clear from the witness statement herewith I can of course be contacted in chambers should anything arise.

So Judgement Jones had not even written his own witness statement. What kind of solicitor apart from a useless one was he?

At least I was not off to prison for two years that was for sure. It spoilt the surprise really, but never mind, I did have the most positive feeling that the Council were not as self-confident as they had been at the last court case when they all lied with smug expressions on their faces. Oh how things had changed!

I started to read the new witness statement of Peter Plonker the Senior Maintenance Technician

I, Peter Plonker, will say as follows:

1. Further to my previous statement dated 10 Sept 10, I would like to add the following, On Tuesday 29 Mar 11 and as a result of a complaint I was requested to attend Camber East Sussex. The complaint received intimated that as an authority the Claimant appears to be taking enforcement action against the Defendant, whilst allowing others to commit offences in that boards and flashing lights advertising a mobile food van, known as A J's Snacks, operating out of a layby on the C24 west of Camber, East Sussex were being ignored.

2. On Wednesday 30th March 2011 in company with the Senior Maintenance Engineer for the area, I attended the Camber area and found one A-board was located west of the above layby, this board was not on the highway and I can produce a photograph of the A-board as an exhibit marked PP/6.

3. There were no flashing lights displayed either on or around the mobile food van which I photographed, this photograph is produced as an exhibit marked PP/7.

4. The claimant often takes action against people who place unauthorised signs on the highway. The above is just one example of this. If the defendant feels she is being singled out, it is because she offends repeatedly and on a more continual basis than anybody else the Highways Department of the Claimant has to deal with The Claimant avers that it is in any event proportionate to monitor the Defendant's compliance, or lack of, with the Injunction Order imposed upon her.

5. On the 30th March 2011, I also noted that the white Peugeot motor vehicle index number J94LDY containing the effigies of various members of the Claimants staff and advertising the Camber Café was parked on the main C24 New Lydd Road near the junction with Lydd Road, the only other A-boards displayed including, one outside the Camber Café, were all placed within the tolerance permitted. The car referred to is shown in a photograph marked PP/8. Even though the sign is on the roof of the car, this is still considered to be on the highway because the terms of the injunction forbid the placing of any signs or posters on street furniture or other structures on the highway or which abut the highway, without the express written consent of the Claimant as the Highway Authority.

6. I now refer to my exhibit PP4 showing a bicycle displaying a café open sign, I have been asked to confirm that this bicycle was on the highway; This bicycle was placed leaning against a utility distribution pole and chained to a metal post, both the distribution pole and the metal post were located on *the highway, therefore the bicycle placed against the front of the distribution pole and with the sign prominently displayed on it was situated on the highway or abutting the highway. The land is considered highway because it adjoins the carriageway. The defendant was told to remove the sign attached to the bicycle by a letter from the Council solicitors dated 6th September 2010 (exhibit REK/3). The defendant in fact removed the sign of her own accord several months ago. In her defence statement she says that she received 'advice from the Citizens Advice Bureau' that she could place the sign at that location. With all due respect, the fact that the CAB (who are not experts in highway law) might have said she could do something does not mean that she has complied with her injunction. In any event I would question why she decided to remove the sign if the Defendant was so convinced that she was legally allowed to place it there.*

That was Peter Plonker's witness statement; he sounded like a child telling tales. He thought I was responsible for Lesley's emails complaining about them discriminating against me. I was annoyed at the comment he had made about the sign on the bike. It was Kerry that kept urging me to remove it and I had really not wanted to and now Peter Plonker had made an issue of it.

I read Rag-Eme-Kale's second witness statement.

I, Rag-Eme-Kale, a Highways Manager employed by the Claimant, in the Transport and Environment Department, will say as follows:

1. Following on from my first Witness Statement dated 25th August 2010, I now produce, signed and dated by me as Exhibit GL/7, two chains of email correspondence from the Defendant to our Legal Services Department on 24th of

January 2011 and 7th March 2011. As can be seen from the emails, the Defendant implies that once the current Injunction expires, she intends to resume placing unauthorised signs in the public highway. The fact that her email of 24th of January 2011 (10.51am) states '...when this injunction order expires in 44 days' time, do I just rip it up and toss it in the bin....does it mean I am free to resume my freedom of doing things like I was before?' would seem to confirm this. Her more recent email of 7th of March seems to be looking forward to the expiry of her injunction and is contemptuous of the Council for bringing this matter to court in the first place. She comments that '...only 33 days to go! Did you see David Cameron on the news yesterday, he said not to take any notice of Council's nonsense regarding small businesses, and I might have to drag him with me to my court case to say it again'.

2. The Defendant has also sent several emails which are fairly contemptuous of the court process itself. In her email of the 24th of January 2011 (14.58) she states that '...besides I'm in no hurry to go and sit all day in a court room with predators and as I understand it, as I am the baddy I get the choice of where I go'. She has also paid very little of the costs awarded against her at the injunction hearing. In her email of 7th March 2011 (12.59pm), she makes a very flippant suggestion that because, in her words, she is unable to pay the Council any money '...I have decided that in fairness to me, you can ask The Tyrannical Clown to give you the cost of my A-boards and café signs which he had removed...I hope you will find this arrangement satisfactory'. This is a reference to the fact that many of the unauthorised advertisements she has placed have been removed along with the wooden boards to which they were attached. When this suggestion is rejected by the Council's lawyer Judgement Jones, the Defendant responds by stating 'Well how am I meant to find the money Judgement

Jones, I suppose I could try selling my body....Why should I have a lengthy prison sentence for not having any money....'. The Injunction ordered the Defendant to pay a sum of £1500 on or before 23rd of April 2010 as well as a further £1000 to pay for the removal of the signs. To date, the Defendant has only paid £285 towards this. The whole tone of her correspondence suggests that the Defendant is not taking this matter seriously and would appear to regard the law as an inconvenience that stands in the way of her 'right' to advertise her business. The fact that these emails were sent after she had received the summons for her committal to prison would appear to confirm this view.

3. I now produce, signed and dated by me as Exhibit·GL/8, a photograph taken on the 14th May 2010 of the existing highway directional signage in Camber that has been defaced by the word 'café' handwritten in permanent black marker. It is an offence under section 132 of the Highways Act 1980 for a person to paint or otherwise inscribe any picture, letter, sign or other mark upon the surface of the highway, on any tree or upon any structure in the highway without the consent of the highway authority. I also exhibit more recent photographs taken on 29th March 2011 of the same highway signage defaced again by the words 'café'. Although it cannot be proved, it is believed that the Defendant has done this to point towards her café.

4. With reference to the Defendant's statement concerning the A-board placed immediately outside the café on 3rd June 2010, 7th July and 8th July 2010; I can confirm that we have never taken this sign away. As it is immediately outside the Defendant's premises, it can be observed through the window and there is a measure of control in that it can be picked up if it blows over. However, it was placed too far into the *carriageway, obstructing traffic flow and forcing southbound vehicles into the path of oncoming traffic. Consequently it was required that the A-board was moved out of the carriageway to behind the double yellow lines. I now produce, signed and dated by me as Exhibit GL/9, photographs taken on the 3rd June 2010 showing the A-board in a position too far out into the carriageway, and photographs taken on 11th July and 2nd August 2010 showing the A-board in a more acceptable position.*

I believe that the facts contained within this statement are true.

Rag-Eme-Kale's second witness statement was all about emails I had sent to Judgement Jones that were nothing to do with him. The photographs of my A-board outside the café were not on the carriageway. There was no purpose to this witness statement and nothing that Judgement Jones could not have contributed himself.

CHAPTER 50

I sent Judgement Jones draft statement, the ugly barrister's advice and predictions and new witness statements to Gary. There were only seven days left till the court hearing, and Judgement Jones was still unsure if I had representation and probably thought that I did not.

Having had the privilege of seeing Judgement Jones instructions from his barrister it was evident that the request for my committal to prison was going to fail hopelessly and surely the reason for these last minute witness statements and exhibits plus the renewal of the injunction order could only serve as an attempt to impede my first witness statement. I was undeterred as there were seven days left which was enough time for me to gather more evidence.

First of all I asked Lesley to write a statement in response to Peter Plonker's comment which implied that either I had written or instigated Lesley's complaint.

It was imperative that I got a photo of AJ's red light on and off to prove that Peter Plonker was lying. It was easy taking a photo with the light on as all I had to do was to pull up just before the layby where he parked his bus and quickly take the photo, but to take a photo of the red light off was a lot harder. I knew he stopped off at the news agent every morning but not always at the same time, usually between 7.45 and 8.30. I had no choice but to sit in wait for him in my car. The first day I waited nearly an hour but he didn't show up. The next day I missed him; just as I got to the top of the road he came driving along New Lydd Road. I waved to him and disappointed I went back to the café. The third day I had my car in position opposite the newsagent and after a few minutes I spotted AJ's bus coming down the road. I opened the passenger window, despite the rain coming in, and put my phone in camera mode. When AJ got out of his bus I pretended I was having a phone conversation with someone. The red light was off and there was no evidence at all that there was an illuminated sign on his bus, so as soon as he went into the newsagent I quickly took a photo and headed back to the café. The photos, although spotted with rain drops, proved beyond doubt that when the illuminated red 'OPEN' sign was off there was nothing but a blank visible which proved Peter Plonker's black and white photo was fraudulent as it clearly showed the outline of the word 'OPEN' as white blobs. Now I had that vital piece of evidence plus the witness statement from the man who owned the fish shop and also a statement from the postman who had been driving the post office van in Beaky's photo.

Lesley wrote her statement:

On 9ᵗʰ March 2011 I sent a complaint to the Highways Agency regarding a red light on a burger van known as AJ's Snacks. I was told in a reply from Rag-Eme-Kale that he agreed that the light was a distraction to motorists and that he would do something about it.
I now understand that when the inspector went to Camber he claims that the van had no red lights on or around it.
I now produce a photo taken on 12ᵗʰ April 2011 which clearly shows a red light being displayed on the front of the van.

I sent Gary Lesley's statement, and he already had the original signed statements of the postman and the fish shop owner. I waited for his response to my extra evidence before I sent the other two bundles.

Gary did respond; he said that Lesley's statement served no purpose as it was nothing to do with me breaching the injunction order, but I argued that as Peter Plonker had mentioned AJ's light in the first place which was also nothing to do with me breaching the order, Lesley's statement was to prove that he was lying. I wanted the judge to know that they had lied and the more proof I had the better it was for me. The same applied to the postman and the fish shop owner's statements. Gary said if that is what I wanted that's the way it would be.

I decided it was time to put Judgement Jones out of his misery by informing him that I did have legal representation for the court hearing. So I sent him a short email saying;

Morning Judgement Jones
I do have someone to represent me on Friday :)
Sally

He replied almost instantly;

Well who is it? Is it a solicitor or barrister?
Also, please note that the statements in these proceedings are
for the attention of yourself and your legal representative
only. They are confidential and privileged legal documents.
The fact that you have circulated them to your friend Lesley
who has written to myself and Rag-Eme-Kale commenting on
their contents is a very serious business, especially as court
proceedings are ongoing. Please do not give any further
documents to Lesley or anybody else, other than your lawyers.
Judgement Jones

What a cheek him saying that I had circulated document contents, especially as it was Lesley who had written the contents in the first place that I had then circulated back to her. I had every right to circulate what I wanted and to whom I chose, he should have been careful what he circulated. I replied;

Judgement Jones
Well, I felt Peter Plonker's statement implied I had written that complaint or that I had instigated it which I hadn't. And anyway it was Peter Plonker who circulated that private document in his statement, so why shouldn't I tell the person who wrote it in the first place? So blame Peter Plonker not me......
I have a barrister representing me called Gary. Is there anything else you would like to know? And if you don't know already I have relocated Tall Paul so he won't blow into the road, he's in next door's garden, OK?
Are you still going to use the first bundle on Friday or are you just going to use these latest ones with the new evidence?
Sally

He emailed back straight away;

Sally
Both bundles will be used as there are two separate applications - one for your committal to prison for breaching the now expired original injunction, the second is a new application for a fresh injunction.

I had the last say on the matter and wrote back;

Judgement Jones
What would be the point of putting me in prison with an injunction order? I will not have the need to put café signs up in prison will I?
How long will all this take, you have stated one whole day for the first bundle for committal to prison so am I to presume we

*will be there all night as well for the second bundle for a
'fresh' injunction order?*
Sally

The next day I emailed Judgement Jones again and
attached the three new witness statements and photographic
evidence of AJ's turned off 'OPEN' sign;

Dear Judgement Jones
*Here attached are three witness statements and exhibits. May
I give your Barrister the signed copies on Friday please? If I
send them to you they will get there too late. If there is a
problem with any of this will you please let me know and
anyway can you confirm that you have received it?*
Thank you
Sally,

Within a couple of minutes Judgement Jones replied;

*I have received them. I suggest you bring the signed originals
to court on Friday.*
I assume you have sent copies to the judge and your Counsel?

He could assume what he liked.
Despite the short notice that he was applying for his 'fresh'
injunction order, I had got everything under control, and after
work I drove to Hastings to hand deliver the extra documents
for the judge.
I had four friends coming to the court to support me and of
course to see the gorgeous Gary.
On the morning of Friday 15th April 2011 I left the café in
Lily's capable hands and set off once again to Hastings
County Court to be committed to prison with a 'fresh'

injunction order.

 As I drove I reflected on what might happen if things did not go my way despite having Gary to defend me. There was always the possibility that the judge might order that I remove all the café signs from their locations and that would include the sign on the car. If that was to be the case the only option I could think of to continue to have a sign to the café was to dress up as Highway Hen, put a chair on the roof of the car and seat myself like Boudicca with a large Café Open sign. I would purchase a large pointing foam rubber hand so when a car approached I would swing the finger to point in the direction of the café.

CHAPTER 51

I dressed in black for my court appearance, with black leggings, long black t-shirt, a very expensive black Laura Ashley cropped cardigan and black Rocket boots. I liked wearing black because it enhanced my white spiky hair.

I was meeting Gary at 9 o'clock at the Court, and I arrived in good time, parked my car and went through the process at the entrance into the court of being zapped and having my bag searched. I reported to the check-in desk. I was getting quite used to this procedure.

As I went up the steps to the waiting area I saw Gary, who came over to greet me, and we went into a side room where it was private. We sat at the table and he explained that he had offered his services for this morning's committal and that is what he was prepared to do. However, he had not agreed to defend me in regard to the new injunction order that the council were seeking. He said as he was already here at the court he would assist me free of charge in dealing with the application to renew the injunction order but he would not assist me further if the application for the injunction order was not concluded this day. If I chose to object to the injunction order and it was to be dealt with at a later date I would have to deal with it myself as he would not be prepared to return here.

I understood totally what he was saying and it was true he had only agreed the £1000 for the day to defend me in the council's quest for my committal to prison. I was not bothered, as if I was given another injunction order it was only a piece of paper after all.

He was happy that I understood and accepted his proposal, and he then said he would go and find the Council's barrister to speak with and I went to look to see if my friends had arrived.

Lesley and Jenny were sitting waiting for me, and they were sure they had seen Kilkenny, Rag-Eme-Kale and Peter Plonker arrive and they too had disappeared into a private side room. Both Jenny and Lesley were impatient to see Gary and then Jo-Anne and Dave arrived to join us. Jo-Anne had never been to a court hearing before and she was quite excited at this new experience. I had made Jo-Anne a book of the poems I had written about the employees of East Sussex Highways so she could read them during the morning and understand the reason for me being in the court in the first place for committal to prison.

Luckily Lesley had brought a packet of mints which we all sucked like crazy, and as we were gathered round I decided I wanted a photo of us in the court so I took one with my phone but as soon as I had taken it the court clerk came and said it was forbidden to take photos in the court and I must delete the photo. I said I would but I did not.

Lesley and Jenny went to buy themselves a coffee from the canteen at the end of the waiting hall and on the way Lesley stopped to read the days listings, and noticed that I was the only person who was appearing in court for committal to prison and as they queued to buy their coffees Lesley saw the 'Black Maria' reversing into its parking space waiting to cart me off to prison if I should go.

Then as time passed Gary came over to us dressed in his gown and wig and said I had to go back into the private side room. He told my friends they could come as well. We all squashed inside the small room, and Gary explained to me what was going to happen. I would be sitting behind him and he would do all the talking. I was on no account to say a word, if I needed to say something he would be standing directly in front of me. I asked him how I would be able to get his attention and I suggested I should poke him in the back but he

was offended by my remark and scowled at me for suggesting
I do such a thing. So the moment arrived and we were called
to the court room. We all piled out and mounted the stair case
and went into the court room; it was even bigger than the last
court hearing I had attended in the depths of the Court
building. Peter Plonker, Rag-Eme-Kale and Kilkenny were sat
in a row at the back of the court room so my friends also sat at
the back on the other side. The Council's barrister was sitting
on the left hand side at the front in all his court regalia with a
mountainous pile of folders and papers in front of him. Gary
went before me and settled down in his place checking his
papers. As I passed the three council witnesses I stopped and
shook hands with Rag-Eme-Kale and Kilkenny who was
wearing his funeral suit again. I gave each of them a big smile
and said how nice it was to see them again so soon. I
introduced myself to Peter Plonker as I had never met him
before. He was certainly in his 60's, a big stocky man with a
silver grey crew cut. I vaguely remembered seeing him in
Camber driving a Highway van and he also fitted the
description that Tommy had given me the day he saw
someone with a clipboard checking round the Peugeot on the
main road. I took my place behind Gary, remembering not to
poke him in the back as I sat down, and turned and looked at
my friends sitting along the back row and then I glanced at the
council witnesses and thought they looked very amusing sat
there in a row trying to look tough.

All of a sudden the clerk told us to stand up which we did
for the judge to enter the Court room; he was such a nice
looking man with a lot of thick wavy white hair and beautiful
blue eyes. He looked kind and smiled at everyone. He told us
to sit and then the two barristers stood up again. All this
standing up and sitting down amused me.

The Council's barrister proceeded to tell the judge all about
my café signs, injunction orders, foul, abusive and defamatory

language and my threatening behaviour towards council staff. I had breached the injunction order again and that is why I was here today for committal to prison and to be given a 'fresh' injunction order for fear of what I might do as the first one had expired and I was free to stick my signs up anywhere unchecked.

He went on to say I had illegally put a sign on the roof of my car and a sign on a bike and the bike was attached to street furniture, I had an A-board outside of the café which was placed on the road causing an obstruction and a danger not only to cars but to pedestrians too. Every so often Lesley disagreed very loudly with what their barrister was saying and every time she expressed her opinion loudly the judge looked at her. When the barrister got to the episode of me believing I was being singled out and he said I was not and everybody was treated the same if they placed unauthorised signs on the highway, Lesley shouted that it was not true they did not treat everyone the same. I turned round and put my finger over my mouth asking Lesley to shush. The barrister just carried on trying to convince the judge I was a persistent offender and I had to be stopped. I had heard it all before the last time, and he went on and on. When their barrister eventually finished his peroration he bowed to the judge and sat down much to everyone's relief and the judge's as well by the expression on his face.

Now it was our turn, Gary stood up and began to point out to the judge how I had not breached the injunction order but I could hardly hear what he was saying; he was speaking to the judge so quietly maybe for fear of me poking him in the back. His speech was much shorter than the ugly barristers and in no time at all he had finished what he had to say and he sat down.

I, along with everyone else waited with baited breathe to hear the judge's response;

The judge removed his spectacles and looked to the back of the room at the three council witnesses and said 'How on earth do you expect me to commit someone to prison for an A-board, a sign on a car and a sign on a bike, and you aren't even calling any witnesses?'

I knew from his first remark that they had failed and what's more the judge's remark had only been meant to humiliate them. I turned round to smile at my friends and noticed Kilkenny was texting like crazy most probably to The Tyrannical Clown keeping him updated on the proceedings.

The judge said that he saw A-boards on nearly every road he drove along and they were a way of life and if they were not visible the businesses would fail. He said that they must surely remember the old butcher's bikes that had signs hanging off the cross bar and he also said that putting signs on car roofs was common practice these days. He had seen signs on large trailers parked in fields and in lay-bys.

Once again he looked over to the three witnesses and asked them what was their definition of 'abutting', it had to be on or off it could not be both? There was silence and no-one responded, so I thought that maybe they did not know the answer. The judge repeated his question 'what was their definition of abutting' and their barrister finally stood up but stooped his body forward and in a very faint voice almost whispering replied ''On' your Honour'.

I turned again to smile victoriously at my friends who were also smiling as the Council's case against me was rapidly disintegrating. The three highway men looked glum; Kilkenny was still texting like there was no tomorrow, probably complaining to The Tyrannical Clown that they were having to endure such degradation. Their barrister suddenly jumped up bowing and stuttering as if he was pleading for his life 'If I may Your Honour' and given permission by the judge he went into great detail of the day I had texted Kilkenny and called him an 'arsehole'. That only made matters worse for them, the judge said 'they were to expect those kind of remarks as it was part of their job'. He continued that he himself had been called far worse things than that and if he took offence every time he had been verbally abused he would have changed profession long ago. He told the three burly highwaymen that they needed to get a thicker skin if they were going to be offended by such a trivial remark.

I had to turn round and snigger at them, how stupid the judge had made them look and rightly so.

Court was adjourned and we stood up as the judge left the court room to consider the evidence.

The three council witnesses shot off out of the court room followed quickly by their barrister and had disappeared completely by the time we reached the hall at the bottom of the staircase. Gary went off to be alone and Jenny and I went outside for some fresh air, leaving Jo-Anne, Dave and Lesley in the court building. Jenny was optimistic that the council were losing and rightly so; she was disgusted with the amount of money they had wasted on my café signs when she had a pothole like a crater right outside her house.

We sat at the bottom of the steps outside the court and whilst we were sitting there discussing the demise of the council's case against me we were joined by Kilkenny, Rag-Eme-Kale and their barrister who had congregated a few steps up from us. Jenny and I ignored them and decided to go back into the court. As we passed them I was surprised that Kilkenny wished me luck. I looked at him and asked if he was sure it was me who needed the good luck.

We were summoned back into the courtroom, and Gary seemed to appear from nowhere. We resumed our places and waited for the judge to come back. We were ordered to rise, the same old routine, we stood up and sat down in turn and the barristers stood up and sat down.

The judge started his brief summary. In his opinion the question of placing A-boards on the highway was not an issue for the Highways Authority but a matter for Rother District Council and therefore he felt that if there was an issue Rother District Council should deal with it and not the County Council. Their barrister stood up and asked for a two year injunction order to be given to me but he requested that the wording be changed from 'towards' to 'towards and about'. The judge said he would place an injunction on me but he would not agree to include the word 'about'. Gary turned to me and asked me if I had understood that I was receiving the injunction order. With all the excitement going on I had forgotten all about the deal we had made earlier in the side room. I told him I did not want it, and he looked really cross and said under his breathe that I had to have it. So I just nodded my head. Then their barrister brought up the subject of the costs and asked the judge to award his clients costs against me. The judge asked him how much the case had cost the council and their barrister looked at his paper and said '£11,600 your Honour' but they were prepared to reduce it under the circumstances.

The judge looked at them and said he thought I had given them enough money already and so he would not be awarding them any costs but they would be put in abeyance and if I breached the injunction order I would have to pay the costs.

The judge looked at Lesley and told her that she must respect the Highways Authority, but she quickly informed the judge that she was not me. He had not even noticed I was sitting there behind Gary and he apologised to Lesley for confusing her with me. I thought it was her own fault because she had spoken out and gesticulated to the judge for the entire duration of the court hearing. He then focused on me and repeated how I must respect the authorities and abide by the laws of the land. I nodded and smiled with my fingers crossed behind my back.

We all stood up as the judge and barristers bowed to each for the last time, the judge let himself out via a door behind him, and the three highway men vanished before I had turned round to leave.

In the foyer outside the court room I jumped for joy. We were all very happy at the outcome. I did not care about getting another injunction order, as it was only a piece of paper after all. Lesley thought the judge had only agreed to it to save their face after the humiliation the three highway men had suffered in front of me and my friends.

Gary beckoned us into the side room and I thanked him. He said he never wanted to see me again, and I said likewise. He gathered up his briefcase and gown and left. I had the feeling that this type of case was rather tame for him. I think he preferred murders and exciting things like that, but he had served me well and was worth every penny and probably more.

Jo-Anne and Dave also left clutching the book of poems I had given them. Lesley, Jenny and I were standing there laughing about the disgraced highway men when Rag-Eme-Kale suddenly appeared and shook my hand saying ' Sally, we knew we couldn't do you for the car and the bike' so I asked him why we were there then, and before he had taken a breath to give his reasons Lesley started on him in a very angry tone. She asked him why so much money had been wasted on my café signs and so little had been spent on repairing the huge pot holes that were really dangerous compared to my café sign on the car, and every time he attempted to answer her she stopped him with more fearful ranting. She said they should justify their actions but Rag-Eme-Kale, who was now sweating profusely, could only stand there and listen, in fact she was quite scary and I felt a bit sorry for Rag-Eme-Kale being on the other end of Lesley's wrath again. He never got the opportunity to explain their actions to Lesley as she walked off in anger. All he could do was to apologise to me; not really the behaviour of someone who had just attempted to have me incarcerated.

I asked Rag-Eme-Kale where Peter Plonker and Kilkenny had gone and he pointed to the canteen and said they were in there having a coffee, but we knew that they were embarrassed and hiding their humiliation.

Jubilant, we left the court and went home.

CHAPTER 52

The next morning I asked Frosty my neighbour if he would take the bike up to the caravan park in the back of his van so I could chain it back onto the scaffold pole. I felt gloriously defiant knowing the highway men could do nothing about it. I also put my sign back onto the fence at the bottom of the sand dunes.

The weather had become unseasonably hot and Camber was packed with day trippers all heading for the beach. Lesley had an idea that would help boost the café turnover. She urged me to invest in inflatables for my customers to purchase after they had had their breakfast. It seemed a good idea at the time, so I looked on-line for the best deals. I found a supplier and I bought 36 rubber rings, 10 crab and lobster rubber rings, 6 ridable whales, 6 ridable hammer-heads and 10 dragon boats at the cost of £250 all of which was debited to my credit card.

So with everything back on track and summer arriving early my thoughts turned to the judge who had been so sympathetic towards me and so unfavourable to the highway men. He had certainly summed them up which they would not have been expecting. I wondered if they had all ganged up on The Tyrannical Clown as it was he who had been out to get me in the first place and their reward for aiding and abetting him resulted in them being belittled and humiliated in front of me and my friends.

Having been told by Judgement Jones that they would not accede to my request for an enquiry against The Tyrannical Clown and Kilkenny I decided to contact the Local Government Ombudsman to see if they would be prepared to investigate my complaint against East Sussex County

Council. I gave a brief explanation of my allegations to the lady, she asked me if I had made a complaint to the Council already and she advised me that they will only investigate when I had exhausted all other channels of trying to get my complaint dealt with. I said that I had complained several times about Council employees and asked for an enquiry which had been refused. She told me in that case to send her the details of my complaint and she gave me a reference number.

I now felt confident that I was right in believing the Council had behaved badly towards me, so I thought I would give Rag-Eme-Kale one more chance;

Dear Rag-Eme-Kale
I am going to say it again, I want there to be an enquiry into why the Highways Authority have behaved in a manner that has caused me unnecessary financial hardship and put my business at risk of bankruptcy.
You yourself said to me at the court that you and your colleagues knew that you could not 'do' me for the car and the bike. I would therefore like to know the purpose of that costly court case. I would also like an investigation to prove that The Tyrannical Clown committed perjury twice, accused me of putting café signs on the highway after 6th October 2009 when he knew very well I hadn't and produced photographs which he knew were taken on 7th October 2009 and not 22nd October 2009 as was said and he accused me of refusing to pay the Council their costs when I had. Also I want to know why Kilkenny made a false witness statement more than once and why they had previously withheld information I had asked for to assist with my evidence for court cases 2 and 3.
Please will you tell me how I go about this to ensure that it will be investigated properly by someone who is to be trusted, not like someone in the complaints department who passed a

private letter I wrote to the Chief Executive who never saw the letter, which instead ended up in The Tyrannical Clown's possession.
Thank you and I look forward to hearing from you soon
Sally

When I had finished and sent the email I was feeling really quite annoyed with them for making me spend all that money to have Gary there and then the audacity of Rag-Eme-Kale saying they knew they couldn't 'do' me for the very things that they had tried to 'do' me for. What was the purpose of it all? They knew they would not frighten me and the more I thought about it the more irritated I became. Despite the second injunction order I had received from the court forbidding me from placing signs on or abutting the highway, the judge had more or less told Rag-Eme-Kale and his chums there was nothing wrong in it. I felt confident that I now had the upper hand in the situation which made me feel compelled to ridicule them like never before.

That day at the court had put a song on my mind, 'A Day Trip to Bangor', except I was hearing 'didn't we have a loverly time the day we went to Hastings'. I decided that I would re write the lyrics to 'A Day Trip to Bangor', download the karaoke version of the song, find some friends to sing it, then make them dress up as the effigies in the car and make a video.

That evening I wrote a song about the day I went to court to be incarcerated but had left victorious whilst the perpetrators hid in the court canteen wishing they had not agreed to do The Tyrannical Clown's dirty work for him.

I named my song 'A Day Trip to Hastings' and within a couple of hours it was finished

Didn't we have a lov-erly time the day we went to Hastings
We got to the court, sucked mints we had brought
Our bags were searched as we went in.....
We sat in a row, looked out for the foe we saw them with their
bundles
They hid in a room so we couldn't see them so we went outside

My barrister came and rounded us up and said he had to see
me
So we put out our fags and brushed ourselves down
Our bags were searched as we went in......
We went in a room he invited my friends so we were all
squashed in there
Soon I'd be off to face the judge so we all piled out.
Didn't we have a lov-erly time the day we went to Hastings
We got to the court, sucked mints we had brought
Our bags were searched as we went in.....
We sat in a row, looked out for the foe we saw them with their
bundles
They hid in a room so we couldn't see them so we went outside

We were told to stand up when the judge came in and then we
all sat down again
The Counsel stood up and bowed to the judge at last it was
beginning
The judge was amazed at the others request to send me off to
jail
For A-board on a car and A-board on a bike he turned quite
pale.
Didn't we have a lov-erly time the day we went to Hastings
We got to the court, sucked mints we had brought
Our bags were searched as we went in.....
We sat in a row, looked out for the foe we saw them with their
bundles

They hid in a room so we couldn't see them so we went outside

*They hadn't a clue what they would do they looked so glum
and stupid*
All in a row with nowhere to go, home would be a good idea
What a terrible waste of time it was what a real disgrace
There's someone we know who's got egg on his face
But we can't say who...
Didn't we have a lov-erly time the day we went to Hastings
We got to the court, sucked mints we had brought
Our bags were searched as we went in.....
*We sat in a row, looked out for the foe we saw them with their
bundles*
They hid in a room so we couldn't see them so we went outside

*They made such a fuss of names I called them the judge
thought they were babies*
*Three burly men behaving like girls were they afraid of old
ladies*
*They sat in a row and they wanted to go back home to their
mummies*
*Now you know why my little white car is full of stuffed
dummies!*

Leave me alone and we can go home
This bird has flown ....

Song finished I needed to gather some friends to sing it for
me. I downloaded the karaoke version of 'A Day Trip to
Bangor' but from then on everything else was done with my
mobile phone.

I thought I could entice potential singers by promising to
ply them with alcohol, so having printed several copies of my
song I then looked for people who would be interested in

singing the sound track for my video. The location for the sound recording was the café and with regular friends Lesley and Jenny, who had no choice but to participate. Lily was always willing to join in and I asked my other neighbour Cindy to come along. I asked Emily if she would come too but she was busy and promised to send her parents instead.

The first part of the rehearsal was not very successful as we were an all-female choir and none of us could sing. Tim and Diana were late and although I knew how the song was meant to be sung the others were not sure and we were not in unison, so I kept topping up their glasses in the hope that the singing quality would improve.

After several attempts we unanimously agreed that we needed a male voice amongst us. So in case Tim and Diana had forgotten I went to find them, and luckily they were at home. I pleaded with them to come and sing with us which they did and at last we had our male voice to guide us along.

What a difference a male bass made to the choir and as we learnt to sing the same line at the same time Tim, apart from leading us, was singing his own version in his deepest, loudest voice and it sounded rather different. Rehearsals done it was time to make the soundtrack. With song sheets at the ready they all huddled round the table, and my mobile phone, being the only source of available recording equipment, was placed strategically in the middle of the table so it would capture every voice. I clicked play on the computer, and turned the volume up to maximum so the choir could hear the backing track. They all leant down towards the mobile phone and sang their hearts out. I contributed my bit from behind the counter.

We only did one recording and it was different, with Tim's distinctive deep voice booming over the girls who sounded like children, but despite that the recording was fit for purpose. All I needed now were some actors, six in all and I would be filming it with my mobile phone.

I had already counted on Lesley to be The Tyrannical Clown and Jenny to be Defrogatory, and Lily was going to be Judgement Jones. I needed a Kilkenny, a Swanoff Swanker and a Highway Hen. Jenny forced her partner Sean to be Kilkenny because all he had to do was to flex his muscles. There were two young brothers who lived up the road, Chris who was in his middle teens and his younger brother Steven who was about twelve. I bribed them with fizzy drinks and they agreed to take part. I beckoned the cast of 'Team Fluffit' to gather in the café on a miserable grey evening in May.

Whilst the others got into their costumes I explained to Chris that his part was to hide behind the counter holding Highway Hen up with a broom handle making her get taller and taller till she towered over the others by the end of the song. I wanted Steven to put his whole body into one leg of the grey leggings I had used to make Swanoff Swanker's body. He dutifully obeyed and with a bit of help we crammed his entire body into one of the legs with only his head visible and I pushed the parrot mask over his head which just left his feet poking out of the bottom. Looking at him I was worried if he fell over he would not be able to put his arms out to save himself and as his legs were squashed tightly together it meant he could only shuffle, so I hoiked the legging up to his hips stretching the fabric to its utmost and telling him he would have to keep his bottom half out of sight. As his role in the proceedings was just to swan around looking cool we decided he could stay behind the counter.

The rapidly planned video would entail the Team Fluffit walking away from the Peugeot which was parked on the café forecourt. Judgement Jones would take the lead carrying a large bundle resting on his forearms, followed by The Tyrannical Clown who would pick up a café sign on his way into the café, followed by Defrogatory and then Kilkenny and somewhere out of sight Swanoff Swanker would mingle amongst them and Highway Hen would already be in the café. That was the plan anyway.

So with the seagulls squawking in the background filming commenced. Take one went smoothly with the Fluffits walking away from the car into the café, with only one hiccough, not really visible: Lily's wig fell off just as she walked into the café. Take two with props: Defrogatory had a large mirror that he had to look in and be 'green with envy'. Judgement Jones sat on the counter with the bundle still resting on his forearms, moving his head from side to side in time to the music. We had stuffed tea towels up Kilkenny's jumper to exaggerate his biceps for him to show off, and Chris was ready with the broom handle which was stuffed up Highway Hen and Steven was ready to swan around behind the counter looking cool.

The music started but it was only to keep everyone in time as the sound recording would be added afterwards. Everyone did their bit but The Tyrannical Clown forgot she was a man and did not hide her femininity very well and worse she was struggling to breathe inside the mask which brought on a claustrophobic attack, but as a true pro she carried on the best she could. Judgement Jones bundle started to slide onto the floor half way through but it did so in time to the music.

Everyone played their parts exceptionally well considering there were no rehearsals beforehand. Chris's arms were collapsing by the time we reached the end of the song as Highway Hen had become so heavy but he stuck it out. Swanoff Swanker did an excellent job of swanning around looking cool.

Exhausted by the demands I had once again forced upon my dear friends they all went home knackered and looking forward to seeing the completed video.

CHAPTER 53

Lily was a clever girl and had the necessary up to date technical skills needed to edit and produce the video. As the singing did not commence right at the beginning of the video Lily asked me how I wanted it to start and I had the idea of using excerpts from the 'interview under caution' tape made at Rye Police Station that The Tyrannical Clown had sent me. I tried over and over again to record onto my phone the bits I wanted to use which was easier said than done but eventually with perseverance I got the sections of the tape I wanted. The opening music I chose was 'Conquest of Paradise' by Vangelis. Lily superimposed The Tyrannical Clown's voice over the top of the music. She added the sound track to the video and then she had the bright idea to write the words to the song rolling up the screen so everyone could sing along with it. At the end of the video we put a photo of the bike, now with a mangled back wheel, having been brutally vandalised by some yobbo but still standing with the sign attached, and The Tyrannical Clown's voice-over telling me to stop laughing.

'The Fluffits sing-a-long' video was launched onto YouTube. I was so pleased with it I wanted them at East Sussex County Council to see it too, so without hesitation I sent the video link to Rag-Eme-Kale to watch and share with his colleagues. There was a view counter with the video on YouTube so it was possible to see how many viewings the video was having.

The inflatables arrived on the day summer had reverted back to winter so they stayed in the box they had arrived in until the week-end. Although the sun was shining it was not beach weather, and there was a cold breeze blowing off the sea but the bikers from Uckfield came for their Sunday breakfast as they did when the weather permitted. I asked them if they would mind blowing up some of the inflatables so at least we could display them on sale. I passed them the box and being the obliging guys they were they got stuck into blowing up rubber rings, dragon boats, hammer heads and sharks by mouth. Danny, the leader of the pack, suggested I bought a pump to inflate them as doing it manually was quite time-consuming and exhausting. Even when there were enough blown up the question was where to put them? They needed to be outside really so I found some string and the guys wove it round the hanging baskets and threaded the rubber rings onto it. The larger things we attached with clothes pegs. It was okay but as the line was sloping all the rubber rings slipped down to the far end. By the time the guys had eaten their breakfasts the whale, dragon boat and hammer head had blown off the string and were blowing round the forecourt and filthy.

Towards the end of May, much to my surprise, I received an email from the Head of Customer & Commercial Development, Economy, Transport & Environment Department, East Sussex County Council;

Dear Mrs Pattinson,
I have been passed your e-mail to Rag-Eme-Kale and would
first like to apologise for the delay in responding to you.
The allegations made in your e-mail are serious. Having
spoken to colleagues in our legal department it has been
decided that this matter should be investigated by one of our
managers rather than our departmental complaints team.
I have asked one of our Policy managers Mr Judas to
investigate this matter and he will be contacting you shortly.
Kind Regards
Mr Spearbrave

Good heavens! I couldn't believe what I had just read, was he serious? If he was, it meant at long last I had the opportunity to expose those perpetrators. Maybe it had been a reaction to the 'Fluffits' video, who knows? We were pretty certain that the video had been well circulated around the Council going by the amount of views it had had. Maybe this was going to be the turning point to my advantage; after all I had my signs back up, and the car with the sign on it was still parked on the road every day without it being scrutinised by highway men, so this had to be the beginning of the end.

A couple of days later I received another email;

Dear Ms Pattinson,
As you are aware from Mr Spearbrave's email, I have been assigned the Investigating Officer in relation to your allegations.
For me to investigate these serious allegations fully, please could you provide me with details of your allegations in writing and any documented evidence that you have in support of these.
Kind Regards
Mr Judas

I was so excited that my allegations were being taken seriously, I answered Mr Judas straight away;

Dear Mr Judas
As I have so much evidence including circumstantial evidence I would prefer to bring all my documents to you in person. That would be much easier for me and I will be able to relate my allegations to you in detail as I want to make certain that you understand them properly.
I look forward to hearing from you

He replied a week later offering me an appointment at County Hall Lewes on the 8th June in the afternoon to go through my evidence, and he reminded me that he would still need written details pertaining to the allegations I had made.

That gave me two weeks to gather it all together, my life was an endless muddle of papers, photocopied letters, pictures, emails and sections of the 1980's Highways Act rules and regulations on where I could and could not stick a sign. I took bits of evidence from the previous court bundles, letters from Judgement Jones, the photos of my signs allegedly taken on 22nd October 2009. More letters from Judgement Jones threatening me with imprisonment and Rag-Eme-Kale's emails reiterating the necessity of me employing a structural engineer with a string of letters after his name to design a safe A-board. I included all the paperwork I considered had been sent to me with intent to intimidate and the witness statements of Kilkenny and the spurious invoices from The Tyrannical Clown.

In the meantime there was a four day dancing event taking place at Pontins - one of the rare occasion when the café did quite well, the down side being that Pontins charged so much for the guests to park on site most of them parked up on the main road for the duration, meaning I lost the parking place for the Peugeot. Consequently I had to put the A-board at the top of Lydd Road or risk losing valuable customers because even if the regular people at the event knew of the café if they could not see anything advertising it they might just assume that the café was closed. As a precaution I attached a café sign to a tree which was opposite the west entrance to Pontins. Then I emailed Rag-Eme-Kale to tell him what I had done with the A-board..

Dear Rag-Eme-Kale
There is nowhere for me to park my car this week-end as there
is a function at Pontins. Because they charge so much for the
customers to park in Pontins, most of them have parked on the
roads so I don't have anywhere to put my car.
So I am letting you know that I have had to put my A-board on
the grass. Please don't mind it's only for the week-end.
Thank you

On 8th June 2011 I left Lily in charge and I set off to
County Hall in Lewes. It was a nice sunny day but windy. As I
drove along Bexhill Road who should be driving in the
opposite direction but Kilkenny, and he spotted me as we
passed and leant forward to stare at me and I in turn stared
back at him. I continued on my journey and when I got onto
the A27 to Lewes I noticed at various intervals along the fast
moving road there were A-boards and signs attached to street
furniture, some advertising 'cherries one mile up the road',
others advertising 'strawberries in the next lay-by', 'summer
fruit' etc. and these were on both sides of the road. There were
a couple of burger vans too with two or three big signs well in
advance of their location.

Were these businesses exempt to Rag-Eme-Kale's
advertising policies I wondered? All the signs I had seen
contradicted everything he had been enforcing upon me.
These signs were remote, vulnerable to wind and the
possibility of being blown onto the main road as most of them
were free standing.

As the A 27 was the main trunk road to Lewes and
Brighton nearly all of the employees in the Ringmer and
Lewes Highways office must drive along this road several
times a week but had evidently ignored these signs that were
placed along this road. I wanted to stop and take photos of

them but it was too dangerous, so I didn't.

I arrived at County Hall in good time and parked in the 'pay and display' car park purely set aside for visitors to County Hall. The car park was surrounded by beech trees billowing in the blustery weather and sounded like the sea on a rough day. I begrudgingly bought a parking ticket, gathered up my carrier bags of papers and set off up a long flight of steps to the entrance.

I introduced myself at the reception and informed the guy that I had an appointment with Mr Judas. I waited some minutes and then Mr Judas appeared asking me if I was Mrs Pattinson.

He told me his colleague would also be at the interview to take notes so nothing would be forgotten. I followed Mr Judas up some stairs into what appeared to be the contact centre where so many of my emails and poems must have arrived. I didn't want to be in this room in case I was identified, so I practically pushed Mr Judas to hurry him up to wherever we were heading. We soon arrived in a small room with a young lady sitting at the table with a note pad in front of her poised with a pen in her hand.

The first thing I asked was how long in his opinion would this investigation take to complete? Mr Judas replied that providing he had all the evidence then his enquiry would be concluded by the end of July. I proceeded to tell him of events regarding my A-boards and café signs, and accusations from Judgement Jones, The Tyrannical Clown, Kilkenny and Rag-Eme-Kale. I produced letters and emails concerning the perjury committed by Kilkenny and The Tyrannical Clown. The poor girl was writing like crazy to get all the facts logged. Amongst the evidence I had brought with me was a copy of the letter I had written to the Chief Executive complaining about The Tyrannical Clown and as my papers were already strewn all over the table I could not find it. I suggested Mr

Judas should go and ask the Customer Care Manager whom I had been corresponding with at the time I had written it back in 2009, but he said she was no longer working for East Sussex County Council. I was concerned when he told me that, and I quickly said that I hoped The Tyrannical Clown had not instigated her dismissal because she had told me he had got the letter that was meant for the Chief Executive. Mr Judas did not say anything to the contrary; he just grunted so I presumed she had been dismissed for telling the truth. If that was the case I felt terribly sad for her, but I was only surmising as I did not know for sure.

Mr Judas had requested various documents that I was going to forward on to him when I got home. I suggested that he ask Judgement Jones for the document that the Council's Barrister had produced at the court on April 6th 2010, accusing me of refusing to pay the fine to the fines office. The interview had taken just over an hour and a half, and I was dreading having to pass all those people sitting out there in the contact centre in case they recognised me.

I shook hands with Mr Judas and warned him that if his investigation was inconclusive I would have no hesitation going to the Ombudsman and lodging a complaint with them, and he nodded so I said good-bye to him and the young girl. He insisted on escorting me to the main entrance. I was quite relieved to be outside and happily drove home counting the number of remote signs that seemed to have missed the attention of Rag-Eme-Kale.

CHAPTER 54

When I had got back to the café there was an email from
Kerry titled; Outstanding Account Re - Planning, A-board
Investigation:

Dear Sally
I am disappointed that you did not advise me of the outcome
of the Court Hearing for the contempt of court and injunction
order. I am equally disappointed that you have not made any
attempt to discharge your liability in relation to this
company's outstanding invoices to the sum owing £2,033.98p
less £400 money you paid on account thus leaving a balance
of £1633.98.
I never put pressure on you to pay this sum and I adopted this
approach to enable you to pay for Counsel who had been
introduced to you by this company.
I had hoped that you would reciprocate that good will gesture
by ensuring that the outstanding debt was paid in full and
therefore I look forward to your proposal on how it will be
resolved without further action.
Kerry

Before I replied to Kerry I needed to send the nine
documents to Mr Judas so he could not make the excuse he
had not received all the documentation he needed to prepare
his report. As far as I was concerned time was of the essence
as I had a gut feeling that The Tyrannical Clown might be on
the move, so I wanted this investigation to be concluded
before he had the chance to get away.

The documents sent to Mr Judas included a copy of the
letter I had sent to the Chief Executive which Mr Judas said
would be easy to prove as every letter that arrived at County

Hall was logged and therefore he could check. He also wanted the correspondence I had had with the lady from the Complaints Department who had said she would come to Camber to discuss the advertising issue with me but never came, and I believed The Tyrannical Clown had stopped her.

The next day I had a conformation email from Mr Judas acknowledging the receipt of all the documentation I had sent to him and a short note to say if he had any further queries he would let me know.

That done I turned my attention to answering Kerry's demanding email;

Dear Kerry
Thank you for your letter but I really am of the opinion that the £600 I have paid you is sufficient for the usable work you supplied.
I believed you were preparing my defence for the court case on 14th December 2010. I had no idea that you imagined I was going to take a case against the ESCC in the High Court until you emailed me on the 14th Dec. 2010 and everything suddenly changed and when I queried your comments you said I wasn't listening.
Apart from two witness statements which I insisted on using in my defence, none of your work was needed or indeed necessary. I do not understand why with all your legal knowledge you would have considered that it was.
Therefore I will not be paying you any more money.
Regards
Sally

That evening I received a short reply from Kerry sent from his Blackberry it said;

See you in court then - don't use people Sally

I had no problem with Kerry wanting to see me in court, as he would only be exposing himself as a con man in as much as misleading me in the way he had by gathering evidence against the Council to take them to court on the grounds of harassment, only for him to tell me at the crucial moment that I was not listening.

He could do what he liked. But a couple of days later I received another email from him now referring to me as Mrs Pattinson.

Dear Mrs Pattinson
Thank you for formally confirming that you did not enter into a contract with this company on the 14th September 2010.
The contract clearly states 'both parties in this agreement can cancel the contract at any time. The contract covers any work carried out in terms of time, travel and expense' All work claimed was in accordance with your instructions.
We last acted as business consultant on the 4th November 2010, you now 10th June 2011 raise as dispute, 'laughable'.
We now place you on notice that if we do not receive in FULL within 14 days of this letter, we will issue court proceedings: no further notice will be given.
Kerry

I very much doubted he would go to all that expense of going to court especially as I had more evidence against him than he had against me. Anyway I did not answer it. I had nothing to say to Kerry, he had taken £600 from me which certainly covered his travel and time he had spent in the café using my computer and drinking tea with toast and Kit-Kats.

I had not heard from Rag-Eme-Kale regarding my A-board which I had put on the grass for the duration of the dance weekend and as there was going to be another one the following week-end I decided to send him another email and tell him of my observations on the A27 when I had gone to see Mr Judas in Lewes.

Dear Rag-Eme-Kale

I don't know why you haven't answered my email asking for your consent to put my A-board on the grass. I will probably be in the same situation next week-end again as there is another function at Pontins when the customers all park on the road. So I am asking you please will you give me your consent for 16th,-20th June 2011 but only if it is necessary to put my A-board on the grass at the top of the road? If the decision is too difficult for you to decide please will you pass it on to someone who can?

By the way I saw signs on the A27 quite near to your place of work one for 'Cherries one mile' and another one 'Strawberries 200 yds." and several advertising 'Hot Food'. Are these signs adjacent or remote? Either way they didn't have your stickers on them.

If you decide that I may not have your consent for my A-board I will have no choice but to claim loss of earnings from you and Lily will be claiming loss of her wages too.

I look forward to hearing from you soon.........

Sally

To my surprise he had answered my email within the hour, it said;

Dear Sally Pattinson

Thank you for your email of 4 June 2011.

First of all, please note that you cannot make retrospective applications. It is not acceptable to place a sign on the highway and then ask for consent after the act. Unless you have express written consent before erecting the sign, you have breached your injunction. To expect immediate consent when you send me an email on Saturday morning is not reasonable.

You do not have permission to place an Advertising board in the verge in the highway. As you will recall from our previous extended correspondence, advertising boards placed remotely from your café will not to be tolerated. You have pleaded guilty in a magistrate's court for this type of offence and are currently under an injunction from the county court prohibiting you from placing unauthorised signs in the highway.

I am also aware of the signs that you have attached to a highway tree. We believe that you have breached the two year injunction already. For the avoidance of any doubt, I attach below the relevant section of the legislation. I also attach photographs of the unlawful sign and a plan of the extent of the highway (the location of the highway tree is shown in green and the extent of the highway is shown in pink with the boundary shown in red). This evidence may need to be produced in court if breaches continue.

Section 132 Highways Act 1980, Unauthorised marks on highways.

(1)A person who, without either the consent of the highway authority for the highway in question or an authorisation given by or under an enactment or a reasonable excuse, paints or otherwise inscribes or affixes any picture, letter, sign or other mark upon the surface of a highway or upon any tree, structure or works on or in a highway is guilty of an offence and liable to a fine not exceeding £100 or, in the case of a second or subsequent conviction under this subsection, to a fine not exceeding £200.

(2)The highway authority for a highway may, without prejudice to their powers apart from this subsection and whether or not proceedings in respect of the matter have been taken in pursuance of subsection (1) above, remove

any picture, letter, sign or other mark which has, without either the consent of the authority or an authorisation given by or under an enactment, been painted or otherwise inscribed or affixed upon the surface of the highway or upon any tree, structure or works on or in the highway.

Please also note that you still owe the Council £2000 from the previous costs order made against you. The judge's recent Injunction does not cancel out the costs from the previous Injunction. I would be grateful if you could resume paying the costs which you have halted since your most recent court appearance.

May I suggest that you give more thought to applying for an advertising sign legally? You will recall from our previous correspondence that I had suggested you approach a sign manufacturer to get a suitable sign design on materials that would be passively safe to be in the highway. If the sign can be sited safely so that it does not distract motorists within 60m of a road junction, or obstruct passage through the highway, then we could approach the Planning Authority, Rother District Council to obtain planning permission. There is a fee of £330 for licensing a private advertising sign to be in the highway. I hope that you will agree in light of the injunction you are under, that this is the right and lawful way to have an advertising sign in the highway. Certainly, I invite you balance the cost of £330 for a lawful sign against the potential for the full £11,600 costs to be awarded against you if you continue to ignore the injunction.

Thank you for the information concerning the 'cherries for sale' signs. I shall look into the matter and whether they comply with this council's policy on seasonal produce signs in rural areas.

If the breaches continue, the Council may feel that it has no choice but to go back to court to make another application for your committal to prison.
Rag-Eme-Kale BEng (Hons) MCIHT
Team Manager, Inspection & Enforcement

I thought I had done the right thing by writing to Rag-Eme-Kale and asking him if I might on the odd occasion put my A-board at the top of the road, but he had been of no help and only threatened me with imprisonment again.

So I wrote an email to Judgment Jones to see if I could get any sense out of him. Subject: 'How do I breach an injunction order without breaching it?'

Dear Judgement Jones,
Please will you tell me who I am meant to ask consent from when I might have need to breach the injunction order on the odd occasion? I thought it was Rag-Eme-Kale. Is it you, The Tyrannical Clown, Kilkenny, Peter Plonker or all of you?
Sally

He replied;

Sally,
If Rag-Eme-Kale alone has provided you with express written consent to place a sign on a particular part of the highway, then that will be enough. Please note that if you have written consent to a sign from Rag-Eme-Kale, you will not be in breach of your injunction order.
Judgement Jones

So that got me nowhere. I did not know how much time it

took Rag-Eme-Kale to prepare his map of dots and crosses which showed me where I had put signs. It was true I had stuck a café sign on a tree opposite the entrance to Pontins. I had never been told that I could not put a sign on a tree, but Rag-Eme-Kale had referred to it as a 'highway tree'. Personally I had never heard of a highway tree. I did look at the dots and crosses on the map and it occurred to me that Rag-Eme-Kale had got his colours confused as it was clear that my sign at the bottom of the sand dunes was absolutely on a white bit therefore exempt from being prosecuted for being on a red or pink no go area. I also noted that there was still the same (but according to Judgement Jones incorrect) maximum fine of £100 for a first offence not £200 as The Tyrannical Clown had informed the Magistrate's in Eastbourne back in October 2009. I knew the information on that first offence matter was true despite Judgement Jones insisting it was wrong. They would have updated their website by now if it was an error and I had brought it to their attention several times.

As for 'summer produce policies' it was quite ridiculous, as a sign advertising a strawberry was no different than a sign advertising a café.

I replied to Rag-Eme-Kale:

Dear Rag-Eme-Kale
Please will you look at your map you sent me yesterday showing the red boundary line. The sign I have in Old Lydd Road is on the white bit and therefore not on the pink bit or the wrong side of the red bit and not in or on or abutting the highway.
Please recall what The Honourable Judge said to you and your colleagues, that anything other than the highways is not your concern.
Sally

Ten days went by before I received a reply from Rag-Eme-Kale,

Dear Sally Pattinson
Thank you for your email of 10 June 2011.
I shall be mindful of the extent of the highway. If you erect an
advertisement on private land beyond the highway that shall
be an issue for Rother District Council the planning authority.
However, just as a note of caution, the highway terrier viewer
only shows a red boundary marker where the extent of the
highway has previously been defined (either through a recent
sale of property, or as a result of a previous enquiry). There
are still many sites where the extent of the highway verge has
yet to be defined. Most frequently these are along rural roads.
When defining the extent of the highway, officers will look for
evidence of frequent passage, public utilities apparatus,
boundary features (fences, hedges, ditches or marker posts)
and changes in level (embankments or steeply sloping land
that the public could not easily traffic). Historical maps and
tithe maps can also help indicate the extent of the highway in
disputed cases.
In our correspondence, I shall endeavour to avoid confusing
issues, or those where the sign is 'abutting' the highway,
unless it becomes a danger to highway users.
Regards
Rag-Eme-Kale

I wanted to know what these tithe maps were that he was referring to, so I googled them just in case he was trying to make things sound more complicated than they were. I found the answer;

Dear Rag-Eme-Kale

*In case you didn't know, tithe maps were not used after the
late 18th Century and were abolished in 1936. Tithes were
taxes paid to the local church which took one tenth of
people's land produce. The maps were marking farm land. So
now I know what tithe maps WERE..... What the hell have they
got to do with my café signs?*
*Well I am going to tell you what that has got to do with my
stolen café signs, as your colleagues stole 100% of my café
signs you must reimburse me 90% of their value according to
your tithe maps....... which I estimate at £2000......*
Sally...

I was not going to be fobbed off by some ancient bylaw
and out of date map and I intended to persist putting pressure
on Rag-Eme-Kale until he regretted bitterly ever mentioning
them.

Dear Sally Pattinson
*I was responding to your email 10 June 2011 concerning the
extent of the defined highway in Old Lydd Road. As you
correctly state, tithe maps were produced predominantly to
ensure that the church could keep track of the monies due
from its congregations. However, these old maps often pre-
date the more accurate Ordnance Survey maps. When
questions arise as to the extent of the highway, the existence
of the way on a tithe map is helpful.*
*With regard to the unauthorised signs that you placed in the
highway, I refer you to my email of 9 June 2011 and Section
132 of the Highways Act 1980. This empowers the Highway
Authority to remove unauthorised signs from the highway.
You have had this explained to you on many occasions and
have even pleaded guilty to the offence in court.*
Yours sincerely
Rag-Eme-Kale

He made me laugh; he kept repeating that things could not be placed on the highway but despite me having sent him so many photos of various signs on the highway which he had ignored.

I had another idea....

CHAPTER 55

Of all the other business sign photos I had sent to Rag-Eme-Kale the most frustrating of them all was the Kiosk in the Western Car Park in Camber whereby the two metal signs were placed directly on the edge of the main road on a daily basis. I had just taken two new photos of them to send to Rag-Eme-Kale again, and I had also been to Rye to take more photos of the three A-boards which straddled double yellow lines outside the restaurant they were advertising.

I had an idea that would put Rag-Eme-Kale into a corner where he would either have to do something about the signs I had sent him photos of, which was highly unlikely, or let me put my A-board back on the grass. Of course he could not stop advertising on A-boards as it would cause uproar amongst the small businesses that were struggling to survive because of the recession and weather. A town without A-boards and signs would look like a ghost town, so I felt no guilt in reporting these businesses as I knew no action would be taken against them.

Dear Rag-Eme-Kale
I have read and re-read your email urging me to apply legally for a café sign and I think you are right, I should apply for a proper sign. So I propose to have a sign like the one in the attached photo of the metal signs belonging to the kiosk in the Western Car Park in Camber which will be just right for my café advert. I have lived in Camber for nearly 9 years and during that time I have seen the two signs either side of the entrance to the Western Car Park on the C24 placed there each day this business is open. So they must surely have the

*necessary consent and planning permission that you so
passionately enforce or they would not be there, would they?
They are adjacent to the same road where mine will be placed
so there's no difference there. They are remote from the café
they advertise so that must meet your approval too.*

*So I'm confident that as you consent to this type of remote
signage you could not possibly refuse the same for me, could
you? So please will you send me the application form for a
remote sign like these and I will be happy to apply and am
100% sure of your consent. After all, you couldn't approve an
application for one person and refuse it for another identical
sign in the same location could you, because you would
appear biased, wouldn't you?*

*So when you have approved my application I will be able to
park my car outside the first entrance to Pontins.*

*How long will it take because I might need it before next
week-end?*

*Incidentally your 'marks on highways' does not mention
chaining bikes to trees and neither does the injunction order
and I thought that I only had to abide by the injunction
instructions. But now you have brought it to my attention I
will try and remember it.*

*I look forward to hearing from you and receiving your
application form.*

Sally

During the next three weeks I heard nothing from Mr Judas.
In the normal scheme of things as a courteous gesture surely
he would have been sending me up dates to assure me that he
was getting on with the job. Neither had I received the
application form that I had requested from Rag-Eme-Kale
which also surprised me as he had implied I should have made
it a priority. So I emailed him to find out what had happened
to it;

Dear Rag-Eme-Kale
what has happened to the application form I requested on the
10th June 2011, I took your advice and told you I would like
to apply for a sign like Mr Forthright in the Western Car
Park?
Why do you tell me to do something and when I do you don't
respond? I don't understand you; you are as confusing as
your highway terrier viewer.....
Are you refusing my request and if so, why? You didn't refuse
Mr Forthright's, or did he ever actually apply for his, or have
you never told him to apply for consent to have his signs in,
on and abutting the highway at a junction, or is it because
he's bigger than you?
Sally

I was keen to see how he was going to wriggle out of the
proposal I had made to him. I did not have to wait long as I
received his reply within a few hours;

Dear Sally Pattinson
I apologise that I have not replied to your last four emails in a
more timely fashion. There is a restructuring process going
on within East Sussex County Council and a significant
proportion of my time has been required to facilitate the
restructuring.
I am very conscious that you did want to discuss a licence for
a permanent advertising sign, and I am very keen that we can
reach a resolution to our outstanding differences of opinion. I
really do not wish to go to court for a fourth time.
Could you make time to meet with me on Tuesday afternoon
next week? At 2pm on 12th July 2011? I suggest that I come
to you at Camber Café, so we can go on site and discuss
visibility issues and potential sign locations. We will need to

discuss sign construction and secure fixings, public liability
insurance and how we contact planning to seek permission for
the advert to be in Camber.
I have not approved a licence for Mr Forthright for an
Advertising board, so I suspect that this is another
unauthorised sign in the highway and I may need to pay a
visit to remove the sign from the highway.
Yours sincerely
Rag-Eme-Kale BEng (Hons) MCIHT
Team Manager, Inspection & Enforcement

I had sent Rag-Eme-Kale photos of Mr Forthright's signs
months ago and he had stated that he would send his inspector
to deal with it and now he was saying he 'may' have to pay
him a visit himself to remove the signs, so he clearly had no
intention of doing anything about them. However, I was quite
surprised that Rag-Eme-Kale had offered to come and see me
and I couldn't help wondering if Mr Judas' investigation had
prompted some positive action to make it appear they were
trying to resolve the situation amicably and so doing would
contradict some of the allegations I had made against them.
Having been told so many times from various council
departments that I would never be permitted to advertise my
café on the highway as it would be a potential danger to
motorists, I had no expectations with this latest proposal.
However, I was curious to see what the outcome would be but
at the same time doubtful that it was going to be anything that
would benefit me.
I replied to Rag-Eme-Kale:

Dear Rag-Eme-Kale
I accept your apology for not answering my emails, but you
could have sent a short one saying you were busy and not

ignoring them and then maybe I would not have thought that you were!
Indeed, I do not want to go to court for a <u>fifth</u> time either......but having said that I feel prison might be a better option for me rather than go bankrupt and be homeless again. Anyway, yes I think you coming to Camber is a good idea, but if you intend to remove all the unauthorised signs you are going to pass 'en route' you had better come in a Pickford lorry as there are hundreds of them........in fact you had better come for a couple of days.
I sent you a photo of Mr Forthright's signs on the 16th May 2011 which contravene section 132 of the 1980's highways act, which you chose to ignore, but you have found the time to remove some of my signs and commandeered the local community officer to steal my sign on the sand dune and made the Sand Dune Ranger rescind his permission that he gave me to put my sign on the sand dune. You have threatened me with prison and £11,600 costs from the last court case. So why have you suddenly decided to do something about Mr Forthright's signs now? And how come you have got to deal with Mr Forthright yourself when you have got inspectors who are supposed to do that sort of thing? They had no problem taking my stuff, oh yes of course, silly me I forgot I am a little old defenceless granny not an ill-mannered oaf. OK, I look forward to seeing you on Tuesday.
Sally.

The following Tuesday I closed the café slightly earlier than usual and cleared everything away for my expected guest. Dead on 2 o'clock I saw the East Sussex Highway Car turn into Denham Way and promptly park on double yellow lines. I left the door open and shot into the back kitchen as I did not want him to know that I had been looking out for him. Then I heard a knock on the side door and a 'hello', but I made him wait a few moments before I went down behind the counter to greet him. Rag-Eme-Kale was accompanied by a tall older man who he introduced as Parry Plotter who had apparently come along to design a café sign for me, although I thought it was more likely because Rag-Eme-Kale was too scared to come on his own and this tall guy was there as his body guard.

I offered them a drink. Rag-Eme-Kale declined at first so I said he could make it himself if he was worried I was going to lace it with poison. He had a coffee anyway and so did I. Mr Plotter on the other hand played safe and chose a bottle of water.

So drinks out of the way we all sat down at the table at the back of the café, Rag-Eme-Kale and Parry Plotter one side and me on the other. I offered Rag-Eme-Kale an ash tray as I had seen him smoking outside the court in April, and he duly accepted and began to roll himself a cigarette. He waffled on about the potential café signs as in the wording and location, design and material, non-corrosive paint, the sub-soil and wind. All the while Parry Plotter had been scribbling in a note pad. I was excited about them designing me my own personal café signs but when he put his pen down I could see that he had drawn three similar café sign designs with numbers barely legible alongside the lines, which presumably were the dimensions. The first drawing consisted of two vertical lines and between these at the top there was one horizontal line, the second drawing was slightly more in 3D and he had written 'Café next Left' on the horizontal bit and the third drawing was the same as the second one but he had written 'Café next Right'. The signs would be non-reflective regulation Council grey paint with black lettering.

Parry Plotter pushed his finished doodles to the centre of the table; we observed them for a moment, and I told him I did not see that a couple of dowdy old signs like those would be jumping out at passing traffic. Rag-Eme-Kale intervened by attempting to justify the significance of having these types of signs to replace my beautiful brightly coloured A-boards and signs which did attract attention. He said I would have to find a reputable sign maker and contact my insurance company about getting liability insurance for remote signs which by law had to be a minimum of 10 million pounds. I was beginning to tire of all this talk about grey paint and prevailing wind, so I changed the subject. I noticed that Rag-Eme-Kale had put on rather a lot of weight, and I asked him what he had been up to since April to cause him to become so fat, As he made his third roll-up he said that he ate too much and drank too much and he liked take-away food too much. He then suggested we went 'on site' to look for suitable locations for the potential official café signs. Just before we left I gave Parry Plotter more copies of the two metal signs placed by the main road daily by Mr Forthright and the A-boards which stood in the road on double yellow lines in Rye, and reminded them that I had provided various pictures of these same signs more than half a dozen times now and they had no excuse not to deal with them. As they gathered up their stuff Parry Plotter put the pictures in his folder along with his so called sign design drawings and they made their way out of the café. I took the dirty mugs back to the kitchen and went to join them. As I locked the door I noticed they had returned to their vehicle and were rummaging around in the back of it, and they reappeared wearing high-vis jackets and white hard hats, although we were only going to walk up Lydd Road to look at potential bits of highway grass. As they came back to join me I laughed at them and asked them why on earth did they need to wear all that clobber to look at grass verges? Needless to say the reply was 'health and safety' they had to wear it; it was part and parcel of their job. I asked them if they had a set to lend me but they had not. No matter, I was brave enough to risk my life walking up the road which I walked up every day without a hard hat and high visibility clothing and had so far survived...

We turned left at the top of the road, crossed over and walked down towards the western entrance to Pontins when suddenly Parry Plotter stopped and began stamping on the grass verge. Rag-Eme-Kale and I watched him then Rag-Eme-Kale said this was a good place for the sign that would have 'Café Next Right' on it. I was beginning to think I wanted more than just three words written on these signs and by the time we had gone back and chosen a suitable place for the other one which really did not look wide enough to put a sign big enough to be seen, I had totally gone off the idea of having official signs anywhere. When I questioned the size of these signs Parry Plotter started to wave his arms about demonstrating the size. I asked him to be more specific because I was going to be asking a sign maker for a quote, he said they were roughly 75mm x 60mm, and Rag-Eme-Kale said something about waiving the application fee of £330.

So places chosen we made our way back to the café, and Rag-Eme-Kale told me to organize the liability insurance for remote signs and reminded me it must be no less than 10 million pounds and I was to find a reputable sign maker for a price quotation and he would make his own enquiries in case he could find a better deal.

When we arrived back at the café Rag-Eme-Kale and Parry Plotter bade me farewell and went off to their car, removed their hard hats and high visibility jackets and drove off.

Just after they had left I received a text from Lily saying she had been offered a job at Pontins and would be starting there at the end of the week. I understood why she would prefer to work there and I quite often had said to her that I didn't think I would survive another winter in the café, as every year was getting harder and harder. So Lily left and sad as I was I did not blame her for going.

CHAPTER 56

Why had Rag-Eme-Kale been so sympathetic to my cause? Surely this had to have something to do with Mr Judas's enquiry, though I was not sure if this strangely suspicious gesture offering me signs with no application fee to pay was just a false show of compassion for the benefit of the investigation or on the other hand I wondered if he had been told to do it to keep me happy.

I did however contact my insurance company to ask how much the premium would increase to cover the £10,000,000 liability that Rag-Eme-Kale had made part of the deal to have the official café signs. I was expecting the insurance guy to say it would go up in hundreds of pounds but instead he laughed and said I was already covered for that. I told him how much it had to be insured for and he said that the chance of an A-board causing a serious accident was so unlikely that it did not increase the premium at all.

On the strength of that good news and to do as Rag-Eme-Kale had ordered I contacted on Lesley's recommendation a sign-maker on the business park in Rye Harbour. I told them the requirements and the sizes of the café signs and asked if they would be able to make them in lime green and the man said they could possibly do that but the council might insist that the signs be retro-reflective which would be an additional cost. He said he would email me the quote soon.

I had done my part of the deal to satisfy Rag-Eme-Kale but with suspicion, and besides I did not really want his official signs anyway. I wanted to keep the car on the road and display my beautiful brightly coloured A-board at the top of Lydd Road.

A few days later the quote arrived by email for the official signs;

Hi Sally,

Further to your recent enquiry I have pleasure in submitting our quotation as follows.

QUOTATION

To supply 2 No. 3mm aluminium signs, size: .75m wide x .61m high (to be confirmed) complete with clip extrusion (fixing rails) to rear), wording: 'Café, Open from 7.30 am, 7 days a week' (to be confirmed), colour: (to be confirmed), 4 No. grey painted aluminium posts 76mm diameter x 2.5m, 4 No. post caps, 4 No. base plates and 8 No. stainless steel fixing clips, **Cost: £315.00 (approx. subject to final sizes, colours and wording etc.)**

Please Note: *The highways department may insist that the signs are retro reflective as this is standard with highway signs. This however, would add an additional cost and limit the choice of colours.*

To fit the above posts and signs in grass/soft ground at Camber, **Cost: £195.00 (approx. subject to position and access etc.)**

ALL PRICES EXCLUDE V.A.T. & DELIVERY.
THIS QUOTATION IS VALID FOR 30 DAYS.

Kind Regards,

Dustin Care (Production Manager, Care Signs)

There was no way I would have the money to pay all that but I forwarded the email to Rag-Eme-Kale anyway in the hope it might jog him into contacting me with an update.

It was time to apply my new idea. I had so many photos of other business signs and I wanted to make a video of them all to remind Rag-Eme-Kale and his inspectors that there were other signs on the highway apart from mine. Molly, who had come to help at the weekends since Lily had gone, wanted to make the video for me as a project for school. I supplied all the photos that were on my computer and she made them into a short film and also added a few photos of my signs as well. I needed some music for the video and found a most suitable song to download from a Disney Film, and the song was called 'What's This'? I wanted to make use of the initials ESCC as in East Sussex County Council and Molly found a picture of the blue ESCC logo. I changed the wording to 'Extreme Saddos Can't Cope' then the appropriate bits of the 1980's highways act were added on the next clip to fit in with the musical introduction of the song. As soon as it was finished we launched it onto YouTube and I sent a complimentary link to Rag-Eme-Kale to help him find those apparently elusive unauthorised signs in the video.

It was getting towards the end of July and I had heard nothing from Mr Judas's progress of his investigation, so it was time to find out how he was getting on with it.

Dear Mr Judas
It is six weeks since I came to see you and as I haven't heard from you I'm wondering how your investigation into my allegations is progressing.
Regards
Sally Pattinson

He replied within the hour saying;

Having interviewed the officers involved in your allegations, I am currently writing up my report of my investigations which I am aiming to finish by the end of next week. I will then need to discuss the content of the report with the Assistant Director for Highways.
Regards

Mr Judas

That sounded positive and I waited with baited breath for the end of the following week to see his completed report. It could only go in my favour with all the evidence I had given him.

I had not heard back from Rag-Eme-Kale. I thought he would have at least confirmed what he had agreed to on his visit two weeks beforehand. As usual he had totally ignored the photos of the signs on the main road advertising the kiosk in the Western Car Park and the same with the A-boards in Rye that straddled double yellow lines.

So for ignoring those signs I had been telling him about for months I made a new A-board and on the inside of it I wrote 'MADE BY SALLY PATTINSON ON THE 23/07/11'. The next day was a Sunday and I pulled the new A-board up the road on my red sack-barrow and placed it on the forbidden grass patch. I did it to see how long it would take them to either remove it or bring to my attention that I had put it there.

I did not have to wait long, for on the next day, Monday 25th July someone saw a highway man taking photos of my new A-board. Straight away I emailed Rag-Eme-Kale to remind him of the other signs he had been going to do something about, but hadn't.

Dear Rag-Eme-Kale
I have noticed that Mr Forthright and the restaurant in Rye are still placing their signs on your highway every day and you don't seem to have done anything about it despite me bringing this matter to your attention on the 14th May 2011 and several times since. What is taking you so long? You are always super-efficient when it comes to taking action against me, for example, taking a photo my new A-board so soon after I made it the screws were still hot. I also noticed that the

*remote pub has got a sign attached to street furniture on the A
259 again.......*
Sally

As I expected the next day I received an email with three
attachments from Rag-Eme-Kale;

I downloaded the attachments first, and laughed at the
great lengths someone had been to to take a photo of the
inside of the A-board showing the confession I had written
saying I had made the A-board on the 23/07/11, and then a
further two photos showing both outsides of the A-board. I did
not understand why they bothered sending me photos of
something I was aware of; did they think I didn't know what I
had done?

Dear Sally Pattinson
*Thank you for your email of 28 July 2011. I shall ask one of
my officers to visit the sites that you refer to and take
appropriate action. Please do not think that other offences by
persons ignorant of the law give you permission to be
contemptuous of the injunction on you not to place
unauthorised signs in the highway.*
*I am disappointed that following my recent meeting with you
on Tuesday 12 July 2011 at Camber to explore the possibility
of licensing signs to be in the highway, you have deposited
another unauthorised advertising sign at the junction of Lydd
Road before my colleague, Parry Plotter has had an
opportunity to forward an appropriate sign design.*
*You do not have permission to place an unsecured Advertising
board in the verge in the highway. As you will recall from our
previous extended correspondence, advertising boards placed
remotely from your café will not to be tolerated. You have
pleaded guilty in a magistrate's court for this type of offence
and are currently under an injunction from the county court*

prohibiting you from placing unauthorised signs in the highway.

I believe that you have breached the two year injunction again. For the avoidance of any doubt, I attach below the relevant section of the legislation. I also attach photographs of the unlawful sign and a plan of the extent of the highway (the location of the unauthorised sign is shown in green and the extent of the highway is shown in pink with the boundary shown in red). This evidence may be produced in court if breaches continue.

Section 132 Highways Act 1980, Unauthorised marks on highways.

(1)A person who, without either the consent of the highway authority for the highway in question or an authorisation given by or under an enactment or a reasonable excuse, paints or otherwise inscribes or affixes any picture, letter, sign or other mark upon the surface of a highway or upon any tree, structure or works on or in a highway is guilty of an offence and liable to a fine not exceeding £100 or, in the case of a second or subsequent conviction under this subsection, to a fine not exceeding £200.

(2)The highway authority for a highway may, without prejudice to their powers apart from this subsection and whether or not proceedings in respect of the matter have been taken in pursuance of subsection (1) above, remove any picture, letter, sign or other mark which has, without either the consent of the authority or an authorisation given by or under an enactment, been painted or otherwise inscribed or affixed upon the surface of the highway or upon any tree, structure or works upon the surface of the highway.

If the breaches continue, the Council will have to go back to court to make another application for your committal to prison.

Regards
Rag-Eme-Kale

Every time Rag-Eme-Kale sent me that section 132 of the 1980's Highways Act it was still quoting the £100 fine for a first offence. I knew what was written was true, so how did they get away with telling the magistrates to give me a £200 fine for each offence and why hadn't that stupid barrister I paid £750 for said something, and although Judgement Jones insisted that the web site was wrong he had made no attempt to have it amended because it was not wrong.

Despite Rag-Eme-Kale's threat of applying to the court again to get me slung into prison the A-board remained on the grass verge and no attempt had been made to remove it.

There had also been no attempt to remove the signs on the main road belonging to the kiosk in the Western Car Park or the A-boards straddled over the double yellow lines in Rye either. I was so infuriated by it I sent Rag-Eme-Kale another email with new photos attached;

You're doing a grand job Rag-Eme-Kale of taking appropriate action regarding the business signs I sent you photos of 92 days ago. I have just taken more photos of them. I believe that you have no intention of taking any action against these people at all and I would very much like to make an opinion for the reason why but sadly I am unable to in case I make you cry.
Photos were taken of my A-board within 24 hours of me putting it on the piece of Council grass when you sent your inspectors to photograph it. How has Peter Plonker got the audacity to say I believe I am being singled out by you people when it's blatantly obvious even to Mr Tovenden (who is blind) that I am.

I should take appropriate action against you......
Sally

I wrote an email to Parry Plotter with more photos of the kiosk signs and the A-boards on the double yellow lines in Rye

Dear Parry Plotter
I have taken another photo (attached) of the signs advertising the restaurant in Rye which are so evidently placed on double yellow lines and more photos of the signs advertising the kiosk in the Western Car Park Camber. Why is this unchecked by you or anyone else? I gave you photos of various signs placed in various places and you have not visited them or taken any action against the owners. I know Rag-Eme-Kale is a wimp and frightened of thug type people but you can't all be the same and just pick on 9 stone old age pensioners like me.....
Why are you taking so long in drawing two poles stuck in two holes and held together with a strip of metal? Are you sure you and Rag-Eme-Kale came to Camber to check out the possibilities for me to have something official or were you just wasting time? I haven't even been sent an application form yet that I asked for weeks ago.
If you are not going to let me have official signs on Lydd Road will you please let me know so I can make another A-board to put on New Lydd Road where you and Rag-Eme-Kale said I could have an official one? And kindly return my photos I gave you as you obviously have no use for them.
Sally

CHAPTER 57

All this waiting for answers had given me an idea for another video, changing the title of The Village People's famous hit YMCA to ESCC. Writing lyrics seemed to come quite easily to me and in no time at all I had re-written the YMCA song to the title of;

THE FLUFFITS CAN STUFF IT

Old men, there's a place you belong
You know
Old men, you have to try and be strong
We said
Old men, you know you are wrong
It is easy to see why you
Need to get a much thicker skin
You will have to, if you're determined to win
To be able to keep up your style
And be jobs worth's all the while

You will be happy in the
ESCC is where it's fun to work
ESCC where you can be a burke
You don't have to worry you can do what you like
But you won't get your hands on one of my bikes
ESCC is where you get your perk
ESCC go off and have a jerk
So big and so brave they keep out of sight
If you come into Camber you might have a fight

Old men, are you listening to me
We said

Old men, why can't you see?
And you
Old men it's so good to be free
And not sad like you old noodles.
Listen to the ones who know best
You can come here but as only a guest
But be careful the road's full of holes
You can keep an eye on your poles

You will stay happy in the
ESCC is where you swan about
ESCC and looking cool no doubt
You can waste all the money that the tax payers pay
But be careful we'll catch you out one of these days
ESCC what are they thinking of
ESCC are they on planet Zog
You'll have to do better than keep taking boards
If you take any more we'll be duelling with swords

Old men why not give it a rest
We said
 Old men you're not doing your best
For us,
Old men just stop being a pest
Go take on a new quest
If you can't stop making a noise
Then you'll have to just brace yourselves boys
And remember what someone has done
Well whose fault all this begun?

Let's hear it for the
ESCC soon we are going see
ESCC all the hypocrisy
Do us a favour and stay out of town

Or something might happen to the Tyrannical Clown
ESCC is where it's going on
ESCC is where we don't belong
Let's try and do something to keep you away
And then we won't miss you, that's all we can say

ESCC we'll say good-bye to you
ESCC and here's some good luck too
Don't be so stubborn and free yourselves up
For what it's worth we think you all suck
ESCC....

I needed to look for the cast. Lesley said she would help out on the day but refused to take part after her attack of claustrophobia wearing The Tyrannical Clown mask, and Jenny did not want to take part at all, but Lily did even though she had moved on elsewhere, and she said she would come and join in. I finally mustered up a group of friends of all shapes and sizes. We needed to record the sound track but there was no Tim and Diana and the first recording was dreadful, so instead of mustering everyone together again I thought it would be a good idea to randomly hand out song sheets to the bewildered customers and make them sing along to the previous recording which gradually formed a much larger choir. The completed soundtrack was futile to say the least but never mind we could make up for it with the YMCA dance.

I called upon Hayley who had worked for me on and off over the years. She was a dancer so I asked her if she would come and choreograph our YMCA dance. Danny the Sunday biker said he would be the camera man and Jan his girlfriend would take part in the dancing. So the cast was set, Lily was to be Highway Hen, Ronnie was The Tyrannical Clown in the feather headdress, Jimmy was Swanoff Swanker in the high-vis jacket and white hard hat, Jan was Defrogatory in the police hat. I had acquired my army outfit from two soldiers who had come in the café one day and I had swapped an egg and bacon sandwich for the trousers from one of the soldiers and another egg and bacon sandwich for an army shirt from the other, so I was Kilkenny as a paratrooper and finally Hayley was dressed as Judgement Jones wearing leggings, a black vest and a leather cap with a chain on the brim.

We had one rehearsal, with Hayley counting to keep us in time and telling us when to change direction. Those of us wearing the masks could not see or breathe and all in all it was quite shambolic and clearly unrehearsed, but never mind, it was done, edited and launched onto YouTube.

The school holidays were coming to an end and I had not heard from Rag-Eme-Kale, Parry Plotter or Mr Judas, the kiosk signs were still on the main road and the restaurant signs were still standing on the double yellow lines in Rye, even my A-board was still standing at the top of the road. The prospect of these official signs ever happening was becoming more unlikely, so I emailed Parry Plotter;

Dear Parry Plotter
It's eight weeks since you and Rag-Eme-Kale came to see me about having official café signs. From your lack of correspondence I take it that you are having difficulty in designing them. Maybe if you design them like an A frame I will then be able to make them myself. You have seen my A frames that I have made in the past, so you know I can make them well.
Whether it's your choice or mine could you please let me know what's happening with them and where are my photos I asked you to return to me, do you need me to send you a stamp to return them?
Sally

Parry Plotter never responded to my email.

The wait for Mr Judas's report was becoming a distant memory, he had said it would be concluded seven weeks ago but still I had heard nothing, I decided I had been patient for long enough so I emailed him.

Dear Mr Judas
It's nearly two months since I last heard from you so I
presume that you have concluded your investigation. When
will I be informed of the outcome?
If you have no further need of my stuff would you please
return it to me?
Thank you
Regards Sally Pattinson

Three days went by and Mr Judas had not answered my email, so on 9th September I sent him another one;

Dear Mr Judas
I emailed you on Tuesday but as I have not had a response
from you maybe you did not receive it.
I was asking if you have finished your investigation and I
would like to have my stuff returned and also when will I
know the outcome of your investigation. Thank you.
I look forward to hearing from you.
Regards Sally Pattinson

I received an out of office reply saying he was not back in his office until the 12th but he would periodically check and deal with emails. The next day the postman delivered a large white envelope which contained a signed complimentary slip from Mr Judas despite him being out of his office until the 12th. He had returned my paperwork minus the proof when taken photos.

So without haste I emailed him again:

Dear Mr Judas

I noticed that you did not return the photos I left with you so I would like to know what's happened to them.

I would also like to know why you have still not told me the outcome of your investigation. I have been very patient but I think now I am entitled to some answers.

I told you that I had already contacted the Ombudsman before your investigation began and that I asked them to put everything on hold while you made your own enquiries. If your findings were inconclusive then I will go back to the Ombudsman and instruct them to continue theirs.

In any event would you please let me know within the next 24 hours how you concluded your investigation?

Thank you

Sally Pattinson

Mr Judas responded three hours later;

Dear Sally,

I am sorry for the delay in responding.

With regard to the photos, I still have these and will put them in the post tomorrow.

With regard to my investigations, I have just finalised the report which, as I highlighted at our meeting, will be sent to the Assistant Director for Legal and Democratic Services for his consideration. I will then need to take advice from him on how he would like the conclusions of my investigations to be presented to you, but I will highlight to him that you are keen to know the outcomes as soon as possible.

I am sorry it has taken so long to conclude my investigations -
it has taken a lot longer than I had envisaged for me to go
through the background information, write up my report and
then bottom out a couple of final queries I had.
As soon as I have been instructed on how my investigations
should be presented to you, I will let you know.
Regards
Mr Judas
Team Manager - Infrastructure and Development
Economy, Transport & Environment Department
East Sussex County Council

Sally? Why the sudden familiarity. His email was full of
excuses, and he did not appear to know what he was meant to
be doing. Why would he have to be instructed on how to
present his report to me? I had asked him at the meeting in
June if he had done an investigation like this one before and
he had said he had but not on such a grand scale. Another
point was why had he been asked to do it in the first place if
he was not capable of passing a non-biased judgement
towards his colleagues?

Early the following week I received the missing photos.
I replied to Mr Judas;

Dear Mr Judas
Thank you for your email of the 13th September 2011 and I
apologise for being impatient but I believed that from your
previous email that you had finished writing your report at
the end of July. Also thank you for returning the photos.
Can you explain why Rag-Eme-Kale and Parry Plotter came
to Camber at 2pm. on 12th July 2011 at their suggestion to
discuss the possibility for me to have authorised café signs on
Lydd Road. It is now the middle of September and I have
heard nothing from them despite me emailing three times to

ask what was occurring with it. They could have at least kept me informed. Rag-Eme-Kale urged me to consider applying for authorised café signs. I don't understand what it was all for, they were here for two hours discussing it! How am I meant to abide by section 132 of the 1980's Highways Act if they suggest something and then do nothing?
Regards
Sally Pattinson

I waited one more month, and Lesley kept urging me to contact Mr Judas. She said I was too patient and so we tried to think of reasons why Mr Judas was taking so long and the possibilities of what the outcome of the investigation was going to be. Could it have been that my evidence was so serious they did not know how to wriggle out of it or on the other hand the delay was intentional to make me believe that a thorough investigation was taking place or was it that my evidence was insufficient? Whatever the reason was for the delay, there was no correspondence from Rag-Eme-Kale nor Parry Plotter who had gone to such trouble and driven an eighty-four mile round trip from Ringmer to Camber to discuss in great lengths the possibility of me having official signs on the main road. In fact Rag-Eme-Kale had been so keen for me to have them he had waived the £330 application fee. Three months had passed since their visit to Camber, I had provided them with the quote for the official signs but still they continued to ignore me. I wanted them to confirm their decision for the signs or tell me if they had changed their minds and I couldn't have them. What's more Mr Judas also ignored my last email, so ultimately on 14th October more than four months after the investigation had begun and three months since Rag-Eme-Kale had agreed to me having official signs to advertise the café, my patience was exhausted and it was time to act. After all actions are meant to speak louder than words, so that day I contacted Hastings County Court to enquire how I went about making an application to take Rag-Eme-Kale to court for failing to abide by the conditions he had set out for me to abide by. I also emailed Mr Judas:

Dear Mr Judas
I now believe that you have had adequate time to conclude
your investigation. I appreciate it took you much longer than
you had envisaged but it has been more than four months
since our initial meeting. I am therefore going to contact the
Ombudsman and ask that they continue their enquiry.
Regards
Sally Pattinson

CHAPTER 58

That afternoon I drove to the Court in Hastings to start my case against Rag-Eme-Kale. It cost £80 and I would have to make up a bundle of evidence. The nice judge who had granted my injunction order was away until February but I had the choice of waiting for him to return to work or see another judge, and that would be within a few weeks. As disappointing as it was that the nice judge was away I opted for sooner rather than later, so I settled for November 1st three weeks later.

I located the three emails for the evidence I needed for my bundle, and once I had found them I prepared my case and I wrote a short statement giving the reason why I had applied to the court.

I wrote that:

On the 15th April 2011 I had been given an injunction order at Hastings County Court forbidding me from placing signs in the highway without the written express consent of Rag-Eme-Kale of East Sussex County Council Highways Department. In June I had applied for an application form but had not received one. Rag-Eme-Kale and his colleague had visited me at my café on 12th July 2011 to discuss the possibility of authorised signs to be placed on Lydd Road to advertise my café, and I understood that Rag-Eme-Kale had agreed as he had not only shown me where the signs would be placed on Lydd Road, he also implied that he would waive the application fee of £330. Since that day I have not been advised as to when the signs would be installed and all my emails have been ignored. I questioned that if Rag-Eme-Kale refused to give me the opportunity to apply for his 'express

written consent', why was it the only condition of the
injunction order?

My bundle was not huge. I put a copy of the injunction
order for the first page followed by the email from Rag-Eme-
Kale he had sent in July suggesting he came to see me to go
on site and discuss visibility issues and potential sign
locations. I also used the three emails I had sent to Rag-Eme-
Kale and Parry Plotter asking what had happened to the
application form for the official signs he was arranging.

Everything had to be in triplicate, one for the court, one for
Rag-Eme-Kale and one for me.

A few days before the hearing I received a document from
Judgement Jones; it was an application notice to make a
counter claim against me. He was asking the court that my
claim against Rag-Eme-Kale be struck out and the claimant
(me) pays the defendant (Rag-Eme-Kale's) costs of the action.
The reasons were that;

1. The application does not state any cause of action
2. It has no prospect of success

His evidence which supported the application was;

1. *No tortious or contractual liability is expressed or*
complied by the claimants claim.
2. *The claimant alleges that the defendant has not responded*
to her emails. This is not a cause of action and should be
dealt with by way of complaint
3. *No civil order can provide the claimant with the remedy*
she seeks

4. The injunction order is not a contract its obligations extend to the claimant only.

I read it and it looked like I did not have a hope in hell of winning and everything he had written was most likely true, but even if I did get lumbered with the costs again they had no chance of ever getting it. I was not going to be put off by the prospect of losing.

It was an early hearing scheduled for 10.15 am on Tuesday 1st November 2011. I arrived early and after the frisking and bag search on the way in I sat and waited but there was no sign of Rag-Eme-Kale.

And then as if from nowhere who should come and sit down beside me but none other than the ugly barrister from the previous two court cases. Why would they need a barrister for such a trivial thing, other than of course to bump up the costs which they most likely were going to be awarded? All I wanted was for the judge to tell Rag-Eme-Kale that he must give me the opportunity to apply for his 'written express consent' as that was the only condition they had given me.

The barrister came over and sat down beside me and asked if he might speak to me. I did not want to speak with him at all so I told him he might not. Consequently no sooner had he sat down than he stood up again and sauntered off to the opposite side of the waiting area and scrutinised a notice board until Rag-Eme-Kale arrived shortly after and then they both stood chatting to each other.

The Clerk to the Court was soon ushering us into the same court room as the last time we were there. Rag-Eme-Kale and his barrister sat on the left and I on the right. We stood as the judge entered the court room; it was a lady this time. She told us to sit but the ugly barrister remained standing and launched into his bowing ritual, then he recited what Judgement Jones had written in their counter claim telling her that my complaint could not be dealt with in a court of law, therefore she should throw my case out and the Council would be seeking their cost of £1800 as well as the money I still owed them from previous costs awarded to them which I had not paid. She nodded her head several times then looking at me she said that she was unable to deal with my complaint and therefore she was dismissing the case in favour of the Council and I was ordered to pay their costs of £1800.

I guessed that would happen but it did not change the fact that Rag-Eme-Kale had done nothing about the official signs he had agreed to in July.

I stood up and explained to the judge that the only way I could advertise my café legally was with Rag-Eme-Kale's consent and since his visit in July he had not even sent me the application form despite me asking for one several times. I asked Rag-Eme-Kale why they had bothered coming to the café and walked round Camber looking for suitable places to put the signs and then had not followed it up.

Then the judge asked Rag-Eme-Kale why they had not proceeded further with the application, and he stood up and told her that the application had not been successful. 'Not been successful?' I asked him indignantly. I reminded him that I had sent him the quote for the café signs and he had told me to obtain and I had checked with my insurance company for the public liability cover, so why was it unsuccessful?

Rag-Eme-Kale claimed that 'Care Signs' was not a recognised sign maker that the Council would consider. Then he pulled a pathetic face, looked at the judge and said I had called him 'fat' when he had visited the café in July and also I had made effigies of them and sat them in my car, I had made corruptions of their names and got my friends to dress up as the effigies and made videos ridiculing them and I had made them public by putting them on YouTube.

To my astonishment the judge did not sympathise with

Rag-Eme-Kale's weight problem; instead she said that YouTube was for all to see including judges and she had also watched my videos.

What was going on? Rag-Eme-Kale snivelling that I had called him fat and the judge saying she had watched my Fluffit videos on YouTube, whatever next!

I said I could not pay the costs as I had no money, but the judge was undeterred and said that was something between me and the Council to sort out. I had not paid Judgement Jones any money for months so a further £1800 was not going to make a huge difference to the debt.

As the barrister was gathering up his papers Rag-Eme-Kale looked up at the judge and told her that he would deal with my application himself and once again he stipulated he would waive the application fee of £330.

I was confused; my case against Rag-Eme-Kale was lost, and in the counter claim from the Council they had won costs, but Rag-Eme-Kale had just vowed before the judge to deal with my application for my café signs which was the reason I went to the Court in the first place, so how could I have lost?

I left the court feeling accomplished, and the next day I rang Mr Judas and demanded that he send me his finished report or I would contact the Ombudsman.

CHAPTER 59

On Saturday 5th November 2011 Mr Judas's report finally
arrived. I could not wait to open it but I was cooking
breakfasts when the postman delivered the large white
envelope and I had to finish what I was doing before I could
read it properly.

I noticed straight away that on the top of the first page it
was dated 2nd November so it seemed that Mr Judas had only
just typed his report despite him telling me on the 13th
September he had finished it and sent it to the Assistant
Director for Legal and Democratic Services for his
consideration.

The report comprised of my meeting with Mr Judas in
Lewes, a list of my allegations, the process of his
investigation and his response to the allegations.

Initially he had done a lot of research into my court
appearances, injunction orders and the fact that I had accused
two council employees of committing perjury whilst I was
forbidden to use defamatory language against council staff.
He highlighted in his report that I had continuously placed
unauthorised signs on the highway which had caused
unnecessary drain on the council's resources.

I was beginning to think that Mr Judas had not quite
grasped exactly what he was meant to be doing with his
investigation, it seemed he had been investigating me and not
the officers I had complained about.

When he did eventually reveal his findings of the officers
he had interviewed, they had clearly lied to Mr Judas and
worryingly it seemed he had quite happily accepted their lies
as he had made no attempt to research or seek proof of the
answers he had been given. He even stated that Kilkenny's
witness statement whereby he had claimed there had been a

complaint about my café signs on the BT pole but then contradicted his own evidence given whilst under oath at the court hearing in April 2010, was not a misrepresentation of the actual events and in any case the judge had accepted Kilkenny's evidence so that was good enough proof that Kilkenny had told the truth

The report included photos that had been The Tyrannical Clown's exhibits of signs which they had removed from the highway, for sale signs, Halloween parties and brand new signs neatly stacked in a room awaiting distribution.

Even though I had provided Mr Judas with the photos of my café signs complete with the dates they were taken, he had found no evidence that the photos were taken on 7th October 2009. But he was able to confirm that an email sent on 8th October 2009 from The Tyrannical Clown to Swanoff Swanker which had been copied to Rag-Eme-Kale and Judgement Jones stated that, 'Yesterday (7th October) I had Camber visited and six signs pertaining to Camber Café were removed to this depot. Now no unauthorised signs remain within the village.' Mr Judas added that there was no mention of any photos being taken when the signs were removed. He had spoken to Judgement Jones who confirmed he had not received the photos by email therefore he could not say for certain when he received the photographs.

In another email from The Tyrannical Clown sent on 3rd November 2009 to Judgement Jones he confirms that the photographs in 'set 1' were taken by the contractor's employee with Peter Plonker's camera as Peter Plonker was driving.

Mr Judas concluded that as part of his investigation he had checked the properties on the electronic versions of the photographs which had a creative date of 8th August 2009, so on the balance of probability he assumed that the photographs were taken in mid-October as he could find no evidence other than the evidence from The Tyrannical Clown to enable him to conclude when the photos were taken therefore the complaint was not upheld as there was no evidence to contradict that of The Tyrannical Clown.

I was interested to see that Mr Judas had provided photo copies from The Tyrannical Clown's and Kilkenny's work schedule diaries. Amazingly The Tyrannical Clown had noted in his diary that he had phoned me on 9th September 2009, having denied it on oath in the court. The Tyrannical Clown admitted to making the call to me but did not remember the content of the conversation and therefore Mr Judas gave the benefit of the doubt to The Tyrannical Clown.

Regarding the photo of the Fish Shop sign I had sent to Rag-Eme-Kale, Mr Judas's observations on the matter were; from the angle I had taken my photograph it did appear that the sign was attached to the lighting column, however, in Rag-Eme-Kale's statement clearly showing the aforementioned photograph it was clearly attached to a separate post on private land as stated by Rag-Eme-Kale in his witness statement. Therefore the allegation was not upheld.

As for the red flashing light on the burger van Mr Judas said I had highlighted the fact that the illuminated sign was on all day and all night and therefore could not be turned off and I was of the view there was no difference between the café sign on my parked car and the flashing red light on the burger van.

Peter Plonker's evidence in court was that there was no flashing light on or around the burger van and he had proved it by taking photographs of the burger van. Mr Judas therefore concluded that if there was a flashing light on the burger van it would have deemed consent and was within Class 9 of the Town and Country Planning Act 2007 (Control of Advertisements) and if the illuminated sign was a distraction it would be a matter for the Police under the Road Traffic Act 1988. Therefore the allegation was not upheld.

In his summary Mr Judas had considered all the evidence I had provided, interviewed the officers concerned in relation to my complaints, and he had concluded that all apart from one should not be upheld but I should be given an apology for the error made by the Fines Office in Brighton regarding the payments I had made and the Council were not at fault as it was the only information they had at the time of the court hearing.

Mr Judas had ignored all the evidence I had provided for him and I could not believe that I had waited five months for Mr Judas to come up with such utter nonsense. He appeared to have forgotten what he was meant to be doing and to only uphold one of my complaints and put the blame on the fines office was laughable.

Mr Judas was not going to underestimate my intelligence, so I sent him an email:

Dear Mr Judas
Your report was full of inaccuracies and was incomplete.
Would you please send me the name of your superior so I can
have this investigation carried out thoroughly?
Regards
Sally Pattinson

I heard nothing from Mr Judas, so I emailed Judgement Jones:

Dear Judgement Jones
Having received Mr Judas's report on the investigation he
carried out, which is full of discrepancies, contradictions and
is incomplete, I would like you to send me the name of his
superior so that my complaint will be investigated thoroughly
and with respect to me.
I will not accept a cover up.

Sally

He replied to my email that evening:

Sally,
I will find out and let you know.
Have you paid any money towards your costs recently? With
the addition of last week's case, I believe over £3000 is
outstanding. I look forward to hearing from you.
Judgement Jones

I expected that kind of patronising answer from Judgement Jones and I had no doubt that he had been advising or threatening Mr Judas on how to present his findings. He knew I had not paid him anything for months, so I wrote an equally patronising email back.

Dear Judgement Jones
Yes. I sent you a jiffy bag with £3292 cash stuffed inside it last
week. I hope you haven't lost it. And by the way, you and your
colleagues owe me £8500 for loss of earnings last year.
I am amazed that none of you people seem to know who your
superiors are. Mr Judas doesn't know who is his and you have
got to find out for him. Is there no organisation in that
establishment? It sounds like you all work in utter
chaos.......but I'm not surprised....that's why you repeatedly
get your facts wrong.
Sally

Straight away Judgement Jones answered:

Sally,

It's a question of who is the most appropriate superior to respond to you. Mr Judas's direct line manager might not be the most appropriate person.
Did you send the envelope with the cash to me directly?
Judgment Jones

That was interesting; did Mr. Judas's direct line manager actually know what Mr. Judas had been doing. Yes indeed that would make sense that it was all done quietly between themselves and that would account for the time it had taken due to Mr. Judas trying to carry on with his normal duties. So keeping my thoughts to myself I replied;

Well Judgement Jones
I don't want someone who is corrupt, who tells lies and commits perjury as your clients do, nor someone who conveniently forgets important things because it is an easy way out of a situation.
There must be one person in that establishment who is honest and decent and will not condone corruption within the Council. So it's up to you to find him. You work there. So if Mr Judas's superior is not appropriate then that is certainly the reason Mr Judas didn't realise what he was meant to be doing. So hurry up please. I want this investigation done properly.
I sent the cash to you in a jiffy bag. Have you sent me my loss of earnings yet and would you like to see the proof of what you and your colleagues are responsible for, regarding my business?
Sally

The next day Judgement Jones sent me another email;

Sally,
The person you need to write to is Lexi Goodfellow, Customer
Information Team Leader, C3F, County Hall, Lewes, East
Sussex. BN7 1UE.
Judgement Jones

It was quite clear Judgement Jones was not going to name-drop, having said he would find out the name for me but now making the excuse he could not as he did not work in that section. I did not trust anybody, regardless of rank, in the Council, so I replied;

Judgement Jones
No Ms Goodfellow is not who I need to contact she has no
authority. I now want the name of your superior and Mr
Judas's superior. You are obliged to give me their names. I
expect the names of these people by return.
Mr Judas's investigation was utter nonsense, condoning
corruption, perjury and lies on the part of The Tyrannical
Clown, Kilkenny, Rag-Eme-Kale and Peter Plonker. I am not
accepting it and I am going to have my complaint investigated
properly. Your honesty is extremely doubtful and needs
looking into. Ms Goodfellow is not capable of doing that.
Please give me the name of your superior.
Sally

I sent Mr Judas an email pointing out my opinion on his feeble effort and failure of carrying out a proper investigation.

Dear Mr Judas
You have not completed the investigation you were meant to
be carrying out. You have NOT made enquiries about the
letter I sent by REGISTERED POST to the Chief Executive
and neither have you provided any evidence that you had

requested from various departments information regarding those spurious invoices.

The photos of the café signs which I provided for you with clear evidence of the dates and times they were taken with my mobile phone you have ignored. But instead you have chosen to GUESS that they were possibly taken in mid-October. In the photos that Judgement Jones sent me it is clearly raining heavily, it was raining on 7th October as I told you, you can check that information with the met office, but it did not rain again until the end of October. 22nd October was grey and windy with NO RAIN. Judgement Jones claims he can't remember when he received the photos as they were sent to him by post. I know very well as you had told me on 8th June, that any post received by the Council is logged, therefore IF Judgement Jones was sent them by post he would have been capable of checking it, but Judgement Jones is LYING. If those photos HAD the wrong date on them, 8th August, it would be showing on the photos Judgement Jones sent me. I know that he was emailed them on 8th October 2009. I am interested to know how in your opinion did these café signs after being removed on 7th October 2010 find their way back to Camber and reinstate themselves on 22nd October 2009 in exactly the same places as they were when I had first put them up in JULY, AUGUST and SEPTEMBER that year? Are you going to guess that as well?????

Regarding the phone call The Tyrannical Clown made to me on 9th September 2009, he denied on OATH making that phone call. He has admitted in your investigation that he DID make that phone call to me. That is proof that he DID commit PERJURY. If you do not acknowledge this admission of The Tyrannical Clown you are aiding and abetting a criminal offence.

Did you get a copy of the witness statement from Judgement Jones which was written by the owner of the Fish Shop regarding the sign on the lamp column? If Judgement Jones did not provide you with it I will get a copy of it myself. If the sign was not on the lamp column why did Rag-Eme-Kale send me this email which I have copied below for you and already given you a copy of? The sign I photographed is clearly attached to the lamp column and I believe you have purposely chosen to ignore my evidence but condone the dishonesty of the officers concerned.

Email from Rag-Eme-Kale:

Thank you for your email of 14 May 2010.
I note that you do not intend to submit a formal application to place a structure in the highway. With this in mind, please re-read the terms of the Court injunction and carefully consider how it applies to your mega-structure.
With regards to your email of 12 May 2010, I am pleased to inform you that we have been in contact with the individual that attached the sign to the lamppost in Rye and it has been removed.
Yours sincerely
Rag-Eme-Kale BEng (Hons) MCIHT
Team Manager, Traffic & Licensing
EAST SUSSEX COUNTY COUNCIL

I replied:

I have contacted the Fines Office in Brighton and they have assured me that all the money I have paid them has been sent to PO BOX 3 County Hall Lewes. Whoever told you that it had been sent to the Children's Services Dept. is lying. The address for that is PO Box 4, County Hall Lewes.
I conclude Mr Judas that either you have not had enough

experience in dealing with these investigations or you are protecting your colleagues. I thought you were meant to do a fair investigation not a biased one.

I am going to make a formal complaint against you if you do not complete this investigation properly or pass it over to someone who can. I suggest you look again at the evidence I provided for you and I recommend also that you consider the answers that the officers in question gave you. They are clearly LYING because they are cowards and because they know they have acted unprofessionally. Or is it because you fear repercussions if you expose these people for what they really are, that being CORRUPT, LIARS AND PERJURERS? Please have the courtesy to respond to this email.

Sally Pattinson

And respond he did at 6pm that evening;

Dear Ms Pattinson,

Thank you for your email. If you wish to pursue your complaint, please contact the Complaints Manager at the County Council who will outline our formal complaints process and the options left within that process.

Regards

Mr Judas

None of this made sense, Mr Judas was now telling me to pursue my complaint about himself to the complaints department. Maybe it was just sheer relief that he was rid of the whole affair and could only mean that Mr Judas was totally unqualified to investigate my original complaint other than to waste time.

Shortly after I received that email from Mr Judas, Lexi Goodfellow contacted me from the Complaints Department;

Dear Miss Pattinson,

I am sorry to hear that you are not satisfied with the complaint investigation carried out by Mr Judas. I understand from Judgement Jones that you feel that the report it is incomplete and contains discrepancies and contradictions. If you wish your complaint be investigated further you will need to follow our formal complaints procedure.

The next stage of the complaint process would be for the case to be referred to a review panel. The purpose of the review panel is to review the complaint to ensure it has been handled according to our procedures; however it is not a re-investigation of the original complaint. The panel would comprise of a chairperson who would be an independent person external to the County Council and an Assistant Director from another directorate within the County Council. You also have the option to take your complaint directly to the Local Government Ombudsman, however sometimes they will ask the complainant to exhaust every stage the local authorities' complaints procedure before they will agree to take the case on.

I see that you also asked for Mr Judas' line manager, please let me know if you are still waiting for those details and I will send them through to you.

I look forward to hearing from you.

Regards

Lexi Goodfellow

Customer Information Team Leader

Governance & Community Services

Although Lexi Goodfellow's email appeared to be quite encouraging I had no confidence in any of the council employees and therefore I was wary of what she was proposing. She had a long way to go to gain my confidence. I replied to her email;

Dear Ms Goodfellow
Thank you for your email.
Mr Judas did NOT investigate my complaint properly; he has condoned the behaviour of and made excuses for the officers and solicitor involved.
So until my complaint is taken seriously and the officers are properly investigated and the evidence is produced, I am not prepared to have a cover up report put in front of a review panel. Do you understand?
Sally Pattinson

Lexi Goodfellow answered my email straight away;

Dear Miss Pattinson,
I certainly appreciate your concerns; however we are obliged to follow the formal complaints procedure that we publish on our website. This is to ensure that we are consistent in our investigations and also because the Local Government Ombudsman will refer to this when investigating complaints against us to ensure we are following our own policies.
Although I am unable to offer you any further choices in terms of your next steps I thought you might find it useful to view our fact sheet on the panel process as it might help you to decide how you would like to proceed.
Please note in my previous email I said that one of the panel members would be an Assistant Director from another directorate. However this was incorrect it would in fact be an Assistant Director from the same directorate i.e. Economy, Transport and Environment but from a different department, please accept my apologies for this error.
Please let me know how you wish to proceed.
Regards

Lexi Goodfellow

I opened the attachment;

EAST SUSSEX COUNTY COUNCIL
TRANSPORT & ENVIRONMENT DEPARTMENT
COMPLAINTS REVIEW PANELS -
GUIDANCE FOR PARTICIPANTS

This is a guide for all those taking part in a Complaints Review Panel. It is in three sections:

General introduction
How to prepare for a review panel
The conduct of a review panel

Taken together, they outline what is required if the Panel is to give a full and fair hearing to someone who has not been satisfied with the action taken by the Department as a result of a complaint investigated under the second stage of the Procedure.

Further advice and information may be obtained from the Complaints Officer.

1. General Introduction

Purpose of a Review Panel

The primary purpose of a panel is to re-examine the response made by officers under the second, formal stage of the Complaints Procedure. It is not a re-play of the entire formal investigation, nor can the Panel consider new complaints. Its purpose is to look at those complaints where the outcome of the second stage was not satisfactory to the Complainant.

The Panel has no legal powers and is not a court of law; neither the complainant nor the Department's representatives may be accompanied by a solicitor or barrister.

The Panel considers whether or not the complaints are justified and will decide if the Department's response was reasonable. It makes recommendations to the Director of Transport and Environment who must give the Panel's findings 'due weight', when deciding what action will be taken by the Department.

The Panel has a secondary purpose, to provide information to the Local Authority, on the effects of service, policy or budget decisions. The Panel may wish to draw general conclusions from the specific cases which come before it. Recommendations should be as concrete and tangible as possible.

General Principle

The Panel conducts its business in such a way that complainants should feel able to present their concerns. The Panel is systematic in its business so that all are heard fully and fairly. The Panel will avoid unnecessary procedural rules.

Usual Panel Attendees

Panel Members

Independent Chair (appointed by Complaints Officer)

Assistant Director, Transport and Environment Department

Complainant (with an advocate or friend)

Departmental Representatives

Group Manager or officer directly involved

Complaints Officer (to act as impartial adviser/clerk to the Panel)

2. How to Prepare for a Review Panel

The Panel Members will wish to prepare themselves beforehand with as much factual material as is necessary, so that at the Hearing they may give full attention to the case put forward by each side. Participants assist themselves, and the Panel by preparing written material to go to the Panel in advance.

Preparation by the Complaints Officer

The Complaints Officer will:
Be impartial
Give advice, when requested, to participants on how the Panel operates and helps the participants prepare
Provide the Panel, and all those attending, in advance with:

a clear written statement of the complaints to be considered
a clear written statement of the outcomes the Complainant wants from the Panel
written material (letters, reports or statements) that the Complainant or the Department's representatives want circulated

a brief factual report of key events and dates, to place the complaint in context. This is usually prepared by the Department's representatives.
a list of the names and occupations of all those who are likely to be mentioned in the written material or the case presentations. This is usually prepared by the Department's representatives.

Arrange the Panel, taking into account any special needs or disabilities of the participants. The venue should be accessible and convenient to all participants, especially the Complainant.

Preparation by the Complainant

Let the Complaints Officer know if you think that there was some misunderstanding at the formal stage. It might still be possible to come to an agreement in advance and so avoid a Panel.
Be clear about your outstanding complaints.
Be clear about what outcomes you want to achieve.
Decide if you want anyone to attend the entire Panel as an advocate or friend and invite them. (Remember that a solicitor or barrister acting in a professional capacity cannot attend). The friend might take an active part, speaking on your behalf, or might simply be present as support to you. Be certain they know what you expect them to do. If you have difficulty finding someone to accompany you, talk to the Complaints Officer, who might be able to suggest supportive individuals or organisations.

Discuss with the Complaints Officer if you want anyone to appear at the Panel to present a particular piece of information.

Provide the Complaints Officer with any written material you want the Panel to have in advance, at least 10 days before the Panel, along with the names of anyone attending with you. Talk to the Complaints Officer if any general information is needed about the process, or is assistance is needed with typing or photocopying. The Complaints Officer will give advice without taking sides.

Prepare your presentation. The Panel will try to make the meeting as relaxed as possible. Even so, you might overlook or forget points that are important to you if you have not written them down. The Panel will ask you and the Department's representative's questions.

Preparation by the Department's Representatives

Let the Complaints Officer know if you think that there has been some misunderstanding at the formal stage. It may be possible to come to an agreement in advance and so avoid a Panel.

Decide who is to be the main representative, presenting the Department's case to the Panel.

Prepare a brief background report for the Panel which should include a list of significant dates and events, and a list of key individuals involved in the complaint. Decide what additional written material you want the Panel to have in advance.

Provide all this documentation to the Complaints Officer at least 10 days before the Panel.

Bear in mind that the Panel will expect the facts to have been well established at the formal stage. Presentations should focus on why the ordinary processes of management and negotiation have not resolved problems.

Prepare background information, on the Department's policies, standards or procedures that applied at the time of the events which the Panel will consider.

Consult with the Complaints Officer if any general information is needed about the proceedings.
Ensure those staff who have an involvement in the complaint, but who will not be attending the Panel are made aware of the outcome.

Preparation by Members of the Panel

- *In reading the material in advance, consider whether there is a potential conflict of interest, and inform the Complaints Officer.*
- *Consider whether there may be general issues which the Panel might wish to explore which might not be anticipated by the Department's representatives, and notify the Complaints Officer.*
- *Prepare questions, bearing in mind that most complainants will not have been to a Panel before. They may welcome questions as a way of bringing out all the relevant details.*
- *Consider and notify the Complaints Officer if there could be elements of the complaint or of the desired outcomes which are outside of the powers of the Panel to consider or recommend.*

3.   The Conduct of a Review Panel

General Principle
Every effort will be made to ensure that the Review Panel is held in a way that encourages a fresh and fair look at the complaint. The time, place, and order of business will allow the participants to state their views fully and directly, without discomfort and intimidation.

Confidentiality
The Panel might hear of private matters, and all participants

should ensure that what is said and written of a confidential nature goes only to those who need to know.

Order of Business

The CHAIR welcomes and introduces the participants, reminds them of the order of business, and emphasises the need to respect the privacy of the information that is brought before the Panel. The Chair should check that the Panel has an accurate statement of the complaints and of desired outcomes.

- *The COMPLAINANT, and/or their friend, presents the matters with which they are dissatisfied.*
- *The DEPARTMENT'S REPRESENTATIVES present the Department's reasons for responding to the formal complaint in the way they did.*
- *Each side is then given an opportunity to respond to or clarify issues which have arisen during the presentation of information. The Panel will ask questions.*
- *The DEPARTMENT'S REPRESENTATIVES are given the opportunity make any final comments.*
- *The COMPLAINANT is given the opportunity to make any final comments.*
- *The CHAIR thanks the participants, explaining the process by which recommendations will be made to the Director. The participants leave.*

The Makings of Recommendations

The Panel members continue, with only the Complaints Officer in attendance, to consider the extent to which the complaints are upheld, and to agree the recommendations. These are put into a report to the Director. The Complaints Officer writes the draft Panel report and the final wording

*must be agreed by the Chair. The report will reflect any area
of disagreement between Panel members on their findings,
although agreement should, wherever possible, be reached
regarding the recommendations. The agreed and signed report
is given to the Director of Transport and Environment within
seven working days.*

*The Panel may on occasions adjourn, for a full review of the
matters before it. The Panel will be aware of the need to
resolve complaints without delay, but may, for example, wish
to have specific information provided by people whose
attendance was not initially thought to be necessary. The
Panel will inform the Complaints Officer if this is the case.
Once the report has been received by the Director, copies of
the report are sent to the complainant, the Panel members, the
Department's representatives, the appropriate Assistant
Director of Transport and Environment, and any other person
who has been identified by the Panel and Complaints Officer
as having a legitimate need to know.*

*The Director of Transport and Environment will decide the
Local Authority's response to the recommendations. The
Director will write to the Complainant, within 27 days of
receiving the recommendations. Copies of this response will
be sent to those who received a copy of the Panel's report.*

Fairness and Courtesy

*The Panel does not operate with strict rules of procedure and
evidence in the way that Courts or Tribunals do, because such
rules might hinder people presenting their case. The conduct
of the hearing is governed by the Chair, who will insist that:*

- *Complainants do not make new complaints or allegations
  at the Panel. The purpose of the Panel is to have a fresh
  look at something that has already been considered but not*

resolved. The Panel, the complainant, and the Department's representatives will have prepared themselves to consider specific issues, and the Chair will limit the Hearing to those issues.

- *Participants will be expected to treat each other with courtesy and respect. The Hearing is not an opportunity for anyone to make derogatory remarks or engage in intimidation, offensive or personally insulting behaviour. Interruptions will be avoided, but the Chair will allow factual questions for clarification. The Chair may terminate the Panel proceedings where there is unacceptable or threatening behaviour by any participants.*

The Role of the Local Government Ombudsman

If still dissatisfied following the response of the Director a complainant may pursue the matter with the Ombudsman. The Ombudsman has a responsibility to consider complaints involving 'maladministration with injustice'. Further details are available from the Complaints Officer.

The Complaints Officer may be contacted at Governance & Community Services Department,
County Hall, St Anne's Crescent, Lewes, East Sussex BN7 1UF

I read the complaints procedure and it was encouraging that my allegations would be put before a panel that were unconnected with the Highways Department and presumably honest people. This was the only option open to me now to prove that the Council employees I had had dealings with were dishonest and corrupt. What did concern me though was, if a review panel would even consider my allegations to be true because of the seriousness of them, would they think that such behaviour would exist in a County Council. I had no choice but to accept the Stage 3 Review Panel before I took my complaint to the Local Government Ombudsman. I replied;

Dear Ms Goodfellow

So what does this panel decide, whether Mr Judas followed the procedure properly or whether he investigated properly? Could you explain that please? I have read the attachment you sent me.

I am however, making a formal complaint to you about Mr Judas as it is my opinion he did not complete the investigation or investigate it thoroughly and he admits he GUESSED some of his conclusions despite me giving him solid evidence.

I have no choice but to follow your complaints procedure although I have very little faith in the people who work for East Sussex County Council.

Regards

Sally Pattinson

CHAPTER 60

For the next few days Lexi Goodfellow did a very good job of gaining my confidence. She emailed me often to make sure I understood the purpose of the Stage 3 Review Panel, and she asked me several questions. One was if I could confirm if during my dealings with the Highway Team any sort of compromise was ever discussed which would have allowed me to advertise my business in a way that could be permitted by ESCC,

I told her that official signs had been mentioned by the Director of Transport and Environment previously and also at great length with Rag-Eme-Kale but his email was so complicated I had not understand what he was talking about, for example; block drawings to scale and sub soil and wind loads and impact and speed limits which meant I was compelled to employ a structural engineer who held a degree with honours. I said I believed he had purposely written in a way that I was not meant to understand it.

I told her that since then Rag-Eme-Kale came to my café on July 12th to discuss the possibility of official signs and on the strength of that visit I thought he had agreed to me having them. However, in the Court a couple of weeks ago I had asked him why he hadn't sent me an application form which I had asked for several times, and he had said the visit had been unsuccessful because I said he was fat and 'Care Signs', who had given me the quote, were not proper sign makers. Then afterwards he said he would come to my café again and fill out the application form with me but he had not come and neither has the application form.

Lexi Goodyear reacted instantly to all my questions and doubts. Soon after I had told her about Rag-Eme-Kale's visit in July she emailed me to apologise on his behalf and told me she had spoken to him and an application form was on its way to me.

I had to decide if I was going to take the Stage 3 option or take my complaint to the Government Ombudsman. I felt I was able to trust Lexi Goodfellow and I felt that she would deal with my complaint honestly. I emailed her and said I would go to the Stage 3 Review Panel and I asked her how long it would take as I was still convinced that The Tyrannical Clown was going to leave the Highways and get away from any consequences which might follow if I should win my case against him.

I accepted to proceed with the Stage 3 Review Panel with my complaint against Mr Judas for the way he had investigated my allegations against the council employees. I was hoping it would not takes months to prepare for it, so I asked Lexi Goodfellow how long it was all going to take; she replied;

Dear Miss Pattinson
It is quite difficult to estimate how long it will take as all of the relevant information needs to be gathered from all parties, the panel established and a date/time needs to be agreed. I regret to say that the actual meeting may not take place until after Christmas. I will make every effort to bring it forward but will be relying on the co-operation of a number of different people.
To start things off I will need a clear written statement from you detailing precisely the complaints you wish to be considered, bearing in mind that this investigation is looking into how your stage 2 investigation was handled. New complaints will not be considered nor will it be a re-play of the entire formal investigation. To speed things up it would be great if you can also begin to gather any evidence that you wish to be considered to support your case.

*Secondly I will need a written statement from you outlining
the outcomes that you want from the panel.*
*Once I have that I will approach the relevant ESCC personnel
and ask them to prepare a response and to gather all of the
information/evidence they wish to be considered.*
*In the meantime I will look into which independent
chairperson is available and which Assistant Director would
be the most appropriate to have on the panel. I really need to
find someone who has had no involvement with your case.*
Please let me know if I can be of any further assistance.
Regards
Lexi

So I had to prepare yet another statement, and as for the
outcome of it all I had not even thought about it. Was I going
to choose their punishments if they were found guilty? That
would be fun.

My statement had to be about the way in which Mr Judas
had carried out the investigation into the behaviour of Council
Employees within the Highways Department and Legal
Department. I had to provide more evidence to support my
allegations and as Mr Judas' report had been in favour of the
people I had complained about, I needed to get hold of
damning evidence against them, proof that they themselves
had contradicted or written something inconsistent to what
they had denied or alleged. Maybe I could ask to see their
work diaries. I doubted whether I could but I could only ask,
so that is what I did. On 25th November 2011, I sent an email
asking if I might have copies of The Tyrannical Clown and
Kilkenny's work diaries for the years 2009 and 2010. Also I
would like a written statement from the man who worked for
the Contracting Company who had apparently taken photos of
my café signs on 22nd October 2009 with Peter Plonker's
camera. Lexi Goodfellow answered the same day saying she

would request the information I had asked for.

In the meantime I prepared my statement in response to Mr Judas' report.

MY RESPONSE TO MR. JUDAS' REPORT

I do not run the Beach Café in Beach Road, Camber as is stated by Mr Judas in the first line of his report. I own and run Camber Café in Lydd Road, Camber. I believe this significant error is an insight which reflects the amount of thought and effort Mr Judas has put into this investigation. Mr Judas states incorrect information right from the start of his report; he says that since November 2008 I had placed unlicensed advertising signs on the public highway. In fact I had told him at the meeting in Lewes that I had written permission from BT to place two signs onto a telegraph pole since April 16th 2007 and there had never been a problem with them until Kilkenny claimed to have received a formal complaint in November 2008.

Officially Mr Judas should have completed his report within 28 days, and I was patient in the hope of him conducting a thorough and unbiased investigation. Mr Judas spent 151 days to produce nothing more than a load of unreliable twaddle.

Six weeks after I had met Mr Judas at County Hall, Lewes I emailed him for an update as I had not heard from him, and he responded on the same day assuring me that he had interviewed the officers and was aiming to finalise his report by the end of July 2011. I did not hear from him again so after waiting a further six weeks I emailed him on 6th September 2011 asking for another update on his progress and as he did not respond I emailed him again on 9th, 12th and 13th September 2011 when he finally sent me an email stating to have just finalised his report which had to be shown to his superior. Again I heard nothing from Mr Judas so on October

8th 2011 I emailed him saying that I considered he had had ample time to complete his report. Once again he did not reply. Eventually I rang Mr Judas on 2nd November 2011 asking for him to send me his report. I received the report on Saturday 5th November 2011.

I believe Mr Judas purposely delayed finalising his report, as it is clear that he spent very little time on the matter of interviewing the officers, investigating the allegations against Council staff and making enquiries based on the substantial evidence I provided for him.

Of the little time he did spend it appears most of it was taken up making enquiries about me and not what he had been commissioned to do. I had provided Mr Judas with bundles of evidence including statements from previous court appearances I had attended so he had all the information he needed.

His report is biased. He has intentionally ignored the evidence that I had provided against the officers. I believe Mr Judas' aim was solely to shield these officers by delaying the outcome of his report to facilitate justification for their behaviour. Whether Mr Judas had been bribed or threatened I will never know, but I am certain that the corrupt officers involved in this matter were the main reason for the delay of the completion of the report.

*The investigation was to deal with complaints from me about ESCC staff, those being; The Tyrannical Clown **Licensing and Enforcement Manager,** Judgement Jones **Solicitor of the Supreme Court employed by East Sussex County Council,** Kilkenny **Highways Inspector,** Rag-Eme-Kale **BEng (Hons) MCIHT Team Manager Inspection & Enforcement** and Peter Plonker **Senior Maintenance Technician** who collectively accused me of things I had not done, producing false evidence and making a threatening phone call which was denied on oath. The Tyrannical Clown's accusation of me* *refusing to pay a fine which I had been paying was done purposely to discredit me before the judge, and had Mr Judas used his common sense and contacted the Fines Office in Brighton himself, he would have been given the correct information, but instead he blamed confusion in the fines office as the cause of the lost payments. He was meant to be investigating, not relying on the word of the people who I had accused of lying.*

Kilkenny had lied when he said he had had a complaint about my café signs. There is no mention of Camber Café on the recorded anonymous phone call report and Mr Judas should have seen that. The service ticket has now been produced and should have been exhibited as evidence in Kilkenny's witness report at the Court case in April 2010.

Rag-Eme-Kale accused me of wasting theirs and tax payer's money because I had reported a sign attached to a lamp column, and he claimed I had purposely taken the picture at an angle to make the sign appear to be attached to the lamp column. I had asked Mr Judas to acquire a copy of the witness statement written by the owner of the Fish shop from Judgement Jones so he would have all the proof he needed to see that I had told the truth, but he did not bother to do so as he preferred to believe Rag-Eme-Kale's account, even though he had sent me an email informing me that the sign had been removed from the light column. I did not take the photo at an angle to make it appear to be attached to the lamp column because that is where it was. Therefore Kilkenny and Rag-Eme-Kale lied and took photographs after the sign had been relocated. I would question why Kilkenny even took a photo of the relocated sign in the first place if it had been moved, as what was the point of doing that apart from the very reason they used the photo for and that was to make another false allegation against me. My colour photo clearly shows the metal strap attaching the sign to the lamp column EXH /4.

The officers concerned know that this is the truth and they have presented contaminated evidence to discredit me. This is yet another example of corruption within East Sussex County Council.

I believed that Peter Plonker had printed a photo of AJ's burger van in black and white to make it appear to have no red flashing lights on it and that is what Mr Judas was meant to be investigating. I had provided photos in colour and black and white and a witness statement from a friend all proving that there were flashing red lights on the burger van. Mr Judas clearly did not investigate this complaint, and he had failed to comprehend the allegation against Peter Plonker. I never said that there were lights flashing on the burger van all day and all night. Mr Judas must have been deluded that day because he had misconstrued legislation by claiming that Class 9 of The Town & Country Planning (Control of Advertisements) (England) Regulations 2007 made it okay for the burger van to have flashing lights on it. Finally on this matter he passed his own personal opinion as to whether the red light was a distraction or not and then concluded that the flashing light was a matter for the police. It was of no importance as to who it was a matter for, he was meant to be investigating Peter Plonker's contaminated evidential photos. Mr Judas did not investigate my complaint at all regarding the letter I had written to the Chief Executive on 4th November 2009, nor did he make enquiries about the information I had asked for several times relating to the invoices that had been billed to me by The Tyrannical Clown for £1045. Of all the allegations I made against council staff only one was upheld and that was blamed on the Fines Office and Mr. Judas thought that I should be awarded an apology. Mr. Judas should have contacted the fines office himself instead of relying upon information given to him by those who had lied about it in the first place.

The Tyrannical Clown did admit to Mr Judas that on 7th October 2009 my café signs were removed, but he would not admit to photos being taken that day. I had provided Mr Judas with photos of those same café signs that had been taken with my mobile phone and showed the dates and times they had been taken. However, with all the evidence I provided and The Tyrannical Clown's admission, Mr Judas ignored what was so blatantly obvious in preference of believing his own deluded personal guess work that the photos taken by the Contractors employee were most likely taken in mid-October. I would insist that, as The Tyrannical Clown states that he himself had ordered the removal of the signs on 7th October 2009, they were without doubt removed on that date. In that case at some point between 8th and 22nd October 2009 how was I able to retrieve and reinstate the same signs in exactly the same position if they were in the depot in Bexhill, the same signs that The Tyrannical Clown had ordered to be removed on 7th October? How was it possible for the Contractor's employee to take photos of these signs with Peter Plonker's camera when the signs were in the depot in Bexhill? Why did it not occur to Mr Judas that the Contractors employee was taking photos of something that was not there?

The phone call that The Tyrannical Clown made to me on 9th September 2009 he denied on oath in the court on April 6th 2010 and this was a clear act of perjury. I accept this cannot be dealt with as an internal matter and therefore if I want to take it further I must make a complaint to the Police although Mr Judas states in his report that The Tyrannical Clown did admit making the phone call to me on 9th September 2009 but his memory had failed him as to why he had phoned me in the first place according to Mr Judas.

Mr Judas has copied sec. 132 of the 1980's Highways Act which states the consequences if someone unlawfully places a

sign on the highway and that the fine would not exceed £100 for the first offence and any subsequent convictions would rise to a fine not exceeding £200. One of my complaints had been that I had been fined £200 instead of £100 for each offence at Eastbourne Magistrates Court. Although Mr Judas had checked the act, it evidently had not registered in his brain as he had failed to connect my complaint to his evidence.
I do not believe that Mr Judas has understood the seriousness of my complaints and allegations, as this report is so inaccurate it is insulting to my intelligence.

Having finished my statement I had to write a list of my desired outcomes. I knew what outcomes I desired but they would be rejected as most of them were physical. So for the time being I wrote;

I wish to be reimbursed the total costs for the A-boards which have been removed from the top of Lydd Road which I believe to have 'deemed consent', and other café signs which had been unlawfully removed by the Highways Authority which were not in their jurisdiction.
I ask for the injunction order to be cancelled.
I wish to be reimbursed the costs of the legal fees I had to pay for a barrister in April 2011.
I want the £1045 billed to me by The Tyrannical Clown cancelled as I believe the invoices were spurious.
I wish to seek loss of earnings incurred upon my business for the tax years 2010/2011 through inadequate advertising.
I want it in writing that The Tyrannical Clown and Kilkenny lied, made false allegations about me and committed perjury.
I want it in writing that Peter Plonker produced contaminated evidence and lied about the red light on the burger van and lied that the photos of my café signs had been taken on the 21st and 22nd October 2009.

Having finished my statement I gathered together all the evidence I had initially provided for Mr Judas, photocopied it all again and sent it to Lexi Goodfellow. I was not really sure what the Stage 3 Review panel was going to achieve. My complaints had been about The Tyrannical Clown and his colleagues, not Mr Judas, but from what I had gathered from Lexi Goodfellow the reason for the Stage 3 was to decide whether Mr Judas had carried out a proper investigation. To my mind he had definitely not, and I was confused as to the purpose of it. If it was agreed that Mr Judas had failed in his investigation what would happen? Although I was annoyed at Mr Judas my main objective had been to expose those bent council employees but it looked as if they would get away with their misdemeanours and then what could possibly happen to Mr Judas, a slap on the wrist? They had asked him to do something he was not capable of doing so he would probably receive compensation and counselling for being put under such pressure.

CHAPTER 61

On 1st December 2011, I received the long awaited letter from Rag-Eme-Kale saying;

I am writing today as agreed at our last meeting in Hastings County Court, I attach a sign design from our contractors. This can be varied to state 'Camber Café next right' for the sign proposed on the western side of the junction and 'Camber Café next left' on the sign proposed on the eastern side of the junction. The signs will be manufactured by our contractor for £96.25 each (plus VAT). This comes to £231.00 for both signs.

Also, as agreed in Court on 1st November 2011 the application fee of £330 shall be waived. However there is a licence fee of £200 for 2 years that shall be required before the licence is granted. In addition East Sussex County Council would be grateful that you pay the costs awarded by the judge on 1st November 2011 of £1077. This sum shall be required before we grant the licence for the signs. In addition it would appear that a sum of £3292 is still outstanding. Although this sum will not be required to be paid in full before a licence for the sign is issued I would be grateful if you would contact Judgement Jones to implement a sensible repayment program to discharge this debt.

I have copied this letter to Rother District Council as section 115 of the Highways Act 1980 requires that I contact the local planning authority for their consent when considering licensing/structure in the highway. If they are amenable to the proposed commercial signs I shall arrange for notices to be erected on site for 14 days to comply with the other requirements of section 115 that road users are consulted.
Yours sincerely

Rag-Eme-Kale

I looked at the map and sign dimensions. The pink part being Lydd Road there were two little green dots showing the site locations of the proposed café signs. All the measurements looked good at first glance until I realised they were in millimetres being 290mls x 230mls which meant the proposed signs were going to be no bigger than lolly sticks. They would not be seen in the all-important summer months as the grass was only cut once a year now since the Parish Council, due to 'cut-backs' had sacked the local man who had kept the common parts of Camber in pristine condition. Instead they had hired a contractor to cut the grass but only once a year due to the cost which far exceeded the wages of the very efficient sacked handy-man. In fact the grass grew so high in the summer months even my A-board was hidden by it. It seemed that all people connected to any type of Council became deluded power freaks with only one aim in mind that was to destroy our green and pleasant land.

Rother District Council had destroyed part of my childhood memories, several beautiful Victorian shelters along Bexhill sea front which I remember fondly had been painted in green and cream shining paint and always had that distinct aroma of paint. These priceless Victorian structures had been demolished and replaced with ugly unsuitable triangular shaped backless benches with triangular roofs which did not keep out the rain. 90% of the residents in Bexhill are retired and therefore need a shelter to rest when out walking.

I was amused at Rag-Eme-Kale's proposed sign designs. I did not know why he had even bothered wasting the paper and his time. I answered his letter by email;

Dear Rag-Eme-Kale
Thank you for your letter of 29th November 2011.
*First of all I would like to thank you for the length of time and
great effort you have put into designing and costing signs for
my café and your generous offer of waiving the application
fee of £330 and your intention to charge me £200 for a
licence with no title.*
*You have said that you will apply to RDC Planning for
permission to display these signs, but I would feel far more
comfortable applying for it myself as I am not confident that
you would not put pressure on them to reject the application.
So if you don't mind I would prefer you to put the application
for your small official café signs in abeyance till further
notice and for the time being I have decided to keep my A-
board in place at the junction of Lydd Road as not only do I
have written permission from RDC to place my A-board at the
top of Lydd Road, it also has Deemed Consent (Class 13) of
the Town & Country Planning (Control of Advertisements)
(England) Regulations 2007 which is sufficient and cost free.
And by the way I sent Judgement Jones £3292.00 a couple of
weeks ago, didn't he tell you or did he forget to log its arrival
again like he did before with The Tyrannical Clown's photos
with invisible dates on.*
Sally

It was not long till I received a reply from Rag-Eme-Kale:

Dear Sally Pattinson.
*You may not put an advertising board on the junction of Lydd
Road as you have been handed down an injunction from the
court specifically to prevent this. I recommend that you re-
read those items that have 'deemed consent' in the Town and
Country Planning (Control of Advertisements) Act 2007, or as
you say, contact Rother District Planning directly for advice.*

The licence that these commercial signs are to be approved under is Section 115 of the Highways Act 1980. Therefore the title of the Licence is a Section 115 Licence to place commercial objects in the highway. Section 115 requires 'walkway consent' to be obtained. You hopefully will recall the discussion we had on site about walkway consent. It requires that I contact the local Planning Authority; however, as you feel that I might put undue pressure on Rother District Council to refuse the application, I shall leave it to you to contact them directly. Please ask them to send me a letter or an email of their consent as I shall require written evidence prior to issuing the licence.

I have seen an email in which you advise that you sent cash in a jiffy bag to Judgment Jones to pay the £3292.00. I sincerely hope you sent this amount of cash by registered post because if it fails to reach us, the debt will remain outstanding.

Yours sincerely

Rag-Eme-Kale

They did make me laugh; they must forward my emails to each other every time I sent one. So I wrote another one for them:

Dear Judgement Jones

I understand from Rag-Eme-Kale you have still not located the missing jiffy bag, so sadly you will have to forfeit your lunch break today and look for the missing jiffy bag I sent you with £3292.00 stuffed in it. Rag-Eme-Kale said I should contact you and tell you that's what you have got to do. When you have found it and counted the contents will I owe you anything else after that?

Happy searching!

Sally

When I had sent that email to Judgement Jones I wrote one in answer to Rag-Eme-Kale's email;

Dear Rag-Eme-Kale

It's you who needs to re-read those items that have 'deemed consent' (class 13). I know my A-board has it, I have a letter from Rother District Council saying I can put my A-board there. If you don't like it that's too bad...

What licence does Mr Forthright have for his abutting signs oh yes and AJ's burger van and The Farm Shop, the passport photo shop in Rye etc. etc. etc?

I have forgotten the discussion we had about walkway consent as that was six months ago. Nobody walks where my A-board is anyway....

I HAD an injunction order; I no longer have it as I have ripped it up, so there.

What are you doing reading emails I sent to Judgement Jones, it might have been private.

I like your joke about sending things by registered post. Once letters arrive at County Hall who knows where they might end up whether they have been registered, recorded or arrived by carrier pigeon! If you don't know ask The Tyrannical Clown.......

I have looked at the measurements of your proposed signs for my café, they are utterly ridiculous. Why not just write Camber Café on a lolly stick?

I will not pay for something so stupid that no one is going to see, my A-board is staying......so you have a nice day.

Sally

PS. What does BEng (Hons) MCHIT stand for?

CHAPTER 62

By the middle of December Lexi and I were on first name terms. She was proving to be very thorough with the organisation of the Stage 3 Review Panel. The date had been set for 17th January 2012 and the panel would be made up of three people chaired by a lady who was a magistrate by profession, plus an independent man with no connection to any Council and another lady from East Sussex County Council who was the head of a department which was nothing to do with the Highways. Also to be present were Lexi Goodfellow dealing with the complaint, Rag-Eme-Kale, Mr Judas, myself, and Lesley who was coming with me for moral support. The review was to take place at Ocean House, St. Leonards-On-Sea, a twelve story office building where the Inland Revenue and other professional organisations were situated.

So with the location in place I gathered as much evidence together as I could, and I was still waiting for The Tyrannical Clown's and Kilkenny's diaries. Lexi had informed me that Kilkenny was no longer employed by East Sussex County Council and The Tyrannical Clown was going to leave shortly. That came as no surprise to me. I did not speculate on the reason for the termination of Kilkenny's employment or indeed the news that The Tyrannical Clown was also departing soon, but it would certainly confirm the reason that Mr Judas had dragged out his investigation. So all the while the Tyrannical Clown was still employed it meant that there was a chance of exposing him.

I had requested several times from Judgement Jones and Lexi copies of the emails between Peter Plonker and Judgement Jones confirming the dates that the photos of my café signs were allegedly taken. I had repeatedly denied putting those signs up after they had been removed on 7th October 2009. Of course the emails could not be produced because they did not exist. Then one morning an email arrived from Judgement Jones to Lexi which she had forwarded to me;

Lexi,
This may help in responding to Sally's query. The photos that she speaks of are attached and the first batch was taken on 21st October - when it was raining, the last two on 22nd October.
They were emailed to The Tyrannical Clown on 27th October (see note below) so they must have been forwarded to me after that date and time, hence the letter I sent on the 28th enclosing the photos.
The photos were taken by Peter Plonker. He noted in his diary that it was raining on 21st October 2009, but dry on 22nd.
We might have to concede that most of the photos were taken on the 21st, but they certainly weren't taken on the 7th.
Judgement Jones
<<C:\Documents and Settings\peterpl\Application Data\FUJIFILM\FinePixViewerS\Temp\1027-162040\DSCF9007.JPG>> S
<<C:\Documents and Settings\peterpl\Application Data\FUJIFILM\FinePixViewerS\Temp\1027-162040\DSCF9008.JPG>> al
<<C:\Documents and Settings\peterpl\Application Data\FUJIFILM\FinePixViewerS\Temp\1027-162040\DSCF9009.JPG>> ly
<<C:\Documents and Settings\peterpl\Application Data\FUJIFILM\FinePixViewerS\Temp\1027-162040\DSCF9011.JPG>> ,
<<C:\Documents and Settings\peterpl\Application

*Data\FUJIFILM\FinePixViewerS\Temp\1027-
162040\DSCF9014.JPG>>*

 <<C:\Documents and Settings\peterpl\Application
*Data\FUJIFILM\FinePixViewerS\Temp\1027-
162040A\DSCF9014.JPG>>*

*These are the photos that Peter Plonker attached to his email
to The Tyrannical Clown on 27th October 2009 which was
then forwarded to me. The photos were taken on the 21st
October (which was a rainy day) and the 22nd. Peter Plonker
logged in his diary when the photos were taken and the
weather on that date.*

Judgment Jones

-----Original Message-----
From: Peter Plonker
Sent: 16 November 2011 09:19
To: Judgment Jones
Subject: FW: Pictures from last week

 -----Original Message-----
From: Peter Plonker
Sent: 27 October 2009 16:22
To: The Tyrannical Clown
Subject: Pictures from last week

Judgment Jones had for some reason provided the
information regarding the dates and the weather conditions on
the day the photos had allegedly been taken. The emails from
Peter Plonker had no content they were just headings, even
the photos had no date on them.

Judgment Jones had told Mr Judas that he had no memory
of when he had received these particular photos as they had
been sent to him by post, but now he is admitting to the day
he had received them by email and had provided the evidence,
albeit false. And to make it worse for himself he was now
saying that the five photos were taken not only by Peter

Plonker over a period of two days, three of the photos when it was raining and two when it was not, he had evidently forgotten that it was the contractors employee who, according to Peter Plonker had taken the photos. What it really amounted to was proof the three of them had lied so much they had tripped themselves up, and none of their evidence made sense. I had not lied about anything and my evidence never changed. And now here was Judgment Jones insulting my intelligence by expecting me to be gullible enough to believe him.

I was having none of it and emailed Judgment Jones;

Judgement Jones,
I see nothing that confirms anything.....it is only confirming that Peter Plonker is a liar. He knows and you know and I know the photos were taken on 7th October. You won't brain wash me so stop trying.
You are hilarious, you have got in such a muddle with your lies that you have finally admitted you are a liar in your email.....
I have included it all in my report for the Review Panel....
Sally

He retorted with another email he had received from Peter Plonker;

-----Original Message-----
From: Peter Plonker
Sent: 21 December 2011 10:38
To: Judgment Jones
Subject: FW: Pictures from last week
Judgment Jones,
I have found the email with photos on have checked diary weather was wet all day and photos were taken 21st October

2009 in the rain but I sent the email on the 27th Oct 09 to The Tyrannical Clown.
Peter Plonker
Senior Maintenance Technician
Transport and Waste Division East Area Office Economy, Transport and Environment Department

I was so happy to receive all these emails which were providing me with more and more evidence against these highly paid council employees with titles who were nothing more than a bunch of liars. They knew I knew they were lying, but between the three of them, that being Judgement Jones, Peter Plonker and The Tyrannical Clown, they were tripping each other up as their lies became more entangled with more lies.

I was not going to accept this nonsense. These were not original emails and I was not going to have my intelligence insulted by idiots. I sent an equally patronising email back to Judgement Jones;

Judgement Jones
Would you please FORWARD me these ORIGINAL emails which I have copied here for you? Also in Mr Judas's report it states that you were sent an email from The Tyrannical Clown 3rd November 2009 I would like to be forwarded that original email as well please. It appears to me that you don't understand the meaning of original so I am going to tell you. 'ORIGINAL' means belonging or pertaining to the origin or beginning of something or to a thing at its beginning. It appears from previous requests I have made that you do not understand the meaning of TO FORWARD either, so I am going to tell you that too.
'TO FORWARD' means directed toward a point.

So you open up the original email that is from the first person who wrote the email you have been asked to forward. Above the email you have the option to forward it on to someone else. So click on that and you then type in the contact to whom you wish to send it and then just click on send; it's easy.
Would you please ask Peter Plonker to forward me the original email he sent to The Tyrannical Clown on 27th October 2009 at 16.22? I have asked for this several times already.
In fact I think I have requested this information too many times now so I hope this will be the last. If you do not accede to my request you are breaking the law by withholding information to which I am entitled. Furthermore this puts you in breach of ESCC's policy on FOI too. I am going to request it every day until you or the officers who sent the emails, provide me with the information I am entitled to.
Did Lexi Goodfellow tell you I have the weather report for October 2009 and it was not raining on the 21st or 22nd. In fact we were enjoying an Indian summer.
-----Original Message-----
From: The Tyrannical Clown Sent: 28 October 2009 09:13 To: Judgement Jones Subject: FW: Pictures from last week
-----Original Message-----
From: Peter Plonker Sent: 27 October 2009 16:22 To: The Tyrannical Clown Subject: FW:
Pictures from last week
-----Original Message-----
From: Peter Plonker Sent: 16 November 2011 09:19 To: Judgement Jones Subject: FW: Pictures from last week
From Sally

In the meantime Lexi had been doing her own investigation into Peter Plonker's photos, and she had noticed discrepancies on the jpeg file. She wrote to me saying;

Dear Sally

None of Peter Plonker's photographs have the date/time stamps on them; all we have is the data from the jpeg file itself.

Peter has told me that the camera's date is now correct but that he cannot tell me exactly how far out it was originally. Even without proof of this it still casts serious doubt over when the photographs were taken.

My thoughts around this are that one set of photos are logged as being taken 28 Aug and the report claims that they were taken on the 27 Oct and another set are showing 8 Aug and you believe that they were taken on the 7 Oct.

There is a pattern there, if the camera was set 2 months plus 1 day out, I believe the dates would concur with what you are saying. However I need proof of this which is why I have asked Peter Plonker to confirm if he is still using his camera and if so what the date settings are. If they are set to 14 October today then you would have what you need. Trouble is I won't find out until 19th December at the earliest as I received an out of office message from him.

I still think the date/time data on the jpg files of the photographs that Judgement Jones sent are important.

The jpg of the pictures that everyone agrees were taken on the 27 Oct have the following file dates:

DSCF9022 28/08/2009 02:26

DSCF9023 28/08/2009 02:27

So the camera was out by 2 months and 1 day.

The photographs that you believe were not taken on the 21st or 22nd but on the 7th Oct are as follows:

DSCF9007 8/08/2009 02:22

DSCF9008 8/08/2009 02:24

DSCF9009 8/08/2009 02:27

DSCF9011 8/08/2009 02:38

DSCF9014 8/08/2009 02:46
If the camera was still out by the same 2 months and 1 day it
means that the photographs were taken on 7th October.
I am going to speak with our IT department. It is important
for me on a professional level that I get to the bottom of this.
Regards
Lexi

Lexi was certainly on the ball and thank goodness for it as she was able to get information on things that I would never have. I still had not received The Tyrannical Clown's or Kilkenny's work diaries which I had asked for as my right to Freedom of Information, nor had the Contractor's employee provided his statement.

I had looked at the photos over and over again. Peter Plonker had claimed he had not taken them as he was driving and it was the contractor's employee who had, but it suddenly occurred to me that all the photos had been taken from the driver's side of the vehicle. In the last photo there was a third highway man in the process of crossing the road in the rain heading towards the bike and sign on my scaffold pole opposite the caravan park. So if Peter Plonker was driving and the photo was taken by the contractor's employee, where had the third man been sitting in the Highway van?

CHAPTER 63

Christmas came and went and it was getting closer to the
Stage 3 Review panel, and I had gathered as much evidence as
I possibly could but I still had not received the work diaries or
statement I had asked for. I had included a local weather
report from a gardener's diary I found on the internet and the
information about the tail end of Hurricane Grace hitting the
South East of England on 7th October 2009, but I wanted
someone more local to back up this vital piece of evidence. I
sent Lexi a list of the contents of my bundle of evidence and
when she approved that everything in it was sufficient for the
Review Panel I sent it off to her by recorded delivery. I hoped
that my request for the diaries they had refrained from
producing might go against them.

Over the next few days there was a lot of correspondence
between myself and Lexi. I asked her for a copy of Peter
Plonker's diary for the month of October 2009 when he
claimed to have taken photos of my café signs and for him to
identify the man crossing the road in the photo that had
allegedly been taken on 21st October 2009. She replied;

Dear Sally
In a meeting with Peter Plonker, I took excerpts from his
diary.
Further to the other diaries, I do need to clarify that even if I
am able to get hold of them I would only be able to provide
copies as due to Data Protection I would have to redact or
block out any personal details of other individuals to protect
their privacy and I can't do that to the originals. We would
have to do the same if your name appeared in it and someone
else requested to see it.

Regards
Lexi

I was not interested in other people, I just wanted to see what had been written in these diaries concerning me, but it worried me that the individuals who I had been dealing with were most likely trying to convince Lexi that she could not copy them for various reasons. I was not going to take 'NO' for an answer and I was determined, so I contacted the FOI office and happily was given a positive result that I was entitled to see them so I quickly emailed Lexi the good news;

Dear Lexi
I have spoken to someone in the FOI office and he told me I do have the right to any information regarding myself that has been entered in those diaries. Also they (ESCC) have 40 days to respond and as I asked for the information on 25th November 2011 that time limit has now elapsed. He advised me to make a complaint but I said I will wait till the end of the week. Please understand that I am not holding you responsible for the lack of response, I know you did ask for the diaries shortly after I requested them.
If you were able to take excerpts from Peter Plonker's diary last week that I can view then surely someone can do the same with the other diaries? After all I only want to see anything that pertains to me or my business.
Regards
Sally

Lexi's reply was disappointing

Dear Sally

Thank you for your email. It would only apply as a Data Protection request if you had specifically asked to see information about yourself, however as you just requested to see the work diaries I did not treat it as such. The person you spoke to was correct that there is a 40 day turnaround but that is counted from when the team receive a completed Data Request form with the £10 payment. In hindsight it appears that I should have treated your request in this way and I am sorry for not advising you to take this course of action. I had not anticipated how difficult it would be to get hold of these documents.

You are absolutely correct about the diaries; if I can get hold of them I can take photocopies of anything you wish to see barring other people's personal information. You have submitted a Freedom of Information request for those diaries now which will hopefully speed up the response. I will speak to Head of Highways when he is back in the office this afternoon to stress the importance of producing the diaries. I am only sorry that I have not been successful in my endeavours so far and I apologise for that.
Regards
Lexi

I was rather surprised that Lexi had not realised that I only wanted what I was entitled to see. Why would I wish to read things about other people, it just meant more delays and I did so want to read the diaries before we went to the Review Panel;

Dear Lexi
Thank you for your email.
In Mr Judas's report in an email sent on 3rd November from The Tyrannical Clown to Judgement Jones it states that the

contractor's employee took the photos as Peter Plonker was driving. May we see the original email please? Also would you ask him to identify the man in the photo who is crossing the road to remove the sign (DSC9007) and ask him if the contractor was sitting on Peter Plonker's lap when the photos were taken (DSC9007 and DSC9008) as they were clearly taken from the driver's side of the vehicle and as he stated in Mr Judas's report that the photos were taken by the contractor as Peter Plonker was driving. How does he explain this?

Regarding the diaries I appreciate that I may not have information about people's private affairs and neither do I want it. I would like to know how many entries in their diaries concern me. I am sure I have the right to know that or there would be no point in the FOI act.

Regards
Sally

I was wondering if Judgement Jones was responsible for holding back the information I had asked for. I checked out the website of the FOI that explained the legal implications if FOI was refused to someone who had requested it, so I pasted it into an email and sent it to him and I copied in Lexi too;

Dear Judgement Jones
Maybe you should read this and then pass it on to your colleagues. I have copied this 'information for authorities' from the FOI official website:

Can I destroy information that has been requested?

In this section
Receiving a request
Time limits

Destroying information
Costs
Confirm or deny
Redaction
Reasons to refuse
Public interest test
How to refuse

It is a criminal offence to deliberately destroy, alter or conceal a record to prevent disclosure of requested information, and to do so could lead to a fine.
If the records containing the information were already scheduled for destruction when the request was submitted you should suspend destruction while the request is considered. For further advice on this, see our guidance on destruction of requested information…
In addition to this information you will be interested to know that I have the weather report for October 2009. The reason it rained so much on the 6th and 7th was because it was the tail end of hurricane Grace which peaked on the 7th which accounts for the heavy rain that day. After that had blown itself away the weather was uneventful, above average temperatures and below average rainfall and the second half of the month we had an Indian summer. It was NOT RAINING on the 21st. or 22nd.
If you and the officers want to continue to lie that is your prerogative, it will be good evidence for me when I take you all to court. In any event all the contaminated evidence your clients have produced for and since Mr Judas's investigation I shall be sending to the ICO
Sally

CHAPTER 64

Threatening Judgement Jones was the way forward as the next morning I received an email from Lexi saying that she had just been informed that the diaries had been found and were on their way to Ringmer where she would go that afternoon and copy all the appropriate information that I had requested. I was delighted, as at last I would be able to see exactly what had been written about me, although it was many weeks since I first asked to see the diaries so they could have quite easily have added or removed entries.

Poor Lexi was going to have to read four diaries and then photo copy the pages, but she had got on with the job and the next day she duly emailed me the copied pages of the diaries. It was five days before the review panel so anything I could use as evidence from the diaries would go against them, but I only had a short time to prepare it. What I wanted was to find entries that Mr Judas should have observed and therefore taken any appropriate action. I printed them off, and they made interesting reading. The Tyrannical Clown had made his first entry on 30th April 2009 mentioning my café signs had been removed. Most of the entries mentioned the whereabouts and removal of my café signs and where they had been taken to. He had discussed the café sign issues with Rag-Eme-Kale and Swanoff Swanker. I read how he was planning to come to Camber to rid the village of my café signs, and after that he was arranging the interview with recording equipment at Rye Police station. He noted that I had lost my temper and thrown my mobile phone and two bunches of keys at him and that I had aimed them in the direction of his face and when he put his arm up to protect himself the keys had hit his arm and drawn blood. What a liar, my keys had only hit his arm because he dived for cover behind his seat like a coward, but he had not written that in his diary.

He had written of contacting the Business Services manager who had sent me reminders for the fraudulent invoices, he had noted that the man had moved to another county and was working for social housing, so in that case he was not working for Sirco when he was sending me the reminders and threats.

The Tyrannical Clown had also contacted a policeman in Bexhill regarding Camber issues. It appeared he wanted to involve him somehow but it obviously did not come to anything.

He wrote several times that he was preparing his papers for the first court hearing at Eastbourne Magistrates Court and he was having meetings about it with Judgement Jones and Rag-Eme-Kale. Kilkenny reported to him about my café signs and the arrangements to remove them. It was quite amusing the amount of destinations my café signs went to. There were three Council locations in Bexhill and one in Ringmer and one in Hailsham.

On 9th September, written at the bottom of the page, was his entry that he had rung me regarding the text message I had sent Kilkenny, having denied it whilst on oath at Hastings County Court in April 2010. Another interesting entry made on 29th September, he had asked Rag-Eme-Kale to put his name on the last invoice for the cost of removing my café signs because I had apparently threatened him by email. I did not recall threatening him or anyone else so I checked the emails I had sent to him in the last four months and all I could find was once I suggested 'he got a life' and after I had received the second spurious invoice I had emailed him telling him I was not stupid and I knew what he was up to. Maybe that had frightened him as it was the third invoice that had Rag-Eme-Kale's name on it and shortly after that I received an email from the highways telling me The Tyrannical Clown was no longer dealing with issues involving me.

But according to his diaries he did carry on dealing with my café issues. He was continuously meeting with Judgement Jones and Rag-Eme-Kale regarding court cases and café signs. He made a huge entry the day of the Court hearing in Eastbourne including the amount of costs that had been awarded and the £2700 fine, and then his entry for 7th October, 3.45pm, 'with Peter Plonker at Sidley Depot, helped with signs taken from Camber today' underneath he had added the name 'Mark' who was the contractor's employee.

So it went on, meeting after meeting re Camber Café in Ringmer with Swanoff Swanker and Rag-Eme-Kale. The last entry for 2009 was 8th December whereby he had a meeting in Ringmer with Rag-Eme-Kale re Camber Café issues which took so long he noted he missed his lunch. All in all between 30th April and 8th December the Tyrannical Clown had made 32 entries in his diary regarding me and my café signs.

Kilkenny's first entry in his diary was on Monday 26th January 2009, when he noted that my café signs were 'still' on the telegraph pole which seemed a strange remark because on this date I had no idea that anything was amiss with my signs, the first I ever knew about it was when they disappeared along with the Wine Bar's signs. His next entry was Tuesday 3rd February when he wrote that my café signs had been returned to me and I had been advised. He had made one more entry in mid-March and just written Camber Café signs and then on April 14th he wrote he had removed 17 signs from Camber. Throughout the rest of April, May and June were entries of him taking my signs and noting that he had advised me. One day in June he had written that I had gone to the depot in Bexhill and demanded my café signs back but only 6 had been returned and the other 14 were 'adrift'.

He entered in the diary when he had rung and advised me but each time in brackets he always wrote (she refused to take the signs down and threatened to put more up if we remove them). When Kilkenny's diary reached the middle of June the entries about Camber Café were being noted on a daily basis. My signs had been photographed on street furniture, the BT pole and the sand dunes fencing. By the middle of July he too was preparing his paperwork for the Magistrates Court of which I knew nothing at that time, so they were clearly planning well in advance.

On 5th August Kilkenny had written quite a paragraph saying that he had been in Camber collecting my café signs when I had pulled up in my car and tried to bribe him with a packet of 'Viagra'. He wrote that I had been suggestive and then in brackets he had written (hard to believe), was this a sign then that he might have been tempted to accept my bribe?

All the entries for the rest of August and beginning of September were about my café signs being removed and papers and photos being prepared for the case. This was interesting because they had clearly decided that they were going to prosecute me and had been preparing their case since July so I did not see the purpose of me going to Rye Police station to be interviewed under caution if they had already decided what they were going to do; it did not make sense. The Tyrannical Clown was wasting more tax payer's money just to try and intimidate me which had back fired on him as I was the one who had done the intimidating and had hopefully scarred him for life.

Then on September 9th I had really upset his day. His entry was 'Received a text from Sally Pattinson saying 'you arsehole I only just put them up it's a good job I have spares' text received at 09.27'. He wrote that I rang him and accused him of ringing me, which he had not, his phone had been resting on the photocopier and the pressure caused his phone to ring mine. He was angry because I had called his private mobile phone and he wanted to know how I had obtained it. He had also noted that he had told me that if I communicated with him again he would take official action.

All the entries up until the court hearing in Eastbourne on 6th October were just about removing my café signs and preparing his statements. On 19th October he had been photographing my café signs which were now located on residents' garden walls and fences.

He had made an entry on 5th November saying that I had accused them of conspiracy and a few days later he wrote 'café signs causing danger in Camber'.

I was amazed to read on 25th November that he had written that he had a meeting with GHB at 4 pm re Camber issues. So that was how he knew so much about my private life. I knew GHB who was married to my friend.

The last entry Kilkenny made in his diary for 2009 was on Wednesday 23rd December and that was one word written in the middle of the page 'Camber'.

After the Christmas break work resumed at the Highways office in Bexhill on Monday 4th January 2010. The Tyrannical Clown's first entry was 'Discussed with Rag-Eme-Kale re Sally Pattinson issues'. On 19th January he had a briefing with Kilkenny and Rag-Eme-Kale who had travelled from Ringmer. The three of them had driven to Camber, and he wrote 'Camber Café sign attached to hoarding in Lydd Road, a large sign on top of a parked Audi outside the church and telegraph pole at the top of Lydd Road and on ESCC fencing on Old Lydd Road. By the end of the month he had discussed Camber Café issues with Judgement Jones, the lady from the Complaints department and Rag-Eme-Kale plus he and Kilkenny had visited Camber on several occasions. (He had not put the true amount of times as it was quite often 3 or 4 times a week). On Friday 29th January he and Kilkenny had removed the sign on the A259 at Guildford which was of course the Christmas card to the 'Merchants from Bexhill' which I had attached to a large signpost and which had been there for 7 weeks before they had seen it.

Mid-February he was out with Kilkenny in Camber, and he noted there was an A-board outside my café, a sign on a car in New Lydd Road, another A-board on Lydd Road and a café sign on the fence in Old Lydd Road. On Monday 22nd February he had a meeting with Judgement Jones and Rag-Eme-Kale and they had decided for another court hearing to apply for an injunction order and he was preparing his statement.

The follow weeks he made entries that his paperwork re Sally Pattinson was prepared, he had been to Camber and he had discussed Camber / Sally Pattinson issues with Judgement Jones.

On 17th March he had written a whole page of his day's events. 'Hastings County Court met Judgement Jones re interim injunction Sally Pattinson. Undertakings given re writing or communication defamatory material against Council Employees. NO injunction granted to stop fly-posting. Full hearing required at a future date. Judgement Jones stated he would get a very good barrister to represent them at the next hearing. He dropped Judgement Jones at the railway station and went back to the office and informed Rag-Eme-Kale of the outcome.

From his entries it appeared he was pestering Judgement Jones to hurry up with the next court hearing. The week after their failure at the court he wrote in his diary that he had spoken to Judgement Jones about ongoing issues re injunction hearing and continual offending and remarks. They were taking many photos as evidence and Peter Plonker had been appointed to take these photos. It was reported that there were still signs up around Camber and one allegedly had a poem written on it so Peter Plonker had been authorised to remove the sign and take it to Bexhill.

I had another whole page to myself on 9th April 2010, when he wrote 'Hastings County Court, very good Counsel to represent us, 12 months awarded costs and damages and fined. Rag-Eme-Kale attended.

On Monday 12th April he and Kilkenny had come to Camber and he noted that there were no Camber Café signs in Camber but then by the end of the week April 16th he and Kilkenny had revisited Camber and removed more Camber Café signs.

By the end of May he had involved Rother District Council as on the 27th May he wrote 'Discussion with Swanoff Swanker and Rag-Eme-Kale re RDC report on Camber and Sally Pattinson.

June 8th he spoke with Judgement Jones re email from Sally Pattinson that he wanted some questions answered, and he had emailed Camber Parish Council re advertising Camber Café on the wall of the Village Hall.

There were no entries regarding me until 20th July when he noted he had checked Camber and there was a sign on a car and another sign on a bicycle which he had found chained to street furniture opposite the caravan park on Lydd Road. During August he continued to repeat the same old thing, that he had taken photos of my café signs and I had breached the injunction. Then on 25th August he had helped Kilkenny with his statement re Camber Café prior to (and the names had been blacked out) statements arriving. One guess at whose statements were arriving, The Old Hag's and Bodger's. He made one last entry on 16th September saying he had reported to Rag-Eme-Kale some information re Camber Café he had received by phone call from Kilkenny.

That was the last entry The Tyrannical Clown made in his 2010 diary.

The next day Lexi emailed me some pages from Peter Plonker's diary for August, September and October 2009. It was obvious at first glance he had added information to his entries. The first time he mentions Camber Café was on 28th August 2009, when he had written '3 hours taking down signs from Camber' then on 9th September (the day my Fish and Chip signs went missing) he had written 'Camber 3 hours to pick up signs from café' in the top right hand corner of the page he had written 'cloudy', well I knew that was wrong because the 9th had been the day I started to sell fish and chips and it was a lovely sunny day. These entries were to coincide with The Tyrannical Clown's spurious invoices as he noted the next day '1 hour take café signs' and the weather was dry. On 15th September his entry 'signs at Camber 2 hours' and squashed in between his other entries the following day on the 16th 'Camber signs 3 hours'. All the entries for the days corresponding with the invoices were written in his diary in a way it was evident that they had been added long after the event. There was no entry concerning Camber Café on 7th October but on 21st October was written 'Camber Photos Café' and he had noted the weather was wet and for the previous day the 20th there was no mention of him being in Camber, he had only remarked that the weather was 'dry'. The next entry regarding Camber was made on Friday 30th October when he noted that he had been in Camber taking photos at 11.35 am but there was no mention of the weather conditions for that day.

It was so obvious that the entries in Peter Plonker's diary were false especially the weather report and why had he not mentioned the signs they had taken on the 7th October but had made a big deal of the photos they allegedly had taken on the 20th and 21st and including a weather report.

Even Peter Plonker's weather reports should have aroused Mr Judas's suspicions as they varied from Dry, Wet or Cloudy depending on the days he was in Camber taking photos. I wondered on the days he had written 'Cloudy' was it a wet or a dry day. These entries were vital evidence that Peter Plonker had lied and Mr Judas should have questioned him about them. I had provided genuine weather reports which contradicted Peter Plonker's account for the weather, and Mr Judas should have spotted and dealt with it, but he had not.

I still wanted some answers despite the fast approaching Stage 3 Review Panel, so I emailed Lexi and asked if she would explain to me what was the order of the day when it came to Peter Plonker's daily schedule, was he allocated a work sheet with jobs to attend or was he instructed verbally on a day to day basis. I asked her if she would enquire as to who had told him to go to Camber on the 21st October 2009 to take photos of my café signs.

Lexi replied later saying that she had received a phone call from Peter Plonker but he had not really cleared anything up although he did say he did not have a schedule he only followed work as it came in throughout the day and he responded as and when needed. He did say that he had not been sent to Camber specifically on the 21st October but The Tyrannical Clown had told him that whenever he was in that area he was to check for café signs and if there were any he should take photographs. Unfortunately he had put nothing in writing to clarify what he had said. He had also told Lexi that he had asked 'Mark' the contractor's employee to confirm in writing that he was with Peter Plonker that day and had taken photos with Peter Plonker's camera.

I knew he was talking nonsense, Lexi might have accepted his answers but I had not and despite the Stage 3 review only a few days away I was going to persist in asking questions until I got satisfactory answers. Next I asked why he had been in Camber that day and if he had removed the café signs that had been photographed, in addition I asked her who communicated with him and who instructed him on his work schedule on a daily basis.

Lexi got back to me after she had spoken to Peter Plonker again and he had told her that he could not recall why he went to Camber that day but he did confirm that they only took photos, and did not remove any of the café signs, but he was not quite sure why they had not. Well I was sure why they had not, because there were none to take.

He also told Lexi that the work for the Reactive Maintenance team generally came through to them from the contact centre as and when members of the public report problems on the highway. This was curious as there did not appear to be any sort of planning or schedule documentation and there had been no explanation why not.

During that day I asked if Lexi had received the promised statement from 'Mark' who had supposedly taken photos with Peter Plonker's camera but Lexi assured me that Peter Plonker was going to email it to her that day and she was expecting it to arrive shortly but it did not, so again I asked Lexi why would 'Mark' be sending an email via Peter Plonker when I had specifically asked Lexi to acquire it and I suggested that it really had nothing to do with Peter Plonker anyway.

She assured me that she would chase the email from 'Mark' but it never arrived which was not a bad thing as it was more proof that Peter Plonker had not only lied about photos being taken on the 21st and 22nd September, he had also lied as to who had accompanied him that day, for there could be no other reason why Mark should not have written a statement saying he took the photos other than that he was not there.

I still had four days left before the review panel, and I was determined to prove that Peter Plonker was a liar, but I knew Lexi could do no more so I emailed Rag-Eme-Kale;

Dear Rag-Eme-Kale

I have asked Ms Goodfellow to acquire the following information, but in case she doesn't get a quick response I would like you as The Tyrannical Clown's manager, to ask him if he had any knowledge of sending Pete Plonker to Camber on 21ˢᵗ October 2009 to take photos of my cafe signs he had removed 14 days previously which The Tyrannical Clown had helped him unload at Sidley depot. If The Tyrannical Clown is aware that this photo shoot took place would you please ask him why he sent Peter Plonker on a mission to take photos of cafe signs that were in Sidley depot? Did you know Pete Plonker had been in Camber on 21ˢᵗ October 2009 taking photos of cafe signs that weren't there? Sally

Rag-Eme Kale answered almost immediately;

Dear Sally Pattinson,
The Tyrannical Clown is on annual leave, returning to the office on 19th January 2012 prior to his retirement on 20 January 2012. I will endeavour to ask your questions before he leaves.
However, I have provided The Tyrannical Clown's diaries for 2009 and 2010 to Lexi Goodfellow so she may be able to find entries for the relevant dates.
Regards
Rag-Eme-Kale

I knew that was going to happen, and I knew that was the reason for Mr Judas taking so long to complete his report. I was sure it was not a coincidence, and I believe that their behaviour had been so unprofessional and my evidence had clearly shown that to be the case, that they had been given early retirement to get them out of the way, so that if I chose to take my complaint further to the Local Government Ombudsman, Kilkenny and The Tyrannical Clown would be unaccountable.

I liked Rag-Eme-Kale's remark about providing The Tyrannical Clown's diaries, when he had made every excuse why I should not see them according to Lexi.

CHAPTER 65

On the morning of the Stage 3 Review I chose not to open the café and instead I stayed at home to prepare myself for that afternoon. I reflected on my circumstances. When I had returned to the UK penniless and homeless, I had worked hard and through that had managed to reinstate myself as an independent woman without the help of anyone and I was proud of that. Yet here I was battling with a corporation which had as far as I was concerned, intentionally tried to wreck everything I had spent the last 8 years accomplishing and I had fought back to protect my livelihood. I had endeavoured to seek permission to advertise the café legally but to every enquiry the response had been a negative one. Now, after five court hearings, thousands of pounds worth of fines, injunction orders and the threat of imprisonment, Rag-Eme-Kale had agreed for me to have official signs to advertise my café, not that I wanted them as I preferred the car and A-board, but I had been seen to cooperate and in any case he had not agreed to that for my benefit; it was purely to make him appear agreeable for the Panel and besides still nothing had materialized from Rag-Eme-Kales promises.

It was time to go, so I gathered up my bundle of papers and drove to Rye to collect Lesley.

We arrived in good time and I found a parking space in Station Approach which was right next to Ocean House. The first person I noticed when we entered the reception hall was Mr Judas, I politely said hello to him and in a way I did feel quite sorry for him. Then I saw Rag-Eme-Kale rummaging through a large bag full of papers, and he had not seen me so I avoided eye contact so I would not have to acknowledge him. We presented ourselves at the reception desk and were told to wait in the seating area, and within moments Lexi Goodfellow introduced herself and said we were waiting for the Chair Person to arrive.

I kept looking at Mr Judas wondering how he was feeling about the situation he had inflicted upon himself, or had had inflicted by someone else. He had a nice face and I felt sorry for him but nevertheless he had failed hopelessly and suddenly I asked him if he had been bribed or threatened. He knew exactly what I was referring to and I could see I had embarrassed him. Rag-Eme-Kale stayed perfectly still listening, then Mr Judas with a disconcerted expression replied, shaking his head 'No, no nothing like that'. He did not convince me and I was sure that his investigation had been hampered in some way or another by those he was investigating.

Then a tall slim trendy middle aged lady came up to me us and introduced herself as Miss Jane Churchill and she would be chairing today's Stage 3 review panel. I had been expecting some old battle axe but this lady looked like an actress with perfect make-up and dark hair cut in a bob, she was friendly and reassuring.

We were eventually ushered up a staircase by Lexi Goodfellow into a large room, warm and light, with a huge oval table in the middle with the exact amount of comfortable chairs around it. The panel sat one side of the table and as well as Jane Churchill there was another lady on the panel who was the Assistant Director for Resources, Economy, Transport and Environment Department from East Sussex County Council and a gentleman who was an independent panel member. Lesley and I sat opposite the panel, to my right at the end of the table sat Mr Judas and to the left of Lesley sat Rag-Eme-Kale and at the far end was Lexi who had organised this afternoon and I realised how much work had gone into the whole process for this meeting. Lexi sat with a pile of papers in front of her as did the panel, Mr Judas and

Rag-Eme-Kale so I followed suit and placed all my folders on the table in front of me. Miss Churchill stood up, introduced herself and welcomed everyone, then in turn the other two panel members introduced themselves. Miss Churchill then proceeded to explain the purpose of today's meeting and emphasised that the panel was only to consider my complaint which was entirely independent from the earlier stages and it was the panel's role to review my complaint not to re-investigate it.

Miss Churchill read out a brief summary of events being that East Sussex County Council had instigated Court proceedings regarding unlicensed advertising signs that I had placed on the public highway. Since that time I had twice placed unauthorised signs on the highway and consequently been subject to two injunction orders in April 2010 and April 2011. These orders forbade me from placing any signs, posters, street furniture or other structures on or abutting the highway without the express written consent from East Sussex County Council and forbade me from using foul, abusive or defamatory language or engaging in threatening behaviour towards any member of Council's staff.

The Council's concern was, and is, to prevent me from placing potentially dangerous, unsecured and unattended sign structures in the highway, that could blow over or fall in the road, becoming an obstruction or a potential hazard to road users, and to prevent me from displaying distracting signs within visibility splays of road junctions.

She continued to say that I had stated that the behaviour of the highways authority had caused unnecessary financial hardship and put my business at risk of bankruptcy. I had accused some officers of perjury but this accusation had been most strongly refuted by Rag-Eme-Kale the Team Manager, Inspection and Enforcement.

I had made a number of allegations against The Tyrannical

Clown, Kilkenny and Peter Plonker and Mr Judas had been assigned as Investigating Officer on 19th May 2011. I had met with Mr Judas on 8th June 2011 and provided him with details of the allegations, but Mr Judas had taken 151 days to complete his report and the copy of the report provided for the panel was unsigned and undated and it ended saying that only one of my complaints was upheld.

I had complained about the length of time Mr Judas had taken to complete his investigation which in my opinion was unprofessional, incomplete and biased, and its omission of any reference to the letter I had written to the Chief Executive on 3rd November 2009.

When Miss Churchill had finished she suggested that she would read out one allegation at a time which we could discuss.

Whilst everyone's papers were still in neat piles in front of them, mine were beginning to spread out over the table as I had been pulling out various bits evidence that I wanted to show the panel, including my accounts for them to see how my annual turnover had reduced by several thousand pounds in the financial year 2009/2010. I blamed the council for removing my A-boards from the top of the road when I was unaware and consequently with no indication to my café even for one day it had lost customers and a substantial amount of money and that was why I had decided to use a vehicle to advertise on as they would not be able to remove it. I showed Miss Churchill my accounts, after she had examined them I shoved them in Rag-Eme-Kales face and as I did so I said 'look what you've done to my business Rag-Eme-Kale, you are responsible for that, does it make you feel good'? I could see that I had clearly embarrassed him as he broke out into a sweat and his face reddened, he did not reply, instead he scrutinised my accounts.

Ever since Lesley had met Rag-Eme-Kale at the court in

April 2011 she had taken an instant dislike to him so finding herself sitting next to him gave her the opportunity to periodically glare at him.

When we got to the allegation of perjury, I explained how The Tyrannical Clown had lied under oath and that I knew he had lied and he knew that I knew. I said Rag-Eme-Kale had been at the hearing and had witnessed what had been said, so he knew that The Tyrannical Clown and Kilkenny had both lied because he knew the truth, as he was their team manager. I asked Rag-Eme-Kale to recall the incident when The Tyrannical Clown had sworn on oath that I had refused to pay a fine, but he said he could not remember. I said if I could remember it why could he not, he had been there and he witnessed it. Lesley said abruptly that blaming his memory was an easy and cowardly way out of a situation. Having just regained his composure from my verbal attack, Lesley's remark incurred another onset of the vapours upon Rag-Eme-Kale. Following The Tyrannical Clown's accusation that I had not been paying the fine and consequently the Fines Office had got the blame as they had allegedly sent the money to the wrong council department, I asked Mr Judas if he himself had checked with the fines office to clarify the information given to him by Judgement Jones. I knew Mr Judas had not contacted the fines office as I had made my own enquiry and had been told that nobody had asked anything about the fine I was paying. In response to my question Mr Judas did in fact admit he had not contacted the fines office but had taken Judgement Jones word. I immediately said to the panel that this was the main reason for the result of Mr Judas's investigation. He had only interviewed the officers and the solicitor and he had accepted their responses as proof, with no justification, therefore he had looked no further to seek the evidence that was required of him.

Miss Churchill agreed with me and I said to her that I

appreciated that it was difficult for Mr Judas to investigate his colleagues but if it was uncomfortable for him he should have told his superior.

During the course of the afternoon Mr Judas had said nothing to defend himself or the actions he had taken during the long process of the investigations and it became clear by his lack of self-confidence why it was he who had most certainly been handpicked for the job. He was apprehensive, a man who could easily be manipulated through his weakness of character. In contrast Miss Churchill was an admirably strong, no nonsense woman, she believed in Justice and she was not going to be fooled by the council's misrepresentations. I felt confident that she, like the nice judge, had disregarded their rank within the Council and seen through these arrogant individuals for what they truly were.

We got onto Peter Plonker's photos of the burger van, I showed the panel my photos of the red light on and off in colour and on in black and white and told them that Mr Judas had completely missed the point of this part of the investigation, it was Peter Plonker's photos that were the subject not whether the red light was legal or not. Miss Churchill passed the photos to Rag-Eme-Kale and asked him to explain the difference between my photos of the red light and Peter Plonker's. I knew she had got him in a corner so I waited in anticipation for his explanation and indeed the onset of another of his hot sweats. He was clearly perplexed by this uncomfortable situation he was in, beads of sweat started to run down his face and neck and Lesley and I stared intimidatingly at Rag-Eme-Kale while he examined the two sets of photos as if his life depended on it holding one of Peter Plonker's photos in one hand and one of mine in the other, and biding his time to think of a feasible answer. Lesley reminded him that she had complained to him by email about the red light being a distraction to drivers. Miss Churchill hurried him up asking him to explain Peter Plonker's photos. Eventually defeated he had no choice but to say he could not explain why Peter Plonker had provided evidence of a red light in black and white which was clearly visible and Peter Plonker had sworn that there was no red light. Lesley immediately uttered to him 'that's only because you can't wriggle out of that one'.

For Rag-Eme-Kale this was a vast contrast compared to the day at Hasting County Court when he had sat behind me listening to the false accusations being made against me, but I had not broken out into a hot sweat, I had been composed and did not retaliate to the lies they told, because I was strong and determined and I had taken their imputations like a woman. Rag-Eme-Kale's reaction to Miss Churchill's questions clearly showed him in true light, he was a liar and a cowardly wimp.

We moved on to the photos of café signs allegedly taken on 21st and 22nd October 2009. By this time much of my paperwork had fallen onto the floor and the rest of it covered most of the table, but amongst the melee of papers I managed to find the photos with the dates and times on, which I had taken with my mobile phone and had provided copies to Mr Judas. Despite my unequivocal evidence he had chosen to rely upon his infinite wisdom and 'guessed' that the photos sent to me from Judgement Jones were taken some time in the middle of October 2009.

I showed Miss Churchill the weather reports I had acquired pertaining to the dates the photos had been taken in torrential rain. I explained to her that on 7th October 2009 when my café signs had been removed it was raining heavily due to the tail end of hurricane Grace which swept across the South of England, although it had rained slightly on the night of the 22nd due to a thunderstorm. With that she took the words right out of my mouth and said 'in that case these photos must have been taken in the middle of the night'. Yes; I knew by that remark she was on my side, but only because of the strength of my evidence and the weaknesses of theirs helped along by Rag-Eme-Kale's inadequacy to explain his colleague's misleading testimonials and botched photographic evidence.

I explained to Miss Churchill that I had requested from Judgement Jones to see the original emails allegedly sent from Peter Plonker to The Tyrannical Clown and from The Tyrannical Clown to Judgement Jones regarding the café signs they had removed as I wanted to see the dates the emails were sent, but they had only provided me with contaminated evidence in the hope that I would believe it. I told her that I had not accepted their evidence as I knew it to be false because they had lied about the dates the photos had been taken which had now escalated into this frenzy of corrupt correspondence. I said I had contacted the FOI Office and they had confirmed I had rights to see the emails so I had informed Judgement Jones of my rights but he continued to provide corrupted emails with the intention of evading the truth I also told Miss Churchill that I had asked numerous times for a statement from 'Mark' who had been with Peter Plonker taking photos on the day my café signs were removed. I said I believed 'Mark' was not with Peter Plonker on that day and that was the reason he had not provided a statement. In fact Peter Plonker claimed to have asked 'Mark' for the statement and also claimed he had an email from 'Mark', but nevertheless nothing had been produced for this review panel.

Miss Churchill said she would like all those emails regarding my requests to Judgement Jones to be sent to her via Lexi, and she turned to Lexi and asked her to send them to her as soon as she received them for the panel to consider.

Then Miss Churchill asked Rag-Eme-Kale if he would like to say something about the evidence I had provided. He said that the duty of the Highways Authority was to keep the highways safe for road users and he and his colleagues were justified in removing my advertising signs from the highway, it was written in section 132 of the 1980's Highways Act. Then I asked him in that case why had they ignored other business signs on the highway when I had provided him on numerous occasions with photographic evidence of Mr Forthright's signs for example, which had never been removed or indeed been subject to any intervention by himself or his Inspectors, he replied with the same old excuse that he would send one of his Officers to deal with it.

Miss Churchill turned to Mr Judas and asked him for what reason had he taken so long to complete his report, and he said that he had a lot of work going on at the same time. Miss Churchill butted in and said 'so what you are saying is that you did not have enough time due to the commitments of your normal job at East Sussex County Council?' to which he agreed.

Miss Churchill ended the meeting by thanking us all for coming and said the panel would make a decision quickly as I had already waited too long for closure on this matter. She said that Mr Judas's investigation lacked important issues, Rag-Eme-Kale's oral evidence had been helpful but the panel were concerned that some of my complaints had been omitted from Mr Judas's investigation. She hoped to complete the panel's decision within 48 hours and she explained to me that she would have to send a copy of the report to the Director of Economy, Environment and Transport as it was he who had the final decision whether he would agree to the panel's recommendations. If he agreed I would then be sent a copy of the Review Panel's recommendations.

There the meeting ended. It was gone 5 o'clock and dark outside, and Lesley and I left confident that the panel had seen through the misguided evidence which had been provided by East Sussex County Council employees.

CHAPTER 66

Next morning I forwarded the seven emails to Lexi for the attention of the review panel, emails I had sent to Judgement Jones asking for the originals he had received from Peter Plonker and The Tyrannical Clown regarding the photos they had allegedly taken on 21st and 22nd October 2009.

Also that morning a letter arrived from Rother District Council from the Planning-Development Management and a copy had been sent to Rag-Eme-Kale;

Dear Mrs Pattinson
CAMBER CAFÉ
I refer to your letter regarding signs for advertising Camber Café, and I apologise for the delay in my response.

Advertisement consent would be required for the erection of the sign as shown within the letter to you from East Sussex County Council. I appreciate your desire to advertise your business, however, the character and appearance of the locality would need to be considered in any application received. The proposed position of the sign is remote from the premises to which it relates and its siting adjoining the highway would be highly prominent in the street scene. This raises two concerns; the first being the visual impact upon the appearance of the street scene and secondly the precedent a remote sign would set in this location. There are a number of businesses located along Old Lydd Road which might seek to advertise on the main road should your application be successful, therefore there could be a proliferation of signs on Lydd Road. As such it is unlikely that I would support a sign in a visually remote position from your business.

Yours sincerely
Mr Sweeny

Having read the letter I was relieved that I would not have to have Rag-Eme-Kale's lollipop sticks to advertise the café on but at the same time I was bemused at the contents of Mr Sweeny's letter. Firstly he had thanked me for a letter which I had not written, he clearly had no knowledge of the circumstances which had led to this request and his ridiculous comment that all the businesses in Old Lydd Road would want to place their business signs on Lydd Road if I had them.

I had specifically asked Rag-Eme-Kale not to write to Rother District Council concerning these official signs, but he had evidently taken it upon himself to do so. It was clear in Mr Sweeny's letter that no strategic planning was in place regarding certain aspects of council policies, which meant consent was most likely given randomly depending on who or what was the mood of the day, if not Mr Sweeny would have chosen a far more technical reason other than everyone with a business in Camber would want to follow suit, apart from that other businesses *did* advertise on the main road already. The injunction order stated that I might not place a sign on the highway without the written express consent from the Highway as the Authority, but evidently that was a misrepresentation as the nice judge had said at the end of the court hearing that advertising my cafe was no concern of the Highways Authority but that of Rother District Council. So The Tyrannical Clown and his conniving colleagues knew full well that I would never get the consent which they had enforced through a court of law. It was absurd, but explained many things, one being why Mr Forthright's metal signs had never been subject to any enforcement laws.

Anyway I was not bothered about that now, I was waiting to hear the decision from the Stage 3 Review panel which arrived six days later by way of attachment from Lexi on Monday 23rd January.

I read it as quickly as I could, the welcoming, the history of the complaint, the nine allegations I had made against members of East Sussex County Council staff, the comments which had been made by Rag-Eme-Kale and Mr Judas and then the all-important decision by the panel was;

The Panel expected to be considering all of the allegations, and recording its findings as to whether each was upheld or not upheld, based on careful consideration of all the documentation and all the oral evidence. The Panel would also record its opinion as to whether the Investigation had examined all of the evidence, and whether the Department's response was reasonable. The Panel would then make Recommendations to the Director.

The Panel paid particular attention to Mrs Pattinson's Desired Outcomes – in particular, that she would like the allegations to be investigated properly.

After a long discussion, the Panel unanimously concluded that the Investigation was flawed.

The Panel had not been provided with any correspondence sent to Mrs Pattinson after the Investigation was completed, and thus did not have the benefit of reviewing any comments that a Senior Manager could have been expected to send to her.

The Investigation would have benefited from an agreed Statement of Complaint, accompanied by details of Mrs Pattinson's Desired Outcomes. As this material had not been constructed, there was some impairment in its focus.

The Panel believed that the Investigation had enough shortcomings to make it inappropriate for the Panel to rely on it.

The Panel took the view that in the specific circumstances of Mrs Pattinson's case, it would have been preferable for the Investigating Officer to have been independent from the Council.

The Panel entirely accepted the duty of the Economy, Transport and Environment Department to ensure the safety of all users of the highways.

The Panel recognised that the relationship between some of the Council's Officers and Mrs Pattinson had deteriorated to the point of becoming dysfunctional.

The Panel entirely understands that the Council's response to complaints and allegations must be proportionate, and with due regard to the resource implications of how matters are investigated.

That said, because of the nature of the allegations, the Panel unanimously recommends that a new Investigation should be undertaken, by an appropriate individual who is completely independent from the Council.

The person appointed to undertake the new Investigation should meet with Mrs Pattinson to draw up an agreed Statement of Complaint and Desired Outcomes. The Investigation should be undertaken without any reference to Mr Judas's Investigation report, in order that the new Investigation considers the allegations entirely afresh.

The new Investigation should be completed within the Department's time-scale of 28 days.

The new Investigation report should be sent to the relevant Assistant Director for a formal response to it, to be prepared and sent to Mrs Pattinson.

It is to be hoped that the new Investigation and the Assistant Director's subsequent response will achieve resolution of the matters raised by Mrs Pattinson.

The Panel suggests that – whatever the outcome of the new Investigation – it might be worthwhile for Mediation to be considered, to try to develop an improvement in the relationship between Mrs Pattinson and the Department, and to establish the way forward, to enable Mrs Pattinson to operate her business satisfactorily in future, without being in breach of any regulations.

The Panel regrets being unable to complete its work, and is reluctant to propose action which incurs additional expenditure for the Council through the commissioning of an external Investigation report; the Panel also regrets the inevitable additional delay that will occur in dealing with Mrs Pattinson's allegations.

This regret is, however, overtaken by the Panel's belief that the Council should deal with the sensitive and serious allegations about some of its Officers, in a manner which is transparent and open, with no risk of there being any perception of bias.

I could not have hoped for more, I knew I had been right and I guessed Miss Churchill's remark about 'dysfunctional' was referring to The Tyrannical Clown and Kilkenny. No wonder they had both suddenly been retired off! I was pleased with the outcome and I just hoped that the Director of Highways would agree to the panel's recommendations. He had 28 days to make his decision.

CHAPTER 67

On Saturday 11th February 2012 I got the response from the Director of Economy, Transport and Environment.

Dear Mrs Pattinson
I have received and reviewed the Stage 3 panel report
regarding the complaint you have raised against East Sussex
County Council in June 2011. I agree with the
recommendations put forward by the panel.
I am sorry that there shortcomings with the original
investigations. Thank you for granting us the opportunity to
reinvestigate. We will appoint an independent investigating
officer who will contact you in due course.
In the meantime our complaints manager, Lexi Goodfellow,
will contact you within the next 5 working days to take you
through how the process works and what to expect.
Yours sincerely

I was of course pleased with his decision but he had made some interesting comments. I had complained to him about The Tyrannical Clown and Kilkenny in June 2010 but he had not been sorry then, in fact he had referred my complaint to Judgement Jones, who consequently had threatened me with imprisonment for breaching the injunction order for accusing council employees of lying and committing perjury.

Thousands upon thousands of pounds of public money, all funded by hard working tax payers, had been unnecessarily wasted since Kilkenny had taken my café sign from the BT pole in January 2009. Yet the roads were full of pot holes, there were cut-backs being made in the social services departments of the council and the grass in common areas had been reduced to being cut once a year. In fact the previous summer the grass had grown so high along the A259 just outside Rye, the residents had attempted to cut it themselves. And now a private investigator was to be commissioned to deal with my complaints against unscrupulous council employees 2 of which were ex policemen. How much was it costing? The Stage 3 Review in Ocean House did not come free and neither did the Panel and a private investigator must surely come at a cost.

The number of my complaints had now increased, as since Mr Judas had failed to resolve the issues he himself had now become a complaint and had also added to the complaints against Judgement Jones for refusing to send me information that I was entitled to. As there was to be a new Stage 2 investigation I was able to add all my new complaints to it thereby increasing my allegations from 9 to 30.

By 17th February Lexi had found an independent investigator by the name of Mr Allen who ran a consultancy from the Isle of Wight. He had agreed to start the investigation from the beginning of the week 27th February and he had assured Lexi of a forensic analysis and a judgement that would be weighed purely on fact.

Well I hoped it would be, providing he was not going to be brain-washed by Judgement Jones as Mr Judas had been.

Whilst I was waiting for the new investigation to commence I continued to chase the whereabouts of Mark the contractor's statement that he had supposedly written via email to Peter Plonker, and I was not going to desist until either I had seen it or Peter Plonker was proven to be the liar I knew him to be. Again I emailed Lexi to ask if she had received it yet as it had been promised and apparently on its way weeks ago. It had not arrived so she suggested I emailed 'Marks' boss, a Mr Long, to ask him to clarify where Mark had been working on 21st and 22nd October 2009

Dear Mr Long

I have been given your email address from Lexi Goodfellow, Customer Information Team Leader, Governance & Community Services for East Sussex County Council.
Several weeks ago I requested via East Sussex County Council, a statement from your employee Mark Holmes which I needed as evidence to produce for a Stage 3 Review Panel concerning certain employees in the East Sussex Highways department.
I have not received the statement from Mark and I do not know if he was asked to produce a statement. However, I would like to know if he was in Camber on 21st and 22nd October 2009 taking photos of my cafe signs with Peter Plonker's camera in the rain. The dates are extremely important and I do have weather reports for those dates and it was not raining.
Is there any way you might be able to assist in this important matter please?
I will possibly need to use his statement as evidence in any legal proceedings that might follow against East Sussex County Council.
Thank you
Sally Pattinson

A week later and Mr Long had not answered my email, so I sent a copy of the email to Lexi for her to see that it was a perfectly polite email and there was no reason for him to ignore it. She then in turn told William Rogers the Head of Highways that Mr Long had not replied to my email. The same day she got back to me saying that William Rogers had contacted Mr Long and told him to get it resolved one way or another. Eventually Mr Long had got back to Lexi saying that 'Mark' had confirmed that he was with Peter Plonker and he will confirm with an email, although Mark had already sent an email previously to confirm this but he will re-send.

Utter rubbish, there was never an email from Mark to Peter Plonker or Lexi. She had been chasing it for weeks now and it did not exist just like Judgement Jones 'original' emails.

Mr Allen contacted me to make arrangements to come to see me at home. I suggested he could park on the cafe forecourt. I saw him arrive but instead of parking his car in front of the café he reversed into my neighbour's driveway. I welcomed him and asked if he realised that he was parked on private property and he said he could not find the café. Well that was one good reason for the necessity of an A-board I told him. Mr Allen was of small build and quite short with receding grey curly hair. He was smartly dressed in a grey suit and he did not accept my offer of a cup of tea or coffee. We talked about the allegations that I had made and he asked me why it had gone to a stage 3 review panel. I thought he would have been aware why, as that was the purpose of him being here. I was also concerned at his surprise by the amount of evidence I had against the council. He said most people did not have any. I showed him several emails that had been exchanged over a period of 3 years and he asked me to forward them all on to him, which was going to be an awful lot of data for one person to take in all at once. He requested a new list of my allegations and a list of unnecessary costs inflicted upon me by the Council.

Mr Allen had clearly timed his visit as precisely 2 hours after he had arrived he abruptly gathered up his papers and prepared to leave before we had finished going through some important issues. I asked him if he would be returning at some point to discuss the rest, to which he replied he might.

When he had gone I wondered if it was all too bewildering for him to take in and I was concerned if he was up to the job of dealing with this sort of thing. Maybe he was one of those investigators who sat in bushes with binoculars spying on people. I was also wondering how he thought he could investigate my allegations if I had no evidence to support them.

As soon as he had left I emailed Lexi in fear of there being a repetition of Mr Judas's cock-up, I suggested to her that Mr Allen might need some guidance as to the procedure he must follow and that we had not covered all of my allegations. She replied almost immediately saying;

Dear Sally
I appreciate your concerns. Mr Allen was given a very brief outline of the complaint and the recommendations of the panel. The rationale behind this was to ensure that he had no preconceived ideas which might prejudice his findings. This formed part of the recommendations by the panel.
I will contact Mr Allen again to ensure that he understands what is expected of him and to let him know that if the complexity of the case means he has to make more trips to see you then that is what we will pay for.
Thank you for letting me know; the last thing I want for another Stage 2 to be carried out with flaws.
Lexi

There were a lot of emails I had to send to Mr Allen so I began in earnest trying to put them in order. I photocopied letters from way back to 2009, there was an immense pile of papers to send and I had no idea how Mr Allen was going to be able to understand it all. I drew up a new list of complaints and allegations.

And so Mr Allen started his investigation. He revisited me two weeks later and we went through things that had been left out the first time. I asked him if he had contacted the fines office to confirm that they had been accused by the council of paying my fine payments into the wrong account. He had not, so determined that no stone was going to be left unturned I phoned the fines office there in front of Mr Allen with the speaker on so he could hear for himself what was being said. I spoke to a girl called Emma who I had spoken with on several occasions previously about the accusations from the Council and she knew what had occurred during the time since I was given the fine. I told her that the council had blamed them for putting the money in the wrong account, she checked again although she had done this twice already for me. She said that there was so much money paid in fines to the council on a regular basis there was a bank account purely for them to pay the fine payments into and therefore it was not possible for there to have been a mistake and my monthly payments had never been paid into any other account than the one it was meant for. She also commented on the fact that I had never missed a payment. Mr Allen witnessed this conversation so there was absolutely no doubt at all that whoever had made the excuse that the fines office was to blame for the council not receiving my money was done for no other reason than to discredit me to the judge on that day in April 2010.

Mr Allen said he had interviewed the officers but The Tyrannical Clown, Kilkenny and Jed Uptland the business manager from Serco had still not responded to the request to be re-interviewed, which probably meant they would not make themselves available to be interviewed by Mr Allen which came as no surprise to me, and anyway they were guilty of everything I had accused them of, if they were honest decent men they would have nothing to hide and be willing to be re-interviewed. So as far as I was concerned if they refused to take part in the investigation they were admitting their guilt.

Before Mr Allen left he told me that he would be interviewing the council employees again as there were certain issues which he was not happy about. He said he would prepare and then send me my Statement of Complaint for me to sign and return to him.

The statement arrived on 19th March:

Statement of Complaint against East Sussex County Council

I have been victimised and bullied by officers of East Sussex County Council to the point that my business has suffered and is in a position where it might not survive if I am not permitted to advertise its presence.

Evidence to support my complaint is in numerous actions by a number of council officers: -

Kilkenny

1. On 6 January 2010 Kilkenny wrote in his witness statement that on 17 November 2008 he had received a complaint about signs relating to my café. He had not received any complaint about my café signs and did not produce any evidence either. When I had the opportunity to question him (9 April 2010) when he was under oath he admitted he had not had a complaint about my café signs and the reason he had taken them was that it would not have been fair to leave mine and take the signs belonging to the Wine Bar.

2. On 13th September 2010 again he made reference to the 'initial complaint' (17 November 2008) in his witness statement and said that I had accused him of perjury, (which I had). However, he considered this to be defamatory language and thereby implied that I was in breach of the injunction order (which I wasn't).

3. He suggested in his witness statement that I might vandalise Beaky's property which I consider to be very insulting.

4. In December 2009 I discovered that Kilkenny had made it his business to pry into my private life by gathering information about me from the previous 35 years. Indeed when I had a chance meeting with Kilkenny in February 2009 he reminded me of where I was living in 1986 and on the subject of other private matters he assured me it wouldn't go any further. Since I have had sight of Kilkenny's work diary by way of the FOI Act I noted from an entry in it on 25 November 2009 that he was to meet Mr H B regarding Camber issues. I know they met in a certain pub in Bexhill-on Sea where Mr H B was the landlord on that date and that Kilkenny wanted information about me. I find this action by Kilkenny an intrusion into my privacy as he obviously went out of his way to acquire information about me. I believe he had no right to do that. Why did he want information about me?

5. I believe The Tyrannical Clown and Kilkenny lied by saying Kilkenny would no longer have anything to do with my café signs from July 2009, solely to inflict financial pressure upon me. However, he did continue to have something to do with my café signs, which is proven by him producing four witness statements after July 2009 and giving evidence at two court cases. If he had not been involved he would have had no evidence or reason to provide these statements.

6. On the 10 June 2010 I received a letter from Judgement Jones saying that having accused two Council employees of perjuring themselves in court (which they had) I would go to prison.

The Tyrannical Clown

1. On 29 October 2009 I received a letter and photographs from Judgement Jones accusing me of placing signs advertising my café on the highway between 6 October and the 22 October 2009 threatening me if I continued to do so they would consider applying to the County Court for an Injunction and an Anti-Social Behaviour Order. I believe The Tyrannical Clown provided Judgement Jones with these photographs knowing that they had been taken on the 7 October 2009. I consider this to be corrupt. I emailed Judgement Jones and asked him who had taken the photographs and he replied that a member of the Council's staff had.

2. Under oath at Hastings County Court on 9 April 2010 The Tyrannical Clown accused me of refusing to pay the council their costs from a previous court case but he produced no evidence to support this. Since this happened they have tried to make the excuse that the fines office in Brighton had sent my payments to the wrong department of the County Council. I made my own enquiries about this and the fines office is adamant that they did not make any mistakes about where my payments were sent to, certainly not the wrong department. This false accusation was made in court to discredit me for the benefit of the judge.

3. The Tyrannical Clown also denied making a threatening phone call to me on Wednesday 9 September 2009 at 1331 hours from telephone number 01424 724555.

4. The Tyrannical Clown produced a false exhibit (pcl/6) of various business signs he said were fakes. I do not believe these signs were fakes but were new signs waiting to be distributed around the area and were exhibited to give the impression to the judge that they were not victimising me. I consider this behaviour to be corrupt.

5. I also believe that The Tyrannical Clown and Kilkenny knew the judge as she said that she had no reason to disbelieve either of them as they were both ex-policemen. No one had mentioned this fact in the Court Room until then. I believe it was unfair for that judge to conduct my case as she obviously knew The Tyrannical Clown and Kilkenny.

6. *According to the Town and Country Planning (Control of Advertisements) (England) Regulations 2007 there are 16 classes that are considered to have 'deemed' consent. Class 13 covers adverts that have been displayed in the same site for the preceding 10 years. My café has been trading since 1984 and all the previous owners displayed A Frames at the junction of Lydd Road. Without a sign of the café's whereabouts it would cease to trade as it is impossible to see it from the main road. None of the previous owners ever had any problems with putting an A frame at the top of Lydd Road. I believe my signs, which have previously been removed from the top of Lydd Road, were taken unlawfully by the highways officers as it clearly shows the A frames advertising my café undoubtedly have deemed consent after 28 years. Class 6 of the Town and Country Planning Regulations 2007 allows adverts on forecourts of businesses. Every time I received written permission to place a sign near my café The Tyrannical Clown stopped it. I believe he was victimising me with the intent of wrecking my business.*

Rag-Eme-Kale

1. *In Rag-Eme-Kale's witness statement he claims that I gave him false information regarding a business sign attached to a lamp column in Rye and that I had wasted their time and tax payers' money. Although initially I believed that Rag-Eme-Kale was given false information from Kilkenny I now believe Rag-Eme-Kale knew that I had told the truth and this is another example of a false witness statement. I did however produce a witness statement from the owner of the Fish Shop confirming they had* been asked by a man from the highways authority to remove the sign off the lamp column.

*2. On 3*rd *August 2009 with permission from the sand dune ranger I erected a café sign on a fence within the location of the sand dunes and not on the highway. These were removed by The Tyrannical Clown and highways officers. At the beginning of June 2011 the ranger who had given me permission to put a café sign on the sand dunes came to my café and said that Rag-Eme-Kale had contacted him and told him he must rescind the permission he had given me (although other businesses place signs on the dunes). Rag-Eme-Kale warned that the ranger might have repercussions regarding his employment. The ranger duly rescinded his permission and handed me back my café sign saying he could not put his job at risk. However, I did replace the café sign. The sand dunes are not on the highway and therefore nothing to do with Rag-Eme-Kale or anyone else connected with the highway authority. Rag-Eme-Kale sent me an email dated the 20 June 2011 with a map showing boundary markers and clearly the place I had my café sign was not on the highway. I brought this matter to Rag-Eme-Kale's attention and he replied saying that he would be mindful of the extent of the highway. In other words he knew that it was not in the highways jurisdiction.*

3. In May 2011 I sent an email to Rag-Eme-Kale with two photographs of other businesses in this area. One was of two metal fish and chip signs which are placed remotely from the business and are advertising the business and are placed in the highway. The other was of a large A frame placed over double yellow lines directly in the road. Although Rag-Eme-Kale says they are unlawful signs placed on the highway and that he would send his officers to deal with it and speak to the owners of the signs he has never approached these people and the signs remain in situ without repercussions from the highway authority. I believe

*this is evidence that I have been singled out by the officers I have
complained about.*

*4. I have asked Rag-Eme-Kale for proof of when the café signs,
which Peter Plonker or Mark the contractor had supposedly
photographed on 21 and 22 October 2009, were removed from the
highway as it would have been accepted and logged at the depot
in Sidley. I believe Rag-Eme-Kale was victimising me.*

Peter Plonker

*1. In his witness statement he produced a photograph of AJ's
Burger van stating that there was no illuminated 'open' sign on
the van. I believe the photo was printed in black and white and
photocopied to give the impression of the light being off when it is
on. Again the judge did not make an issue of this although he
could clearly see the light was on.*

*2. After stage 2 of the complaints process was completed I asked
on numerous occasions to be forwarded the 'original' email
correspondence between The Tyrannical Clown, Peter Plonker
and Judgement Jones regarding the removal of the café signs I
was accused of erecting after 6 October 2009. I have been sent
falsified emails that these people have composed themselves onto
an email with the intention of making me believe the contents are
true and the emails are the 'originals'.*

*3. I was led to believe that Mark Watson, who works for May
Gurney, went with Peter Plonker on 22 October 2009 to take
photographs of my café signs. I was told that Mark Watson took
the photographs as Peter Plonker was driving. It is clearly visible
in the photos that some of them were taken from the driver's side
of the vehicle.*

4. *After I had proved that it was not raining on 22nd September 2009 Judgement Jones informed me that two of the five photographs were taken on 21st September when it was raining and two were taken on 22nd September when it wasn't raining (despite the fact that it is clearly raining in all the photos). I asked when the fifth photograph was taken but they have not responded.*

5. *I acquired two weather reports. It was raining heavily on 7th October 2009 due to the tail end of hurricane Grace. It was not raining on 21st or 22nd October apart from in the early hours of 22nd, when there was a thunder storm. On 25th November 2011 I requested a statement to be written by Mark Watson confirming that he was with Peter Plonker on 21st and 22nd October 2009 taking photographs of my café signs but although Peter Plonker claimed to have obtained the statement from Mark the contractor it has never been produced. I believe that Mark the contractor was not asked by Peter Plonker to produce a statement as I had requested. They will not send me the original emails because they cannot, because they do not exist. This proves that the café signs were removed and photographed on 7th October 2009 in the rain as I have always claimed (The Tyrannical Clown made an entry in his diary on 7th October 2009 that he had ordered the café signs to be removed and that he had helped Peter Plonker and Mark unload the van). I believe I was intentionally accused of something I clearly had not done and I believe this was an act of bullying by The Tyrannical Clown and Judgement Jones.*

Judgement Jones

1. *On two occasions Judgement Jones has asked the court to place injunction orders on me for using foul and abusive language and threatening behaviour. I have never used foul or abusive language or threatened physical violence toward any member of* *the council's staff. This request was granted by the judge and consequently blackened my name as if I were an unruly thug.*

2. *I have, since the stage 2 investigation was completed, asked Judgement Jones to send me the original emails between himself, The Tyrannical Clown and Peter Plonker that would prove their contention that Mark the contractor and Peter Plonker photographed my café signs on 21ˢᵗ and 22ⁿᵈ October 2009. Judgement Jones has sent me fraudulent correspondence. He will not send me the correct data from the camera with which the photographs were taken. It is claimed that the wrong date was displayed on the camera, i.e. 8ᵗʰ August 2009.*

3. *On 6ᵗʰ October 2009 I appeared at Eastbourne Magistrates Court for unlawfully placing unauthorised signs on the highway. I pleaded guilty and was fined £200 for each offence. Since that time I have been sent and have seen on the East Sussex County Council website Section 132 of the 1980's Highways Act that for a first offence the fine is £100. I remember that in the court the Magistrate asked what the maximum fine was and either The Tyrannical Clown or Judgement Jones replied £200. I believe it was The Tyrannical Clown who answered. Although I have queried this with Judgement Jones he tells me that the website and Section 132 is wrong and that the maximum fine can be £2,500. I do not believe that as my first offence I should have been fined £200 for each offence.*

4. *Judgement Jones frequently told me I could or would go to prison for a maximum of two years. An example of this is in a letter I received from him on 6ᵗʰ September 2010 in which he says they will apply to the court for my immediate committal to prison unless I remove all café signs including the one outside my café and Tall Paul, in which case they would take no further action. I believe this was to intimidate me. I believe Judgement Jones knew*

I was being victimised and that he condoned the behaviour of the officers.

Requests for Evidence Ignored

1. I asked Judgement Jones on 29th and 31st March 2010 for a copy of service tickets 58061, 62709, and 64741 as I needed them as part of my evidence. He ignored my requests. I also asked him that a witness statement to be written by Peter Plonker regarding the removal and the photographs he took of my café signs on 22nd October 2009. Judgement Jones ignored both of my emails and I am still waiting.

2. On 15th February I emailed the Highways Contact Centre with questions regarding the contractors who had removed my café signs. I received a reply the next day saying my query had been passed to the Business Systems Manager. After five weeks without any response I emailed the contact centre again reminding them that I was still waiting for my answers. Two years on I am still waiting.

3. In November 2009 I contacted the CAB and told them that The Tyrannical Clown was victimising me and on their advice I wrote a letter of complaint about him to the Chief Executive of the County Council. I sent the letter by recorded delivery and I wrote Private and Confidential on the envelope. I never received any confirmation of my letter being received and neither did I get an answer. In January or February (I can't remember the exact date) I spoke to the Customer Care Manager and from the questions I asked her she responded in a way that I understood that the letter I had written had not been given to the person for whom it was intended but had been passed to The Tyrannical Clown in Bexhill.

Mr Judas

1. The Tyrannical Clown and Kilkenny have escaped any repercussions of the complaint investigation because they are no longer employed by the local authority. I am convinced that Mr Judas delayed completion of his investigation in order that these two men could retire.

2. If Mr Judas says he did not have the time to complete it he should have informed his superior and the investigation should have been passed on to someone else, but as he emailed me in July 2011 and said his report would be finalised by the end of the following week I doubt if the time factor is really to blame.

Desired Outcome

What I would like to see happen as a result of the independent investigation is: -

1. I wish to be reimbursed the total cost for the A-boards which had deemed consent and were removed from the top of Lydd Road; and other café signs which were unlawfully re moved by the Highways Authority which were not in their jurisdiction.

2. I wish for the injunction order be cancelled regarding me using foul and abusive language and threatening behaviour toward council employees.

3. I wish to be reimbursed for the cost of legal fees I incurred when I had to pay for a barrister to appear in Court on 15th April 2011. I had not breached the injunction order.

4. I want the cost of £1,045.00 that I was invoiced for the removal of café signs cancelled because I believe the invoices are spurious.

5. *I wish to claim loss of earnings incurred upon my business for the tax year 2010/2011 through lack of signage.*

6. *I want it in writing that The Tyrannical Clown victimised me, committed perjury, lied to the judge to discredit me and made false allegations against me.*

7. *I want it in writing that Ken Walker lied when he said he had a complaint about my café signs on the telegraph pole and I want him to apologise for prying into my private business.*

8. *I want it in writing that Peter Plonker lied about the red light on AJ's burger van, lied that the photos of my café signs had been taken on 21st and 22nd October 2009 and when he claimed Mark had taken the photos with Peter Plonker's camera because Peter Plonker had been driving; and also lied when he said he had acquired a statement from Mark the contractor to assist in this investigation.*

9. *I want it in writing that Judgement Jones lied when he said he could not remember how he received the photos of my café signs which were taken on 7th October 2009 and that he sent me deceptive copies of emails I asked for. I want Judgement Jones to apologise for threatening me with committal to prison purely to*

intimidate me.

10. *I want an apology from Rag-Eme-Kale for accusing me in his witness statement of wasting their time and tax payers' money and saying that I had given him false information.*

11. *I want the Chief Executive of ESCC to be informed that I had written to her and that The Tyrannical Clown had intervened and had the letter redirected to himself.*

12. *As a result of the 2 year delay from the point I initially requested an inquiry and which has resulted in The Tyrannical Clown and Kilkenny no longer being employed by the County Council, and therefore unaccountable, I want the local authority to pay all legal costs for when I take legal action against The Tyrannical Clown and Kilkenny.*

I read it twice and signed it.
Then I made a list of what I believed was the cost of materials and time regarding the café signs which I had to replace every time they took one.

The cost of the A-boards and signs they took is as follows.....

VAT was 15% when I was buying the wood and costs are including VAT...
Approximately 13 x sheets of plywood x 4'x 8' £15.29 = £198.77
Baton prepared timber 2'x 1' £1.00 per metre = £96.00
Box of screws 1' £3.31 x 2 = £6.62
Box screws 2' £4.04 x 2 = £8.08
Hinges x 2 per pack £2.63 x 16 = £42.08
Paint 2 1/2 litres £24.99 a pot x 3 = £74.97
Liquid pens small 1 packet of liquid pens per board prices varied £300.00
Liquid pens large x 30....... £180.00
Electricity to charge my cordless drill 8 hours @ £1 x 15 hours = £15.00
Petrol to collect material to make the signs approx. £60.00
Labour @ minimum wage £5.75 x Approx. 4 hours per A-board = £368.00
Approx. 3 hours per flat sign = £345.00
Total = £1694.52

But of course that did not include other expenses the Council had cost me. I put it all together in a large envelope and sent it off to Mr Allen by recorded delivery.

It was just over two months since the Stage 3 Review panel had taken place. Lexi kept me up to date with Mr Allen's progress. She told me she had written again to The Tyrannical Clown, Kilkenny and Jed Uptland from Serco but none of them had responded. She told me of the various dates Mr Allen would be going to Lewes to interview the 5 remaining council employees, each interview would last for 90 minutes. Then she had received a call from The Tyrannical Clown who had declined the request to be involved. It was now April and there had been delays as some of the employees were on annual leave when Mr Allen went to interview them and Easter held everything up too. Now Lexi had emailed me saying that due to the complexity of the case Mr Allen hoped to complete his draft report by the first week in May. Kilkenny had also declined to be interviewed which had disappointed Mr Allen.

Mr Allen was taking forever to complete his draft report, though he had been thorough and quite often asked me to repeat things I had already told him. Whether this was to check my honesty or whether he had genuinely forgotten what I had already told him I knew not, but what I did know was that Mr Judas had not asked me anything when I had been to meet him in June the previous year or after or during the time he was making his report. I wondered more why Mr Judas had even been asked to carry out an investigation and I wanted to know, so I asked Lexi and she answered;

Hi Sally,
I believe I can answer quite a lot of this and regrettably once again it doesn't reflect well on us here. I was in the post of Complaints Manager when your initial complaint to Rag-

Eme-Kale on 6th May 2011 was passed through to the Economy, Transport & Environment Formal Complaints Team.

I was very concerned about the serious nature of the accusations and sought advice from my manager at the time, and our legal team, as I didn't feel qualified to deal with a complaint relating so closely to court proceedings. Judgement Jones advised that we should refer you to the police as it was concerning perjury. However the Assistant Director for Legal Services said whilst he didn't think it should go through the normal complaints process, it should be considered by the Department and he recommended that a manager be selected to investigate. This was the last I heard about it until Mr Judas sent me an email last November asking me who needed to sign off his Stage 2 investigation. I advised that Mr Taylor, Assistant Director, should sign it off but that it should go out from the Complaints Team so that we could check it too. I understand that Mr Taylor did see it but then Mr Judas sent it directly to you bypassing us again.

In hindsight, I believe that removing your complaint from the normal complaints procedure was a poor decision and it was one of the main reasons that it was so badly executed. Mr Judas was not supported throughout this time by anyone who had in depth knowledge of the procedure and nobody chased his progress. I feel responsible for this as it was me that invited that decision by escalating it to more senior management and I apologise for my part in that. If it had stayed within our control it would have been managed in the same way as it is being managed now.

I hope that goes someway to answering your questions. Please let me know if you need any further information.
Regards
Lexi

It was the beginning of June and Mr Allen was making slow progress although he had implied that his report would be finalised by the end of May. Then out of the blue he suddenly wanted all kinds of information, asking the same questions such as how was I aware that Kilkenny had met HB in a pub. Could I verify that Kilkenny had lied about a complaint from an anonymous caller regarding my café signs he removed and do I have proof that he contradicted his statement whilst on oath in court? Did I have photographs of the metal Fish and Chip signs on the main road in Camber and of the A-board which straddled the double yellow lines in Rye. Mr Allen said that nobody knew about fraudulent emails I had been sent from Judgement Jones, where had I obtained the weather reports from and when did Peter Plonker say he had received an email from Mark saying he took photos on 21st and 22nd October 2009?

I was ready to ask Lexi to sack Mr Allen. She could have quite easily provided the evidence Mr Allen had requested. I knew Kilkenny had met HB in a pub because the person he met had told me of the meeting and what had been said and secondly when I received the copies of Kilkenny's diaries he had made a note for Friday 25th November 2009 that he was meeting HB at 4pm regarding Camber issues. I had already sent him the photos along with the emails I had sent Rag-Eme-Kale concerning the location of these signs and Peter Plonker's and Judgement Jones emails had already been sent to Lexi. I had told him that the Councils Barrister had written in his prosecution statement that I had refused to pay the fine and The Tyrannical Clown had, under oath accused me of not paying it. I had sent him all the fraudulent emails from Judgement Jones claiming they were sent from Peter Plonker and The Tyrannical Clown. If Mr Allen wanted the evidence that had taken place in the court room he could have asked for a transcript of the hearing. Everything over and over again, was he so forgetful or just checking up on me, whatever the reason my patience had run out.

Then I received an email from Lexi saying the finance manager had been asked to trace the movements of the payments that East Sussex County Council claim which went astray but the manager needed some details from me. Did I have a record of the dates the money was paid and the exact amount. Mr Allen already knew this information and I had told him several times already that the monthly amount of £50, which I was paying by direct debit and the initial £1000 I had paid with money I had saved towards the rent. He had listened to the conversation I had with Emily from the fines office, so why had he asked for information he already knew and why was the finance manager asking me for answers? If my integrity was in doubt, if they wanted positive answers they should contact the fines office for that information. I suggested to Lexi that that was what they should do, and I provided her with the contact number of the fines office and told her to speak to Emily. I also threatened that if Mr Allen's report was not finalised by the end of the week I shall contact the local Ombudsman

A week later and I had heard nothing so I emailed Lexi asking her if someone had contacted the fines office to which she replied that she had tried but only got an engaged tone but she had passed the number on to the finance manager to deal with. As for the completion of Mr Allen's report, he was still waiting for a couple of updates, also she was going to be on annual leave the following week and if I needed to contact her she had asked her colleague to deal with any questions I might have as he was aware of the history of my complaint.

It meant more delays and of course Lexi was entitled to a holiday but I was so fed up with waiting, as it was a year since I had the first meeting with Mr Judas and now Mr Allen's investigation was going round and round in circles, that suddenly I had a feeling inside of me that I had never felt before, a feeling that I just wanted to explode like a bomb of decaying vegetables all over Mr Allen and his never ending report. I was so overwhelmed with frustration that I emailed him:

Dear Mr Allen

On 1st June I was asked by Lexi to provide her with information regarding the payments I had made and still make to the fines office as the finance manager of ESCC had been asked to check the dates when the payments had been made for the duration of the time I was accused of not paying. I provided her straight away with the contact number for the fines office. I emailed her last Friday a week later to ask if the manager of the finance department had been successful in getting the information I presume you had requested. She replied that she had tried contacting the fines office herself without any luck but had passed the number to the finance department. Today as I'm sure you are aware is 11th June and it appears that still no contact has been made to the fines office for this information. I am amazed at this late stage into the investigation that this should now be addressed. Surely this would have been the first and most obvious beginning to that part of the investigation regarding these payments, not the last.

I also understand that you are waiting for 'a couple' of updates. What updates? You were ready to finalize your report at the beginning of May. I am concerned that this investigation is going the same way as Mr Judas's and the reason I believe his took so long was to give the Council the opportunity to make excuses for the conduct of the officers and wriggle out of what they had done.

I suggest that if you need proof of what was said in the court room you ask for a copy of the transcript then there will be no doubt of what I was falsely accused of.
Lexi is now on annual leave till 18th June so how are you going to be updated with information when she is absent from work.... and so another week will go by....

Mr Allen sent a short reply within the hour;

The report is almost ready for signing off and I am making absolutely sure I have every angle covered. That is why there are further bits of information I have requested. So please do not align that with thoughts of excuses for officers' conduct. It is manifestly untrue. Wait until you see my report and the council's adjudication

.

I had waited months for this enquiry to be completed so I could wait another week or two or three just as long as Mr Allen proved those individuals I had complained about were corrupt, but Mr Allen was taking too long to finish his report. The rule set out for this inquiry was 28 days, and while I appreciated that there were many issues for Mr Allen to deal with that was his job and he knew he had a schedule to keep.

I wanted to know what this information was that Mr Allen was waiting for, so I emailed Lexi's colleague;

Dear Mr Daniels
Although I was feeling optimistic this morning about Mr Allen's report being completed this week, he tells me that he is still waiting for updates....We are now 57 days past the 28 which as you are well aware was the allocated time for this investigation to be completed.

Please can you explain why it is taking so long? I understand there was a lot involved, but I think the time has come to bring this to an overdue conclusion. What updates is Mr Allen waiting for that he hasn't had time to update during the last 57 days and why has it taken so long to decide to make the most obvious decision to check with the finance department the whereabouts of the money I regularly paid? That should have been the first thing to do not the last.....and why didn't Mr Allen ask me that himself?

Unfortunately this is an official complaint and I really must insist that this investigation concludes this week.....

Regards

Sally

Mr Daniels also replied within the hour:

Dear Sally,

I am very sorry for the length of time it is taking to conclude this process. In terms of your complaint I need to inform you that Mr Allen is waiting for an update from our Finance team regarding the issue of payments. I have just spoken to Finance, who are currently investigating the issue and will provide an update as soon as possible.

There is one other aspect Mr Allen is waiting to hear back from, and that is regarding the ESCC owned dunes at Camber. I will chase the team manager responsible now to see if I can speed up the process.

The report is in its final stages, and we believe it will be signed off by The Director of Economy, Transport & Environment later this week.

Kind regards

Silas Daniels

Lexi was on leave so even if Mr Allen's report was signed off sometime this week there was little chance of me getting a copy of it until Lexi was back at work.

CHAPTER 68

It was now the third week in June and if I did not get Mr Allen's report this week I was definitely going to seek advice from the Ombudsman. I thought Lexi would have emailed me on the Monday with an up-date but she did not and neither did she on the Tuesday. It was now Wednesday 20th June and I could wait no longer so I emailed Lexi;

Dear Lexi
I consider the 93 days I have waited since I signed the Statement of Complaint and Desired Outcomes on 19th March 2012 has long exceeded the 28 days which was within the Departments time-scale and recommended by Miss Churchill in her report written on 19th January 2012.
My patience is exhausted, so either conclude Mr Allan's investigation and get it signed off today or alternatively return all the evidence you have and the paperwork which I provided for Mr Allan so I can take my complaint to be investigated by the local Government Ombudsman.
Sally

Lexi soon replied she said;

Dear Sally
I am very sorry for the delay. The report is complete and with the Director of Economy, Transport and Environment now. I do appreciate that it has taken far longer than anyone would have wanted, however, there were 30 separate aspects to consider and Mr Allen has been very thorough interviewing council officers multiple times when things didn't add up or new evidence came to light.

You can expect to receive the report directly from him very
soon.
Regards
Lexi

At last, but that didn't mean it was imminent and before I
would get to see it the Director of Economy, Transport and
Environment would have to read it and approve of the
contents. I wanted to know how long he had to read it so I
asked Lexi how long had Mr Allen's report been with the
Director and if there was a time scale for him to read it she
replied;

Dear Sally
I passed it through to him today. I received the first full draft
on Monday but upon reading it, I felt that some matters
needed clarification and I asked Mr Allen to make the
necessary changes. He sent the final one to me this morning,
which I passed straight through to the Director
In normal circumstances the sign off would be included in the
28 days so we have no set time limits for this part of the
process. However, I have stressed to the Director how
anxious you are to receive the report and highlighted how
long it has taken to reach this point.
Regards
Lexi

It was 22nd June and I feared that the longer the document
was in the hands of the Directors the more it was vulnerable to
corruption without my knowledge. I put nothing past the
Council not even the Director, my experience had taught me
that Councils are not to be trusted in anything. I asked Lexi if
she could email me a copy, she said she had asked the

Assistant Director of Legal Services as he was ultimately responsible corporately for complaints but as yet he had not given her a reply. She said she understood completely my suspicions and mistrust of the people dealing with my complaint.

On Thursday 28th June 2012 I received an email from Lexi informing me that the Director of Economy, Transport and Environment's personal assistant had just confirmed to Lexi that the report had been posted to me that day and I should receive it either tomorrow or Saturday at the latest.

It did not arrive the next day but it did on Saturday 30th June. I was busy in the café owing to a week-end function at Pontins and a lovely sunny day of all the days I would have wished not to be busy but I was and these type of days were rare and as keen as I was to read Mr Allen's report I had to concentrate on what I was cooking before I had the chance to read it, seeing the large white envelope sitting there on the work top was satisfying enough.

When the rush had passed it was early afternoon and I sat down and opened the envelope. On the top was a letter from the Director of Economy, Transport and Environment;

Dear Mrs Pattinson
I am pleased to provide you with the final report for the Stage 2 investigation into your complaint, undertaken by Mr Allen. I am sorry for the time it has taken to complete. This was a complex case, with 30 separate aspects of your complaint, each requiring thorough examination.
I have carefully considered the points that you have raised and the recommendations put forward by Mr Allen.
Firstly, I would like to offer you a formal apology on behalf of East Sussex County Council for the way in which your case has been handled. It is very regrettable that the situation was permitted to continue for so long without an amicable

resolution being sought. Please be assured that this is not how we wish to interact with our customers. We have learnt a great deal from this investigation and have changed how we work to prevent a situation like this developing again.

I would like to offer you the sum of £5000, without prejudice, in recognition of distress and inconvenience we have caused you over the last 3 years.
Finally, it is clear that your belief that you need to advertise your business for it to survive, lies at the heart of this complaint. In view of this, I propose that we licence an advertising sign to enable you to inform passing trade of your presence, in a manner that does not present a hazard to other road users.
Please let me know if you would like to accept my offer and I will make the necessary arrangements.
If you are not satisfied with my response and wish to take the matter further, you can discuss your concerns with the Local Government Ombudsman.
Yours sincerely
Director of Economy, Transport and Environment

The report consisted of 71 pages. I read it and found it disappointing, contradictory and on occasions totally wrong where Mr Allen had misconstrued important issues and consequently not upheld the complaint. Out of the 30 allegations I had made Mr Allen had only upheld 8 and partially upheld one other.

Those employees who had been interviewed had continued to lie. Peter Plonker was undoubtedly a compulsive liar to the point that he truly believed his own lies. Judgement Jones, as the Council's solicitor working with these devious individuals, had successfully transformed the negative issues I had made against his conduct to make himself appear as the victim and by applying this tactic he had beguiled Mr Allen as he had Mr Judas.

All the allegations made against The Tyrannical Clown and Kilkenny that related to the perjury they had committed in the court had not been upheld because of the apparent lack of evidence. Mr Allen had specified that to prove each of the allegations he would have had to acquire the transcript from the court which would have cost the council £1500 and therefore he did not acquire it as he considered that to be an unreasonable cost to the local authority.

He had checked the service ticket which recorded the alleged complaint about my café signs and of course there was no mention of Camber Café only the Wine Bar, that complaint was upheld and I had been right all along. None the less, despite Kilkenny writing in his witness statement that he had had a complaint about my café signs on 17th November 2008 Mr Allen chose to over-look that part of my complaint and clearly condoned Kilkenny's perjury.

My complaint against the Highway Authority regarding Mr Forthright's fish and chip signs and the A-board straddled across the double yellow lines in Rye was upheld as there was no direct evidence that any action had been taken against the proprietors of these businesses.

Mr Allen upheld my allegation about Peter Plonker producing contaminated evidence. Mr Allen commented that the original complaint had come from Lesley therefore he did not understand the relevance of my complaint as it was of no consequence to my circumstances. When Mr Allen had asked Peter Plonker why, if this complaint had been from Lesley, he had included it in his witness statement, Peter Plonker had replied that he could not recall why. After further questioning it was established by Peter Plonker that the red light was on but had not been flashing. The point of my complaint was that Peter Plonker had written in his witness statement that the red light was off and his only proof was a contaminated exhibit which had been printed in black and white and photocopied several times. It would have been very difficult, nigh on impossible to prove a light was flashing on a static photograph.

The complaint about the photos which I knew were taken on 7th October 2009 and had been denied by Peter Plonker and Judgement Jones by saying they were taken on 21st and 22nd October 2009, was upheld because, according to Mr Allen's report, they were unable to verify irrefutable evidence of when the photos were taken and as they had changed who and when the photo's had been taken it was easy to be sceptical about any of the accounts they had given.

The next complaint to be upheld was referring to the weather conditions on 7th October 2009. Mr Allen had commented that I had provided two sources of evidence one from the Meteorological Office and the other from a local Entomologist both confirming that on 7th October 2009 ex-Tropical storm Grace brought heavy rain to Southern England, and also confirming that on 21st and 22nd October 2009 the weather was cloudy and dry with night time thunderstorms.

When Mr Allen questioned Peter Plonker about the weather on 21st October he replied that it had been raining all day, he knew that because he always noted the weather conditions in his diary, when Mr Allen asked him why he kept a note of the weather Peter Plonker had replied that it was a legacy from his farming days.

At a later stage of the investigation, records had been recovered from Sidley depot and amongst them photographs that were said to have been taken on 27th October 2009. The electronic dating on these pictures shows 28th August 2009 which tied in with calculations made by the complaints manager Lexi Goodfellow that the mechanism on the camera was out by two months and a day.

Extrapolating from this, Lexi Goodfellow said the photographs taken by the camera as 8th August 2009 were therefore likely to have been taken on 7th October 2009 and are in fact pictures Peter Plonker claimed were taken on 21st October 2009, therefore there was a strong possibility that the photographs were not taken later in October 2009 as claimed by The Tyrannical Clown in his message to Judgement Jones on 28th October 2009.

In Mr Judas's report The Tyrannical Clown is quoted as saying that he had Camber visited on 7th October 2009 and signs were removed. There is no reference to signs being photographed. Mr Allen questioned Peter Plonker where he was on 7th October 2009 and he had said he was in Three Oaks in the morning following a complaint about flooding and at 2pm he had an appointment in Rye, a short drive from Camber. Peter Plonker had written in his diary that the person he was due to see had not turned up. This would have left him with nothing scheduled after 2.30 pm that day.

Also confirming the fact that Peter Plonker was in the vicinity of Camber that day was an email from The Tyrannical Clown sent to Swanoff Swanker on 8th October 2009 saying:

'Yesterday I had Camber visited and six signs pertaining to Camber Café were removed to this depot as Peter Plonker was in the Rye area yesterday'.

Mr Allen had asked Peter Plonker whether he had requested Mark the contractor to write a statement confirming he had been in Camber on 21st and 22nd October 2009 taking photos of Camber Café signs. Peter Plonker had replied that he had not been asked to get one.

Mr Allen concluded that part of his report by saying;

'Testimony from Peter Plonker is of

*questionable value and none of his evidence can be
corroborated and his verbal testimony cannot be backed up
by contemporaneous recording'.*

Weighed against him also were the dates on the camera
setting and The Tyrannical Clown's documentation that the
signs had been removed on 7th October 2009.

The Tyrannical Clown's spurious invoices had no
supporting evidence so consequently my complaint was
upheld.

After that part of Mr Allen's report his findings became
distorted and contradictory. My complaint against Judgement
Jones falsified emails of photographs and signs taken on 7th
October was not upheld, although Mr Allen had previously
upheld the allegation of the date Peter Plonker had taken the
photos and signs which had been the subject in the emails. It
did not make sense. Then as part of this enquiry Mr Allen had
asked the IT department two questions, the first whether a
search could be made of electronic records and second to
verify the message Peter Plonker says he sent to The
Tyrannical Clown on 27th October 2009. The answer was
*'Emails were found in Peter Plonker's sent items and The
Tyrannical Clown's inbox. Emails are automatically archived
once they have been in a mail box for 6 months'.* Of course
that was going to be the case and I believe that the answer
given was a generalisation and Mr Allen had only referred to
the one email that contained correct information I had
admitted to, that on 27th October 2009 I had put an A-board at
the top of Lydd Road. The point of this part of the
investigation was to prove that information which had been
written in recent emails was not authentic and had been
written with the intention to provide false information. It was
easy to see that the author of these emails had changed the
font to make it appear that the email was a copy, for anyone

with the slightest bit of common sense it was obvious apart from Mr Allen, although he had already upheld my allegation that the photos had not been taken on 22nd and 21st October 2009, but nevertheless Mr Allen had concluded the emails could not have been tampered with I can only assume that Mr Allen had chosen to disregard my evidence for reasons known only to himself and that allegation should have been upheld.

From all the evidence I had submitted to Mr Allen he had only upheld 8 of my complaints and partially upheld one other. 16 aspects of his investigation were not upheld because there was not enough evidence to support them and there were no findings made on 5.

Mr Allen did not investigate to any great extent the letter I had sent to the Chief Executive he stated that it was not possible to make a finding as it could not be established with sufficient certainty whether the letter was passed to The Tyrannical Clown but if it was it would have been illogical given that he was implicated in the allegation of victimisation. Had it really not occurred to Mr Allen that The Tyrannical Clown wanted the letter to destroy it so as to avoid his behaviour being brought to the attention of the Chief Executive?

My evidence was substantial, and Mr Allen had vowed to base his findings on 'Forensic Evidence' but he had not adhered to this.

I know beyond all doubt that The Tyrannical Clown, Kilkenny, Peter Plonker and Judgement Jones lied, committed perjury and falsified legal documents. I can only imagine that Mr Allen was limited to the amount of allegations he could uphold and I believe that the eight and a half complaints were upheld on the strength of my evidence I had provided. He had made excuses and opinions to justify not upholding the majority of my allegations.

My friend's husband denied all knowledge of passing information about me to Kilkenny or that such a meeting even took place. That was understandable I would certainly have done the same for a friend, but Mr Allen seemed to have over looked the fact that Kilkenny had written the appointment in his diary.

One of my desired outcomes had been to take legal action against The Tyrannical Clown and Kilkenny for the perjury they had committed and that East Sussex County Council pay the court costs, Mr Allen's opinion was that there would be no purpose in this as it would be as if the Council were prosecuting themselves. Mr Allen had not done his best and as it was the Council who were paying him this explained why his report was biased in as much as it appeared that he had gone to great lengths to invalidate my allegations but he had too easily condoned their interpretation of events.

Overall Mr Allen's report was disappointing. Although Jed Uptland had refused to be interviewed about The Tyrannical Clown's invoices my complaint was upheld through lack of substantial evidence, but he had made no enquiries, especially as the sum of £1045 had been added onto the fine I was given on the day of the Court hearing. If he had investigated properly he would have discovered the person responsible for sending the invoices in the first place had clearly committed a deliberate act of fraud. Judgement Jones lied beyond belief, and I did not accept his excuse that he was acting on behalf of his clients, far from it, he was most likely advising them on ways to detach themselves from their misconduct. Judgement Jones should have been thoroughly investigated not just believed on the strength of his status. There was no acknowledgement of my complaint about Mr Judas at all. Peter Plonker lied himself to the point of diminished responsibility and Kilkenny had disappeared into the sunset. If Mr Allen alone had decided not to ask the Court for a copy of the transcript purely to save the Council money it was preposterous. I believe it was more likely that the transcript of those Court proceedings on 6th April 2010 would not only have proved beyond any doubt that perjury had been committed that day but also equally question the integrity of that judge. Mr Allen was being paid to conduct an investigation but his findings clearly demonstrated that he had favoured those guilty Council employees, which puts the whole investigation procedure into question as in this aspect of my complaint the perpetrators had become the victims who were worthy of protection.

Apart from that I had so wanted retribution for those individuals who were free to commit perjury, lie, deceive and abuse the power of their job titles and worse are employed on trust but are free to waste public money unchecked.

I had no regrets in standing up to these horrible people and I am glad that I had ridiculed them and I would do it again if I felt my livelihood was threatened.

I did have the choice of starting my complaint all over again with the Local Government Ombudsman but I do not think that the outcome would have been any different.

The whole episode had never caused me stress or anxiety. Instead I rose to the challenge, but their disgusting behaviour along with the worst recession since the 1930's had had a severe effect on my financial situation. That aside I answered the letter from the Director of Economy, Transport and Environment;

Dear Sir
I acknowledge receipt of Mr Allen's report and your offer.
I am prepared, in recognition of the distress, inconvenience and extreme financial pressure which were inflicted upon me by your officers during a period of nearly four years, to accept £7500 without prejudice.

I accept your apology and offer of licence to enable me to
inform passing trade of the presence of my business.
There are many discrepancies and contradictions in Mr
Allen's report which I am not happy about. I am not a liar and
I have not lied throughout this whole process. I hope I will not
have to take my complaint further.
Yours sincerely
Sally Pattinson

The next day I received his reply;

Dear Mrs Pattinson,
Thank you for your swift response. I am pleased to hear that
we are in a position to bring this matter to a resolution.
I have carefully considered your proposal. Bearing in the
mind the length of time that it has taken to reach this
conclusion I am prepared to increase the payment, without
prejudice, to the sum of £7,500.
As soon as I receive your agreement I will make the necessary
arrangements for the payment to be made and for a member
of my team to contact you regarding the licensing of your
sign.
Yours sincerely

So that was that!, I got my cheque and I got an
unnecessary licence for my A-board. Sadly the perpetrators
did not get their comeuppance as I would have wished, but I
was keen to know what changes had taken place within the
Council from the lessons they had learned from their
experience of picking on the wrong woman, so I emailed Lexi
one more time and she replied;

Dear Sally

Thank you for your email. The investigation of your complaint exposed a number of issues within the Highways teams in terms of how they interact with customers. Since this time all of the customer facing teams have attended a full day's customer service training course in conjunction with Sussex Police.

William Rogers, Head of Highways, is very customer focused and has invited me to work closely with him and his managers to help them improve the way that they and their teams interact with customers and handle complaints. Further to this we are currently reviewing our Corporate Complaints procedure to look at ways of reducing timeframes and making whole experience better for our customers. Once the new process is in place, myself and my team will be providing regular training sessions and guidance to all Highways staff. Lastly I provide William Rogers with a weekly report of his team's open customer enquiries and complaints, highlighting any that I feel require his personal attention.

I hope this provides you with some reassurance that we are working on how we deal with people's concerns and complaints.

Regards
Lexi

THE END

Written by Sally Pattinson

September 2014

Readers who would like to see the videos
mentioned in this book can find them at:

https://www.youtube.com/watch?v=jRVBP6OCMQE
https://www.youtube.com/watch?v=eOhMDQCphuw
https://www.youtube.com/watch?v=GSxXOthphzk
https://www.youtube.com/watch?v=_mr77fNR-e8

Printed in Great Britain
by Amazon

70022787R00322